Magnification and Miniaturization in Religious Communications in Antiquity and Modernity

CONTEXTUALIZING THE SACRED

Editorial Board

Elizabeth Frood, *University of Oxford*
Rubina Raja, *Aarhus University*

VOLUME 12

Previously published volumes in this series are listed at the back of the book.

Magnification and Miniaturization in Religious Communications in Antiquity and Modernity

Materialities and Meanings

Edited by

Elisabeth Begemann, Diana Pavel, Georgia Petridou,
Rubina Raja, Anna-Katharina Rieger, and Jörg Rüpke

BREPOLS

British Library Cataloguing in Publication Data

A catalogue record for this book is available from the British Library.

© 2023, Brepols Publishers n.v., Turnhout, Belgium

All rights reserved. No part of this publication may be reproduced,
stored in a retrieval system, or transmitted, in any form or by any means,
electronic, mechanical, photocopying, recording, or otherwise,
without the prior permission of the publisher.

D/2023/0095/36
ISBN: 978-2-503-60479-4
e-ISBN: 978-2-503-60480-0
DOI: 10.1484/M.CS-EB.5.132481
ISSN: 2565-8093

Printed in the EU on acid-free paper

Contents

List of Illustrations vii

Abbreviations xiii

1. Magnification and Miniaturization in Religious Communications
   in Antiquity and Modernity: Materialities and Meanings
   ELISABETH BEGEMANN, DIANA PAVEL, GEORGIA PETRIDOU,
   RUBINA RAJA, ANNA-KATHARINA RIEGER, and JÖRG RÜPKE 1

Miniaturization

2. Look Closely and You Will See: Banqueting Tesserae
   from Palmyra and Small-Scale Iconography
   RUBINA RAJA 9

3. The Material Record of Micro-Shares: An Archaeological
   Case Study on Sanctuary Transactions in Ancient Sicily
   NATASCHA SOJC 17

4. What Do Tiny Objects Want? A Case Study with Miniature Pottery from Pompeii
   ANNA-KATHARINA RIEGER 43

5. Are the Same Objects Desirable for People and for Gods?
   Material and Dimensional Interchangeability
   ELISABETH TRINKL 69

Monumentalization

6. Scaling Altars in the Etruscan Funerary Sphere
   DIANA PAVEL 87

7. Urban Monumentality and Religion
   JÖRG RÜPKE 103

8. Perceptions of Changing Religious Landscapes in Augustan Rome
   DEVMINI MALKA WIJERATNE 117

9. The King and the Population as Protagonists of the Oath:
   Intermediatory Semantics in Ancient Near Eastern Treaties
   ELENA MALAGOLI 127

Domestic Space

10. Small, Versatile, Numinous: Pagan-Mythological Statuettes at the End of Antiquity
    INE JACOBS 145

11. The Dancing Deity: Diminishing the Goddess Libertas on the Palatine
    ELISABETH BEGEMANN 165

12. *Di Penates*: From Small Objects to Anthropomorphic Gods
    PETER SCHERRER 177

The Fragmented and the Augmented Body

13. The Eyes Have It: Materialities, Monumentality, and Meanings in
    Eye-Shaped Modern Greek *tamata* and Ancient Greek *anathemata*
    GEORGIA PETRIDOU 197

14. A Triangle of Mary: Relating Religious Artefacts to Non-Religious Lorry Drivers
    MANUEL MOSER 211

Index 225

List of Illustrations

2. Look Closely and You Will See: Banqueting Tesserae from Palmyra and Small-Scale Iconography — *Rubina Raja*

Figure 2.1.	Tessera with a male bust and a blank side. Copenhagen, Ny Carlsberg Glyptotek, inv. no. I.N. 3260	11
Figure 2.2.	Tessera with a bust of Athena and a blank side. Copenhagen, Ny Carlsberg Glyptotek, inv. no. I.N. 3229	11
Figure 2.3.	Tessera with a rosette (side A) and a seal impression of a male bust (side B). Copenhagen, Ny Carlsberg Glyptotek, inv. no. I.N. 3264	11
Figure 2.4.	Tessera with a bust of Poseidon (side A) and a half-figure of Beltî (side B). Around both are various symbols, for example a star and a globe. Copenhagen, Ny Carlsberg Glyptotek, inv. no. I.N. 3196	11
Figure 2.5.	Tessera with an inscription and astral symbols (side A) and a male bust surrounded by various astral and religious symbols (side B). Copenhagen, Ny Carlsberg Glyptotek, inv. no. I.N. 1141	11
Figure 2.6.	Tessera with the busts of two gods inside a crescent (side A) and a camel with a packsaddle (side B). Copenhagen, Ny Carlsberg Glyptotek, inv. no. I.N. 3193	12
Figure 2.7.	Tessera with a Palmyrene Aramaic inscription (side A) and symbols (side B). Copenhagen, Ny Carlsberg Glyptotek, inv. no. I.N. 3190.	12
Figure 2.8.	Tessera with a priest bust (side A) and a Greek inscription (side B). Copenhagen, Ny Carlsberg Glyptotek, inv. no. I.N. 3216	12
Figure 2.9.	Tessera with a hieroglyphic cartouche (side A) and a seal impression with a female bust (side B). Copenhagen, Ny Carlsberg Glyptotek, inv. no. I.N. 3227	12
Figure 2.10.	Tessera with a bust of a priest and an inscription (side A) and a seal impression with a bust (side B). Copenhagen, Ny Carlsberg Glyptotek, inv. no. I.N. 2772.	12
Figure 2.11.	Tessera with a bust of a priest flanked by palm leaves (side A) and a seal impression of Athena surrounded by a wreath (side B). Copenhagen, Ny Carlsberg Glyptotek, inv. no. I.N. 3215.	12
Figure 2.12.	Tessera with the head of a ram (side A) and a priest bust (side B). Copenhagen, Ny Carlsberg Glyptotek, inv. no. I.N. 1142	12
Figure 2.13.	Tessera with a standing priest between two bulls (side A) and a bull and a sheep below a seal impression (side B). Copenhagen, Ny Carlsberg Glyptotek, inv. no. I.N. 3200	12
Figure 2.14.	Tessera of a seal impression surrounded by a wreath and an inscription below (side A) and a standing priest next to a star and a palm branch (side B). Copenhagen, Ny Carlsberg Glyptotek, inv. no. I.N. 3206.	12

Figure 2.15. Tessera with two reclining priests on each side. Copenhagen, Ny Carlsberg Glyptotek, inv. no. I.N. 3209. ... 12

Figure 2.16. Tessera with a reclining priest under vines (side A) and a seal impression of a standing male, surrounded by animal heads (side B). Copenhagen, Ny Carlsberg Glyptotek, inv. no. I.N. 2771. ... 13

Figure 2.17. Tessera with a reclining priest under vines and a garlanded arch (side A) and servants mixing wine with a seal impression of Apollo above (side B). Copenhagen, Ny Carlsberg Glyptotek, inv. no. I.N. 3208. ... 13

Figure 2.18. Tessera with a priest bust (side A) and a male god wearing a kalathos (side B). Copenhagen, Ny Carlsberg Glyptotek, inv. no. I.N. 3217. ... 13

3. The Material Record of Micro-Shares: An Archaeological Case Study on Sanctuary Transactions in Ancient Sicily   *Natascha Sojc*

Figure 3.1. Deposition of a cooking vessel into the natural soil during excavation, view from west. Agrigento, S. Anna. Fifth century BC. ... 18

Figure 3.2. Akragas and the extra-urban sanctuary of S. Anna, the investigation area of Augsburg University indicated hatched. ... 19

Figure 3.3. Extra-urban sanctuary of S. Anna, areas of investigation. ... 19

Figure 3.4. Deposition during excavation: an olpe (top) found over a black-glazed oinochoe (middle) and drinking vessels (bottom). Agrigento, S. Anna. Fifth century BC. ... 20

Figure 3.5. *Aes rude* (bronze). Agrigento, S. Anna. Fifth century BC. ... 24

Figure 3.6. Pieces of bronze from deposition (arrowhead, finger ring, and fragment of a furniture attachment). Agrigento, S. Anna. Fifth century BC. ... 25

Figure 3.7. Ancient depositing activities, 1960s excavation. Agrigento, S. Anna. ... 27

Figure 3.8. Deposition of two black-glazed handles belonging to two different vessels. Agrigento, S. Anna. Fifth century BC. ... 28

Figure 3.9. Deposition of a bronze coin covered by a vessel fragment next to a tile fragment. Agrigento, S. Anna. Fifth century BC. ... 29

Figure 3.10. Drinking vessel, placed bottom up, held in place by a sherd. Agrigento, S. Anna. Fifth century BC. ... 30

Figure 3.11. Deposition of a female terracotta protome fragment during excavation. Agrigento, S. Anna. Fifth century BC. ... 30

Figure 3.12. Complex deposition, lower part, with miniature vessel, vessel bottom fragment and *aes rude* laid down against a setting of stones. Agrigento, S. Anna. Fifth century BC. ... 31

Figure 3.13. Complex deposition, upper part, with knives and drinking vessels. Agrigento, S. Anna. Fifth century BC. ... 31

Figure 3.14. Ancient depositing activities, University of Augsburg excavation, US 43, US 49, and US 61 in trench A. Agrigento, S. Anna. ... 32

Figure 3.15. Female terracotta figurine, fragment of torch.
Agrigento, S. Anna. Fifth century BC...33

Figure 3.16. Female terracotta figurine, fragment of chest with jewellery.
Agrigento, S. Anna. Fifth century BC...33

Figure 3.17. Female terracotta figurine, head fragment with characteristic
broken edge. Agrigento, S. Anna. Fifth century BC..............................33

Figure 3.18. Female terracotta figurine, fragment of feet and pedestal.
Agrigento, S. Anna. Fifth century BC...33

Figure 3.19. Deposition containing a female terracotta figurine fragment missing
the feet and pedestal. Agrigento, S. Anna. Fifth century BC...................33

Figure 3.20. Roof tile fragments covering a deposit with subsequent
depositions above, Agrigento, S. Anna. Fifth century BC.......................34

Figure 3.21. Glass beads found in depositions. Agrigento, S. Anna. Fifth century BC............34

Figure 3.22. Deposition of beads and a bronze pin. Agrigento, S. Anna. Fifth century BC.......35

Figure 3.23. Terracotta loom weight. Agrigento, S. Anna. Fifth century BC. 35

Figure 3.24. Ancient depositing activities, University of Augsburg excavation,
US 33, US 80, and US 93 in trench A. Agrigento, S. Anna......................36

Figure 3.25. Depositions during excavation, terracotta roof tile as marker.
Agrigento, S. Anna. Fifth century BC...38

4. What Do Tiny Objects Want? A Case Study with Miniature Pottery from Pompeii — *Anna-Katharina Rieger*

Figure 4.1. Gulf of Naples with Pompeii and Stabiae......................................44

Figure 4.2. a. The plan shows the terrace and remains of walls at the sacred
place of Privati with the 'fossa' containing the deposited material;
b. the terrace and the 'fossa' between walls..47

Figure 4.3. a. Accumulated material, mainly from clay at the sacred place of Privati
(fourth to first centuries BC); b. the vessel object made from nine cups or
plates, a stand at the bottom, and an *olla* on top; c. miniature cups and jugs.......47

Figure 4.4. Small-scale pottery, mainly *unguentaria* and *balsamari*, from the necropolis
at the Porta Nocera from tombs of the mid-first century BC....................48

Figure 4.5. *Unguentaria*: a. from the sacred place at the Fondo Iozzino together with
a multi-handled *kylix*; b. a set of toiletry items from the Casa Imperiale;
c. workshop VII.4.24–25, which can be dated to the second century BC..........48

Figure 4.6. A special form of miniature object, the *coperchi*, and miniature *calici*/
goblets from Insula VI.1...51

Figure 4.7. Small-scale plates from I.8.9, containing pigments (first century AD)............51

Figure 4.8. Miniature pottery from houses: a. Casa di Lesbianus (I.13.9), where four miniature vessels were kept in an *armarium* in the central room; b. from a *thermopolium* in I.14.15, where a single miniature cup; c. a so-called *culla*, a *bruciaprofumo*, with figurative protome at the end was found together with b; all material can be dated to the first century AD. 53

Figure 4.9. Miniature pottery in house contexts: a. Casa delle Vestali VI.1.6–8, miniature goblets from below the *tablinum* (third/second centuries BC?); b. Casa di A. Octavius Primus (VII.15.13) from a trench in the *triclinium* (saggio A in *triclinium* i): findings of a miniature cup and the lower parts of two female statuettes. 54

Figure 4.10. a. Niche in the facade on the street or at the entrance of a house in VI 2.16–21 with material, among which is a *kylix* in a pit below the altar and miniature pottery from the large pit a little to the north of the altar; b. street altar to Salus in IX.8.8 with find material: in a pit to the south a single *kylix* was found, to the north fragments of miniature pottery and fragments of an entire *coperchi* were found. 56

Figure 4.11. Insula VI.1 a. Find-spots of miniature vessels; b. the trench at the southern end of the insula; c. the well house and the fountain, between which ran the trench (b), where numerous *coperchi* were found in the pre-Augustan layers; d. the paintings from the Augustan period on the well house with altar in front, preserved in an engraving by Mazois from the nineteenth century, attest to its function as compital shrine. 57

Figure 4.12. Accumulations of Hellenistic clay materials from Fondo Iozzino, Temples, Sanctuary Fondo Iozzino. 61

5. Are the Same Objects Desirable for People and for Gods? Material and Dimensional Interchangeability — *Elisabeth Trinkl*

Figure 5.1. Late Geometric/Early Archaic bronze figurine dedicated to Apollon by Mantiklos. Museum of Fine Arts, Boston, inv. no. 03.997. 70

Figure 5.2. Delos, Colossus of the Naxians. 72

Figure 5.3. Ensemble of miniature vessels from Pheneos. 74

Figure 5.4. Mock vessels from Pheneos. 75

Figure 5.5. Dresses in miniature from the temple repositories in Knossos, replica. 76

Figure 5.6. Relief table in miniature, Olympia, inv. no. T 202. 76

Figure 5.7. Wreaths made from lead from Pheneos. 78

6. Scaling Altars in the Etruscan Funerary Sphere — *Diana Pavel*

Figure 6.1. Tomb of the Typhon, Monterozzi necropolis, Tarquinia. Painted facsimile (1911–1912) of Elio D'Alessandris with one of the renditions concerning the painting present on the altar. 88

Figure 6.2. Plan of the Tomb of the Five Chairs, Banditaccia necropolis, Caere. Reproduction of a nineteenth-century drawing. 95

| Figure 6.3. | The Grande Ruota tumulus located within the Grotta Porcina necropolis. | 99 |
| Figure 6.4. | The circular altar within the stepped area from the Grotta Porcina necropolis. | 99 |

7. Urban Monumentality and Religion — *Jörg Rüpke*

| Figure 7.1. | Kaogongji from the Song-era Xindingsanlitu. | 109 |

10. Small, Versatile, Numinous: Pagan-Mythological Statuettes at the End of Antiquity — *Ine Jacobs*

Figure 10.1.	Portrait bust holding a statuette of the Aphrodite of Aphrodisias, from the Atrium House, Aphrodisias (inv. no. 1986-1). Geyre, Aphrodisias Museum. Fourth century (?).	147
Figure 10.2.	Barberini diptych. Paris, Louvre. Sixth century.	148
Figure 10.3.	Axiometric view of the House of the Painted Inscription at Hierapolis.	151
Figure 10.4.	Amor and Psyche from the House of the Painted Inscription at Hierapolis after partial restoration. Fourth century.	152
Figure 10.5.	Fragments of a statuette of Apollo found on the colonnaded street at Sagalassos. Ağlasun, Sagalassos Excavation House depots.	153
Figure 10.6.	Statuette of Hygeia with Hypnos from the excavations of the colonnaded street at Sagalassos, after restoration. Burdur Museum. AD 250–260 or later.	153
Figure 10.7.	Torso of Aphrodite from the excavations of the colonnaded street at Sagalassos, after conservation. Ağlasun, Sagalassos Excavation House depots. Second century (?).	154
Figure 10.8.	Street fountain with column base, underneath which the Aphrodite torso was found.	155

11. The Dancing Deity: Diminishing the Goddess Libertas on the Palatine — *Elisabeth Begemann*

| Figure 11.1. | Terracotta statuette of a girl dancing, *c*. 299–200 BC. | 169 |
| Figure 11.2. | Dancing *lar*. Bronze, Roman, third century AD. | 170 |

12. *Di Penates*: From Small Objects to Anthropomorphic Gods — *Peter Scherrer*

Figure 12.1.	Denarius of C. Sulpicius C.F., 106 BC. Obverse: *D(i) P(enates) P(ublici)*; garlanded busts of two young men. Reverse: Lavinian Sow.	183
Figure 12.2.	Denarius of C. Antius C.f., 47 BC (Westfalenmuseum Muenster); reverse: busts of two youths with the legend *DEI PENATES*; obverse: Hercules.	184
Figure 12.3.	Map of the settlement on Magdalensberg (Noricum; Carinthia) with find-spots of face beakers: 1) kitchen in the high-security building; 2) *fabrica auraria imperialis*; 3) storeroom of a Roman merchant.	185

Figure 12.4. Face beakers from Magdalensberg (Carinthia, Austria), Tiberian period. a) upper row: trading goods from the warehouse; b) lower row: beakers from the high-security building. 186

Figure 12.5. Above: face pot from a tumulus grave in Kematen/Ybbs, Noricum, with three miniature vessels attached at the upper part of the handles, and engraved animals, plants, and *caduceus* on the body. Below: so-called snake-vessels. Left side: from Pocking, Raetia, with small faces at the lower part of the handles and miniature *turibula*; right side: Vindonissa, Germania Superior, with tree-like plants on the body and small dishes as upper end of the handles..187

Figure 12.6. Face pot from Bonn, found in 2018 inside a wooden barrel in a private Roman house...188

Figure 12.7. Italian Terra Sigillata with face or mask applique. 189

13. The Eyes Have It: Materialities, Monumentality, and Meanings in Eye-Shaped Modern Greek *tamata* and Ancient Greek *anathemata* — Georgia Petridou

Figure 13.1. Modern Greek *tamata* from the author's collection...199

Figure 13.2. Top: Yiannis and Dimitris Yiagtzis in their workshop in Athens; bottom: Yiannis Yiagtzis polishes a modern Greek eye-shaped *tama* from the Yiagtzis workshop. 199

Figure 13.3. Coloboma is a congenital defect of the iris, which usually means that the pupil is longer than it should be, occasionally acquiring a keyhole-like shape......201

Figure 13.4. The θαυματουργός 'miracle-working' icon of Ἁγία Παρασκευή Κομοτηνής ('St Paraskevi of Komotini'), heavily adorned with *tamata*......................203

Figure 13.5. Marble votive plaque found near the Eleusinian Telestērion depicting a radiant Demeter (IG II² 4639) dated roughly to the fourth century BC. 203

Figure 13.6. Silver votive plaques from the Sanctuary of Demeter in Mesimvria-Zone. They were discovered next to the eastern wall of the city and date to *c*. the fourth century BC...207

14. A Triangle of Mary: Relating Religious Artefacts to Non-Religious Lorry Drivers — *Manuel Moser*

Figure 14.1. Three entities that share a common name: the first is Mary, the driver, the second is Mary, the icon, and the third is Mary, the mother of G*d. 217

Figure 14.2. Connections between religious artefact, driver (now explicitly a particular long-distance one), lorry, and the family left at home. 218

Abbreviations

Ancient Authors and Works

Amm. Marc.	Ammianus Marcellinus, *Res gestae*
Anth. Pal.	*Anthologia Palatina*
Aristid.	Aelius Aristides
Arnob.	Arnobius, *Adversus nationes*
Aug., *Civ.*	Augustine, *De civitate Dei*
Cic., *Att.*	Cicero, *Epistulae ad Atticum*
Cic., *Dom.*	Cicero, *De domo sua*
Cic., *Fam.*	Cicero, *Epistulae ad familiares*
Cic., *Leg.*	Cicero, *De legibus*
Cic., *Nat. D.*	Cicero, *De natura deorum*
Cic., *Pis.*	Cicero, *In L. Pisonem*
Cic., *Scaur.*	Cicero, *Pro M. Aemilio Scauro*
Cic., *Sest.*	Cicero, *Pro P. Sestio*
Cic., *Verr. 1, 2*	Cicero, *In Verrem actio 1, 2*
Cod. Theod.	*Codex Theodosianus*
Dion. Hal., *Ant. Rom.*	Dionysius Halicarnassus, *Antiquitates Romanae*
Fest.	Festus
Gell., *NA*	Gellius, *Noctes Atticae*
Hes., *Op.*	Hesiod, *Opera et dies*
Hes., *Theog.*	Hesiod, *Theogonia*
Hippoc., *Vid. ac.*	Hippocrates, *De visu/De videndi acie*
Hor., *Carm.*	Horace, *Carmina*
Ioh. Mal.	John Malalas, *Chronographia*
Jer	Jeremiah
Liv.	Livy, *Ab urbe condita*
Macrob., *Sat.*	Macrobius, *Saturnalia*
Mart.	Martial, *Epigrams*
Naev.	Naevius
Nep., *Att.*	Nepos, *Life of Atticus*
Ov., *Fast.*	Ovid, *Fasti*
Ov., *Tr.*	Ovid, *Tristia*
Paus.	Pausanias
Pers.	Persius, *Saturae*
Petron., *Sat.*	Petronius, *Satyrica*
Plaut., *Merc.*	Plautus, *Mercator*
Pliny, *HN*	Pliny the Elder, *Naturalis historia*
Plut.	Plutarch, *Vitae parallelae*
R. Gest. div. Aug.	*Res gestae divi Augusti*
Sall., *Iug.*	Sallust, *De bello Iugurthino*
Schol.	Scholia to the author in question
Serv., *Aen.*	Servius, *Commentarius in Vergilii Aeneida*
Suet., *Aug.*	Suetonius, *Divus Augustus*
Str.	Strabo, *Geographica*
Tac., *Ann.*	Tacitus, *Annales*
Varro, *Ling.*	Varro, *De lingua latina*
Varro, *Sat. Men.*	Varro, *Saturae Menippeae*
Verg., *Aen.*	Vergil, *Aeneid*
Vitr., *De arch.*	Vitruvius, *De architectura*
Zos.	Zosimus, *Historia nova*

Epigraphic corpora

AE	*L'année épigraphique* (Paris, 1888–)
CEG	Allen Hansen, P. (ed.). 1983–1989. *Carmina epigraphica Graeca*, 2 vols (Berlin: De Gruyter)
CIL	*Corpus inscriptionum latinarum* (Berlin, 1893–)
CSE	*Corpus speculorum Etruscorum* (1981–)
CSE Vaticano	*Corpus speculorum Etruscorum: Stato della Città del Vaticano*, I: *Città del Vaticano, Museo Profano della Biblioteca Apostolica Vaticana* (Rome: L'Erma di Bretschneider, 1995).
CTH	Catalogue of Hittite Texts. S. Košak, G. G. W. Müller, S. Görke, and C. Steitler (eds) <https://www.hethport.uni-wuerzburg.de/CTH/> [accessed 12 February 2023]
CVA	Corpus vasorum antiquorum <https://www.cvaonline.org/cva/> [accessed 12 February 2023]
EA	*Epigraphica Anatolica* (1983–)
EDCS	Epigraphik-Datenbank Clauss / Slaby (University Eichstaett–Ingolstadt): <http://db.edcs.eu/epigr/epi.php?s> [accessed 12 February 2023]
IDR	*Inscriptiones Daciae Romanae* (Bucharest, 1975–)
IG II²	Kirchner, J. (ed.). 1913–1940. *Inscriptiones Graecae*, II and III: *Inscriptiones Atticae Euclidis anno posteriores*, 2nd edn (Berlin: De Gruyter)
InscrIt	*Inscriptiones Italiae* (Rome, 1931–)
RIB	Roman Inscriptions of Britain: <https://romaninscriptionsofbritain.org/> [accessed 12 February 2023]
RTP	Ingholt, H., H. Seyrig, and J. Starcky (eds). 1955. *Recueil des tessères de Palmyre* (Paris: Geuthner)
TLL	*Thesaurus latinae linguae* (Leipzig 1900–)

1. Magnification and Miniaturization in Religious Communications in Antiquity and Modernity: Materialities and Meanings

Elisabeth Begemann, Diana Pavel, Georgia Petridou,
Rubina Raja, Anna-Katharina Rieger, and Jörg Rüpke

Measuring the World against the Body

Even if human agents are not the measure of all things, their bodies and their bodily dimensions often serve in this role. Whether life-sized, over-sized, or under-sized, representations of the human body and its parts impact the ways in which we conceive of, interact with, and relate to nature, as well as how we construct and reconstruct the man-made environment, that is to say, how we relate to the world. Up- or down-scaling, monumentalization or miniaturization, serve as strategies in the creation of anthropogenic 'products' that are employed in religious rituals, allowing for increases in attractiveness, astonishment, or deterrence, for reaching further out of or deeper into the world. As Hartmut Rosa puts it, 'Any elementary analysis of the ways in which human beings come to relate to the world, experience and perceive it, act and orient themselves within it, cannot but begin with the body.'[1] This is the starting point for the notion of scale that sits at the heart of the present volume.

This book, and the contributions collected within it, has its roots in a conference organized by the International Graduate School 'Resonant Self–World Relations in Ancient and Modern Socio-Religious Practices' (IGDK 2283/W 1265) — a joint project between the University of Graz and the Max Weber Centre for Advanced Cultural and Social Studies of the University of Erfurt — in collaboration with the Department of Archaeology, Classics, and Egyptology of the University of Liverpool and the Centre for Urban Network Evolutions (UrbNet) at Aarhus University.[2] Taking its cue from Rosa's sociological theory of resonant self-world relations and its particular emphasis on our bodily relations to the world, the conference and the contributions that have emerged from the papers delivered there engage closely, and from a number of different disciplinary angles, with the agents and forces that drive phenomena of magnification and miniaturization in Antiquity and modernity.

Against a background of recent advances in the fields of embodiment and lived religion,[3] materiality, memory studies,[4] and cultural perception of the body,[5] as well as research addressing the problem of scale,[6] our contributors address two main foci. On the one hand, the contributions examine artefacts that are either magnified (e.g. oversized inscriptions, architectural elements, statues, buildings) or miniaturized (e.g. coins, imagery, miniaturized religious gifts, or other miniaturized elements in religious contexts, such as amulets or anatomical votives). On the other hand, they study the semantics of monumentalization and miniaturization on the microscopic level (e.g. ekphrastic narratives, summary descriptions, schema of synecdoche, *pars pro toto* dedications, and rituals) and the macroscopic level (e.g. colonization, globalization, parochialism, social alienation and xenophobia, individualization, etc.).

Such complex issues can only be addressed adequately in an interdisciplinary context. Accordingly, this volume brings together experts from a wide range of disciplines, including Ancient Near Eastern Studies,

---

[1] Rosa 2019, 47.

[2] Funded by the German Science Foundation (GRK 2283) and the Austrian Science Fund (W 1265-G25), and the Danish National Research Foundation (DNRF 119), respectively.

[3] E.g. McGuire 1988; Morgan 2010; Raja and Rüpke 2015; Rüpke 2018.

[4] Meskell 2008; Boivin 2008; Drazin and Küchler 2015; Küchler 2019.

[5] Mol 2002; Rebay-Salisbury, Stig Sørensen, and Hughes 2010.

[6] E.g. Krämer 2009; McMahon 2013; Roberts 2016.

Archaeology, Classics, History, Philology, Religious Studies, and Sociology. The many and diverse examples discussed here show similarities and differences in their approaches to size and scale, assigning importance or meaning to objects based on size, and speaking about the materiality and immateriality of experience and practice in a variety of religious contexts. The main focus is on ancient Mediterranean material culture and architecture. However, glimpses beyond this area and period are offered by chapters reflecting a range of broader perspectives, from the History of Religions of the Ancient Near East to contemporary practices in medical emergencies and risky jobs. As can be seen in the ensuing contributions, the shared methodological focus benefitted from close engagement with a broad range of sources from different historical periods, enabling advances in interpretation as well as theoretical modelling.

This volume contains thirteen contributions arranged across four sections: 'Miniaturization', 'Monumentalization', 'Domestic Contexts', and 'The Fragmented and the Augmented Body'. While each section has a different focus, they are connected by the following key research questions: What were the essentials of magnification or miniaturization? What elements were eliminated, retained, or emphasized in these processes such that the end product remained recognizable? How did, and does, size relate to shape and material, and how were the materials and the objects made from them 'charged' by the respective scale? How did under- or over-life-sized modes of representation or dimensions influence the short-term experiences or long-term habitualizations of human agents? What were the wider socio-political ramifications of architectural minimizing or maximizing processes? And, finally, what was and is the impact of these processes on human perception and understanding?

Miniaturization

The section on miniaturization consists of contributions by Rubina Raja, Natascha Sojc, Anna-Katharina Rieger, and Elisabeth Trinkl, each of whom addresses issues of miniaturization in ancient material.

Rubina Raja's chapter 'Look Closely and You Will See: The Banqueting Tesserae from Palmyra and Small-Scale Iconography' tackles issues of definition of what is 'small', or what is 'not to scale' and how changes in dimensions trigger meaning and reaction. Motifs change size and place, allowing new or shifted meanings to be ascribed. Potential — and varying — meanings are offered due to the abstraction and formal reduction of the altars and niches, whereas in the case of small-scale imagery it is only the size, but not the details, that is reduced. Abstraction plays no part in the process. Rather, the reduction in size goes hand in hand with an increase in elaboration, detail, and artistic finesse. This approach to abstraction and reduction is traced by Raja above all through the tiny Palmyrene banqueting tesserae on which a myriad of signs, symbols, and iconographic elements appear.

In her contribution 'The Material Record of Micro-shares: An Archaeological Case Study on Sanctuary Transactions in Ancient Sicily', Natascha Sojc enquires into the religious and socio-economic implications of the archaeological record. Using the example of deposits in the sanctuary of S. Anna at Agrigento, Sojc distinguishes different ways of sharing with the gods: tiny manufactured things, fragments, parts of sets, or tiny natural objects. Drawing on analogies with Indian temples and offering rituals, she interprets the fifth-century BC contexts as the remains of a redistributive system that, over the course of a century, established a community that was subtly organized through the various options for micro-sharing. Traditional approaches that explain these objects in terms of *pars pro toto* offerings or the reciprocity of resource distribution fall short in view of the 'objectal' range of the deposits. It is rather choices and selections in 'gift-transactions' that dominate the scene and point to a close and deliberate cooperation between the worshippers.

Issues relating to the fuzziness of functions, ascriptions of meaning that are less than clear, and the imposition of overdetermined archaeological labels are central to Anna-Katharina Rieger's contribution, 'What Do Tiny Objects Want? A Case Study with Miniature Pottery from Pompeii'. This chapter examines the miniaturized pottery employed in various contexts in Pompeii (houses, street shrines) and in shared sacred places in the region. Size is not the only criterion for determining whether something is miniaturized or magnified. On the contrary, quantities must be taken into account as well, which, in turn, appear as both accumulations and as specific aggregations of ceramic products, thus widening the spectrum of interpretations. The role and purpose of individual tiny pots or collections thereof in ritual communication must be further differentiated. The ludic aspects of tiny vessels arising from their usage by children might sometimes provide an explanation. However, the fine nuances of the production processes, the change of bodily perception for an adult user, and the relation of container to content — in the case of very small containers making it appear as if the content fills the entire pot — are all factors that play into the various meanings of miniature vessels.

In her chapter 'Are the Same Objects Desirable for People and for Gods? Material and Dimensional Interchangeability', Elisabeth Trinkl starts from the question of what deities would like to receive as gifts from humans and how size and materials matter in this exchange. To exemplify the significance of the material and shape of offerings to the gods in archaic and classical Greece, Trinkl uses two images of Apollo — the Mantiklos Apollo, a tiny bronze statuette, and the Colossus of the Naxians, the largest *kouros* ever made. In both cases, the remarkable dimensions do not matter, but the material and expectations of the dedicator do. The practice of exhibiting and thereby offering such objects brings Trinkl to the importance of the intention of a consecration. Size and material underline an effectual expression in these acts of offering a gift. Material and size must be employed in such a way that the *kosmos* is maintained in the relationship between deity and humans. However, the intention is also transmitted through the skilful transformations objects may undergo. Trinkl uses examples of miniature pottery from Pheneos (Peloponnese), which play with size to successfully perpetuate former religious acts. Meanwhile, foodstuffs, flowers, and textiles are mimicked and produced in different materials (e.g. faience, clay) in a way that helps us see that gifts to the gods were most effective in ancient Greece when they transgressed the borders of different sizes and materials.

Monumentalization

The section on 'Monumentalization' consists of four chapters, by Diana Pavel, Jörg Rüpke, Devmini Malka Wijeratne, and Elena Malagoli. These chapters address the impact of magnification on issues pertaining to the size and number of religious objects, as well as on issues related to socio-religious strategies.

In 'Scaling Altars in the Etruscan Funerary Sphere', Diana Pavel focuses on the various forms and dimensions of altars in Etruscan necropoleis, showing that no pattern can be identified in the relation between size, shape, and location (inside a burial chamber, on top of a tumulus). According to Pavel, no hierarchy is at work here, but rather an intentional difference in the ways in which human agents interact on a practical (ritual and bodily) level with the altars. A distinctively bodily engagement can be associated with the differently dimensioned objects in Etruscan necropoleis that provided a medium for communication with the divine or the ancestors. The question of why some of the altars are so monumental cannot be answered. However, one may see elements of theatricality and an interaction with the surrounding landscape as possible factors that influenced the monumental design of certain tomb-connected altars.

Issues of monumentality are central to Jörg Rüpke's contribution on 'Urban Monumentality and Religion'. Rüpke asks why religious places in cities often become monumental and what this phenomenon says about the relationship between human agents and their gods, suggesting that it might be a tool by which humans exerted control over otherwise unattainable deities. The magnification of houses into large-scale temple buildings as well as the construction of city walls that visibly include and exclude led Rüpke to a view of the city as a monument. Aspects of socio-economic and political hierarchies also play an important role here, in that monumentality is created not only by density and largeness but also by the lack of these qualities (e.g. empty spaces, such as plazas or roads). The second part of the contribution goes on to discuss in depth how we can conceptualize monumentality when facing 'low density urbanism' (Fletcher 2009) and how control and urban diversity relate to each other.

As Devmini Malka Wijeratne shows in 'Perceptions of Changing Religious Landscapes in Augustan Rome', the interplay between size and number is of great importance. When Augustus's *Res gestae* mentions the renovation of more than eighty temples, what is at issue here is not just the work carried out on each or the size of any particular temple but rather their sheer number. Monumentality comes into existence through the amassing of quantity and comes to mean more than the sum of the individual parts. Larger audiences that are addressed and embraced in monumental events, in spaces, and by the objects and architecture displayed there, also play a role in this kind of *in situ* magnification, as well as in the process of magnification in general.

The final contribution in this section is Elena Malagoli's 'The King and the Population as Protagonists of the Oath: Intermediatory Semantics in Ancient Near Eastern Treaties'. Malagoli's chapter shows how textual strategies, metaphorical language, and associations with and hints at physical figures, spaces, cities, and monuments all work together to weave a textual tapestry on which both parties to a treaty can draw. Such evocations influence the imagination, imagined dimensions, meanings, and the reception and effect texts had or have on people. Malagoli enquires into the position of the

Hittite king and interprets him as a *pars pro toto* of his people. This process of association may have started in the mid-second millennium BC, but the phenomenon of conceptualizing a leader as a 'multiple body' can be traced throughout time (for example, in medieval Europe). However, in the course of Malagoli's inquiry the term '*pars pro toto*' is questioned, especially since the king in these types of treaties is presented as an active leader, and as acting on behalf of his people, rather than as a heroized, distant figure.

Domestic Space

In a chapter entitled 'Small, Versatile, Numinous: Pagan-Mythological Statuettes at the End of Antiquity', Ine Jacobs tackles aspects of the phenomenon of smaller-than-life-size statues and statuettes in late antique and Byzantine times (from the fourth to the seventh centuries AD, approximately). These figures are often thought of as the remnants of a polytheistic past or as elite décor that speak volumes about the owners' keen interests in Classical Greek *paideia*. However, in the context of Aphrodisias, as well as late antique houses and sanctuaries in other parts of the Mediterranean, Jacobs questions this view and maintains that the deliberate exhibition and reproduction of the statuettes of deities demonstrates an ongoing renegotiation of imagery that proves to be both 'functional' and powerful (emanating a type of 'efficacious endurance') as far as the communication with the divine is concerned. This new interpretation captures the religious dynamics in Late Antiquity much better than the traditionally held view of a 'falling back on "pagan beliefs"' or a 'resistance towards new beliefs'. Stressing the prospective rather than retrospective aspects that such imagery entailed, the author offers more than a simple black and white image of late antique religion.

Elisabeth Begemann's contribution, entitled 'A Dancing Deity: Diminishing the Goddess Libertas on the Palatine', shows how Roman authors play with seeming or real diminution (*exempla* in Valerius Maximus) or smaller and larger images of deities that are intended to function through contrasts. While Cicero's highly political speech *De domo sua* makes use of associations between moral categories (good/bad) and sizes (large/small), the ascription of these categories depends on content (Lar/Libertas) and Cicero builds his argument on associative allusions. The concept of Libertas, the goddess of freedom, venerated on the Palatine and, in principle, perceived to be good, is pejoratively moved towards a meaning of *licentia* and equated with a foreign *meretrix*, whereas Cicero's *Lares*, even if small as objects, attain a huge significance in the Roman context.

Peter Scherrer's chapter '*Di Penates*: From Small Objects to Anthropomorphic Gods' shifts the focus of this section of the volume by discussing anthropomorphic representations of a rather under-defined group of deities, namely the *Lares* and *Penates*. This group of deities are in turn situated within the wider context of vessels with heads found in provincial household contexts, the so-called *Gesichtsgefäße*, which are often found together with miniature receptacles or food shares. These objects may represent the *Di Penates*, who were called upon for the protection of livestock and the well-being of the household (as distinct from the *Di Penates publici*, who were called upon as gods by whom oaths were sworn). For all Romans, the individual family's *Di Penates* were important. With reference to Cicero's description — which aimed to discredit Verres's behaviour — of how the *Di Penates* normally received their shares of food in small receptacles, Scherrer explains the need for provincial inhabitants to make these *Di Penates* easily conceivable by the invention of *Gesichtsgefäße*. The process of anthropomorphization enables the construction of an addressable entity. The portability of the pots on which the faces of the deities were applied is crucial for this choice and product. Thus, Scherrer's chapter on *Lares* and *Di Penates* picks up a common thread in the contributions of Jacobs, Rieger, and Sojc, namely the contestation of forms and artistic production, as well as the socio-religious framings of provisioning, stockage, and reproduction in material culture.

The Fragmented and the Augmented Body

The last two chapters of this volume, by Georgia Petridou and Manuel Moser, make a number of bold and cross-cultural comparisons across a very wide range of periods, foregrounding the monumental impact of magnification and miniaturization in the process of establishing significant self–world relations with inanimate objects, the transcendental other, and other socio-religious agents.

In Georgia Petridou's chapter, 'The Eyes Have It: Materialities, Monumentality, and Meanings in Eye-Shaped Modern Greek *tamata* and Ancient Greek *anathemata*', the Greek Orthodox *tamata* to St Paraskevi are compared to the ancient eye-shaped dedications (*anathemata*) that were offered to Demeter and Kore. The common denominator between these groups of objects is that they both represent miniaturizations of internal and external human body parts. The comparison reveals that, in both Antiquity and modernity, a paradoxical coexistence of processes of miniaturization and magnification was and continues to be central to the meaning-making mechanisms of these objects. Despite both types of objects being effectively miniaturized versions of human bodies or its parts, they exercise monumental power in the eyes of both the dedicants and the deities to whom they are offered. In addition, comparing these seemingly incomparable eye-shaped dedications, Petridou argues, allows for an *ad fontes* analysis of the lived experience of ophthalmological illness in both Antiquity and modernity.

In 'A Triangle of Mary: Relating Religious Artefacts to Non-Religious Lorry Drivers', Manuel Moser presents material from a modern socio-religious study conducted in the (East) German trucking milieu. Moser argues that inquiring into the employment of religious objects offers unique insights into the process of establishing significant self–world relations with various social agents: the trucks, the drivers, the people close to them, and also a transcendental other. Moser sets these agents into relation, using the notion of 'assemblage' to frame a discussion of object agency — a topic that has also been addressed in papers on late antique statuettes and pottery, such as that of Jacobs in this volume. This object agency, Moser shows, can be found on many different physical scales: from the small-scale images or portable objects dear to the drivers, on the one hand, to the truck itself, on the other, as the ultimate assemblage.

Synopsis

To summarize, in some chapters of this volume, the body not only emerges as the canonical measure for objects, but is itself fragmented and fluid and in need of stabilization in complex socio-religious processes, while always standing in relation to magnified or miniaturized objects (Jacobs, Petridou, Raja, Rieger, Scherrer). Other chapters explore the all-important power relations pertaining to age and socio-economic factors, which can also be textually and/or visually expressed by differences in size (Begemann, Malagoli, Pavel, Sojc, Trinkl). Finally, several of our contributions reveal different but equally important parameters of the agency of both miniaturized and magnified objects in their shaping of the natural and man-made environments of human action (Moser, Rüpke, Wijeratne). Taking their cue from Rosa's sociological theory of resonant self–world relations and its particular emphasis on our bodily relationships,[7] all the papers collected in this volume engage closely, and from a variety of disciplinary perspectives, with the agents and forces that drive phenomena of magnification and miniaturization in Antiquity and modernity. Together, they make a substantial contribution to the wider scholarly debate regarding how the perception and meaning of undersized or oversized forms and structures is shaped and changed synchronically and diachronically by our inquiry into the human body and its size, and how this type of inquiry has an impact on modern and ancient processes by which humans develop resonant and muted relations self–world relations.

---

[7] Rosa 2019, 83–109.

Works Cited

Boivin, N. 2008. *Material Cultures, Material Minds: The Impact of Things on Human Thought, Society, and Evolution* (Cambridge: Cambridge University Press).

Drazin, A. and S. Küchler (eds). 2015. *The Social Life of Materials: Studies in Materials and Society* (London: Bloomsbury Academic).

Fletcher, R. 2009. 'Low-Density, Agrarian-Based Urbanism: A Comparative View', *Insights*, 4.2: 1–19.

Krämer, S. 2009. 'Gibt es maßlose Bilder?', in I. Reichle and S. Siegel (eds), *Maßlose Bilder: Visuelle Ästhetik der Transgressionen* (Munich: Fink), pp. 17–36.

Küchler, S. 2019. 'Some Thoughts on the Measure of Objects', in J. Davy and C. Dixon (eds), *Worlds in Miniature: Contemplating Miniaturisation in Global Material Culture* (London: University College London Press), pp. 176–88.

McGuire, M. B. 1988. *Ritual Healing in Suburban America* (New Brunswick: Rutgers University Press).

McMahon, A. 2013. 'Space, Sound, and Light: Toward a Sensory Experience of Ancient Monumental Architecture', *American Journal of Archaeology*, 117.2: 163–79.

Meskell, L. 2008. 'Memory Work and Material Practices', in B. J. Mills and W. Walker (eds), *Memory Work: The Materiality of Depositional Practice* (Santa Fe: School for Advanced Research Press), pp. 233–44.

Mol, A. 2002. *The Body Multiple: Ontology in Medical Practice* (Durham, NC: Duke University Press).

Morgan, D. (ed.). 2010. *Religion and Material Culture: The Matter of Belief* (London: Routledge).

Raja, R. and J. Rüpke (eds). 2015. *A Companion to the Archaeology of Religion in the Ancient World* (Malden: Wiley-Blackwell).

Rebay-Salisbury, K., M. L. Stig Sørensen, and J. Hughes (eds). 2010. *Body Parts and Bodies Whole: Changing Relations and Meanings* (Oxford: Oxbow).

Roberts, J. L. (ed.). 2016. *Scale* (Chicago: University of Chicago Press).

Rosa, H. 2019. *Resonance: A Sociology of our Relationship to the World* (Cambridge: Polity).

Rüpke, J. 2018. *Pantheon: A New History of Roman Religion* (Princeton: Princeton University Press).

MINIATURIZATION

2. Look Closely and You Will See: Banqueting Tesserae from Palmyra and Small-Scale Iconography

Rubina Raja

Everything Which Is Physically in the World Must Be Measured against Something Else

The banqueting tesserae from Palmyra, most of which were found scattered across the site, but with large concentrations in the sanctuaries of the city, remain one of the best sources for the diversity of the religious life of Palmyra. While a corpus was published in 1955, which gave a solid overview of the more than 1100 types of tesserae, these small tokens have only recently begun to be studied in a systematic way that allows us to say much more about the implications that they carry for our understanding of Palmyrene religious life.[1] The small objects, usually made of clay and not measuring more than a few centimetres in diameter, hold a rich and varied iconography connected to the oasis city's cults, deities, priesthoods, priestly groups, and ritual practices.[2] The small scale of these objects combined with their detailed iconography is the topic of this contribution with a focus on scaling, the meaning of small objects and the even smaller, but wide-ranging, iconographic repertoire. The combination of small objects and detailed iconography raises questions about the societal meanings of the tesserae and the broader societal implications of this unique phenomenon from this oasis city in the Syrian Desert. How are we to imagine that people would have perceived these objects? And do we have to imagine that they looked as closely at them as we do today when we study them? Or did the images on them not matter, as long as people knew that they were in possession of the right tessera in order to gain entrance to the religious banquet for which it served as a ticket? Or to receive the food and drink, which they would have given access to?

Big versus Small — Sanctuaries versus Tesserae

The so-called banqueting tesserae from Palmyra are our richest source to the oasis city's religious life.[3] The extremely rich and varied iconographies imprinted on them give information about the cults and their deities, priestly groups and individual priests, who organized religious banquets and paid for them, events which took place in numerous of the sanctuaries across the city and perhaps also outside those.[4] One should briefly explain the terminology attached to the tesserae, since these received their name only in modern times due to their rectangular shape taken from the Latin word *tessera*, meaning square or dice. This Latin word was introduced for such small square token-like ancient objects already in the eighteenth century.[5] When scholars began to publish on the Palmyrene objects they simply adopted this modern name for these small objects, whose antique name we do not know, since no sources from Palmyra mention them.[6] The earliest publications on the tesserae were mainly focused on the inscriptions that are found on numerous of them. Almost all of these, with only very few exceptions, were written in the local Palmyrene Aramaic dialect and related to names of individuals, priestly groups, or deities. A few give dates and measures of food and drink to be distributed. It was only much later that scholarship turned to the iconography on the tesserae in any depth, with big pushes being made in the publications from 1955 and 1944/1962.[7] Judging from

---

[1] Ingholt, Seyrig, and Starcky 1955. For the newest overview and research programme of the tesserae, see Raja 2022b.

[2] Raja 2015a; 2015b; 2016.

[3] Kaizer 2002; Raja 2019b; 2019c.

[4] Al-As'ad, Briquel-Chatonnet, and Yon 2005; Raja 2019a.

[5] Ficoroni 1740 with reference from Rostovtzeff 1897, 463; Crisà, Gkikaki, and Rowan 2019, 1–3.

[6] E.g. Spoer 1905; Simonsen 1889a; 1889b (the same publication in Danish and French, respectively).

[7] Ingholt, Seyrig, and Starcky 1955; du Mesnil du Buisson 1944; 1962.

their iconographic repertoire, they all stem from the first centuries AD. However, their chronology is in no way tightly defined yet, but is rather based on a few, in fact only five, that are dated by year. These datings span from AD 89 to 188 with some insecurities within that span as well.[8] The tesserae were usually made in terracotta and very seldom in other materials — other materials, however, might also be lost to a larger extent than the clay tesserae.[9] They were mould-made, which means that two moulds were made for each tesserae series — one for each side. The clay was then pressed into these moulds, taken out to dry, and then fired. The tesserae were made in series and currently more than 1300 types exist, of which numerous examples are extant of several series.[10] Within these about 1300 types more than ninety different shapes can be traced, which underlines that even when it came to the form of the tesserae, they were diverse. Furthermore, it renders the term tesserae inappropriate, since there are plenty of round, triangular, and other shapes within the repertoire.[11] Only one series, consisting of 125 examples of the same type, which is taken to be a complete series, has been found in an archaeological context.[12] They do not measure more than from a few centimetres to up to five centimetres in diameter and about one centimetre in thickness. So it is fair to say that they were very small objects. It is therefore even more interesting that so much attention seems to have been paid to the iconography on these objects, and that it was as composite as it appears to be, when other realms of Palmyrene art seem to be fairly streamlined and keep within certain iconographic borders.[13]

The tesserae were so to say on the absolutely opposite trajectory to the monumental sanctuaries in which they were used, such as the Sanctuary of Bel, the *temenos* of which measured more than 200 by 200 m.[14] Other sanctuaries were fairly large as well.[15] It is within the framework of these large spaces that we have to recontextualize the small objects that the banqueting tesserae were. How would people have perceived these when they were handed them? And where and in which contexts would these objects in fact be handed over? We have absolutely no evidence that gives us a clue about the distribution pattern of these objects. Nor do we know much about the collection patterns — apart from the one series of 125 tesserae mentioned above. As they were found buried in a pot in the Sanctuary of Arsu, they have been interpreted by the publishers as having been collected upon entrance to the sanctuary. Would the handing out have happened at other religious events? Or in public settings? Or rather in private settings? Would the inviter go around to those being invited handing them an object each? It is hard to imagine, since one could question what the idea would be with handing out entrance tickets to people you knew already and could recognize when they tried to gain entry. On the other hand, these tokens might simply have had the function of neat invitations, invitations to be remembered and perhaps kept. However, this does not explain why numerous of them were found in the drains of the banqueting hall in the Sanctuary of Bel, or why the series found in the Sanctuary of Arsu is interpreted as a series which had been collected already.[16] Perhaps we simply do not have enough archaeological knowledge to speculate further about the distribution patterns of tesserae, since the knowledge we have is at its best tied to the collection practice — and even that is poor evidence. In fact, the preface to the 1955 corpus may give the best explanation for our lack of archaeological contexts for these objects:

> En 1929 le Service des antiquités commença le déblaiement du sanctuaire de Bêl et M. Robert Amy, qui dirigeait ces travaux, put acquérir des paysans un nombre si considérable de tessères que le publication du recueil dut être différée.[17]

When the French mission cleared out the village in the Sanctuary of Bel, in which several hundred of local Tadmorians had lived until then, these objects would have sprawled out of the ground in the *temenos*, if they had been left there by attendees in Antiquity or collected by people guarding the entrance. The locals would have sold these finds to the French, while they were dis-

---

[8] Colledge 1976, 54. For dated examples, see: *RTP* 785 = AD 89/90 or AD 92/93; *RTP* 737 = AD 107/108; *RTP* 645 = AD 108/109 or AD 187/188; *RTP* 691 = AD 118/119, and *RTP* 32 = AD 132/133.

[9] Ingholt, Seyrig, and Starcky 1955, 5–6.

[10] Ingholt, Seyrig, and Starcky 1955 for more than 1100 types and Kubiak-Schneider and others (forthcoming) for another approximately two hundred types currently under publication.

[11] Raja 2022b, table 2.1.

[12] Al-As'ad, Briquel-Chatonnet, and Yon 2005.

[13] Raja 2017a; 2019d.

[14] Amy and Seyrig 1936; Seyrig, Amy, and Will 1968; 1975.

[15] Raja 2022a, 42–48 for further sanctuaries and their sizes as well as further references.

[16] Raja 2015a.

[17] Ingholt, Seyrig, and Starcky 1955, preface by Henri Seyrig.

Conceptualizing and Viewing the Subjects on the Tesserae

mantling their own houses in order to be moved to new accommodation in the new village outside the *temenos*.[18]

While the tesserae were small objects, they could be elaborate in terms of their iconography.[19] Furthermore, no two series were alike. What must it have been like to conceptualize these images? What were the processes behind developing them? And how did the small scale of the objects play into the conceptualization process? What did it feel like to hold these in one's hand and what would one do with them after coming into possession of them? How would they be kept safe until they were to be used? And if they were just meant to be discarded upon entry or buried upon collection, why does it then seem to have been important to have them made in such elaborate designs?

The iconographic patterns ranged from basic patterns to complex scenes. The basic types, such as a signet seal imprint on one side and nothing on the other, are rare (Figs 2.1–2.3). The most elaborate tesserae could hold complex scenes on one side and scenes with a multitude of religious symbols on the other (Figs 2.4–2.6). Tiny inscriptions could be placed on both sides of the tesserae, almost exclusively in Palmyrene Aramaic (Fig. 2.7) with a few examples in other languages (Greek: Fig. 2.8; Egyptian: Fig. 2.9). The iconographic repertoire was extremely varied and creative but was almost always connected to the religious realm. Numerous religious symbols, architecture, images of deities and of religious banqueting are found on the tesserae. Palmyrene priests, identified by their distinct hats, were also very common motifs of the tesserae.[20] The priests were either shown in bust-style frontally (Figs 2.10–2.12) or standing, also frontally shown (Figs 2.13–2.14). However, most often they were shown reclining on a banqueting couch, usually alone, but sometimes also together with another priest (Figs 2.15–2.17). They could be accompanied by inscriptions giving the names of the priest or the priestly group to which they belonged. Sometimes these inscriptions state that the priest invites to a banquet, or the inscription simply states that people should 'come', so

---

18 Baird, Kamash, and Raja 2023.
19 Ingholt, Seyrig, and Starcky 1955; Colledge 1976, 54–56.
20 Raja 2017b; 2018.

Figure 2.1. Tessera with a male bust and a blank side. Copenhagen, Ny Carlsberg Glyptotek, inv. no. I.N. 3260

Figure 2.2. Tessera with a bust of Athena and a blank side. Copenhagen, Ny Carlsberg Glyptotek, inv. no. I.N. 3229.

Figure 2.3. Tessera with a rosette (side A) and a seal impression of a male bust (side B). Copenhagen, Ny Carlsberg Glyptotek, inv. no. I.N. 3264.

Figure 2.4. Tessera with a bust of Poseidon (side A) and a half-figure of Beltî (side B). Around both are various symbols, for example a star and a globe. Copenhagen, Ny Carlsberg Glyptotek, inv. no. I.N. 3196.

Figure 2.5. Tessera with an inscription and astral symbols (side A) and a male bust surrounded by various astral and religious symbols (side B). Copenhagen, Ny Carlsberg Glyptotek, inv. no. I.N. 1141.

Figure 2.6. Tessera with the busts of two gods inside a crescent (side A) and a camel with a packsaddle (side B). Copenhagen, Ny Carlsberg Glyptotek, inv. no. I.N. 3193.

Figure 2.7. Tessera with a Palmyrene Aramaic inscription (side A) and symbols (side B). Copenhagen, Ny Carlsberg Glyptotek, inv. no. I.N. 3190.

Figure 2.8. Tessera with a priest bust (side A) and a Greek inscription (side B). Copenhagen, Ny Carlsberg Glyptotek, inv. no. I.N. 3216.

Figure 2.9. Tessera with a hieroglyphic cartouche (side A) and a seal impression with a female bust (side B). Copenhagen, Ny Carlsberg Glyptotek, inv. no. I.N. 3227.

Figure 2.10. Tessera with a bust of a priest and an inscription (side A) and a seal impression with a bust (side B). Copenhagen, Ny Carlsberg Glyptotek, inv. no. I.N. 2772.

Figure 2.11. Tessera with a bust of a priest flanked by palm leaves (side A) and a seal impression of Athena surrounded by a wreath (side B). Copenhagen, Ny Carlsberg Glyptotek, inv. no. I.N. 3215.

Figure 2.12. Tessera with the head of a ram (side A) and a priest bust (side B). Copenhagen, Ny Carlsberg Glyptotek, inv. no. I.N. 1142.

Figure 2.13. Tessera with a standing priest between two bulls (side A) and a bull and a sheep below a seal impression (side B). Copenhagen, Ny Carlsberg Glyptotek, inv. no. I.N. 3200.

Figure 2.14. Tessera of a seal impression surrounded by a wreath and an inscription below (side A) and a standing priest next to a star and a palm branch (side B). Copenhagen, Ny Carlsberg Glyptotek, inv. no. I.N. 3206.

Figure 2.15. Tessera with two reclining priests on each side. Copenhagen, Ny Carlsberg Glyptotek, inv. no. I.N. 3209.

Figure 2.16. Tessera with a reclining priest under vines (side A) and a seal impression of a standing male, surrounded by animal heads (side B). Copenhagen, Ny Carlsberg Glyptotek, inv. no. I.N. 2771.

Figure 2.17. Tessera with a reclining priest under vines and a garlanded arch (side A) and servants mixing wine with a seal impression of Apollo above (side B). Copenhagen, Ny Carlsberg Glyptotek, inv. no. I.N. 3208.

Figure 2.18. Tessera with a priest bust (side A) and a male god wearing a kalathos (side B). Copenhagen, Ny Carlsberg Glyptotek, inv. no. I.N. 3217.

that they should attend the event for which the tessera was an invitation.

The priests must have been the commissioners of the tesserae. They were the ones who sponsored the religious banquets.[21] How often or how exactly these events were organized, the evidence from Palmyra does not tell us much about, but these events would have offered the opportunity for socializing under the auspices of the deities who would have been celebrated and to whom sacrifices would have been made at these events.[22] Signet seals are found commonly on the tesserae. These would have tied the tesserae closely to one individual, namely the owner of the signet ring.[23] The signet seals usually carried motifs in Graeco-Roman styles, quite different from the styles otherwise shown on the tesserae or in general found in Palmyrene art. This is not so odd, since such seals and potentially even the rings they were set in would have been imported from other places. There are, however, also seals with motifs that look more local in style. This brief overview of motifs is not in any way exhaustive, but just outlines the diversity and range of combinations of images, which could be found on these very small objects.

Gazing with the Gods

Dining to celebrate the gods or even dining with the gods was a common religious practice in Antiquity, also in Palmyra. The Palmyrene tesserae literally reflect this situation in the cases where they carry reclining priests at banquets, sometimes with the gods above their heads and more usually with deities depicted on the other side (Fig. 2.18).[24]

In Palmyra, several banqueting halls are found in sanctuaries as well: one in the courtyard of the Sanctuary of Bel, one in the Sanctuary of Baalshamin, and two banqueting halls outside temple complexes. The banqueting hall in the Sanctuary of Baalshamin, immediately north of the *cella* of the Temple of Baalshamin, is known through an inscription.[25] However, the largest banqueting hall in Palmyra was located in the courtyard in the Sanctuary of Bel.[26] It is also in this banqueting hall that by far most of the tesserae were found in the underground drainage system.[27] The complex measured approximately 33 by 10 m, excluding the kitchen annexe to the north.[28] More than a hundred people would have

---

21 Kaizer 2002, 220–29.

22 Kaizer 2002 as well as Raja 2015a; 2015b; 2016; 2019a; Gnoli 2016.

23 Raja 2022b, table 2.2 for the signet seal impressions.

24 For examples, see Ingholt, Seyrig, and Starcky 1955, *RTP* type 17 (reclining priest with bust of a god above); *RTP* type 118 (reclining priest on one side, standing gods Bel, Iarhibôl, and Aglibôl on the other side); *RTP* type 284 (priest bust on one side, standing Hermes on the other side).

25 Kaizer 2002, 229–34.

26 Seyrig, Amy, and Will 1975.

27 Seyrig, Amy, and Will 1975.

28 Nielsen 2015, 51.

been able to dine at once in there. Several other banqueting halls are known through inscriptions from the site.[29] While banquets would of course have taken place in the halls built for such events, they might also have taken place outside, potentially in the sanctuary courtyards under the open sky. It would have been in these spaces that the sacrifices, from which the meat for the banquets and other foodstuffs would come, as well as ritual actions would have taken place. Maybe people would have moved from the open space into the closed dining hall depending on the size of the event, or maybe only some people, the specially invited, would have moved inside to dine while others would have dined outside. We simply do not know. However, what we can be sure of is that these events would have been connected to ritual actions, sacrifices, and worship. And the gods would have been called upon to be present and therefore also take part in the ritual dining with the living. Could one imagine that the gods cared for the imagery on the tesserae? Might this be one of the explanations for their elaborateness? That these were not only objects meant for the living, but also meant for the gods? As a sort of secondary sacrifice or token of appreciation and worship, which would have taken place both as preparation for the event and at the event?

The Role of Technology in Downscaling Objects and Upscaling Iconographic Complexity

I have recently argued that it might be entirely unnecessary to try to come up with a systematic typology of the iconography of the tesserae.[30] It simply does not exist, despite the fact that numerous elements were used over and again on the tesserae. The importance was in the combination of the different elements, and the commissioners or the producers must have had a very good overview of which types had been produced already — an aspect which never has been discussed in the discourses on these objects. Some iconographic elements were very common, such as priestly representations, images of deities, inscriptions, religious symbolism, and all were connected to the religious sphere, whereas the signet seal impressions rather reflected the personal identity of the owner of the signet ring. The overall designs of each single series should be seen as either a personal choice or a choice made by a group — but a choice which was then realized and produced by someone else, namely the mould-maker. This is where the concept of urban heterogeneity comes into the picture. As a feature of urban societies, heterogeneity can be understood in different ways. It can be used to describe a society marked by diverse social composition, including a wide variety of ethnic, class, religious, or gender groups. But it can also denote economic variation, which would have grown on a basis of labour specialization and division. If we take the term to imply social as well as economic differentiation, then this has implications for the way in which we may be able to view the tesserae as outcomes of urban heterogeneity in Palmyra. Through a focus on heterogeneity, we may in fact become more able to explore networks, which often are not that visible in the archaeological record, such as the 'weak ties', described as the social connections that go beyond the 'strong' bonds of kinship in the evolution of urbanism.[31] S. M. Sindbæk suggested that such connections may be a critical component of urban societies, and a factor that helps to focus and explain some of their social characteristics and developmental paths.[32] Through a large-scale study of the funerary portraits from Palmyra such issues have recently been explored, demonstrating clearly that it often only took one event pivoting around a few individuals to change the fortune of a city and seal its fate.[33] So might we also begin to study the tesserae in such a light? Namely as a phenomenon resulting from a high degree of urban heterogeneity in place at Palmyra, a heterogeneity that also was dependent on 'weak links' such as the presence of 'mould-makers', individuals who in reality would have been highly skilled craftsmen and artists carving highly detailed moulds.

Often translating such sociological terminology into the archaeological realm is difficult. Even if 'heterogeneity' is an actual and determinate quality of societies, the question remains how, and if at all, we can approach it through archaeological evidence. Where cities were places of choice for elites, the diversity of the material culture found there may be a poor guide to the heterogeneity of these places as compared to the wider regions or communities.[34] But might the tesserae from Palmyra again here be exactly a group of material, which offers an approach to consider economic heterogeneity? If so,

---

[29] Kaizer 2002, 220–29.

[30] Raja (forthcoming).

[31] Granovetter 1973; Sindbæk 2022.

[32] Sindbæk 2022.

[33] Raja, Bobou, and Romanowska 2021; Romanowska, Bobou, and Raja 2021.

[34] Raja and Sindbæk 2023.

the work of W. Brian Arthur presents a lens through which we might begin to explore the social processes and trajectories inherent in the tesserae as objects of social entanglements.[35] Arthur describes technology as 'assemblages of practices and components' brought together as 'a means to fulfil a human purpose'.[36] Basically he considers technologies both in the narrow sense of 'devices and engineering practices' and social or organizational techniques. He explains that new technologies tend to develop by 'combinatorial evolution' — a process that is instigated by the problems or opportunities encountered by humans, and typically, perhaps even universally, realized by combining and recombining previously known technologies for new ends.[37] This means that technologies often develop in protracted processes of experiment and refinement, of trial and error. When viewed through such a lens, technological evolution basically is the coming together of needs or wants, of skills and knowledge, and evidence for experimentation and tinkering with ways-of-doing. Such processes are the essence of heterogeneity. The ideal locations for the development of such are thus characterized by 'combinatorial' evolution and in the end effect carries an unmistakable correspondence to the traits seen as hallmarks of urban societies in archaeological studies and to the heterogeneity of sociological definitions of urbanism. Might this in fact be the key to understand the complexity of the tesserae, as outcomes of urban heterogeneity understood in its broadest sense? If this is the case, we have to study these not only as religious tokens or entrance tickets, but as outcomes of a societal process, which implied a highly heterogenic community on all levels. Only through the coming together of economic resources, religious complexity, the need for social control (of the entrance to ritual banquets), social stratification, and labour specialization could the tesserae have come into being. And the downscaling of the images to sizes almost unimaginable — and then in terracotta, which was not a precious material at all — very neatly encompasses all these trajectories and elements in one item.

Universal Heterogeneity: Bringing the World of the Living and the World of the Gods Together through 'Smallness'

With the risk of overstretching the concept of heterogeneity, one might go as far as to view the tesserae as objects which intend to bridge the world of the living and the world of the gods through their complex iconographic expressions. These tiny objects, so easily lost, so easy to carry, so easy to hide, so easy to forget, so easy to bring with one, could be seen as attempts at encompassing the entire Palmyrene way of doing or understanding religion, while at the same time giving us — when viewed as evidence for urban heterogeneity — a nuanced insight into the complexities of Palmyrene society, both culturally, socially, and religiously speaking. In an abstract way, the smallness of the tesserae brought down the heavens to the people, who could carry around astral symbolism and images of gods in their pockets or in their purses. In that way, people had the religious world embodied in a tiny object, which could mean the world — even if only for a certain period of time or even only for a moment.

---

35 Arthur 2009.
36 Arthur 2009, 28.
37 Arthur 2009, 18.

Works Cited

al-As'ad, K., F. Briquel-Chatonnet, and J.-B. Yon. 2005. 'The Sacred Banquets at Palmyra and the Functions of the Tesserae: Reflections on the Tokens Found in the Arṣu Temple', in E. Cussini (ed.), *A Journey to Palmyra: Collected Essays to Remember Delbert R. Hillers* (Leiden: Brill), pp. 1–10.

Amy, R. and H. Seyrig. 1936. 'Recherches dans la nécropole de Palmyre', *Syria: archéologie, art et histoire*, 17: 229–66.

Arthur, W. B. 2009. *The Nature of Technology: What It Is and How It Evolves* (New York: Free Press).

Baird, J., Z. Kamash, and R. Raja. 2023. 'Knowing Palmyra: Mandatory Production of Archaeological Knowledge', *Journal of Social Archaeology*, 23.1: https://doi.org/10.1177/14696053221144013.

Crisà, A., M. Gkikaki, and C. Rowan (eds). 2019. *Tokens: Culture, Connections, Communities*, Royal Numismatic Society Special Publications, 57 (London: Spink).

Colledge, M. A. R. 1976. *The Art of Palmyra* (London: Thames & Hudson).

du Mesnil du Buisson, R. 1944. *Tessères et monnaies de Palmyre* (Paris: Bibliothèque nationale de France).

——. 1962. *Les tessères et les monnaies de Palmyre* (Paris: Bibliothèque nationale de France).

Ficoroni, F. 1740. *I Piombi antichi* (Rome: nella Stamperia di Girolamo Mainardi).

Gnoli, T. 2016. 'Banqueting in Honour of the Gods: Notes on the Marzeah of Palmyra', in A. Kropp and R. Raja (eds), *The World of Palmyra*, Palmyrene Studies, 1 (Copenhagen: Royal Danish Academy of Sciences and Letters), pp. 31–41.

Granovetter, M. S. 1973. 'The Strength of Weak Ties', *American Journal of Sociology*, 78.6: 1360–80.

Ingholt, H., H. Seyrig, and J. Starcky. 1955. *Recueil des tessères de Palmyre* (Paris: Geuthner).

Kaizer, T. 2002. *The Religious Life of Palmyra: A Study of the Social Patterns of Worship in the Roman Period* (Stuttgart: Steiner).

Kubiak-Schneider, A. and others (forthcoming). *The Palmyrene Tesserae: An Update to the RTP* (Turnhout: Brepols).

Nielsen, I. 2015. 'The Assembly Rooms of Religious Groups in the Hellenistic and Roman Near East', in M. Blömer, A. Lichtenberger, and R. Raja (eds), *Religious Identities in the Levant from Alexander to Muhammed: Continuity and Change*, Contextualizing the Sacred, 4 (Turnhout: Brepols), pp. 47–74.

Raja, R. 2015a. 'Cultic Dining and Religious Patterns in Palmyra: The Case of the Palmyrene Banqueting Tesserae', in S. Faust, M. Seifert, and L. Ziemer (eds), *Antike. Architektur. Geschichte: Festschrift für Inge Nielsen zum 65. Geburtstag* (Aachen: Shaker), pp. 181–200.

——. 2015b. 'Staging "Private" Religion in Roman "Public" Palmyra: The Role of the Religious Dining Tickets (Banqueting *tesserae*)', in J. Rüpke and C. Ando (eds), *Public and Private in Ancient Mediterranean Law and Religion: Historical and Comparative Studies* (Berlin: De Gruyter), pp. 165–86.

——. 2016. 'In and out of Contexts: Explaining Religious Complexity through the Banqueting Tesserae from Palmyra', *Religion in the Roman Empire*, 2.3: 340–71.

——. 2017a. 'Going Individual: Roman Period Portraiture in Classical Archaeology', in A. Lichtenberger and R. Raja (eds), *The Diversity of Classical Archaeology*, Studies in Classical Archaeology, 1 (Turnhout: Brepols), pp. 271–86.

——. 2017b. 'You Can Leave your Hat on: Priestly Representations from Palmyra – Between Visual Genre, Religious Importance and Social Status', in R. L. Gordon, G. Petridou, and J. Rüpke (eds), *Beyond Priesthood: Religious Entrepreneurs and Innovators in the Imperial Era* (Berlin: De Gruyter), pp. 417–42.

——. 2018. 'The Matter of the Palmyrene "Modius": Remarks on the History of Research of the Terminology of the Palmyrene Priestly Hat', *Religion in the Roman Empire*, 4.2: 237–59.

——. 2019a. 'Religious Banquets in Palmyra and the Palmyrene Banqueting Tesserae', in A. Kropp and R. Raja (eds), *The World of Palmyra*, Palmyrene Studies, 1 (Copenhagen: Royal Danish Academy of Sciences and Letters), pp. 221–34.

——. (ed.). 2019b. *Revisiting the Religious Life of Palmyra*, Contextualizing the Sacred, 9 (Turnhout: Brepols).

——. 2019c. 'Revisiting the Religious Life of Palmyra: Or Why It Still Matters to Focus on Ancient Religious Life within the Context of a Single Site', in R. Raja (ed.), *Revisiting the Religious Life of Palmyra*, Contextualizing the Sacred, 9 (Turnhout: Brepols), pp. 1–6.

——. 2019d. 'Stacking Aesthetics in the Syrian Desert: Displaying Palmyrene Sculpture in the Public and Funerary Sphere', in C. M. Draycott and others (eds), *Visual Histories of the Classical World: Essays in Honour of R. R. R. Smith*, Studies in Classical Archaeology, 4 (Turnhout: Brepols), pp. 281–98.

——. 2022a. *Pearl of the Desert: A History of Palmyra* (Oxford: Oxford University Press).

——. 2022b. 'Revisiting the Palmyrene Banqueting Tesserae: Conceptualization, Production, Usage, and Meaning of the Palmyrene Tesserae — Perspectives for a New Corpus', in R. Raja (ed.), *The Small Stuff of the Palmyrenes: The Coins and Tesserae from Palmyra*, Studies in Palmyrene Archaeology and History, 5 (Brepols: Turnhout), pp. 5–68.

——. (forthcoming). 'The Banqueting *tesserae* from Palmyra Tokens for Religious Events', in R. Raja (ed.), *Handbook of Palmyra* (Oxford: Oxford University Press).

Raja, R., O. Bobou, and I. Romanowska. 2021. 'Three Hundred Years of Palmyrene History: Unlocking Archaeological Data for Studying Past Societal Transformations', *PlOS ONE*, 16.11: e0256081.

Raja, R. and S. M. Sindbæk. 2023. 'Urban Heterogeneity', *Journal of Urban Archaeology*, 8.

Romanowska, I., O. Bobou, and R. Raja. 2021. 'Reconstructing the Social, Economic and Demographic Trends of Palmyra's Elite from Funerary Data', *Journal of Archaeological Science*, 133: 105432.

Rostovtzeff, M. 1897. 'Étude sur les plombs antiques', *Revue numismatique*, 1: 462–93.

Seyrig, H., R. Amy, and E. Will. 1968. *Le temple de Bel á Palmyre: album* (Paris: Geuthner).

——. 1975. *Le temple de Bel á Palmyre: texte et planches* (Paris: Geuthner).

Simonsen, D. 1889a. *Sculptures et inscriptions de Palmyre à la Glyptothèque de Ny Carlsberg* (Copenhagen: Lind).

——. 1889b. *Skulpturer og Indskrifter fra Palmyra i Ny Carlsberg Glyptotek* (Copenhagen: Lind).

Sindbæk, S. M. 2022. 'Weak Ties and Strange Attractors: Anomalocivitas and the Archaeology of Urban Origins', *Journal of Urban Archaeology*, 5: 19–32.

Spoer, H. H. 1905. 'Palmyrene Tesserae', *Journal of the American Oriental Society*, 26: 113–16.

3. THE MATERIAL RECORD OF MICRO-SHARES: AN ARCHAEOLOGICAL CASE STUDY ON SANCTUARY TRANSACTIONS IN ANCIENT SICILY

Natascha Sojc

Introduction

With the ongoing excavation by the University of Augsburg of an extra-urban sanctuary belonging to the ancient city of Akragas on Sicily, the issue of scale is literally being addressed from the bottom up.[1] In the archaeological contexts discovered so far, varied forms of miniaturization prevail. The adjoining city, however, was adorned with a skyline of temples and one of the largest temples of the Greek world ever built, the Olympeion.[2] In the case of Akragas,[3] the study of the small and fragmented finds in the extra-urban sanctuary can fortunately be carried out against the background of monumentality of the city sanctuaries.

Based on the general findings on monumentalized sacred zones in the Greek world, it can be assumed that Akragas's city sanctuaries were places where the social status of the worshippers was expressed through the erection of buildings, statues, stelai, and inscriptions. The architecture and monuments functioned as media with a high representational value that served communication on two levels. The individual worshipper interacted with the deities on the one hand and on the other with the other people visiting the sanctuary.[4] It is further assumed that the social relations and hierarchies of the polis were represented or mirrored in the religious sphere of their sanctuaries, because the prestigious architectures and monuments were put up by competing politicians or elite families and remained visible for a long period.

Regarding the evidence of the extra-urban sanctuary, however, the argument is not readily applicable, which makes it necessary to choose another approach that focuses on instances of miniaturization.[5] These could be discussed for the built structures found there but can above all be investigated through numerous depositions, on which the following contribution will focus (Fig. 3.1).[6] The donations, which probably were not on display before being buried, show a remarkable wide range of smallness resulting from destruction and fragmentation to separation and dispersion. The materiality of reduction, in turn, seems to have transported miniaturization in a figurative sense as well. Since no written sources or inscriptions for the extra-urban sanctuary exist, the investigation of religious transformation of downscaling can only start from the finds and their contexts, from which ritual actions can also be deduced.[7]

---

[1] For comments on a draft of this paper, the author wishes to thank the organizers of the symposium 'Measuring the World against the Body: Materialities and Meanings of Magnification and Miniaturization in Religious Communications in Antiquity and Modernity', as well as the colleagues who joined in the discussion. For the productive discussions on the final version, I thank Anna-Katharina Rieger, Michael Schaper, and Caroline Veit, as well as Carolin Meckes for photographic processing.

[2] Cf. e.g. Parello 2020.

[3] Although the ancient city of Akragas on the southern coast of Sicily has been resettled in its northern part since the Middle Ages, where it is covered by the modern city of Agrigento, many important functional areas of the polis have been preserved. In the twentieth century, an active excavation and research activity in the urban sanctuaries, public areas, and necropoleis led to the ancient remains on an area of 934 ha being declared a UNESCO World Heritage Site in 1997, so that the ancient city is available for scientific research in the long term. It is also an advantage for archaeological research that several ancient authors report on the city of Akragas. Thus, the historical and political development of the polis from its foundation in the last decades of the sixth century BC, when it originated from the Sicilian city of Gela to its refoundation as Agrigentum by the Romans at the end of the third century BC, is recorded: De Waele 1971, 155–57; Adornato 2011.

[4] Cf. Frevel and von Hesberg (eds) 2007.

[5] This is not to exclude the possibility that similar communication processes also took place in the large city sanctuaries, but so far, depositions from urban sanctuaries have hardly been documented in a way that studies finds and ritual practices.

[6] Complex deposition in trench evolving around a locally produced Ola (US 112).

[7] As argued elsewhere, the archaeological record of the extra-urban sanctuary allows — to a certain extent — for the reconstruc-

Figure 3.1. Deposition of a cooking vessel into the natural soil during excavation, view from west. Agrigento, S. Anna. Fifth century BC. Photograph/3D model by C. Meckes.

By comparing the ritual treatment of objects like ceramic drinking vessels with the handling of their miniaturized counterparts, i.e. the fragments of a drinking vessel, the phenomena that motivated the miniaturization can be studied. As the material for the investigation derives from depositions, it is furthermore important to consider that these contexts reveal specific ancient choices which sanctuary attendants made with regard to the combinations of objects and rituals. The result amounts to a religious product that is more than a simple equation of the parts, for there definitely remain indications of temporal and spatial relationships between the finds, as well as of agency, inscribed in the contexts.[8] In order to do better justice in the analysis to this specific relationship between object, actors, and depositional activity, it seems helpful to draw on an anthropological model that conceptualizes such combinations between objects and rituals as shares the worshippers held in the sanctuary.

From such a perspective, besides the transformative quality of the rituals, the economic component of the religious process is emphasized, where not only material values were transformed into immaterial ones, but transactions in the manner of appropriations from the worshippers to the deity also took place. In a transfer of the anthropological model, the artefacts from the sanctuary that are reduced in size (e.g. the vessel fragments) and that are measured against the bodies of the worshippers of the sanctuary, will be considered 'micro-shares'. First, however, the extra-urban sanctuary of S. Anna and its research status will be briefly presented (Fig. 3.2).

S. Anna: An Extra-urban Sanctuary

Archaeologically conclusive remains of an extra-urban sacred site were discovered in 1965 during construction work on a private property in the Agrigento suburb of S. Anna. On the excavation area of about 1550 m², two architectural structures were uncovered, which are only preserved in foundation layers and one first course of the rising walls. Near and inside the buildings, several deposits were found in the ground, in which ceramic small

---

tion of spatial and temporal relationships between individual finds, cf. e.g. Sojc 2020a.

[8] Cf. Meskell 2008, 237–42 for the dialectic between objects and people.

3. THE MATERIAL RECORD OF MICRO-SHARES

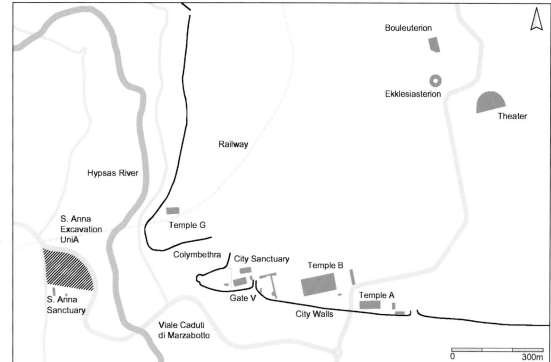

Figure 3.2. Akragas and the extra-urban sanctuary of S. Anna, the investigation area of Augsburg University indicated hatched. Map by A. Rheeder.

finds and terracotta figurines were well represented.[9] New surface finds made north of the sanctuary of S. Anna during 2011 suggested a significantly larger extension of the sacred area. This has since been confirmed by geoprospection, an archaeological survey, and excavations; since 2014, a team from Augsburg University has been researching this area of 15,686 m² (Fig. 3.3).[10] During the 2014–2021 campaigns, the remains of walls, stone settings, artefacts made of various materials, and

---

[9] Fiorentini 1969; Trombi 2017, 101–03.

[10] The author would like to thank the persons responsible for the Parco Archeologico e Paesaggistico della Valle dei Templi Agrigento, especially the directors Giuseppe Parello and Roberto Sciarratta, Maria Concetta Parello, and the management of the Soprintendenza BB.CC.AA. di Agrigento for the permission to conduct research in the area of the so-called Sanctuary of S. Anna. I would like to express my special thanks to the landowners, the Segreto family, for their interest and kind cooperation. Special thanks go to the University of Augsburg for funding the research. Further thanks go to all the students and graduates who participated in the excavation and finds processing campaigns at S. Anna. The findings summarized here would not have been possible without the dedicated participation of various specialists who provided the basis for this. Linda Adorno and Valentina Garaffa are responsible for the ceramic finds; Clemens Voigts took over the building research; the animal remains were examined by Roberto Miccichè and the botanical remains by Barbara Zach.

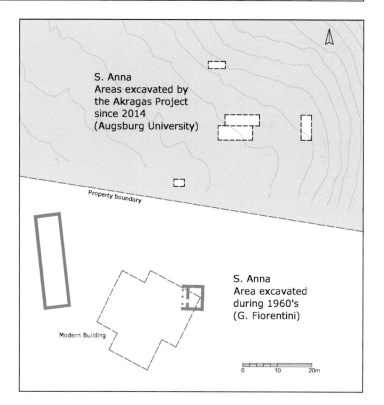

Figure 3.3. Extra-urban sanctuary of S. Anna, areas of investigation. Map by A. Rheeder.

Figure 3.4. Deposition during excavation: an olpe (top) found over a black-glazed oinochoe (middle) and drinking vessels (bottom). Agrigento, S. Anna. Fifth century BC. Photographs by A. Bell.

organic substances from the end of the sixth century BC to the beginning of the fourth century BC were excavated on the plateau.[11] The abundant finds can be interpreted as remaining traces of sacrifices, both votive offerings and festive meals.[12]

Characteristic for the S. Anna sanctuary are simple built features, mostly made of unworked arenite stones, and subsurface depositions, in large numbers and often filled with objects in a fragmented state (Fig. 3.4).[13] Since the publication of the first excavation in 1969, the sanctuary was attributed to Demeter in analogy with similar finds in other sites on Sicily.[14] Even if only a few of those could be linked to the goddess with the help of inscriptions or graffiti, the common trait of the sanctuary seemed to be the lack of costly *anathema* and a dominance of unexpensive, locally produced votives, like mould-made female figurines, buried in the ground. Arguably due to the low economic worth of the dedicated objects and the absence of monumental architecture, these sanctuaries in general and S. Anna in particular have been thought in earlier research to have been used by marginalized groups of society,[15] either as a venue for women's worship of the goddess, i.e. as a Thesmophorion, or alternatively as a place for cultural encounters between the Greek settlers and the local 'indigenous' people in a religious setting.[16] Meanwhile, the deconstruction of such a perspective and a broader material basis allows other interpretations to be considered as well.[17]

An interesting parallel to be considered for S. Anna is the new attribution which has recently been advanced for a cult site near Syracuse formerly identified as a Demeter sanctuary. Based on a broader knowledge of figurine iconography, the extra-urban sanctuary 'Belvedere-Santuzza', hitherto also known mainly for its deposits, was attributed to Artemis.[18] Furthermore, recent interpretations for inland sanctuaries (e.g. Sabuccina, Entella, and Morgantina-S. Francesco Bisconti) that likewise were earlier attributed to Demeter and characterized by a multitude of deposits in the ground, point us in the direction of hero or ancestor cults being practised there.[19] Finally, because a closer look at the depositions in S. Anna reveals that the material value of the archaeological finds must rather be considered heterogeneous instead of 'just cheap', a more general analogy can be proposed as well.[20] In cult places located near settlements on Crete, comparable heterogenous find spectra have been convincingly interpreted as an indicator for religious spaces with an integrative function and associated with broad social strata of the population participating in the rituals.[21] In addition, it has been suggested that these suburban sanctuaries served for rituals of transition from adolescence to adulthood. In general, Zeus, Apollo, or Hermes are conceivable as sanctuary gods for the rites of passage of young men, while Athena, Artemis, or Demeter could have acted as divine protectors for young women.[22]

In the light of these diverse interpretations, it seems promising to approach the sanctuary's remains at S. Anna from the perspective that the heterogeneous spectrum of deposited objects indicates a socially broad community active at the place. The fact that there still is no conclusive identification of the patron deity of S. Anna

---

[11] The natural plateau lies at an altitude of approx. 62–66 m a.s.l. above a river valley, cf. Sojc (ed.) 2017. Until 2019, an area of approximately 140 m² was excavated.

[12] During the investigations, great importance is given to the documentation of the spatial location of finds, which — together with their contexts — are being understood as remains of ancient activities.

[13] The upper layer of a depositional context was discovered in trench A in US 96 with the horizontally placed olpe (F 465). Directly under it, in US 111, lay a black-glazed oinochoe (F 483), two glass beads (F 486, F 489), and a second olpe (F 494) containing another glass bead (F 495). Further excavation revealed the deposition of other vessels and fragments. Prominently positioned among those was a two-handled cup placed bottom up (F 497). For an overview of finds and findings, see Sojc 2020a.

[14] Fiorentini 1969.

[15] This criticism already voiced by Hinz 1998, 232 while commenting on earlier research.

[16] Cf. Hinz 1998, 92; De Miro 2008, 53–59; Parisi 2017, 151.

[17] Cf. Sojc 2021 for the argument in detail.

[18] Alfieri Tonini 2012. Alfieri Tonini also suggested that the worship of Artemis in a kind of communal cult (sometimes also together with Persephone) could also be considered in other Demeter sanctuaries.

[19] For a reinterpretation of inland sanctuaries formerly addressed as Demeter sanctuaries, see Öhlinger 2015, 76–85 and 169–71.

[20] Beside pottery and terracotta, pieces made of bronze and glass were also dedicated at S. Anna, and next to locally produced goods some imports can also be found. For a general discussion about the cheapness of miniaturized votives, see Foxhall 2015.

[21] For suburban sanctuaries on Crete, cf. Prent 2005, 476–502.

[22] A further possible comparison for the S. Anna sanctuary is the extra-urban sacred site of the Apoikia Selinous in the 'Gaggera' area, which is in fact, as inscriptions reveal, a sequence of sanctuaries with areas dedicated to the worship of Demeter Malophoros, Zeus Meilichios, and Hecate. Cf. Spatafora 2020.

nor of the primary ritual function of the sanctuary is not an obstacle to this approach.[23] The variety of possible interpretations shows that the deposits at S. Anna were in their time most likely not considered deficient and were probably not compared to the monumentality of the inner-city sanctuaries of Akragas. On the contrary, the structured depositions must have felt to be appropriate for the religious context of this extra-urban sanctuary. Archaeological analysis must therefore consider the remains of the rituals in S. Anna as the material expression of a distinct performative dynamic in this sacred place. The depositions that are documented in the excavation are very diverse — both in terms of content and the sequence of ritual acts — and were carried out over several generations. Thus, it can be assumed that at the sacred site a salient set of values applied to the votive offerings probably aimed to integrate worshippers through ritual activities performed for the deity of the sanctuary. Thus, the religious habitus should focus on the horizontal communication among fellow worshippers, which could have primarily expressed social communality, instead of agonistic messages.

Ritual Object and Ritual Handling Understood as Share

To gain a fresh perspective on the transactions at the S. Anna sanctuary, it seems useful to turn to anthropology, where structures and performances in religious communities have been documented together with all the material props. A model that represents ritual processes in an entirety that we miss in the archaeological record could be used to tentatively reconstruct the processes of transformation and help us understand better what role the objects in the depositions played in the wide spectrum of donation, votive, and sacrifice.[24]

The different ways and means of establishing social cohesion in the religious sphere of a sovereign deity have been studied in great detail by Arjun Appadurai for a south Indian Hindu Vaishnavite temple.[25] A multitude of rituals and tasks in the temple, as well as a broad spectrum of gifts to the deity, have been documented, analysed, and merged into an anthropological model that can be tried out in an adapted version to the archaeological contexts at hand in S. Anna. In the framework of the polytheistic Hindu religion, each temple is understood as the realm of a sovereign deity which is at the centre of material and immaterial transactions. These activities include preparing meals for the deity, feeding the deity, clothing it, saying different prayers at special times of the day, and singing songs. Donating small or large amounts of cash or land is also part of the process. Gifts to the deity range from leaves and flowers to all sorts of objects and utensils,[26] embellishment of shrines, and vehicles for processions. In a sense of economic autonomy, the deity is considered the owner of all the goods which are either saved or redistributed in its name. In the process of worship, gifts and services to the deity are carried out in association with others and converted into immaterial values. Each of the many worshippers is in a relationship of exchange with the deity and is therefore considered to have a 'share' in the sanctuary. This is also recognized by the other members of the religious community through respect for the importance of every role played in the temple, tasks carried out together, and certain 'honours'.[27] Their symbolism is primarily relational,[28] like being allowed to approach the image of the deity or hanging a garland in its shrine, the preparation or distribution of food during a religious festivals, and the right to consume a special amount of food during communal feasts.[29] The right to donate, to give gifts, and to perform rituals, i.e. to have a share, is conceived as such an honour. It is also good to be close to the deity because the deity offers protection in the broadest sense, and protection can also be asked for in a specific form. Protection can also mean a purification of the devotee, a mediation in a conflict, or a safeguard for the ongoing relationship between the worshipper and the deity. In a cultural sense, the redistributive process centring on the temple deity organizes the vast and varied congregation, establishing and strengthening the religious ties between the worshippers by their joint ritual actions and the materiality of their contributions to the temple.[30]

---

[23] Because of the many zoobotanical remains, one could also think of an agricultural celebration; for the range, cf. Isager and Skydsgaard 2013, 157–98.

[24] For the importance of agency and ritual practices in the lived religion approach, see Albrecht and others 2018.

[25] Appadurai 1981.

[26] Even if none of these objects is involved in the practice of sub-surface depositions, the broad range of things, many of them seemingly mismatched, is notable for transfer and applicability.

[27] Appadurai 1981, 212. Cf. Graeber 2001, 30–33.

[28] The share also means that the rest — the whole — is 'outside', i.e. the deity, the human being, and the whole are connected by the rite.

[29] Appadurai 1981, 145–47.

[30] Appadurai and Appadurai-Breckenridge 1976.

The form of organization that is at work here and is authorized solely by the sovereign deity is not a pyramidal hierarchy but rather an orchestration of a complex set of shares and honours, which does not necessarily mirror the social status held outside of the temple.[31] Individual devotees experience and reaffirm their own position in the temple community in these processes and in relation to the deity while interacting with others. Most of the communication in the temple is focused on the expression of these relationships. Finally, the cohesion of the religious community is based on a general consistency between the self-assessment of the attendants and the recognition by others in the congregation and, of course, the deity.

The anthropological model opens up possibilities to reconstruct some of the missing links in the archaeological record at the sanctuary of S. Anna. Above all, it can be proposed that the objects together with their contexts — that is, the depositions (Fig. 3.1) — can be understood as the remains of ancient worshippers' shares in the sanctuary. It can be hypothesized that for the ancient worshipper the right to participate in the creation of a deposition would make the relationship with the deity of the sanctuary visible and be equal to an honour in the religious community. The broad range of objects that was brought to the deity and handled in different ritual ways could be further read as an immense archive of transactions and a network of relations.[32]

Let us therefore assume that the artefacts such as ceramic vessels, terracotta figurines, glass, metal, food, and liquids, as well as natural objects like plant seeds or seashells, were considered to hold value for the receiving deity.[33] The archaeological context of these items could be understood as a variety of performative acts that were seemingly able to bring about the transformation of the objects into shares.[34] We could for example envision the following process. First, a space was allotted for the deposit and then fellow worshippers were chosen to either assist or witness the ritual. Next, a pit was dug in the ground; it was then decided which artefacts and natural things should be placed inside, if the object should be given whole or only in fragments, or if a libation or a faunal offering should be added to the deposition. All sacrificial material had to be positioned, fixed, or stacked in an appropriate order; the deposit had to be closed; and finally it had to be determined whether it should be marked above ground and in which way.[35] The many possible combinations of objects and transformative acts suggest that there was a great variety of possibilities available to connect with the deity and to hold and maintain this connection in the sanctuary of S. Anna.

Starting out from the objects gifted to the deity in S. Anna, the many instances of fragmentation, like small pieces of metal, ceramic, and terracotta, stand out as part of the depositions. Cases of miniaturization achieved through the separation of individual pieces from larger sets like loom weights and glass beads are also characteristic finds from the excavation of the sanctuary. Therefore, in the course of the following, such micro-parts of the sanctuary will be presented and some of their prominent characteristics will be discussed.

Nothing Is too Small or too Light: Miniaturized Bronze Artefacts

One of the finds that the S. Anna sanctuary is known for in research since the 1960s is the discovery of a *pithos* of indigenous production in which *c.* 150 kg of bronze pieces of different shapes, sizes, and provenances were deposited.[36] Beside Greek vascular attachments, there are Sicilian *lettucci astragaloidi* and a sword pommel from France, as well as melting stock, intermediate products, and perhaps also copper ore.[37] Some of the 729 items date back to the seventh century BC and are thought to have circulated for a long time before being deposited at S. Anna.[38] The objects contained in the *pithos* come in varied states of technical or craft treatment and usages.[39] Even if many pieces are of Greek and Sicilian manufacture, the deposition assembles objects of different origins relating to various areas geographically,

---

[31] Appadurai 1981, 61–62.

[32] Cf. Rieger 2016, who highlights the collective memory function of the depositions in sanctuaries.

[33] Frequently, natural objects and substances also form part of the deposits; these will be discussed elsewhere.

[34] The concept of the share underlines how important it is to document the archaeological finds in combination with the context that can supply information of the ritual handling. Without this evidence, the transformation from material to immaterial is lost.

[35] The complexity of some of these ritual handlings leading to the creation of a deposition seem to be the result of worshippers working together.

[36] For an image, see <https://ausstellungen.deutsche-digitale-bibliothek.de/akragas-projekt/#s12> [accessed 12 February 2023].

[37] Baitinger 2017.

[38] Trombi 2017, 97.

[39] The usage probably also included the cutting of bronzes to enable smaller bargains.

Figure 3.5. *Aes rude* (bronze). Agrigento, S. Anna.
Fifth century BC. Photograph by L. Götz.

culturally, and temporally, as well as items that seem technically and typologically unmarked (e.g. rectangular bronze plates).[40] Moreover, the bronzes show a noteworthy range of scale, from heavy, fist-sized items of 2 kg to pieces with dimensions of only a few centimetres and weighing a few grams.[41] With regard to bronze pieces of various forms (e.g. rings), *aes rude* (Fig. 3.5), and scrap, recent research has shown that for Sicily as well as for central Europe, bronze still held exchange value for long-distance and intra-island trade at least up to the fifth century BC.[42] This means that any bronze object or fragment held a quasi-monetary value and could be used for trading, even alongside coinage.[43]

The bronze 'sanctuary treasure' was discovered in the middle of a rectangular building, of which only the earthen floor and the first course of blocks of the walls remain.[44] The *pithos*, which had a wide opening, was embedded in the ground up to two-thirds of its height,[45] and it would have protruded about 15 cm out of the floor.[46] The partial immersion in the floor indicates that the treasure remained accessible for retrieval of pieces when needed throughout a longer period.[47] Above the bronze filling the *pithos*, a deposition was found consisting of two iron knives, a miniature vessel, and a black-glazed *phiale*. This deposition is considered to be the sealing of the sanctuary treasure. It is dated to the end of the fifth century BC, when the whole building is thought to have been destroyed during the Carthaginian attack on Akragas; a destruction layer formed over the *pithos* and the deposition.[48]

Although there is no archaeological indication if the bronze was donated during one large ritual or if it was filled up in the course of time though repetitive ritual practice, the physical and performative elements can be considered comparable.[49] The worshipper had to choose a piece of bronze out of his or her own possession,[50] enter the building, walk up to the *pithos*, and bend down to reach it. Although the heavy and big pieces would have to be put down with caution to not break the vessel in the act of deposition, the small objects would have to be handled with another form of care. Perhaps a piece of metal scrap was first displayed in the open palm of the hand and then taken up with only the fingers to place it in the storage vessel, next to the other bronzes. Alternatively, it could be veiled by the hand and then placed in the interior of the *pithos*, thus concealing the donation that then vanished among the other pieces. Together with the act of donating, the conversion of a

---

[40] Archaeometric analysis of metal alloy could supply new information on the scrap metal used for the intermediate products where no attribution through visual characteristics is possible. A PhD project at the University of Augsburg by Giovanni D'Elia is underway to investigate these questions.

[41] Trombi 2017, 97. Cf. 97 n. 21 for a summary on the up-to-now inconclusive debate about if there existed a bronze weight system similar to a coinage system.

[42] Verger 2003; Baitinger 2016.

[43] Baitinger 2013.

[44] Fiorentini 1969, 63, 68–76. If the structure of 27.5 m × 7.5 m is to be considered as an enclosure or as roofed remains open. The material in the foundation trenches of the rectangular building can be dated somewhat later, namely between the middle of the sixth century BC and the beginning of the fifth century BC. Dating elements are terracotta fragments of Daedalian style, Corinthian pottery, and their local imitations; see Fiorentini 1969, 66 with n. 6. The rectangular structure can therefore only be safely assumed to date from around 500 BC: Hinz 1998, 71; Baitinger 2017, 109. A Bronze Age or indigenous pre-colonial sanctuary, as suggested by Fiorentini

1969, 75 as a forerunner at this site, can be ruled out according to current knowledge, because no earlier material was found either in the excavations nor during the extensive surveys; see Adorno 2017; Sojc 2020a.

[45] The vessel's remaining height is *c.* 48 cm and the opening is *c.* 59 cm wide; cf. Fiorentini 1969, 71. The earthen floor level of clayey composition in the building was found to be consistently *c.* 10 cm deep and spread over the natural ground, which is likewise clayey: Fiorentini 1969, 65–67 with fig. 1. To position the *pithos* into the ground, a hole must have been dug through the floor level and into the natural soil.

[46] This reading is supported by the positioning of the other depositions inside the building, which were found interred into the floor.

[47] Baitinger 2017.

[48] Fiorentini 1969, 71; Baitinger 2017, 112.

[49] For investigating the embodied experience of past action as approach in the research of rituals, see Lee 2005.

[50] Personal belongings as offerings, cf. Hughes 2017 and below.

3. THE MATERIAL RECORD OF MICRO-SHARES

Figure 3.6. Pieces of bronze from deposition (arrowhead, finger ring, and fragment of a furniture attachment). Agrigento, S. Anna. Fifth century BC. Photograph by D. Stante.

piece of bronze into a share held in the sanctuary was achieved. It seems that nothing was too light or too small to be considered suitable, as such a share or that size did not matter so long as it was any piece of bronze. Other rituals were carried out, because both containers deposited above the bronze — the miniature vessel and the black-glazed *phialai* — might have been used for libations of small amounts of liquids, cereals, or food offerings. The two iron knives might have been used for food preparation or for sacrificing animals, and they perhaps point us towards two persons acting together in these rituals. Additionally, it could be hypothesized that the retrievability of the bronze from the treasure also indicates that the process of donating into the treasure could have been ongoing. In such a scenario, the sealing of the treasure could have been enacted not only once, when the container was considered 'filled', but each time metal was put in or retrieved. Taking this line of speculative thought a step further, such a ritual could mean that perhaps someone had to witness the positioning of the piece of bronze.[51]

Beside the donations in the sanctuary treasury, bronze is present as a dedication in many depositional assemblages. Some of them were encountered in close proximity to the *pithos* in the 1960s excavation, interred either in the floor of the building or directly outside it, buried under the pebble pavement. Among the bronze items that form a part of these depositions are *phialai*, many times in a miniaturized or fragmented state, a type of object that has not been noted in the content of the *pithos*.[52] One deposition found *c.* 1.5 m to the south-west of the pithos contained not only two miniaturized *phialai*, one of them fragmented, but also two small rectangular bronze plates as well as pieces of bronze scrap.[53]

Comparing the bronze recovered in the treasure and the over three hundred pieces in the many depositions excavated since 2014 in the north-eastern area of the sanctuary, it is remarkable that only the small, light ones are a common find (Fig. 3.6). In fact, the bronze offerings with a few grams of weight in many depositions can still be lighter than those with the lowest weight in the storage vessel (at least 5 g).[54] It can be observed that the transformation of small and light bronze objects into micro-shares was undertaken mainly in combination with other objects. For example a piece of *aes rude* was found deposited together with a seashell in a locally produced, unpainted drinking cup with a hemispherical body; these were subsequently covered.[55] It seems likely that the place for the deposition was pointed out to the worshipper, who would have had to kneel down to enact the transformation and to carefully handle the

---

[51] One can think of a priest or priestess or some dignitary of the religious community. Alternatively, questions of permission could be brought into play, e.g. a dignitary taking the piece of bronze from the devotee and putting it into the vessel. It is intriguing to imagine that any donation of bronze into the treasure would also require other rituals to properly transform a piece of bronze into a share or micro-share, which would require at least one other person's assistance to enact.

[52] A revisitation of the content of the *pithos* remains a desideratum. Beside the *phialai*, other categories of bronze objects absent from the *pithos* but encountered in the numerous depositions found in a north-eastern area of the sanctuary are coins, graters, and rings.

[53] Deposition 5: cf. Fiorentini 1969, 70–71.

[54] Since 2014, bronze pieces have been found in deposits and in so-called sacred rubbish contexts, e.g., depositional pits, with weights up to *c.* 200 g.

[55] Sojc 2020a, 241. The *aes rude* (F 273), the seashell, and hemispherical cup (F 279) are embedded in a layer of objects (US 34 in trench A) before being covered with earth to create a new, higher sanctuary floor level.

bronze and the shell before protecting it in the body of the drinking cup. The drinking vessel in turn refers to another ritual — a feast or a libation — that might have preceded the laying down of objects. Nearby were found other deposited drinking cups; thus it might be that more than one devotee participated in and witnessed the ritual.[56] In another instance a miniaturized *phiale* was placed on the pebble pavement of the sanctuary and subsequently covered with earth and small stones.[57] The gift seems to have been deposited in one single act, perhaps indicating that a tiny amount of liquid was libated from it before it was deposited.

As most of these depositions of bronze were covered by earth, stones, or roof tile fragments, it is unlikely that these metal objects were meant for later retrieval. Instead, these micro-shares were supposed to rest for good in the sanctuary. Once more taking up the hypothesis formulated above — namely, that the bronze in the treasure was not deposited in one moment in time but that donation was an ongoing process — this could indicate for the small pieces of bronze that perhaps attendants had a choice. They could perhaps have decided whether their bronze should become part of the treasure or of a deposition.[58] Alternatively, it can be imagined that, when gifting bronze, there would have to be a piece for the treasure and one that went into the deposition in the ground. Based on the current trends in the evidence, which indicate a chronological coexistence of both the *pithos* and the depositions, a hypothetical conclusion would be that the small pieces offered more possibilities for ritual transformation. They could have been either laid down or given as contribution to the sanctuary property. For the bigger bronzes, i.e. those with higher economic value, one could perhaps postulate ritual rules that only permitted their transfer to the communal sanctuary treasure. Every size has a certain meaning, and the micro-shares do relate in quite a few ways to the deity, the community, and the donator. This number and diversity of links could be understood as ongoing ritual communication.[59]

Tiny Bits and Pieces: Fragments of Ceramic and Terracotta

In the material record of the S. Anna sanctuary, ceramic miniature vessels and doll-sized anthropomorphic terracotta figurines are found frequently.[60] These two forms of miniaturization are considered to be characteristic finds by archaeological research that, when present in significant numbers in an excavation, allow the site to be identified as a sanctuary. The question of what role the miniature vessels and the figurines played in the Greek sanctuaries is a subject in itself;[61] the focus in the following will be on the depositions of fragments of vessels or terracotta. Such items found in the sanctuary of S. Anna have been identified not only as dedicated objects in their own right but also as components used to 'construct' depositions.

Vessels

In the sanctuary of S. Anna, drinking vessels — above all, the locally produced unpainted cups with two horizontal handles — have been laid down in a variety of depositional contexts, both as entire vessels and also in fragmented states.[62] The handle of a *kotyle*, for instance, was deposited together with a bronze patera fragment,

---

[56] Be this as it may, the archaeological context indicates that at least in this one instance additional substances would have to be brought along beforehand and preparations, a sacrifice, and a meal would be held perhaps in other areas of the sanctuary before visiting the ashlar building with the bronze deposit.

[57] The *phiale* (F 278) was positioned on the pavement US 38 in trench A. It was made from a plate *c.* 2 mm thick with a diameter of *c.* 9 cm. The *phiale* broke *in situ* and not all fragments could be recovered, because it was seemingly damaged by another deposition that was buried next to and partially over it, possibly at a later time.

[58] For the large bronze pieces, it seems instead to have been considered inappropriate that they should go subsurface, and only the ritual transfer into the sanctuary treasure could turn them into a share.

[59] Referring to the ritual practice of depositing bronze as a widespread practice since the Bronze Age (cf. Leonard 2015; Fontijn 2020), it would seem worthwhile to compare and contrast depositions from S. Anna and other similar finds from Greek sanctuaries with Bronze Age contexts diachronically to find out about these ritual intentions in the *longue durée*. Perhaps up to now we have tended to overlook continuities in religious behaviour handed down from generation to generation well into the Archaic and even the Classical Age because of the divide between academic disciplines.

[60] Cf. Fiorentini 1969; Hinz 1998; Trombi 2017; Adorno and Garaffa (forthcoming); Eimer (forthcoming).

[61] For miniature vessels, see e.g. Ekroth 2003; Tournavitou 2009; Rieger 2016, 314–18; Pilz 2011. For terracotta figurines, see Albertocchi 2004; van Rooijen 2019.

[62] For the whole vessels, cf. Sojc 2020a on the various depositions of these cups, mostly *kotylai* or so-called two-handled cups, in S. Anna. For the general role of fragmented pottery in Graeco-Roman sanctuaries, I base myself on the landmark paper of Rieger 2016. Cf. also Patera 2015 for patterns of substitution.

3. THE MATERIAL RECORD OF MICRO-SHARES

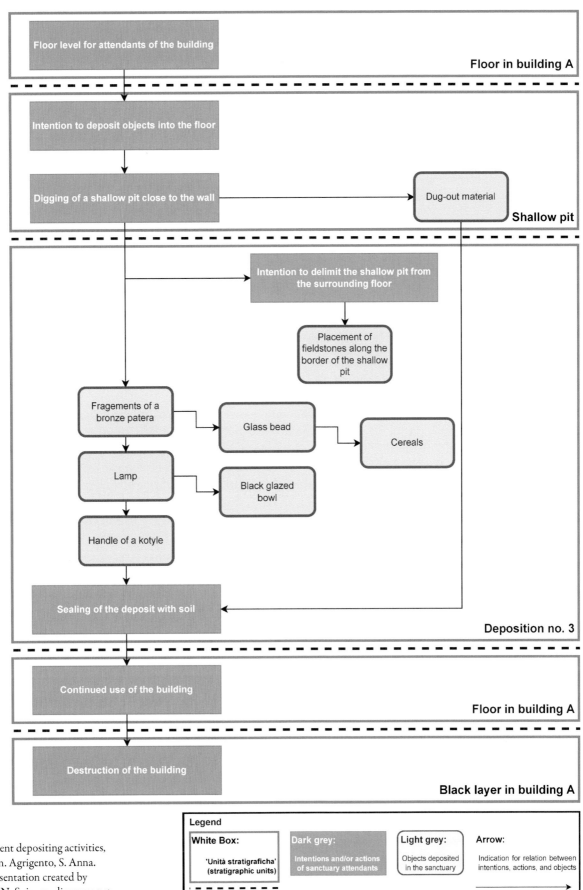

Figure 3.7. Ancient depositing activities, 1960s excavation. Agrigento, S. Anna. Schematic representation created by M. Schaper and N. Sojc. on diagrams.net.

Figure 3.8. Deposition of two black-glazed handles belonging to two different vessels. Agrigento, S. Anna. Fifth century BC. Photographs by C. Meckes and T. Dworschak.

a lamp, a small bowl, and cereals.[63] The objects were put in a shallow pit that had been dug in the floor and lined with stones and covered with earth (Fig. 3.7).[64] In another case, two handles, each of a different black-glazed cup, were deposited on the sanctuary floor in close proximity to one another and carefully covered by a fragment of a roof tile (Fig. 3.8).[65] Lastly, the structure seems to have been levelled in such a way that the floor remained walkable.

The handle alone — as well as the entire vessel — in a deposition alludes to other ritual acts, drinking during a feast, offering food, sacrificing cereals, or a libation from the cup.[66] The handle indicates prior transformations: namely, the breaking of the vessel in a way that the handle remained whole, contrary to the body of the vessel which, after breaking, could no longer fulfil its original function as a cup. At the same time, the handle had also lost its functionality — there was nothing left to 'handle' with it. Next in the process came the separation of one handle from the rest of the vessel fragments. For the remaining handle, it can be envisioned that it could have been kept, used another time, or taken home as a material reminder of the ritual activities.

Alternatively, if it was still attached to a larger piece of the vessel's body, as is the case in some instances of finds, this part could have still been used as a container for smaller amounts of liquids in libation rituals.[67] The question of where the rest of the fragments went is to date open for the individual finds, but some of the levelling layers in the sanctuary were filled with 'sanctuary trash'.[68]

For such and similar activities, the fragments could have been kept and reused: for example, in the 'construction' of depositions. In the same way that we find individual whole drinking vessels deposited together with another object, with the cup functioning as a cover for that other object; fragments or bottoms could also be used to protect a dedicatory object. In these instances, however, we as excavators are up to now less inclined to understand the sherd as a dedication in its own right.[69]

---

[63] See Fiorentini 1969, 70. Deposition 3: Fiorentini 1969, Tafel 34.1 nos 1, 4, 6, 7.

[64] This and the other diagrams presented in the text schematically depict the stratigraphic layers in which the objects were deposited. The spatial and temporal references of actions that can be reconstructed from object and context are also shown. Stratigraphic layers are represented starting from the deepest, i.e. oldest layer, which are to be read from top to bottom (white squares) to mirror the chronological sequence of actions. The objects creating a context (light grey boxes) are connected with arrows which indicate relations between the objects. Finally, the dark grey boxes suggest an interpretation of the ritual practice or agency that derives from the excavated object in its context.

[65] The handles and the tiles were excavated in trench A in US 74. A video documenting the excavation of two handles can be viewed at <https://akragasproject.philhist.uni-augsburg.de/Tile_US74.html> [accessed 12 February 2023].

[66] At S. Anna, the fragmentation was also applied to miniature vessels.

[67] This can be proposed because the miniature vessels or bronze *phialai* that were used in the rituals could hold also minimal amounts of liquids.

[68] Cf. Sojc 2020b, 130–34. In another case, one depositional pit in the sanctuary predominantly contained bottoms and handles of vessels, see Sojc 2020a, 234–37. For sacrificial trash, cf. Rieger 2016.

[69] Cf. Mills and Walker 2008, who argue for a more flexible boundary between ritual and other practices in the sanctuary depositions.

3. THE MATERIAL RECORD OF MICRO-SHARES

For example, a locally produced unpainted half of a cup with one handle still attached was found to cover the donation of a single bronze coin (Fig. 3.9).[70] Then again, smaller sherds were used to stabilize depositions that were positioned on the sanctuary's earthen floor so that they remained in place when they were covered with earth or stones. In one instance, next to a wall-like structure, a drinking vessel was placed upside down on a tile fragment covering several animal bones.[71] The cup was not only held in place by a vertical ceramic sherd, but was also separated from a nearby architectural structure by it (Fig. 3.10).

In comparison with whole vessels, the fragments show the same possibilities for ritual transformation. They could be handled for libations, for protection and dividing spheres in depositions, and even act as stand-in for the whole vessel. Being marked by the ritual of destruction and the separation from other parts, the fragment held additional options for ritual performances and therefore for the transformation into a share.

In general, one can imagine that five pieces resulted from the vessel's destruction: two handles, the bottom, perhaps two larger and some smaller parts of the body. These were then at hand for distinct deposition as well as for the various acts in the sacred place. The many instances of the integration of tiny bits into deposits shows how much cultic activity was based on the use of micro-shares in the sanctuary of S. Anna. A relationality is at work here that referred to size or acquired different meanings through size. The fragmentation of the vessel into different parts ended in an irreversible destruction of its integrity on the one hand, but on the other hand multiplied its potentiality to be included in depositions and the number of sanctuary transactions worshippers were involved in.

Figure 3.9. Deposition of a bronze coin (bottom) covered by a vessel fragment (top) next to a tile fragment. Agrigento, S. Anna. Fifth century BC. Photographs by A. Bell.

Figural Terracotta

Something similar can be said for miniaturized female figures or protomes that were a common and favoured votive gift, presumably due to the appealing design.[72] In the sanctuary of S. Anna, the figurines depicting either a deity or a worshipper have been found mostly in the form of Athena Lindia, the gift-bearing and torch-carrying type.[73] The deposition of entire figurines,[74] how-

---

[70] The bronze coin (F 499) was found in trench A (US 111).

[71] The two-handled cup (F 297) contained in US 33 formed part of complex depositional situations in trench A, cf. Sojc 2020a, 232–34 and below, Fig. 3.20.

[72] For this aspect in general, cf. Martin and Langin-Hooper 2018, 3–6.

[73] For the typology of figurines in Akragas, cf. van Rooijen 2019.

[74] See Trombi 2017, 101–02 figs 9–10.

Figure 3.10. Drinking vessel, placed bottom up, held in place by a sherd. Agrigento, S. Anna. Fifth century BC. Photograph by C. Meckes.

Figure 3.11 (above and left). Deposition of a female terracotta protome fragment during excavation. Agrigento, S. Anna. Fifth century BC. Photographs by D. Stante and T. Dworschak.

ever, is far exceeded by the number of the figurines deposited only in a fragmented state.[75] Of the identifiable figurine parts, the fragments of heads have been found in stratigraphic layers that could possibly be connected with the ritual closures of sanctuary areas, that is, in contexts that are known from other sacred sites to contain fragments of figural terracotta.[76] A part of a female terracotta protome was, for example, retrieved that had been deposited over a possible collapse layer. It had been placed face up and covered by earth and horizontally placed tile fragments (Fig. 3.11).[77] In other instances, figurine heads in the S. Anna sanctuary are encountered as parts of depositions buried in the ground;[78] other times, they were laid down and embedded in larger and complex depositional contexts.[79] The pedestals in turn, which sometimes show the feet, were likewise selected by the worshippers for inclusion in depositions. A pedestal, for example, was found in the bottom layer of a depositional complex. The terracotta fragment was

---

[75] Bell 2019 for the ratio of whole figurines to fragments.

[76] Cf. Kistler and Mohr 2015, 387–90 for finds at Mont Iato and with reference to a comparable argumentation for other finds by LaMotta and Schiffer 1999; Hughes 2018, 51–53, referring to the finds of De Lucia Brolli and Tabolli 2015 at the Sanctuary of Monte Li Santi-Le Rote a Narce.

[77] In trench A under the agricultural layer US 0, closed by horizontally placed tile fragments, the upper half of protome F 39 was found together with ceramic vessels placed bottom up and objects F 1–28, F 30, F 32, F 34, F 35, F 36–38, F 218. The objects were placed on top of the possible collapse layer US 2 and could therefore have been a deposition laid down in some sort of closing ritual.

[78] Deposition 1: Fiorentini 1969, 68 n. 14; cf. Trombi 2017, 96–97.

[79] In trench A, two depositional compartments were found that were filled in layers with sacrificial matter and individual objects (US 52). Among those, the fragment of a terracotta head (F 354) was found embedded, cf. Sojc 2020a, 238–40 fig. 8.

3. THE MATERIAL RECORD OF MICRO-SHARES

Figure 3.12. Complex deposition, lower part, with miniature vessel, vessel bottom fragment and *aes rude* laid down against a setting of stones. Agrigento, S. Anna. Fifth century BC. Photograph by C. Meckes.

Figure 3.13. Complex deposition, upper part, with knives and drinking vessels. Agrigento, S. Anna. Fifth century BC. Photograph by C. Meckes.

found near to a piece of *aes rude*, an iron fragment, a vessel bottom, and a miniature vessel positioned upside down (Fig. 3.12). The objects were placed against a small built structure of arenite stones and covered with roof tile fragments, earth, and stones. Above this were laid three iron knives and a large ceramic shard of cooking ware with a few stones (Fig. 3.13). On top of these, three more knives were placed together with a loom weight, a lid, and at least five drinking cups, some placed upside down (Fig. 3.14).[80]

Other parts of terracotta figurines have been documented among the remains of depositions as well, especially fragments of torches (Fig. 3.15), the offerings (e.g. piglets or birds), and the jewellery on the chests of the figurines (Fig. 3.16).[81] Interestingly, the heads show fractures which do not correspond to the breaking points that would be predetermined through the process of production (*Sollbruchstellen*).[82] Since the broken edges are characteristic and similar, it can be assumed that there was a distinct way of acting, whereby the heads were broken or cut off the figurines similarly (Fig. 3.17).[83] The pedestals in turn seem to have been broken off the figurine in a fairly regular way (Fig. 3.18).[84]

The smallness and fragmentation of the terracotta objects, in connection with the many different ways in which they were handled, processed, and deposited, underlines the high transformative and communicative value of these micro-shares. After having separated the head and the pedestal from the figurine, the worshipper could have proceeded to chip off other sections of the figurine's torso. These fragments — the offerings, torches, or the figurine's bejewelled chest — show a wide array of fracture edges.[85] To a lesser extent, the clothing parts

---

[80] The deposition in trench A consisted of three layers. On the floor US 61, positioned against the stones of USM 50, a piece of *aes rude* (F 377) was covered by a roof tile next to a bottom-up miniature vessel (F 378), the pedestal with feet (FB 308), a piece of iron (F 383). On the middle and upper layer, defined as US 49, three knives were found (F 339, F 343–44) covered by a large ceramic shard and three more knives (F 335–37), a loom weight (F 340), and at least five two-handled cups (F 338).

[81] Bell 2019. Cf. van Rooijen and others 2017, 159.

[82] Cf. Bell 2019.

[83] Terracotta head (F 175), found in US 13 in trench A, shows a typical breaking edge like it had been cut. Bell 2019 found that from the eighty-five figurine heads found in the sanctuary of S. Anna, more than half show the same characteristic breaking pattern.

[84] Terracotta pedestal (F 476), found in US 101 in trench A.

[85] The important point seems to have been to keep the icono-

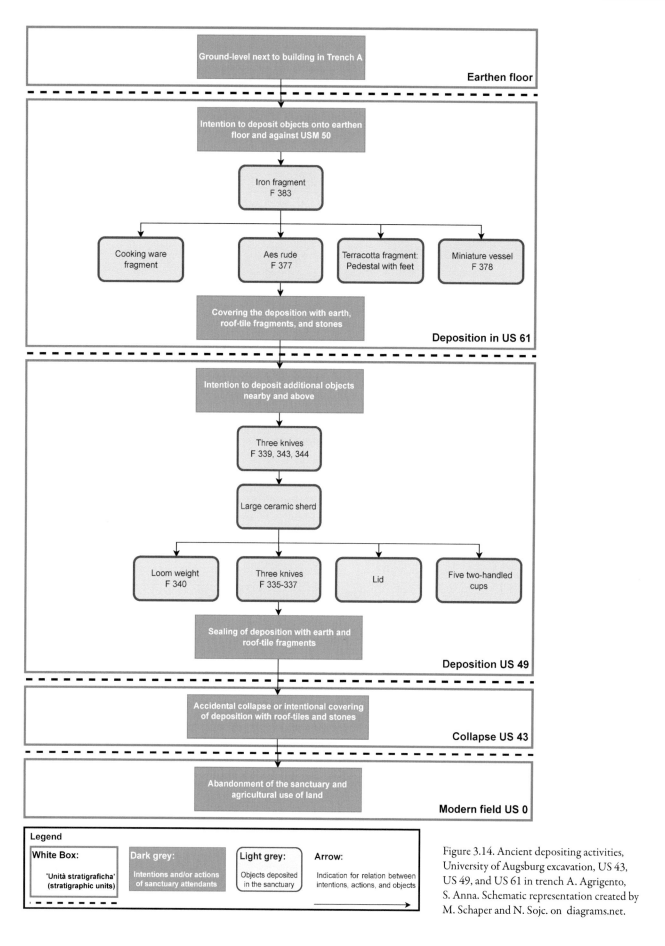

Figure 3.14. Ancient depositing activities, University of Augsburg excavation, US 43, US 49, and US 61 in trench A. Agrigento, S. Anna. Schematic representation created by M. Schaper and N. Sojc. on diagrams.net.

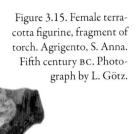

Figure 3.15. Female terracotta figurine, fragment of torch. Agrigento, S. Anna. Fifth century BC. Photograph by L. Götz.

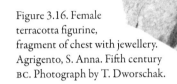

Figure 3.16. Female terracotta figurine, fragment of chest with jewellery. Agrigento, S. Anna. Fifth century BC. Photograph by T. Dworschak.

Figure 3.17. Female terracotta figurine, head fragment with characteristic broken edge. Agrigento, S. Anna. Fifth century BC. Photograph by D. Stante.

Figure 3.18. Female terracotta figurine, fragment of feet and pedestal. Agrigento, S. Anna. Fifth century BC. Photograph by T. Dworschak.

Figure 3.19. Deposition containing a female terracotta figurine fragment missing the feet and pedestal. Agrigento, S. Anna. Fifth century BC. Photograph by M. Schaper.

of the figurines have been recovered as fragments contained in the deposits and were seemingly treated as individual pieces. Each irrevocably broken figurine could have yielded five iconographically distinct parts: the head, the pedestal, the chest with jewellery, the offering, and a part of clothing. The important point seems to have been to ensure the details on the fragments were still recognizable. Alternatively, a deposit was found to contain a figurine with only the pedestal and the feet missing (Fig. 3.19).[86]

Up to now, the figurines' back sides have not been found to warrant such deliberate handling but were observed to be part of the same 'sacrificial trash' areas in the sanctuary which were already mentioned above, e.g. as levelling layers. The whole terracotta figurines with their multifaceted symbolism — a perfect whole body, richly clothed and adorned, carrying the appropriate attributes for religious activities — are viewed by research as a representation or substitute for ritual performances. The tiny pieces recovered from the depositions seem to extend this chain of signifiers. If a figurine carrying a piglet could be dedicated instead of a piglet sacrifice, then a terracotta fragment of a piglet would refer both to a whole figurine and

---

graphic details visible on the fragments, perhaps to still be able to enter the imaginary of cultic activity that the figurines alluded to. For the phenomenon in general, see Alberti 2013, 49–50.

[86] The figurine fragment (F 363) is carrying a piglet as offering. The figurine fragment was broken *in situ* in a deposition (US 7) in trench D; see Schaper (forthcoming).

Figure 3.20. Roof tile fragments covering a deposit with subsequent depositions above, Agrigento, S. Anna. Fifth century BC. Photograph by C. Voigts.

Figure 3.21. Glass beads found in depositions. Agrigento, S. Anna. Fifth century BC. Photograph by D. Stante.

able. With layered depositions, roof tile fragments were used to seemingly close a ritual phase by covering it in a plain, so that the items appear to be stacked (Fig. 3.20).[87] At the same time, the roof tile fragments marked the location of depositions above ground, standing out easily among the surrounding earth and stones. That the roof tile fragments were an integral part of the deposition's construction is beyond doubt, but perhaps they should also be considered as part of the depositional assemblage. In this case, the tiles would also represent a form of micro-share. A large variety of roof tile fragments was found in the sanctuary of S. Anna heaped on the sanctuary floor next to a wall and in the vicinity of depositional contexts.[88] The roof tile fragments could be either part of the sanctuary's ritual apparatus, where the fragments could be picked up before being used in the course of the deposition rituals, or the mound of fragmented roof tiles could have been a proper deposition, where, for example, attendants brought fragments of their houses' roofs to the sanctuary as gifts for the deity.[89] Alternatively, one can think of the roof tiles being destroyed in the course of the deposition ritual, during which some parts were used for the construction of the depositions and the leftover fragments were subsequently collected in this one area.

Another fragment of a roof, part of a lateral geison, was found placed in a probable single-act deposit on the pebble pavement and covered with earth and tile fragments. Its form and decorative scheme show close parallels to the roof of the first phase of the nearest temple in the city, Temple G (Fig. 3.2).[90] The assumption that

the piglet sacrifice, as well as to the ritual breaking of the figurine and to perhaps five other fragments, which may have been distributed across the sanctuary in other depositions. This could be likened to a dispersion of dedications, which created a network of ritual communications. As mentioned above, up to now the finds of figurine fragments outnumber those dedicated in their entirety, so that one can consider that the transformation in the form of micro-shares was the prevalent transaction form — with a potent agency as a ritual signifier.

Roof Tiles and Roof Terracotta

Fragmented roof tiles are omnipresent in the sanctuary of S. Anna as part of the construction of depositions. Roof tile fragments were stood up vertically, delimiting and structuring depositions, together with stones (cf. Fig. 3.9). The tile fragments were also put horizontally over single-item depositions and sometimes also pushed into the ground so that the floor stayed walk-

---

[87] The deposition of hemispherical cups (F 279–81) in trench A (US 34).

[88] The heap of rooftile fragments found in trench A along the eastern side of the south end of USM 39 consisted of batches US 64, US 72, US 77.

[89] This would be in line with the fact that a whole roof tile was considered a commodity in that period. Cf. Sioumpara 2019 for roof tiles listed as property in sanctuary inventories in Greece and stored on site.

[90] The geison fragment (F 315) was found in trench A, positioned on pavement US 38. For an analysis of the lateral geison and

3. THE MATERIAL RECORD OF MICRO-SHARES

Figure 3.22. Deposition of beads and a bronze pin. Agrigento, S. Anna. Fifth century BC. Photograph by C. Voigts.

Figure 3.23. Terracotta loom weight. Agrigento, S. Anna. Fifth century BC. Photograph by D. Stante.

one of the pieces was brought from Temple G to S. Anna to be deposited at an extra-urban veneration place is intriguing.[91] The case of the geison points us to a variety of relations with the temple itself, the temple's roof, and the destruction of that temple to make place for a new larger building. The micro-share deposited in S. Anna is charged with symbolic meaning, perhaps referring to another sanctuary and a variety of ritual actions.

One Piece of a Set: A Glass Bead, a Loom Weight, a Counter

In the excavation of S. Anna, over 350 brightly coloured glass beads have been found (Fig. 3.21). However, the twenty-eight beads deposited together on the floor under a drinking cup, which were probably deposited in the form of a bracelet or even a necklace, are an exception (Fig. 3.22).[92] Most beads were found as individual items integrated in a multi-object deposition (cf. Fig. 3.7).[93] One can perhaps imagine that it was first required to take off a piece of jewellery and then to unthread a bead off a strand. After retying the string and putting the jewellery back on, it was finally possible to carefully position the bead in the deposition. We are dealing here with the transfer of a personal ornament to the deity and also with the worshipper parting with a piece that was part of a larger entity. This means that the absence would have been noticeable when one returned from the sanctuary to everyday life. Even if the bead was easily replaceable in economic terms,[94] the dedication could be equalled to the worshipper's conscious creation of a gap in the ongoing everyday, a disruption that was accepted in order to integrate this piece into the chain of signifiers of the sanctuary. A similar argument could be made for other dedicational objects deposited in S. Anna that were part of a set. Individual loom weights were part of depositions

---

the discussion of its assignment to a specific roof, cf. Rheeder 2019, 55, 203–05 (Roof 4); the fragmented remains were uncovered in the filling of the foundation of the second phase of Temple G.

91 Equally tempting is an alternative scenario: the geison fragment comes from the destruction or renewal of a canonic roof at the S. Anna sanctuary itself that was similar in size, decoration, and date to that of Temple G, but has not yet been identified.

92 In trench A (US 33) under a bottom-up hemispherical cup (F 286) the twenty-eight eye-motif glass beads were found. Next to the beads one bronze pin or needle of *c.* 11 cm length was recovered

(F 290) and another cup, as well as fragments of cooking ware and drinking vessels.

93 Single glass beads have also been documented as laid down paired with one other item. Beside the votive assemblages, the beads have also been discovered scattered in 'sacrificial trash' contexts. For general considerations in regard to the separation of single beads and their reassembling in new constellations in the context of Bronze Age depositions, see Brück 2019, 73–79.

94 The glass beads found in the sanctuary of S. Anna were probably imported from Carthage or Egypt; see Meckes 2021; (forthcoming).

Natascha Sojc

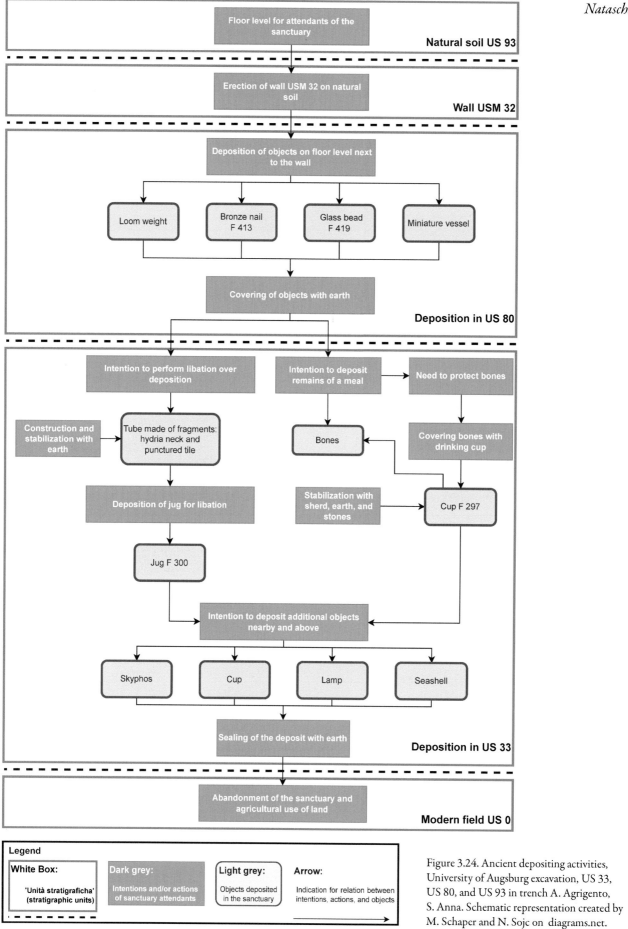

Figure 3.24. Ancient depositing activities, University of Augsburg excavation, US 33, US 80, and US 93 in trench A. Agrigento, S. Anna. Schematic representation created by M. Schaper and N. Sojc on diagrams.net.

as well (cf. Fig. 3.14). A loom weight would therefore be missing from the loom, as around thirty loom weights would be required for weaving (Fig. 3.23).[95] Here again it would require an active choice to remove one of the items and carry it to the sanctuary for dedication and then return home and be reminded by the vacant spot of the ritual and the micro-share held instead in the sanctuary.

Another part of a set discovered at S. Anna is a simple counter made from terracotta.[96] The board game from which it was removed might have been a game with a set of five, thirty, or sixty counters.[97] With the separation of one piece from its set, the themes of irretrievability, irreparability, and irrevocability pertaining to the miniaturized and fragmented pieces of bronze, ceramic, and terracotta items, which were converted into micro-shares, reoccur in the lack of the item.[98] However, while the individual pieces were certainly missed, their absence established and embodied a connection with the sacred place. The link to the deity, one can imagine, perhaps guaranteed the continued existence of the remaining items and, in a more general sense, guarded against all forms of irreversibility and of loss.

As we have seen above, the micro-shares amplify symbolic references, since the small size usually came about through a larger number of ritual performances. The miniaturized size comes to equal a concentration of transformative agency, and the micro-shares were therefore more flexible and powerful signifiers. These small parts, their distribution and diverse usability, and the many relations that micro-shares open up expand the chains of signifiers many times over. This effectively gave a higher meaning to the religious actions and reaffirmed the authority of the sanctuary's deity.[99] At the same time, the number of ritual actions increased the chain of signifiers, so that the always-open end of these chains of signifiers threatened to be exposed. The many contingencies created through the variety of objects and depositional modes might have bordered on arbitrariness. It can be assumed that this could have also been risky, were it not for the burial in the earth. Or did this allow for more interaction, since one could think more about what and where to put it, or what meaning one wanted to give to the piece in the here and now? Therefore, it was perhaps even more necessary to anchor these signifiers through a situational re-enactment for ascribing meaning, which was done through the ritual transfer of the object into the realm of the deity in the sanctuary.

Communal Activities: When One Small Thing Joins Another

In the sanctuary of S. Anna, some of the more complex depositions show not only one but a number of micro-shares chosen, treated, prepared, combined, and dedicated. In one case already described above, a loom weight, a bronze nail, a glass bead, and a miniature vessel were deposited next to a wall as the bottom layer of a deposit, which prompted other depositions at a later moment in time on top of it (Fig. 3.24). A similar agency of micro-shares is evident in a context where the bottom layer consisted of piece of iron, a piece of bronze (*aes rude*), a miniature vessel, and a pedestal (fragment of a figurine), covered by stones and earth (Fig. 3.14). In both cases, the different micro-shares are very noticeable and could have been an intended ritual feature, perhaps to concentrate the symbolic charge of the depositions and amplify the links to other ritual actions, like the breaking of a votive figurine, giving up of one piece of quasi-monetary value, or parting from a utensil or a piece of personal adornment. These micro-shares might be, in each instance, the donation of one worshipper, who would then have been missing items from not only one sphere of life; they could likewise be connected to a group of attendants, even to single-act depositions accumulated over time. A number of worshippers acting at the same moment in time seems the more plausible interpretation when the next layer of the deposition with the pedestal fragment is considered, where six knives and at least five drinking vessels were laid down together with a large sherd of cooking ware, a loom weight, and a lid.[100] These refer to animal sacrifice (communal drinking and eating), destroying a cooking pot and depositing its fragments, and giving up parts of a storage container and of

---

[95] Cf. e.g. Pfisterer-Haas 2006, 108–11.

[96] The counter found in the depositional pit US 29 remains a singular find up to now. For the depositional pit, cf. Sojc 2020a, 234–37. For the problem of recognizing counters in the archaeological record, see Wilson 2018.

[97] See Bendlin and Hurschmann 2006.

[98] Cf. Depner 2013, 84–88.

[99] Of course, this means that the meaningless reality of existence was likewise effectively concealed.

[100] Interestingly, lids of *pixides* and cooking ware are found integrated in depositions, not used in their original function as covers, but added like e.g. loom weights or a vessel's handle. Perhaps this was understood as the first separation, as the container could no longer fulfil its original function.

Figure 3.25. Depositions during excavation, terracotta roof tile as marker. Agrigento, S. Anna. Fifth century BC. Photograph/3D model by C. Meckes.

a loom.¹⁰¹ The micro-shares in such a single deposition point us to the active participation of groups of individuals in rituals and feasting and other depositional activities as indicated by the fragmented objects.¹⁰² These, to offer one more interpretation, could also be imagined to be divided amongst a group, where each person then could go on to dedicate a fragment in another ritual.

To sum up: the layers of the deposition tell us that it was an ongoing ritual process in which small things were joined, and that these depositions prompted other actions. The diversity of donations and the recurrence of objects (knives, cups) leads us to assume that several people were involved. As shown above, it can also be inferred that these things could enter into multiple relationships. They were predestined to be embedded in communal activities; one could also see them as objects of communication and social cohesion.

Taking into consideration that up to now the chronology of the excavated depositions at S. Anna show an ongoing depositional process from the end of the sixth to the fourth centuries BC, such a potent integration of worshippers into the sanctuary's community must have taken place intergenerationally. Taking up the different propositions for the composition of the sanctuary community at S. Anna — women, heterogenous groups of Greek settlers, and the local 'indigenous', the people of Akragas — perhaps none of these groups can be excluded.¹⁰³ On the contrary, starting out from the perspective of micro-shares, I think one would have to even widen the scope. In the same way that a handful of people acting together in a ritual could integrate any of the above-named ritual communities, this would also hold true for the participation of extended families. One can think of the groups represented on the dedicational reliefs of later times, including servants, slaves, and a variety of

---

¹⁰¹ It seems highly unlikely to me that one person would leave six knives and five drinking vessels; similarly I hesitate to imagine that every object was contributed by a different person, which would mean the participation of at least eighteen people. A more cautious calculation of six to nine worshippers can be envisioned, coming from the number of cups and knives and thinking of other ritual functions. For other communal depositions of drinking vessels in the sanctuary of S. Anna, see Bell (forthcoming).

¹⁰² For the general phenomenon of group formation through interaction in a religious setting, see Lichterman and others 2017.

---

¹⁰³ The range of possible cultic functions: veneration of Demeter, of Demeter and Persephone, of Artemis, as a religious meeting place for different cultures, in a religious setting, ancestor's or hero's cult, place for rites of passage from youth to adulthood, cf. above.

family members, including adolescents and children. Recent research has stressed the early integration of children into rituals and sanctuary life.[104] However, the active participation of children in cultic activities has so far been precluded on the grounds that they did not have any economic means. As the pieces are small, why not also propose children as the ones who laid down the head of a figurine?

Material Record of Micro-shares

The large, imposing inner-city temple precincts document how political powers of the polis expressed themselves through monumental temples, statues, stelai, and inscriptions. In contrast, the extra-urban sanctuary of S. Anna allows us to study how the communicational value of the shares that the worshippers held in this sacred site was directed inwards, towards a ritual community building. The sanctuary was important for the people from Akragas, because they could properly 'talk' with each other as well as with the deity in a way that put the mutual engagement in ritual activities at the centre. As shown above, the importance of size was relative in depositions of the extra-urban sanctuary, as is implied by the material record of fragments and separated pieces of a set. Miniaturized by different actions and ritual performances, these items came to exercise an extraordinary agency. Even if one had also to invest some economic resources into these micro-shares, it was rather their worth as personal item or the act of giving something away that made them suitable for the depositing rituals.

The orchestration of the laying down of things in communal activities with other attendants of the sanctuary organized but above all bonded the congregation. Additionally, the discreet nature of depositions, which required objects to be covered and sealed, guaranteed an ongoing communication with the deity of the sanctuary through the embedded donation long after the ritual was over and only stones or roof tile fragments marked the place of deposition (Fig. 3.25).[105]

One would perhaps remember who brought a glass bead or how one witnessed the breaking of a terracotta figurine and the distribution of its fragments. Surely, the memory of treating and positioning things, down to the bodily actions one had to go through to bury them in the ground, would keep. But perhaps at the same time one would already be wondering about the next sanctuary transaction: What should be brought along and how could it be transformed into a micro-share?

---

[104] Sommer and Sommer 2015; Dillon 2020. Cf. Lillehammer and Murphy 2018.

[105] Deposition in a shallow pit, trench A (US 102).

Works Cited

Adornato, G. 2011. *Akragas arcaica: modelli culturali e linguaggi artistici di una città greca d'Occidente*, Archeologia e arte antica (Milan: LED).

Adorno, L. 2017. 'Agrigento. Ricognizione di superficie in località S. Anna. I reperti', in N. Sojc (ed.), *Akragas: Current Issues in the Archaeology of a Sicilian Polis*, Archaeological Studies, Leiden University, 38 (Leiden: Leiden University Press), pp. 159–71.

Adorno, L. and V. Garaffa (forthcoming). 'Ceramica in contesto: metodo di lavoro e prospettive di ricerca', in M. Schaper and N. Sojc (eds), *Exploring an Extra-Urban Sanctuary of Akragas: Excavations at S. Anna 2014–2019*.

Alberti, B. 2013. 'Archaeology and Ontologies of Scale: The Case of Miniaturization in First-Millennium Northwest Argentina', in B. Alberti, A. M. Jones, and J. Pollard (eds), *Archaeology after Interpretation: Returning Materials to Archaeological Theory* (Walnut Creek: Taylor & Francis), pp. 43–58.

Albertocchi, M. 2004. *Athana Lindia: le statuette siceliote con pettorali di età arcaica e classica* (Rome: Giorgio Bretschneider).

Albrecht, J. and others. 2018. 'Religion in the Making: The Lived Ancient Religion Approach', *Religion*, 48.4: 568–93.

Alfieri Tonini, A. 2012. 'Culti e templi della Sicilia sud-orientale nelle iscrizioni. Apollo e Artemide', in F. Copani (ed.), *Convivenze etniche e contatti di culture: atti del Seminario di Studi Università degli Studi di Milano, 23–24 novembre 2009*, Aristonothos. Scritti per il Mediterraneo antico, 4 (Trento: Tangram), pp. 187–208.

Appadurai, A. 1981. *Worship and Conflict under Colonial Rule: A South Indian Case Study* (Cambridge: Cambridge University Press).

Appadurai, A. and C. Appadurai-Breckenridge. 1976. 'The South Indian Temple: Authority, Honour and Redistribution', *Contributions to Indian Sociology*, 10.2: 187–211.

Baitinger, H. 2013. 'Sizilisch-unteritalische Funde in griechischen Heiligtümern. Ein Beitrag zu den Votivsitten in Griechenland in geometrischer und archaischer Zeit', *Jahrbuch des Römisch-Germanischen Zentralmuseums Mainz*, 60: 153–296.

——. 2016. 'Metallfunde in sizilischen Kontexten des 8. bis 5. Jahrhunderts v. Chr.: Anzeiger von Identität oder "Internationalität"?', in H. Baitinger (ed.), *Materielle Kultur und Identität im Spannungsfeld zwischen mediterraner Welt und Mitteleuropa = Material Culture and Identity between the Mediterranean World and Central Europe: Akten der internationalen Tagung am Römisch-Germanischen Zentralmuseum Mainz, 22–24 Oktober 2014*, Römisch-Germanischen Zentralmuseums Tagungen, 27 (Mainz: Verlag des Römisch-Germanischen Zentralmuseums), pp. 33–48.

——. 2017. 'The Metal Votive Objects from the Sanctuary of S. Anna in their Sicilian Context', in N. Sojc (ed.), *Akragas: Current Issues in the Archaeology of a Sicilian Polis*, Archaeological Studies, Leiden University, 38 (Leiden: Leiden University Press), pp. 109–27.

Bell, A. 2019. 'Medien in der Antike – die Botschaften kleiner Votivfiguren' (unpublished master's thesis, Universität Augsburg).

——. (forthcoming). 'Set in a Row. Depositions with Multiple Drinking Vessels', in M. Schaper and N. Sojc (eds), *Exploring an Extra-Urban Sanctuary of Akragas: Excavations at S. Anna 2014–2019*.

Bendlin, A. and R. Hurschmann. 2006. 'Board Games', in H. Cancik and H. Schneider (eds), *Brill's New Pauly* <http://dx.doi.org.ez.statsbiblioteket.dk:2048/10.1163/1574-9347_bnp_e219920> [accessed 3 March 2022].

Brück, J. 2019. *Personifying Prehistory* (Oxford: Oxford University Press).

De Lucia Brolli, M. A. and J. Tabolli. 2015. *I tempi del rito: il santuario di Monte Li Santi-Le Rote a Narce* (Rome: Officina edizioni).

De Miro, E. 2008. 'Thesmophoria di Sicilia', in C. A. Di Stefano (ed.), *Demetra: la divinità, i santuari, il culto, la leggenda; atti del I Congresso Internazionale, Enna, 1–4 luglio 2004*, Biblioteca di Sicilia antiqua, 2 (Pisa: Serra), pp. 47–92.

Depner, A. 2013. 'Worthless Things? On the Difference between Devaluing and Sorting out Things', in H. P. and H. Weiss (eds), *Mobility, Meaning and Transformations of Things: Shifting Contexts of Material Culture through Time and Space* (Oxford: Oxbow), pp. 78–90.

De Waele, J. A. 1971. *Acragas Graeca: Die historische Topographie des griechischen Akragas auf Sizilien*, I: *Historischer Teil*, Archeologische Studiën van het Nederlands Historisch Instituut te Rome, 3 (Den Haag: Ministerie van Cultuur, Recreatie en Maatschappelijk Werk).

Dillon, M. 2020. 'Children in Archaic and Classical Greek Religion. Active and Passive Ritual Agency', in L. A. Beaumont, M. Dillon, and N. Harrington (eds), *Children in Antiquity: Perspectives and Experiences of Childhood in the Ancient Mediterranean* (London: Routledge), pp. 326–43.

Eimer, Q. (forthcoming). 'A Different Perspective: Finds of Miniature Vessels in the Sanctuary of S. Anna', in M. Schaper and N. Sojc (eds), *Exploring an Extra-Urban Sanctuary of Akragas: Excavations at S. Anna 2014–2019*.

Ekroth, G. 2003. 'Small Pots, Poor People? The Use and Function of Miniature Pottery as Votive Offerings in Archaic Sanctuaries in the Argolid and the Corinthia', in B. Schmalz, M. Söldner, and K. Schauenburg (eds), *Griechische Keramik im kulturellen Kontext: Akten des internationalen Vasen-Symposions in Kiel vom 24. bis 28.9.2001, veranstaltet durch das Archäologische Institut der Christian-Albrechts-Universität zu Kiel* (Münster: Scriptorium), pp. 35–37.

Fiorentini, G. 1969. 'Il santuario extraurbano di Sant'Anna presso Agrigento', *Cronache di archeologia*, 8: 63–80.

Fontijn, D. 2020. *Economies of Destruction: How the Systematic Destruction of Valuables Created Value in Bronze Age Europe, c. 2300–500 BC* (Abingdon: Routledge).

Foxhall, L. 2015. 'Introduction: Miniaturization', *World Archaeology*, 47.1: 1–5.

Frevel, C. and H. von Hesberg (eds). 2007. *Kult und Kommunikation: Medien in Heiligtümern der Antike* (Wiesbaden: Reichert).

Graeber, D. 2001. *Toward an Anthropological Theory of Value: The False Coin of our Own Dreams* (Basingstoke: Palgrave).

Hinz, V. 1998. *Der Kult von Demeter und Kore auf Sizilien und in der Magna Graecia* (Wiesbaden: Reichert).

Hughes, J. 2017. 'Souvenirs of the Self: Personal Belongings as Votive Offerings in Ancient Religion', *Religion in the Roman Empire*, 3.2: 181–201.

——. 2018. 'Tiny and Fragmented Votive Offerings from Classical Antiquity', in S. R. Martin and S. M. Langin-Hooper (eds), *The Tiny and the Fragmented: Miniature, Broken, or Otherwise Incomplete Objects in the Ancient World* (Oxford: Oxford University Press), pp. 48–71.

Isager, S. and J. E. Skydsgaard. 2013. *Ancient Greek Agriculture: An Introduction* (London: Routledge).

Kistler, E. and M. Mohr. 2015. 'Monte Iato. Two Late Archaic Feasting Places between the Local and the Global', in E. Kistler and others (eds), *Sanctuaries and the Power of Consumption: Networking and the Formation of Elites in the Archaic Western Mediterranean World; Proceedings of the International Conference in Innsbruck, 20th–23rd March 2012*, Philippika, 92 (Wiesbaden: Harrassowitz), pp. 385–415.

LaMotta, C. V. and M. B. Schiffer. 1999. 'Formation Processes of House Floor Assemblages', in P. M. Allison (ed.), *The Archaeology of Household Activities* (New York: Routledge), pp. 19–29.

Lee, D. B. 2005. 'Ritual and the Social Meaning and Meaninglessness of Religion', *Soziale Welt*, 56.1: 5–16.

Leonard, K. 2015. 'Arranged Artefacts and Materials in Irish Bronze Age Ritual Deposits: A Consideration of Prehistoric Practice and Intention', in C. Houlbrook and N. Armitage (eds), *The Materiality of Magic: An Artifactual Investigation into Ritual Practices and Popular Beliefs* (Oxford: Oxbow), pp. 23–36.

Lichterman, P. and others. 2017. 'Grouping Together in Lived Ancient Religion: Individual Interacting and the Formation of Groups', *Religion in the Roman Empire*, 3.1: 3–10.

Lillehammer, G. and E. M. Murphy. 2018. 'Introduction – Across the Generations. The Old and the Young in Past Societies', in G. Lillehammer and E. M. Murphy (eds), *Across the Generations: The Old and the Young in Past Societies; Proceedings from the 22nd Annual Meeting of the EAA in Vilnius, Lithuania, 31st August–4th September 2016* (Stavanger: University of Stavanger), pp. 11–19.

Martin, S. R. and S. M. Langin-Hooper. 2018. 'In/Complete. An Introduction to the Theories of Miniaturization and Fragmentation', in S. R. Martin and S. M. Langin-Hooper (eds), *The Tiny and the Fragmented: Miniature, Broken, or Otherwise Incomplete Objects in the Ancient World* (Oxford: Oxford University Press), pp. 1–23.

Meckes, C. 2021. 'Glass Bead Production in the 6th to 4th Century BC Using the Case Study of a Greek Colony' (unpublished master's thesis, University of Augsburg).

——. (forthcoming). 'Beads for the Gods', in M. Schaper and N. Sojc (eds), *Exploring an Extra-Urban Sanctuary of Akragas: Excavations at S. Anna 2014–2019*.

Meskell, L. 2008. 'Memory Work and Material Practices', in B. J. Mills and W. H. Walker, *Memory Work: Archaeologies of Material Practices* (Santa Fe: School of Advanced Research), pp. 3–24.

Mills, B. J. and W. H. Walker. 2008. 'Introduction: Memory, Materiality and Depositional Practices', in B. J. Mills and W. H. Walker, *Memory Work: Archaeologies of Material Practices* (Santa Fe: School of Advanced Research), pp. 234–44.

Öhlinger, B. 2015. *Ritual und Religion im archaischen Sizilien: Formations- und Transformationsprozesse binnenländischer Kultorte im Kontext kultureller Kontakte*, Italiká, 4 (Wiesbaden: Reichert).

Parello, M. C. 2020. 'Introduction to the Study of Sacred Spaces in Ancient Agrigento', in M. de Cesare, E. C. Portale, and N. Sojc (eds), *The Akragas Dialogue: New Investigations on Sanctuaries in Sicily* (Berlin: De Gruyter), pp. 79–98.

Parisi, V. 2017. *I depositi votivi negli spazi del rito: analisi dei contesti per un'archeologia della pratica cultuale nel mondo siceliota e magnogreco*, Supplementi e monografie della rivista Archeologia classica, 14 (Rome: L'Erma di Bretschneider).

Patera, I. 2015. 'Objects as Substitutes in Ancient Greek Ritual', *Religion in the Roman Empire*, 1: 181–200.

Pfisterer-Haas, S. 2006. 'Penelope am Webstuhl. Die Macht der Gewänder', in I. Kader (ed.), *Penelope rekonstruiert: Geschichte und Deutung einer Frauenfigur* (Munich: Museum für Abgüsse Klassischer Bildwerke München), pp. 97–120.

Pilz, O. 2011. 'The Uses of Small Things and the Semiotics of Greek Miniature Objects', in A. S. Smith and M. E. Bergeron (eds), *The Gods of Small Things* (Toulouse: Presses universitaires du Mirail), pp. 15–30.

Prent, M. 2005. *Cretan Sanctuaries and Cults: Continuity and Change from Late Minoan IIIC to the Archaic Period*, Religions in the Graeco-Roman World, 154 (Leiden: Brill).

Rheeder, A. 2019. 'Architectural Terracottas from Akragas. Investigating Monumental Roofs from the Archaic and Classical Periods of Akragas' (unpublished doctoral thesis, Leiden University) <https://scholarlypublications.universiteitleiden.nl/handle/1887/70760?solr_nav%5Bid%5D=4bbd3491f5e4694d5c2c&solr_nav%5Bpage%5D=0&solr_nav%5Boffset%5D=0> [accessed 12 February 2023].

Rieger, A.-K. 2016. 'Waste Matters. Life Cycle and Agency of Pottery Employed in Graeco-Roman Sacred Spaces', *Religion in the Roman Empire*, 2: 307–33.

Rooijen, G. van. 2019. 'Goddesses of Akragas: A Study of Terracotta Votive Figurines from Sicily' (unpublished doctoral thesis, Leiden University) <https://scholarlypublications.universiteitleiden.nl/handle/1887/81576?solr_nav%5Bid%5D=170e11ad9479966d5a0c&solr_nav%5Bpage%5D=0&solr_nav%5Boffset%5D=0> [accessed 12 February 2023].

Rooijen, G. van and others. 2017. 'Figuring out. Coroplastic Art and Technè in Agrigento, Sicily. The Results of a Coroplastic Experiment', *Analecta praehistorica Leidensia*, 47: 151–62.

Schaper, M. (forthcoming). 'Trench D', in M. Schaper and N. Sojc (eds), *Exploring an Extra-urban Sanctuary of Akragas: Excavations at S. Anna 2014–2019*.

Sioumpara, E. 2019. *Managing the Debris: Spoliation of Architecture and Dedications on the Athenian Acropolis after the Persian Destruction* (Athens: Acropolis Museum Editions).

Sojc, N. (ed.). 2017. *Akragas: Current Issues in the Archaeology of a Sicilian Polis*, Archaeological Studies Leiden University, 38 (Leiden: Leiden University Press).

——. 2020a. 'Depositions of Sacrificial Material and Feasting Remains from the Extra-urban Sanctuary of S. Anna (Agrigento). Appendix: A Note on Characteristic Finds by Linda Adorno', in M. de Cesare, E. C. Portale, and N. Sojc (eds), *The Akragas Dialogue: New Investigations on Sanctuaries in Sicily* (Berlin: De Gruyter), pp. 221–51.

——. 2020b. 'Beseitigung, Verwahrung oder Kreislauf? Zum stofflichen Potenzial deponierter Materialien in antiken griechischen Heiligtümern. Das Beispiel des extraurbanen Heiligtums S. Anna bei Agrigent (Sizilien)', in C. Schliephake, N. Sojc, and G. Weber (eds), *Nachhaltigkeit in der Antike: Diskurse, Praktiken, Perspektiven*, Geographica historica, 42 (Stuttgart: Steiner), pp. 117–42.

——. 2021. 'Das außerstädtische Heiligtum von S. Anna und seine räumliche und zeitliche Beziehung zur polis Akragas', in J. Fornasier and A. V. Bujskich (eds), *An den Ufern des Bug: Deutsch-ukrainische Ausgrabungen in Olbia Pontike im Kontext internationaler Forschungen zu antiken Migrationsprozessen* (Bonn: Habelt), pp. 75–94.

Sommer, M. and D. Sommer. 2015. *Care, Socialization and Play in Ancient Attica: A Developmental Childhood Archaeological Approach* (Aarhus: Aarhus University Press).

Spatafora, F. 2020. 'Il santuario di Zeus Meilichios a Selinunte. Dati e materiali inediti per la rilettura del contesto', in M. de Cesare, E. C. Portale, and N. Sojc (eds), *The Akragas Dialogue: New Investigations on Sanctuaries in Sicily* (Berlin: De Gruyter), pp. 291–314.

Tournavitou, I. 2009. 'Does Size Matter? Miniature Pottery Vessels in Minoan Peak Sanctuaries', in A. L. D'Agata, A. Van de Moortel, and M. B. Richardson (eds), *Archaeologies of Cult: Essays on Ritual and Cult in Crete* (Princeton: American School of Classical Studies at Athens), pp. 213–30.

Trombi, C. 2017. 'Il materiale votivo e di uso rituale nel Santuario di S. Anna (Agrigento). Note sugli aspetti cultuali e socio-politici', in N. Sojc (ed.), *Akragas: Current Issues in the Archaeology of a Sicilian Polis*, Archaeological Studies, Leiden University, 38 (Leiden: Leiden University Press), pp. 95–108.

Verger, S. 2003. 'Des objets gaulois dans les sanctuaires archaïques de Grèce, de Sicile et d'Italie', *Comptes-rendus des séances de l'Académie des inscriptions et belles-lettres*, 147.1: 525–73.

Wilson, G. 2018. *Playing with Things: The Archaeology, Anthropology and Ethnography of Human-Object Interactions in Atlantic Scotland* (Oxford: Archaeopress).

4. What Do Tiny Objects Want?
A Case Study with Miniature Pottery from Pompeii

Anna-Katharina Rieger

From Inter-artefactual Relations to Relations between Body and Artefact

In his article 'What Do Objects Want?', Chris Gosden draws attention to the 'formal properties of artifacts' that allow objects 'to have social effects on people'.[1] Against the conceptual background of agency of objects and their affordances, Gosden claims that inter-artefactual relations, i.e. the 'forms of objects, the historical trajectories of the class of objects' and the development and recognizability of object classes and styles, shape 'people as socially effective entities'.[2] This view embraces that we studying the material culture of Graeco-Roman Antiquity must acknowledge that objects have their own rules along which they act and which — in changing and adapted forms, functionalities, and materials — can transgress artefactual borders. Hence, they can establish specific relations to human agents.[3]

Gosden's approach, asking for the 'the obligations objects place upon us', can be applied to a particular phenomenon of ancient 'object classes' — objects with extreme dimensions, either downscaled or upscaled.[4]

I will look through the lens of inter-artefactual relations and frictions as well as agency and affordances on downscaled pottery objects from religious contexts in Hellenistic and Roman Campania in order to determine their relations to human agents. This approach helps to reveal their meanings and enables us to deduce why and for what purposes pottery objects are miniaturized and how they might be socially effective.

Even though Gosden is interested in understanding why styles often have a long continuity and how traditions are established or change against the backdrop of the debates on 'Romanization' in Britain,[5] I start from the assumption that his analytical layout of '*inter*-artifactual' relations, for example of different types of pottery in a certain time span, can be applied to size and dimensions as a particular inter-artefactual relation. In contrast to his aim, I am not primarily interested in *inter*-cultural exchanges, but remain in a rather '*intra*-cultural' setting, looking for the relation of differently sized pottery from contexts in Campania in a certain time span, mainly the fourth century BC to the first century AD.[6] Moreover, like others, the tiny clay objects appear *en masse* and might also be investigated under the aspect of a potential 'mass power of objects'.[7]

---

[1] Gosden 2005.

[2] Gosden 2005, 193. He explores 'what might be called an object-centred approach to agency' based on Gell 1998 and Gell 1992 (the concept of agency resulting from recognizable styles of objects and their relations), as well as Gibson 1979 (affordances as 'action possibilities' that are given in our objectual environment — and perceived by human agents as such). Object agency gained much momentum in the last years (cf. Hicks and Beaudry 2010; Hodder 2011; Witmore 2014; Stockhammer and Hahn 2015; Schreiber 2022). However, there are differentiated views on this non-anthropocentric cultural history and anthropology (cf. Ingold 2007 with a plea for bringing together theoretical and practical approaches to materials and materiality; Schreiber 2022 with a focus on practice theoretical approaches when dealing with material culture) and also a shift back to a more human-centred anthropology, archaeology, and history (cf. Ribeiro 2016; Cole 2013 from a philosophical perspective; Hahn 2015 from an anthropological perspective).

[3] Gosden 2005, 209.

[4] Gosden 2005, 193. For upscaled phenomena and objects, see Rüpke's and Waldner's contributions to this volume.

[5] Gosden 2005, 194: 'looking less at objects as indicators of ethnic groups and their boundaries and more at the ways styles of objects set up universes of their own into which people need to fit.'

[6] An inter-cultural aspect plays a not-unimportant role insofar as Latium and Campania between the fourth and the first centuries BC are concerned: political and cultural change occurred that was phrased as 'Roman colonization' and revisited recently, see Roselaar 2011; Stek 2013; 2015; see also below, pp. 62–63. Other examples, including some I refer to later, are San Omobono at Rome, Lavinium, Pantella, Satricum, and San Leucio close to Canosa (see Canopoli 2020; Lanzi 2019; Moser 2019).

[7] Gosden 2005, 193. The multiplicity and quantities of the objects play a role in Gosden's argument.

In the following paragraphs I will explore 'the obligations objects place upon us' — what they want — with regard to tiny objects in a twofold approach:[8] from an etic perspective, we as archaeologists have to be clear about categorizations and labels in order to respect the 'obligations' an object carries with it. From an emic perspective — as far as we can take the perspectives of an object or an ancient context — we must find access, which means a methodology, to infer from these 'obligations' the understanding ancient users and producers of tiny objects may have had of them and what meanings they attributed to them.

By looking at miniaturized and miniature pottery objects from the Campanian city of Pompeii and the small sanctuaries in the wider area (Fig. 4.1), I explore in detail:

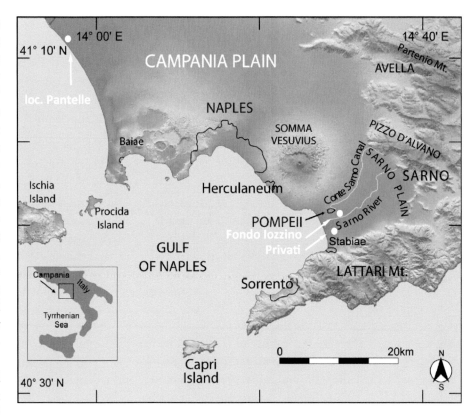

Figure 4.1. Gulf of Naples with Pompeii and Stabiae. White dots mark the sacred places of Privati, south of Stabiae, at the foot of the Monti Lattari; Fondo Iozzino, south of Pompeii; and at the località di Pantelle close to Mondragone (Senatore, Falco, and Meo 2016, fig. 1).

— **Categories**, or what a miniature or miniaturized vessel or object is: this section deals with the problems of archaeological categories and denominations. In order to deduce meanings from tiny objects, I first need to be clear about what object or object class was labelled as 'miniature' and who (ceramologist, archaeologist, religious historian) gave or used the label.

— **Contexts**, or where such tiny pottery objects were used and/or found: this section starts from descriptions of the narrow archaeological contexts in which miniature pottery occurs and their wider characterization, also regarding functional contexts and analogies. The question behind this is whether we can distinguish a main utilization of the place they were found in — for example, a religious or a mundane one. The differentiation of number and kind of pieces (quantities and forms), the place of deposition (subsoil, on soil, pit, layer), and associated findings (other pottery, other materials) represent a first step to an interpretation which also accounts for the employment of tiny pottery items as oscillating between religious and profane practices.

— **Connotations**, or how we can unravel what tiny vessels and objects 'want', especially in religious contexts: this section is an attempt to explore the dimensions of meanings the miniature pottery could have had (in the presented cases) for people in Campania. Here, the human body — its size, abilities, and limitations, but also the epistemic and imaginative capacities of humans — take centre stage. Light will also be shed on both realms in which the tiny items from clay were embedded: the production process and the consumption process.

— **Chronologies**: in a final step, I will briefly touch on the issue of the decrease in use of miniature pottery from the Classical and Hellenistic to the Roman periods and will try to explain it through Gosden's claim that 'periods of change are important in bringing out the relationships between people and their object world'.[9]

---

[8] See Gosden 2005, 194.

[9] Gosden 2005, 193–94.

Categories: What Is a Miniaturized Object?

What characteristics must a vessel, thing, or tool have to be a miniature? If we determine something that we find in an archaeological excavation to be small, miniaturized, or tiny, or if we label it with diminutives such as *brocchetta*, *krateriskos*, *arula*, *statuette*, and so on, this already implies a decision on the object's functional aspects and therefore also on its interpretation. However, function can be twofold. On the one hand, it depends on object-immanent features independent of the size: an open or even flat form of pottery can be used as a container for more solid items or content; a closed form is suitable for keeping liquids. On the other hand, function is also related to size, since size says something about its 'handiness' when it comes to using or moving the object: a statuette can be moved and carried by one person, in contrast to a statue, which needs more persons' hands and power. The same is true for vessels which are mobile and portable up to certain dimensions and weight. The affordances of the object determine some of its utilizations and functions which goes beyond mere touch and gaze.[10] Beside these basic affordances related to the size of an object which influence what to do with it, there are more options to imply certain interpretations by labelling the phenomenon.

In studies of miniatures, a common and useful distinctive description is that of models, diminutives, and tokens.[11] These terms centre on different aspects of the tiny things. A model entails a reference to something larger and/or fully functional; a diminutive says something both about the process during which the thing became small and its relation to a larger object of which it is a shrunken version; token taps into its symbolic aspects — that the tiny thing stands for or represents something different.

I will sketch only briefly the interpretations by archaeologists — and I refer to those from European, Mediterranean, and Near Eastern prehistory and antiquity — ranging from Pilz, who called this the indexical character of miniatures, establishing relations between a signifier and a signified, to Mack, who focused on their capacities of imagining an ideal invisible world.[12] Barfoed works with all three categories (model miniature, diminutive, and token miniature), differentiated by size, and ascribes an active use to the first two and a passive use to the last category.[13] In opposition to such limiting formalizations, Knappett and Kiernan see the need for a dynamic view on miniaturizations from the ancient Mediterranean in definition as well as consequently in interpretation, not predetermined by a label.[14]

Whatever name we give to an object, the criteria to work with are its size, its larger-scaled reference, and its functionality. All terminologies and metaphoric labels on miniaturized objects oscillate between an emic (object-based) explanation and an etic (context- and meaning-based) explanation (such as 'abstraction', 'compression').[15] We have to be aware of these main differences when moving towards an interpretation focused on the side of the object (entailing its production) or on the side of the contexts (entailing its consumption).[16]

To shed light on the subtleties of nomenclature in relation to objects, I draw on examples from Pompeii

---

[10] See n. 1; Hughes 2018, 65.

[11] See this distinction in Bailey 2005, 29–30, refined and used e.g. by Barfoed 2018, table 2. Knappett 2012, 100 expresses his doubts: 'however, there are surely grounds for questioning this distinction: surely any model, however precise, is an abstraction of sorts, given the evident loss of functionality?'

[12] Hughes 2018, 65 operationalizes the concept of iconic sign and indexicality of the miniaturized objects, referring to Peirce: 'The concept of indexicality becomes particularly relevant here, insofar as an indexical sign "refers to its object not so much because of any similarity or analogy with it [...] as because it is in dynamical connection both with the individual object, and with the senses or memory of the person for whom it serves as a sign" (Peirce [1902] 1955, 107)'; Mack 2007.

[13] Barfoed 2018. In contrast to this, Langin-Hooper 2015, 3 works with the rather vague term of 'slightly larger miniatures' which 'endearingly conform in size to the human hand's ability to grasp easily-provoking intrigued awe, as well as comforting familiarity'.

[14] Kiernan 2009; Knappett 2012.

[15] Bailey 2005, 32–36, puts it rather poetically by saying that small objects make people 'indulge in flights of fantasy' or open 'alternative worlds' (34), and sees miniaturization as 'abstraction and compression' in formal, spatial, and temporal regards (34–36), allowing for physical intimacy (Bailey 2005, 38); see also Langin-Hooper 2015, 62; Meskell 2015, 14 and 15 fig. 9. Knappett 2012, 87 speaks about the 'dynamics of material culture meaning' and the directly and indirectly perceived functions and meanings. He also focuses on a topological and partly quantitative approach for interpreting the facets of miniatures (distance, fidelity, directionality, and frequency), as well as dynamic qualities (Knappett 2012, 92–93, 104). Kohring 2011 in turn reflects on the production side of miniature pottery, where she sees the start of 'enchantment' and particular meaning. See below pp. 58–62 and Trinkl in this volume, pp. 73–76.

[16] The two angles of view are conflated by the third, represented by Mitchell 2004; Gosden 2005; Meskell 2015 and myself, asking deliberately the not-immediately plausible question about what the objects or pictures want.

and its surroundings: the sacred place of Privati at Stabiae, find contexts from houses, compital shrines, and a necropolis in Pompeii, drawing comparisons to the sacred precinct of the Fondo Iozzino outside its walls and to Pantelle close to Mondragone (Fig. 4.1).[17]

Grasso (2004), who published the most thorough study of Pompeian miniature pottery, starts with a differentiation of 'ceramica miniaturistica e ceramica a piccole dimensioni', which she bases on mathematical grounds — the measurements of the smallest diameter or height.[18]

Is a 'Compilation' of Miniature Vessels Still a Miniature?

What if the measured size of an object is not all that counts or makes an object a miniature? A peculiar object from the small sacred place of Privati close to Stabiae exemplifies the paradox between size in dimensions but miniature in concept (Fig. 4.2). A huge number of objects was brought to light by the excavators at this sanctuary.[19] Terracotta figurines, bronze objects, and pottery form the main corpus of finds at this place, which was in use from the fourth to the second centuries BC (Fig. 4.3a). Many miniatures are only slightly longer than 2 cm.

Among the countless miniature pottery items, one object stands out. It is a pile of ten small cups or plates produced and fired as one piece that reaches almost 30 cm (Fig. 4.3b–c). Their size diminishes the higher their position. The top of this cup-tower is formed by a miniature *olla* (jar or jug). The piece itself is not small and was at this height not even easy to handle, but the parts it consists of are miniature vessels. Each vessel might not be higher than 3 cm, and they have maximum diameters of 9–10 cm at the bottom and 5 cm at the top of the pile.

---

[17] Most contexts and findings are taken from Grasso 2004; for Insula VI.1 I refer to Cool and Griffiths 2015. Larger sacred precincts and funerary contexts play a more marginal, comparative role in the scope of this contribution.

[18] Grasso 2004, 15 and 18, visualized as Gaussian curves in her figs 1 and 2; on miniature pottery from Pompeian and Campanian contexts, see also D'Alise 2019 and Osanna 2021 (Fondo Iozzino); Gallo 2012 (an archaic bothros in IX.1.29); Lanzi 2019 (on the sacred place of Pantelle).

[19] Miniero and others 1997, esp. 39, nos 49–52 for four more miniature vessels (*skyphos*, jug, cups) and no. 57 for the object given here in Fig. 4.5. Other objects are also very small, like the *olpetta*, no. 40, which is only 6.4 cm high, and the *coppe*, nos 33–34, which might be called 'miniaturized'.

In the catalogue of the material from Privati, it is called a 'thimiaterion',[20] which would entail its utilization for burning incense, such as resins or herbs. The missing ventilation holes and the closed and high form of the *olla* on top, however, speak against this interpretation, at least in a functional manner.

Whatever the pile of cups and the vessel on top were used for, it was buried in the soil around the second century BC along with terracotta figurines and other downscaled pottery. The object itself is not a miniaturized pottery form — it has in its appearance no normal-dimensioned references — but the potter deliberately gave it a shape which epitomizes what happens with the individual pieces of miniature pottery in the small sanctuary: they accumulate as remainders of people's ongoing and repeated religious activities of offering, dedicating, and praying.

This object, which stands out through its shape and appearance, demonstrates that the pile of different numbers and sizes cannot be dealt with separately and have to be set into relations with each other.[21]

Is a Small Vessel for Small Amounts of Expensive Goods a Miniature?

So-called *balsamari* and *unguentari*, widespread small-scale containers, are tiny pottery objects, but they do not pertain to the group of miniaturized forms, since they have no larger siblings (Figs 4.4–4.5). People in Graeco-Roman Antiquity, including Pompeians, used these vessels for keeping perfumes and precious cosmetic or medicinal oils and liquids. To put it more objectively, their size only allows for small amounts of emulsions or liquids to be kept, so that we assume they were made for precious contents or substances of which only small quantities were used at a time. They can have prolonged, spindle-shaped, or rounded bodies; not all have a bottom on which they can stand, so that they were kept hanging, lying, or in racks.[22]

---

[20] Miniero and others 1997, 38–39 no. 57.

[21] The combination of qualitative and quantitative characteristics is not only relevant in the case of miniaturization, but more often than we tend to think and consider it. This compiled object in comparison to the rest of the material from Privati offers a good example for this; for Near Eastern Archaeology, see Pollock and Bernbeck 2010. Such piles of objects are also known from Greece in the Archaic and Classical periods (see Bouzek 2017), to which Elisabeth Trinkl has drawn my attention.

[22] The term *unguentarium* is more often applied to an elongated, thin form with a bulge at its central part; see Anderson-Stojanović

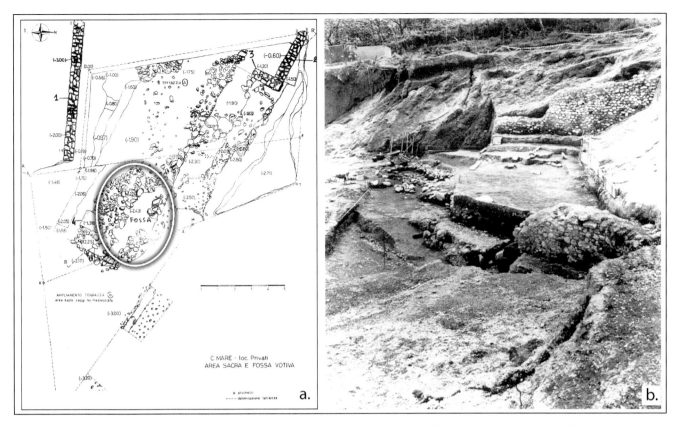

Figure 4.2. a. The plan shows the terrace and remains of walls at the sacred place of Privati (north down) with the 'fossa' (red circle) containing the deposited material with many terracotta statuettes and both full-scale and miniature pottery; b. the terrace (right) and the 'fossa' (left) between walls (1 and 2 in the plan) (Miniero and others 1997, figs 2 and 3).

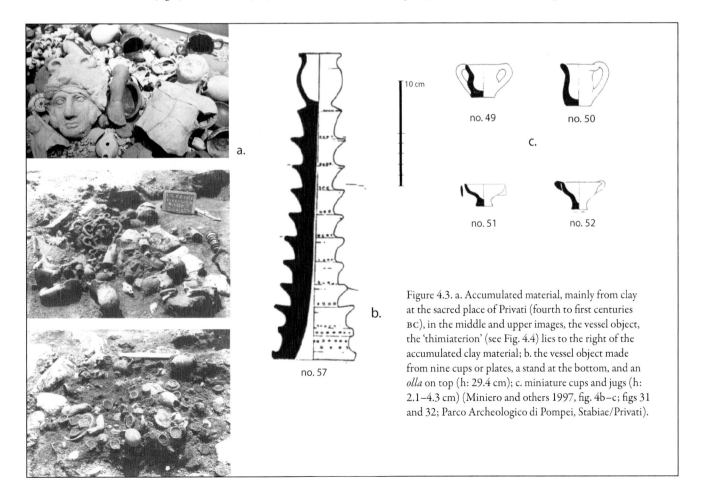

Figure 4.3. a. Accumulated material, mainly from clay at the sacred place of Privati (fourth to first centuries BC), in the middle and upper images, the vessel object, the 'thimiaterion' (see Fig. 4.4) lies to the right of the accumulated clay material; b. the vessel object made from nine cups or plates, a stand at the bottom, and an *olla* on top (h: 29.4 cm); c. miniature cups and jugs (h: 2.1–4.3 cm) (Miniero and others 1997, fig. 4b–c; figs 31 and 32; Parco Archeologico di Pompei, Stabiae/Privati).

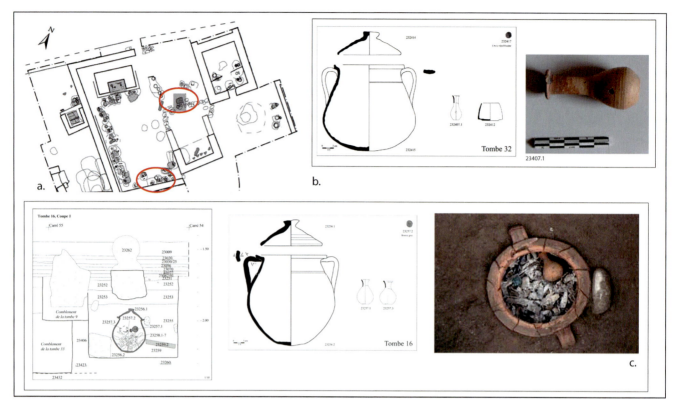

Figure 4.4. Small-scale pottery, mainly *unguentaria* and *balsamari*, from the necropolis at the Porta Nocera from tombs of the mid-first century BC: a. enclosure 23/25 with tombs 16 and 32 marked by the red circles; b. the urn of tomb 32 and a miniature vessel and a *balsamario* from its pit. The first was found behind the stele, turned upside-down, the latter in the filling above the urn, in a detail picture to the right; c. the urn of the tomb 17 in its pit; on top of the ashes lay two *balsamari* (Van Andringa, Duday, and Lepetz 2013, a. p. 326 fig. 212; b. p. 1087 fig. 49; p. 193 fig. 148; c. pp. 327–28 fig. 212b–c).

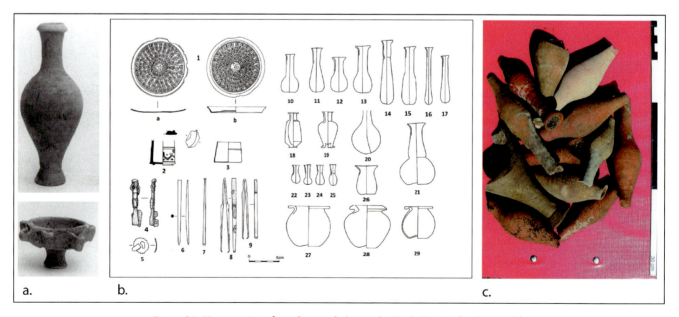

Figure 4.5. *Unguentaria*: a. from the sacred place at the Fondo Iozzino (without scale) together with a multi-handled *kylix*; b. a set of toiletry items from the Casa Imperiale (I.11.17); c. workshop VII.4.24–25, which can be dated to the second century BC (a. D'Ambrosio 1993, fig. 3; b. Berg 2017, fig. 9; c. Ribera and others 2012, fig. 7).

This type of small container is often found in burials; recently well-contextualized examples were found in the excavations in the necropolis of Porta Nocera (Fig. 4.4).[23] Individual *balsamari* were also dedicated at sacred places, such as the sanctuary at the Fondo Iozzino (Fig. 4.5a);[24] they were also used in personal hygiene and toiletry and as such are parts of household inventories (Fig. 4.5b).[25] A third place where they occur in high numbers in Pompeii is in Insula VII, east of the Forum (VII.4.28, Fig. 4.5c).[26] The quantities of *balsamari* in this zone seem to be the result of a production site located here, which made the excavators call it the 'perfume quarter'.

The *balsamari* and *unguentari* do not reach larger dimensions than 7 cm high.[27] There is no doubt that these containers can be called proper miniature pottery, although they miss one determining factor to be a fully-fledged miniaturization: they do not have large or normally scaled 'siblings'. Yet, one could still argue that they are miniaturized because their size is adapted to their purpose as carrier of small amounts of (precious) liquids — shrunk according to the amount of content or their carrying capacity. Another aspect is that this size of container can be handled easily and delicately. Still, they are just tiny, not miniatures or miniaturizations.

How human agents could handle and interact with the *unguentaria* is similar to miniaturized pottery from sacred or mundane contexts. That is why one should include them when searching for the meanings and interactions of tiny objects with humans, more precisely with Pompeians in the Hellenistic and Roman periods — even though they lack the larger references.[28]

According to their various applications — as burial objects, in sanctuaries or houses, or for individuals for personal hygiene as well medical and cosmetic treatments (Figs 4.4–4.5) — their involvement in practices differs. They might have been given to the deceased as personal belonging or as the remains of anointment of the body or the scents used in funerary rituals and in festivals for the dead;[29] similar reasons might explain their presence in sanctuaries — as remainders of ritual anointments for example of statues. When found in houses, the *balsamari* and *unguentaria* have no actual religious purpose, since they are rather parts of toiletry sets.

In all contexts, however, these containers not only have certain affordances because of their size (and possible fragility) but also because of their functional aspects of keeping precious substances. Because of their dimensions and their contents, the tiny objects provided particular 'action possibilities' to their users. In handling these containers, the users could practically and epistemically perceive their specific delicateness.[30]

A Lid, a Token, a Cymbal, or a Cymbal for Children?

Since miniaturization is a relational term that we use — rather unconsciously — in relation to a modern western adult human being, we should be careful if the reference, such as the person's body handling the object, might be smaller — if it is, for example, a child, who has smaller hands. Independent of time in history or cultural context, miniature objects can often be found in the context of play, through which children get an understanding of their environment, learn behavioural schemata and modes of the utilization of things and their social embedding, and socially appropriate habits.[31] Functionality is not always a criterion of these objects, since toy vessels, for example, are often solid and cannot contain anything. They share this characteristic with models or tokens, whose referential aspects and 'as if'-aspect prevail over functional aspects. Hence, it is not always possible to draw a line of distinction between a miniaturized object for

---

1987. For content analysis of an Etruscan ointment see Colombini and others 2009. They occur also in sanctuaries with not entirely clear usage, e.g. in the Sanctuary of Zeus Labraundos in Asia Minor in the Hellenistic period and of Hekate at Lagina; see Williamson 2021, 136 and 291 with n. 169; Hellström 1965, 23–27.

[23] Duday, Van Andringa, and Creissen 2019; Green 2008. For such containers from burials in the Porta Nocera necropolis, see S. Fontaine in Van Andringa, Duday, and Lepetz 2013, 1169–201, catalogue 1202–31, here Fig. 4.4. More examples with clay *balsamari* are tombs 17, 46, 47: see Van Andringa, Duday, and Lepetz 2013, 204 fig. 153, 206 fig. 144, 356 fig. 228.

[24] See also below, n. 76, on the *unguentarium* found in the room with a compital shrine in VIII.4.24.

[25] Allison 2004; Berg 2017; 2020; Cool 2016.

[26] See Ribera and others 2012; Bustamante-Álvarez and others 2017.

[27] Cf. Anderson-Stojanović 1987 and S. Fontaine in Van Andringa, Duday, and Lepetz 2013, 1169–201, catalogue 1202–31.

[28] Grasso 2004, 21 includes them in her catalogue without discussing this issue.

[29] Use in funerary rituals see Pliny, *HN* XII.41.83: in the name and application of roses (as violets at the *Parentalia*) of one of the festivals for the dead, the *Rosaria*, scent is alluded to.

[30] See above, pp. 43–44.

[31] On play and ludic learning, see Dasen and Vespa 2021; Schwartz 2019; Weiss 2015. On miniature mock vessels, see also Trinkl in this volume.

smaller humans such as children and a token or model.[32]

In Pompeii, a particular item among the pottery findings is the so-called *coperchi*, which do not have straight parallels elsewhere and could pertain to the above-mentioned category of 'small item for small hands' (Fig. 4.6).[33] These tiny, slightly conical objects from a coarse clay measure 3 cm in diameter. Their height reaches *c.* 2 cm. The handle or upper part where it can be taken and held is a narrow and thin rim, which seems to have been made by pressing the clay between the fingers during production. Such objects were found in the excavation of the Tempio Dorico on the Foro Triangolare in layers belonging to the Hellenistic phase; one example came from the area of the Temple of Apollo or the House of Ganymede (VII.13.4); and the most recent finds — in large amounts — originate from the excavations in Insula VI.1 and at the compital shrine of IX.8.8.[34]

Grasso as well as Cool and Griffith detected differences in the fabric used for miniature cups (*calici*) or jugs (*brocche*) and for the *coperchi*.[35] Not only by their differing fabric do they stand materially (and visually) apart from other miniature pottery, but they also occur rarely in the same contexts or associated with the shapes they could have been meant for, if we assume them to be lids.[36] If the term 'lid' for these tiny objects is suitable as a formal descriptive label but is functionally wrong, what then could they have been made and meant for? Are they 'token miniatures' since they have only a 'passive usage' with a merely symbolic meaning and no functional aspects?[37] Is this a suitable and comprehensive explanation for a 'hand-some' thing?

When experimenting with how to handle these objects, Cool and Griffiths found out that the rim on top is suited to being held between two fingers, either the forefinger and middle finger or, as they propose, forefinger and thumb (which seems less convenient). The affordance given by their shape is key to understanding their function, even though they are so tiny. Holding them, the fingers cover the convex shape. A known object that is held like this is a cymbal.[38] Even though it is not easy to find parallels, since they differ widely in forms and sizes (and not least material), and they have rings to pull them over a finger, this interpretation is not too far-fetched. With their diameter of 3 cm, however, they seem to have not been made for adults' hands and should still be seen as miniaturized. Were they made for children's hands?

To get a clearer idea of their function and utilization in the case of the tiny objects such as the *coperchi*, it might be useful not only to look at their affordances but at their find contexts.[39]

Contexts of Meaning of Pottery with Downsized Features: What Is Clear and What Is Religious?

The examples so far presented show that the label we pin to a tiny object *ex post* can be determined by its affordances that are determined by its material characteristics and its culturally defined and appropriated production- and utilization-process. The 'thimiaterion', the *unguentaria*, and the *coperchi* also showed how many variations and uncertainties remain.[40] This makes any interpretation or ascription of meaning uncertain and variable as well, as demonstrated by the case of the *coperchi*, which could also be for children's hands.

---

[32] It is not stringently possible to allocate objects for play into the scheme of Barfoed 2018, table 2 which was developed on archaic and classical Greek material (mostly from the Peloponnese). Trinkl in this volume discusses some of this evidence. On the significance of the 'as if'-effect, see the conference from 2022 entitled '"As if" in Ancient Religions', organized by Felix Budelmann and Esther Eidinow.

[33] Grasso 2004, 32–33 found at the Tempio Dorico, at the Temple of Apollo, and in the Casa di Ganimede (VII.13.4). Outside Pompeii, some similar items dating to the Hellenistic period were found at the sanctuary Roccagloriosa or Cupra Marittima, which are not considered as close enough by Cool and Griffiths 2015, 7.

[34] Duhn and Jacobi 1890, 13; Eschebach and others 1995, 188; de Caro 1986, 27 n. 65; Cool and Griffiths 2015.

[35] Cool and Griffiths 2015, 7: (Fabric V003) which is coarser than for the *calici* from the same context; Grasso 2004, 32: 'argille grezze di colore marone rossastro con inclusi lucenti neri'. For their interpretation as cymbals, it would be of interest to know whether this fabric is apt to produce a certain kind of sound possibly as a result of its hardness. See below, Fig. 4.11, for the findings at Insula VI.1, but also Fig. 4.10 for the ones at the shrine IX.8.8.

[36] Cool and Griffiths 2015, 8, for their discussion.

[37] See the terminology in Barfoed 2018, table 2.

[38] Cool and Griffiths 2015, 13–14.

[39] See below, pp. 54–56, for further implications of the archaeological context and material. It is a longer way to argue in favour of cymbals or even more precisely for small-scale cymbals for children's hands. Clay cymbals are rare in catalogues; sizes go up to 18–20 cm. The purpose of an easily produced sound-creating object might be in the foreground for the *coperchi*. See Wardle 1981, I, 133, 330, 339. The smallest pieces she mentions are 5.3 cm, the largest 15 cm.

[40] At the overlaps of different cultural settings, the affordances of an object open options to discern meaning, utilization, and sensual perception by material and form, see e.g. Langin-Hooper 2015 and her approach to identity negotiated in Seleucid terracottas from Babylonia; see also Foxhall 2015, 2.

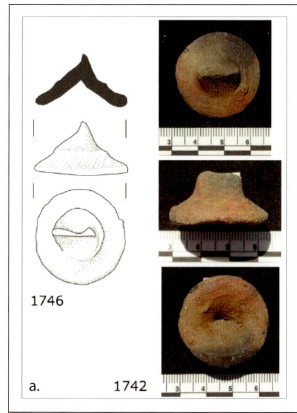

Figure 4.6. A special form of miniature object, the *coperchi*, and miniature *calici*/goblets from Insula VI.1 (Cool and Griffiths 2015, figs 6–7).

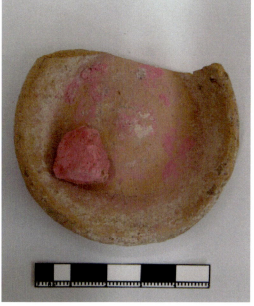

Figure 4.7. Small-scale plates (diam: 10 cm and 6 cm) from I.8.9, containing pigments (first century AD) (Osanna 2016, figs 14–15).

Archaeological Contexts of Pottery with Downsized Features, Functions, and Again Labels

As size is important for the functional aspects of pottery products, we learn from this property about their practical functionality. When ceramic products have open or closed forms, when they are very small or very large, specific purposes and applications are implied. Yet the contexts we find objects in often predetermine how we label them. If a pot with a rounded shape is found close to a spot of ashes, we tend to call it a cooking pot whether it has a burnt surface or not. Only the analysis of the fabric and its characteristics when exposed to high temperatures could change this label. Therefore, we have to be clear on the interwovenness of naming and putting an object into a category. Keeping the process open as long as possible or reopening it and thinking of options to rename an object — in the case of the pot, it could be a storage pot set into the ground — allows for new interpretational approaches to the utilization, function, and purpose of the objects.

If we want to be aware about categories and give attention to the reasons why we call a tiny ceramic object a miniature or miniaturized pottery, we have to look closer at the specific contexts where such pieces occur — in our case, at Pompeii and its surroundings. What the find context — its associated structures and findings as well as chronologies — can tell us about the meaning of the tiny pottery items will be first limited to the more general question of how to detect a religious or a profane meaning of objects before we can then ask about the specific meaning of tiny objects. In general terms, the areas from which the objects dealt with in the following come are houses and sidewalks, as well as shared sacred spaces.

But how far are descriptions of a context predetermined and in turn predefine all subsequent interpretations? The common method of attributing find material to contexts follows first the stratigraphical unit, then the trench, followed by the functional space of the city — houses, sacred areas, tombs — which has an impact on any further interpretation. If, as I said before, the presented material stems from houses, sidewalks, and shared sacred spaces, this already anticipates or evokes certain ideas and expectations on what the structures, layers, and material around the tiny pottery look like and were used for. The attribution to features such as 'house', 'sacred area', or 'tomb' can only be given if the chronological setting is cleared and an allocation possible.[41] The intention and the actual utilization of a piece of pottery might still remain open, however, since areas of use can overlap: for example, in houses with workshop areas or, vice versa, workshops with dwelling functions, or sacred areas that might have been houses in an earlier phase.[42]

Only a close look at the associated objects and structures or installations, the material and fabrics they are made from, their characteristics, and their chronology have an impact on the interpretation, not least its numbers and quantitative relations.

(Almost) Clear Contexts of either Religious or Profane Function of the Miniature Pottery: Houses, Workshops, and Other Sites of Consumption

The assemblage and layer in which a piece of pottery (or other material) is found or was deposited can tell us much about its usage — at least in this moment of its 'pathway'.[43] Since the use and demand of small-scale pottery (apart from toiletry items) decreased from the Classical and Hellenistic to the Roman periods, I start from the youngest contexts, which show a continuity of their usage, although the continuous stability of their meanings, 'transported' a long way down chronologically, must be questioned.[44]

A clear indication of their profane purpose can be found in the case of two small plates on which pigments are preserved, from a shop (I.8.9) dated to the first century AD (Fig. 4.7). The practical application — like the *balsamari* — for carrying or keeping tiny amounts of any matter determines the size of the pottery. Judging only from size, however, one would call this container, with its *c.* 6 cm diameter, miniaturized. Yet the lucky preservation conditions of contextual data determine its use (and categorization or label).

The purpose of tiny pottery pieces from the Casa di Lesbianus (I.13.9) is almost obviously religious to judge from the associated finds (Fig. 4.8a): two small jars (*brochette*), a cup, and a lamp were kept in an *armarium* in the central room of the small house together with various objects of glass, bone, and bronze and two statuettes of deities (Liber Pater and Venus?). Statuettes of a dove and a sheep were also among these objects.[45] The embedding of the pottery objects into the ritual activity of the household is indicated by the assemblage with the statuettes of deities in the last phase of Pompeii in the first century AD.[46]

---

[41] This leads to predetermined interpretations, especially in cases of material deprived of its find context or with unclear provenances. The findings of miniature vessels from the Porta Nola (Grasso 2004, 52–53, 80–81) could be interpreted as part either of a liminal cult at the city gate or of rituals pertaining to funerals and care for the dead, because of the gate's closeness to the adjoining necropolis. Downsized objects were found at the Porta Stabia in a clearly ritual setting close to an altar with a niche above in the passageway (second century BC, see Ellis and others 2012; Ellis and Devore 2008, 318–19), for a small votive cup containing a small amount of carbonized remains from the first century BC.

[42] Overlap of household production, workshop, and living/dwelling is common in Pompeii, see e.g. Flohr 2011.

[43] The term 'pathway' (borrowed from biochemistry for the step-by-step reactions and transformation of substances) seems to me more suitable as description of the point in time we look at or use an object, instead of the 'animated' term 'biography', see Rieger (forthcoming).

[44] See e.g. Grasso 2004, 84–85.

[45] Grasso 2004, 56–57 with ns 120–22.

[46] The location, even in the central room of a small house,

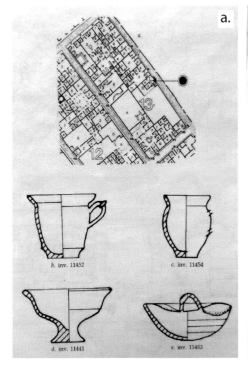
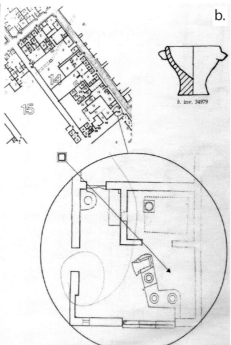

Figure 4.8. Miniature pottery from houses: a. Casa di Lesbianus (I.13.9), where four miniature vessels were kept in an *armarium* in the central room; b. from a *thermopolium* in I.14.15, where a single miniature cup; c. a so-called *culla*, a *bruciaprofumo*, with figurative protome at the end was found together with b; all material can be dated to the first century AD, even though the pottery types were in use from the third century BC onwards (Grasso 2004, tavoli 19 and 20; Elia 1962, fig. 6).

Another example for the use of miniature vessels in religious contexts was found in a *thermopolium* in I.14.15 (Fig. 4.8b). A miniature *calice*/goblet was associated with a *bruciaprofumo* in the form of a 'cradle' in this house's layers from the eruption of Mount Vesuvius in the first century AD (Fig. 4.8c). The specific form of the *bruciaprofumo* is commonly related to the *patella* used in the cult of the *Lares*. Since the tiny goblet was found associated with this incense burner with a small female bust, we may assume that the *familia* living here also used the tiny goblet in religious practices for the household gods.[47]

One of the unclear but probably religious contexts of evidence comes from the Casa delle Nozze d'Argento (V.2.i), where eight small-scale pottery pieces were found in mixed layers from cleanings in the area of the *piscina* of the thermal complex and its surroundings.[48] This bathing complex adjoins the *hortus*, the garden, of the house. Because of the mixed layers, it is difficult to fix a chronology of the miniature cups or the original location of the pieces. According to Grasso, they originate from the beginning of the third century AD.[49] If their find-spot in a secondarily composed layer in the garden correlates to their first place of utilization, they might have belonged to a niche for the household gods, which are common in gardens and could have been a part of the organization of this space.[50]

More examples of clear or not-so-clear religious or profane employment of miniaturized pieces could be added, since often contexts of the objects from older excavations are missing or found in mixed find layers because of the many phases of houses and buildings at Pompeii. However, since the main question asked and to be answered is what the tiny objects want and what obligations they 'place upon us',[51] we should focus on contexts where their specific size and dimensions might help to clarify their meaning. For this purpose, I turn to archaeological contexts outside of houses — in the streets, particularly the sidewalks.

---

correlating to atria in larger houses, where household shrines were often situated, is not a compelling argument in favour of a religious meaning.

[47] Grasso 2004, 57–58. See Elia 1962 for this type of *bruciaprofumi*. The association of tiny altars with statuettes of always small *Lares* and statuettes of other deities as well as small portable altars shrink the entire household ritual to a miniature dimension.

[48] Sigges 2002, 284. Grasso 2004, 61 and 110 (table) Tav. 23 bottom, where she indicates a wrong find-spot — it was in room 1 and 2 close to the thermal complex and the kitchen (room s) in an area that could have been a garden; see Sigges 2002, 320–23 Taf. 77 and 80 with miniature pieces, and 335–39 with more findings and the interpretation of the area of the house.

[49] Grasso 2004, 61 n. 168.

[50] Kastenmeier 2007, 69–79 on the place of religion in the service area of the houses.

[51] Gosden 2005, 193.

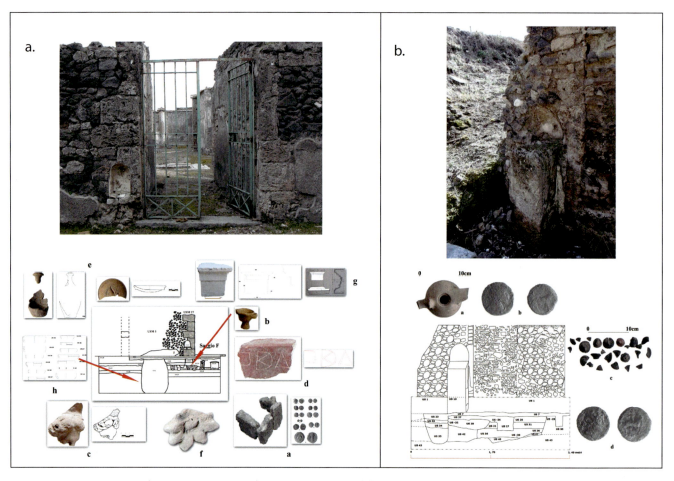

Figure 4.9. Miniature pottery in house contexts: a. Casa delle Vestali VI.1.6–8, miniature goblets from below the *tablinum* (third/second centuries BC?); b. Casa di A. Octavius Primus (VII.15.13) from a trench in the *triclinium* (saggio A in *triclinium* i): findings of a miniature cup and the lower parts of two female statuettes (a. Bon and others 1995; 1997, figs 5.14–15; Coarelli and others 2005, fig. 44).

Clearly Religious Contexts in the Streets: Foundation Deposits

Miniaturized or miniature pottery has been found so far at three religious installations along the streets — compital shrines — at Pompeii. Anniboletti (2008b), who conducted excavations in front of the facades of the houses VI.2.16–21 and IX.8.8 as well as in a room at VIII.4.24, studied these contexts and findings of compital shrines in the course of her thesis (Fig. 4.9).[52]

The niche to the left of the entrance of VI.2.16–21, with an internal box for offerings, was in use between the mid-second century BC and the end of the first century BC (Fig. 4.9a). The material includes a miniature *calice*/goblet found in a pit beneath the niche. This context correlates to the findings at the shared sacred space at Privati not only in its chronology (mentioned above) but also in the form and size of the miniature vessel (b in Fig. 4.9a).[53] However, in contrast to Privati, where more people were active and their offerings of tiny pottery were part of ongoing practice, the goblet from this installation at VI.2.16–12 is the only piece which people or their representative religious specialist offered in a kind of foundation pit.[54] It is (like in the next example) related to the sacralization of the place of communication with some deities of the locality, the *domus*, or its the entrance situation at the niche.[55] As such, it represents the unique ritual and one moment in the existence

---

[52] Anniboletti 2007; 2008a; 2008b; Van Andringa 2000.

[53] See above, p. 46.

[54] Anniboletti 2007, 2–3 fig. 2 indicates the 'fossetta sacrale' beneath the niche as provenance of the single *kylix* (not glazed), which in Anniboletti 2008a, 211 fig. 3 is only mentioned in the caption.

[55] Anniboletti 2008a, 210–12 fig. 3; Van Andringa 2000, 62 no. 27.

of the sacred place, its creation. In contrast, the more numerous pieces of black-glazed miniature pottery from the larger pit to the north of the niche could represent the remains of religious gatherings embracing people from the street or neighbourhood group (Fig. 4.9a.b).

Another niche in the wall can be seen at the facade of the Casa del Centenario (IX.8.8) (Fig. 4.9b). In this case the installation is enlarged by a block of Sarno limestone as an altar below it. Altar and niche are located at a former doorway, which was blocked in the time of the Late Republic.[56] It is one of the few street altars where the remains of the last sacrifice were not cleaned away, so that in the moment of the eruption of Mount Vesuvius they still lay there. The entire sacred location was, at least in the last phase, dedicated to *Salus*. A faint inscription is preserved above as well as the painting of two cornucopia with a garland which can be dated to the phase after the middle of the first century AD.[57] In looking for the earlier phases, Anniboletti retrieved material of a kind of foundation deposit from trenches in the sidewalk below the level of the altar's setting. In a pit to the north of the altar lay a miniaturized *kylix*, a Hellenistic lamp from the last quarter of the third century BC, and a bronze coin from the first half of the third century BC — all with traces of fire. To the south were several small pits on the level of the foundation of the altar filled with bones, but one also with one tiny *kylix*.[58] On a younger layer, a horizon of utilization consisting of soil mixed with ashes, occurred more than twenty miniature *kylikes* as well as six *coperchi* and the fragments of several more (c in Fig. 4.9b).[59] At the end of the first century BC, the *sacellum* on the street close to the former entrance is maintained and the level raised, despite the closure of the entrance.

The material attests not only that altar and niche were installed and used from the beginning of the second century BC, but it also shows the differentiated employment of miniature pottery.[60] Even though the same types — the *kylix* and the *coperchi* — appear, the numbers make all the difference. For the foundation ritual, people deposited the individual item (two individual kylixes in two different pits, respectively) in the soil. For later recurring rituals, they used higher numbers of pottery, mixed *kylikes* and *coperchi* — maybe related to the higher numbers of participants in as well as repetitions of the ritual.

In VIII.4.24, the location and layout are different to the niches of VI.2.16–21 and IX.8.8 since it is an installation in a room with an entrance from the Via Stabiana, not merely a niche or an altar on the sidewalk.[61] Inside the room (3 × 2.30 m) stands an altar on a podium, or rather, built into it. In the gap that the podium fills between the altar and the rear wall of the room there are two *pozzi* — holes of *c.* 20 × 20 cm. From these *pozzi*, material such as bones, shells, and pottery were retrieved that seem to originate from continuously practised sacrifices.[62] In one of the many deposits interred in the floor level of the room, a 'coppetta miniaturistica a orlo rientrante in ceramica a vernice nera' was found (US 40 in the north-western corner). This piece can be dated to the second century BC, in the second half of which the *sacellum* was installed; it was renovated in the Augustan period and remained in use until AD 79.[63] A niche in the northern wall (to the right when coming into the room) which still existed at the moment of the excavation could have been used for the image of the *Lares* or other deities.[64]

Like in IX.8.8, the find of one single tiny container of clay in VIII.4.24 shows that in sacred places related to entrances, streets, and sidewalks, miniaturized vessels were not employed *en masse* like in sacred places such as Privati, where more people came to practice their religious communication. In the latter, the tiny vessels could accumulate to manifest the repetition and actualization of the rituals, whereas the individual pieces at the compital shrines or niches at entrance ways belong instead to rituals of foundation or sacralization, which both mark the transition from a one kind of utilization to another, as well as rituals marking liminal zones where spatial transition takes place, such as the doorways.[65]

---

56 Anniboletti 2007, 6–9; 2008a, 215–18; Van Andringa 2000, 52 no. 10.

57 *CIL* IV 3774: *Salutei sacrum*; for the painting see Mau 1900, 240 (with wrong location).

58 Another one contained a coin (*semuncia*) from the end of the third century BC, Anniboletti 2008a, 217.

59 Anniboletti 2008a, 8.

60 Anniboletti 2008a, 217.

61 Anniboletti 2008b, 3–4 fig. 7.

62 Anniboletti 2008b, 5–6 figs 8 and 9. See also below, n. 74, on the *unguentarium* found there.

63 Anniboletti 2008b. The first phase is dated to the mid-second century BC according to the tufa altar found in the *sacellum* (Anniboletti 2008b, 3 fig. 6).

64 Mau 1900, 217 Tafel 107 describes the niche in the north wall (see his drawing) which could have housed statuettes of *Lares*, *Genius*, or other deities, not paintings, as Anniboletti 2008b, 1 reports.

65 Rüpke 2015. See also below, pp. 62–63.

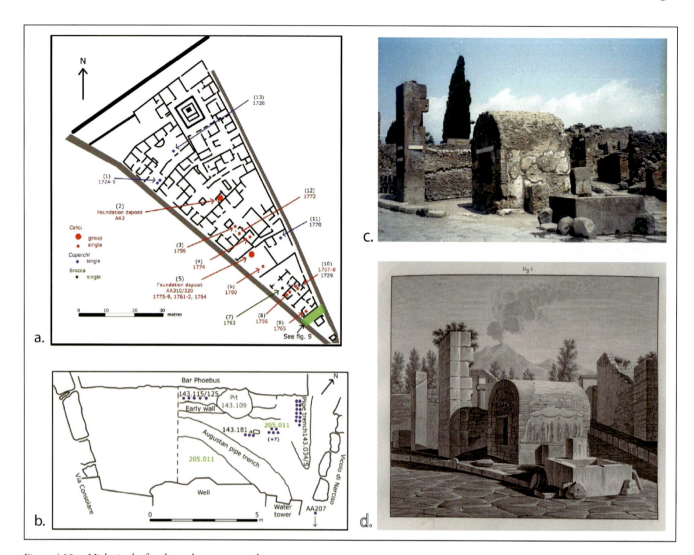

Figure 4.10. a. Niche in the facade on the street or at the entrance of a house in VI 2.16–21 with material, among which is a *kylix* in a pit below the altar and miniature pottery from the large pit a little to the north of the altar; b. street altar to Salus in IX.8.8 with find material: in a pit to the south (to the left of the altar, in unità stratigrafica 34 or 35?) a single *kylix* was found, to the north (to the right of the altar, unità stratigrafica 36 or 42?) fragments of miniature pottery and fragments of an entire *coperchi* were found (a. Anniboletti 2008a, figs 1 and 10; b. Anniboletti 2008a, fig. 3 and <www.pompeiiinpictures.com>, Altars, IX.8.8, © Jackie and Bob Dunn, by permission of the Ministero della Cultura — Parco Archeologico di Pompei, retrieved 15 May 2022).

These contexts Anniboletti unearthed in facades, on sidewalks, and along the streets again convey the employment of miniature pottery not only as offerings addressed to gods and *numina* but rather in foundational rites conducted when the niches and altars were installed or changed. VIII.4.24 does not fully match this explanation, since the tiny vessel was not deposited below the altar or in the *pozzi*. However, it could have been a deposition related to the niche in the north wall.

An Almost Clearly Religious Context: *Lares*

The *coperchi* at the altar for Salus in front of IX.8.8 are clearly connected with the religious practice of offering and depositing objects to this deity or her predecessor when the street altar was installed. They also occur in layers of the houses and sidewalks in Insula VI.1.

In the contexts in VI.1, however, these specific pieces of pottery cannot undoubtedly be related to religious practices. So far — following Cool and Griffith — they might be explained as tiny cymbals or similar sound-making objects. But what could they mean beyond this functional explanation, considering the high numbers in which they occur in the trenches of the southern part of Insula VI.1? What did the *coperchi* want in these trenches, or more justifiably asked: Why did Pompeians put or leave them there, and what does this tell us about the meaning of their dimensions or size (Fig. 4.10)?

The twenty-seven pieces found at the southern end, in comparison to only eleven in the rest of the insula, can

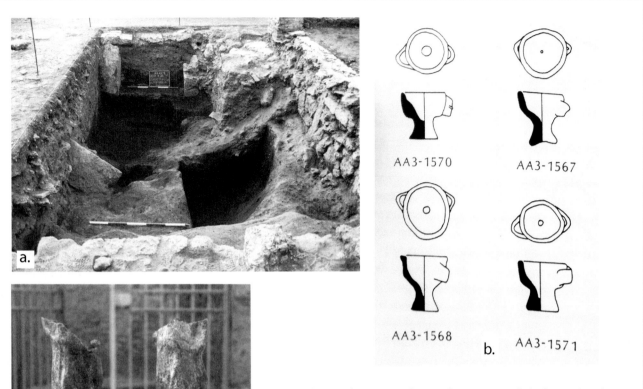

Figure 4.11. Insula VI.1 a. Find-spots of miniature vessels; b. the trench at the southern end of the insula; c. the well house and the fountain, between which ran the trench (b), where numerous *coperchi* were found in the pre-Augustan layers (each dot an example); d. the paintings from the Augustan period on the well house with altar in front, preserved in an engraving by Mazois from the nineteenth century, attest to its function as compital shrine (Cool and Griffiths 2015, figs 8–9; <www.pompeiiinpictures.com>, VI.1.19, © Jackie and Bob Dunn, by permission of the Ministero della Cultura — Parco Archeologico di Pompei, retrieved 15 May 2022; Mazois 1824, pl. 2.1).

be interpreted as a sign of intensive usage of these objects at this part of the insula, if we do not assume that they were collected and disposed here (Fig. 4.10a–b).[66] A set of them was found in a ditch that was dug for water pipes and a water tower in the Augustan period (Fig. 4.10b). The well at the southern end of the insula, dating back to the second century BC, was by then redundant.[67] However, it was reappropriated, at least its southern wall was, as a compital shrine with a painted scene depicting a group of *magistri* sacrificing to the *Lares* (Fig. 4.10c–d).[68] The interpretation as an intentional deposition of the *coperchi* in this *fossa* is arguable. Yet, if they have not been deposited here intentionally, the tiny objects in a larger number were at least not removed when the area was cleared for the water pipes. This might be related to their meaning. Moreover, the Augustan compital shrine on the former well-house, close to the water tower at the corner, allows for the assumption of a continuing religious significance of this place, to which the *coperchi* also contributed in their invisible subsurface location.[69]

---

[66] Cool and Griffiths 2015, table 2. The entire insula offers interesting material concerning religious depositions, as for example underneath the *tablinum* of the Casa dei Vestali (VI.1.6–8) — a fill not of domestic waste, but with four miniature *calici*/goblets and the remains of a juvenile pig, dated to the third and second centuries BC (Bon and others 1997), see here Figure 4.9. It resembles a pit with the remains of a foundation ritual, which in contrast to the ones beneath the niches employs more than one miniature vessel.

[67] Cool and Griffiths 2015, 11–12.

[68] Cool and Griffiths 2015, 13: 'a curious feature is the number of *coperchi* found within the eastern trench for the piped water supply'. Even though it is not clear whether this was a casual or an intentional redeposition, they have been around in the soil or the surface when people worked there.

[69] See Rieger 2016 on agency of pot sherds in sacred places even when they become invisible.

In analogy to the street altar at IX.8.8 (Fig. 4.9b), the tiny *coperchi* of VI.1 might also be interpreted as objects used by the Pompeians in religious practices in the neighbourhood (and maybe in the houses, as the other findings in VI.1 suggest; Fig. 4.11).[70] It cannot of course be fully clarified whether they functioned as cymbals making sounds in the cult of the *Lares vicinales* or *compitales*, or if they represented only the potential to make music in their miniaturized form and the inhabitants of this area of the city did not use them in practice.

Yet there is a third option, since we know that children played a role in the cult of the *Lares compitales*, whose festival was also meant to confirm the belonging of the individual inhabitants to this group or neighbourhood. The custom of appending woollen dolls to the compital shrines when the Compitalia were celebrated meant to represent every member of a household in front of the neighbourhood, employed again a diminutive form: the doll as a substitute for the human being.[71] So the *coperchi*-cymbals — if this interpretation is correct — might be the diminutive form of the musical instruments accompanying the rituals of appending tiny human images, the dolls, to the shrines. They could have been practically used by children who partake in the rituals.

Connotations:
What the Size of a Tiny Object Can Mean

After having outlined and given examples for the etic and emic ascriptions to miniaturized, miniature, or just tiny pottery vessels and their occurrence in Pompeii and the wider area, I will now try to search for the specific meanings of these tiny objects. If a religious context for the above-mentioned pieces of tiny pottery items could be determined through the archaeological context, their significance in religious practices must again consider the particular affordances of the miniaturized format and what it imposed on or evoked in people using them.

Let us return to the outstanding piece of pottery from the beginning of this paper, the pile of tiny cups with the *olla* on top from the sacred place at Privati (Fig. 4.3a–b) and the question about the relation of size, number, and meaning. The 'thimiaterion' represents an 'objectified' accumulation of tiny pottery. Number and size — of the entire piece and of its individual parts — interact in a meaningful play both internally and externally with a potential user. What do these tiny objects, their number, and their combined forms and assemblages tell us?

Creating Meaning by Using Miniature Pottery in Large Numbers

Looking at the chronologically earlier findings of the fourth to second centuries BC, we are often confronted with large amounts of vessels of all sizes accumulating at sacred places. Not only miniaturized pottery but also anatomical votives or terracotta statuettes were common offerings in most areas of the Italian Peninsula in the Classical and Hellenistic periods.[72] Although they decrease in number in the Roman period, not only overall but also at the individual find-spots and contexts, the tradition is not interrupted.

The accumulation is on the one hand the result of long-lasting activities and repeated practices, so that the tininess of some of this material is counterbalanced by the sheer number of objects (Figs 4.3, 4.12). This applies both in the case of Pompeii at the sacred place of Fondo Iozzino and at Privati close to Stabiae, where not only small groups but also larger crowds practised the cult in the third to first centuries BC.[73] In the earlier find contexts in late Republican houses, the numbers also surpass the 'one MNI' (minimum number of individuals) and can reach the 20 MNI (Figs 4.8a, 4.11a–b).[74] In the compital shrines — if we follow the interpretation as outlined above

---

[70] Bon and others 1995, 165, where bones of piglets and some miniature cups were found in a pit beneath the later *tablinum*. A single *kylix* was found in VII.14.15, together with the lower part of two female statuettes (which have their only parallel in those from Privati), see Coarelli and others 2005, 201–02.

[71] Flower 2017, 169, see also 202: '*Compita* could in turn presumably have yielded counts of individuals (by sex and by legal status) from the dolls hung at Compitalia and possibly even the number of brides who had offered bronze coins at each crossroads shrine during the previous year, if that information was also recorded locally.'

[72] The so-called 'votivi di tipo etrusco-laziale-campano' were not limited to these regions, see e.g. Comella 1981, fig. 1; Draycott and Graham 2020; Gentili 2005; Stek 2017.

[73] At Privati, Miniero and others 1997, 35 say about the findings: 'La maggioranza dei materiali rinvenuti è costituita dalle coppette (microcalici): se ne sono rinvenute alcune migliaia.' Also at the Sanctuary of the Fondo Iozzino, a bulk of the material is miniature vessels; see D'Ambrosio 1993, 201 'migliaia di frammenti'; D'Alise 2019. From the first century BC onwards, a decrease is recognizable, see Lanzi 2019, fig. 3 visualizing the pottery finds at Pantelle; at the sanctuary on the Largo Argentina in Rome, the miniature pottery comes to an end in the second century BC (Moser 2019, 66–81); this is in line with the decrease of miniaturized pottery at sanctuaries of Privati, Stabiae, or Fondo Iozzino, Pompeii.

[74] Casa di Pansa (VI.6.1), see Grasso 2004, 65–66; the Casa di Nozze d'Argento (V.2.i), see above n. 33; or in the Casa dei Vestali (VI.1.6–8), see Bon and others 1997.

— larger numbers of the tiny objects could also occur. The southern parts of the Insula VI.1 offers evidence for this in the first-century BC levels before the renovation in the time of Augustus of the location at the crossroads and the well that made it a fully-fledged compital shrine. The same is true for the second-century layers below the niche and altar at IX.8.8 or VI.2.16–21 (Fig. 4.9).[75]

A clear difference in numbers already occurs in the centuries BC in the pits or layers that belong to the initial sacralization of an area. In the case of IX.8.8, the single piece of a small cup, located at the level on which the altar rests, is part of the foundation rite.[76] Only in the Roman period do the numbers generally decrease, and people seem to have used only one or two miniaturized goblets when offering in the streets. Again IX.8.8, in the layers dated to the Augustan period, is an example of this development.[77]

The custom of using miniaturized pottery in ritual acts continued; only their multiplicity decreased. Their use in sacred places shared by many groups ceased and was substituted by statuettes, coins, and written confirmations of offerings preserved as inscriptions.[78] In compital and household shrines, people continued to use them to offer gifts they put into them. Here, the number of cups, goblets, or plates was never high because of fewer people offering; that is, only one household was involved.

At their peak in the fourth/third to the first centuries BC, the tiny objects allowed for an impressive accumulation by sheer quantity, though of course not in factual volume. Their number represents the many donors and people that acted for and communicated with the deities. Yet, when interpreting only their numbers, their meaning goes beyond the quantity. It is the multiplicity — the power of the many — in which they can be present at a sacred space together with other small-scale dedications, such as statuettes, pieces of metal, stones, and flowers. Instead of the volume or size, it is the individual tiny piece brought by a worshipper which has a particularly meaningful character.[79] The term 'democratization of the Sacred', introduced by Moser, rephrases the phenomenon in a suitable way:[80] a substitution for the full-scale altars as a place of sacrifice, so that more people could partake in communal rituals.[81]

Meanings by Producing and Using One or More Miniature Pottery Items

What tiny objects may have meant and 'wanted' can be grasped by approaches that are in line with Knappett and Kiernan, who argue in favour of a dynamic creation of meanings for these objects as well as an understanding of miniatures as a polysemic group of objects.[82] I would like to bring this dynamic approach to bear on what Gosden says about intercultural and inter-artefactual meanings (referring to Gell's 'inter-artifactual' capacities of objects as outlined at the beginning of this contribution).

By combining the views of these authors with the material from Pompeii revisited here and by considering both sides of production and of consumption, various layers of meaning of the tiny pottery objects can be differentiated.

---

[75] Anniboletti 2008a, 210–12 and 215–17. The 'fossa di scarico' in VI.2.16–21 contained miniaturized pottery material from the second half of the third to the second half of the second century BC, which in Anniboletti 2007, 2–3 fig. 2 is indicated with its unità stratigrafica; in Anniboletti 2008b, 211 fig. 3, it is not.

[76] One *unguentarium* which can be dated to the Hellenistic period was deposited in unità stratigrafica 76 in the *sacellum* VIII.4.24 close to the 'pozzi'; see Anniboletti 2008b, 4 with fig. 7.

[77] In the later phases of VIII.4.24, for example, no miniaturized objects occur (Anniboletti 2008a, 217). However, this place stands out through its numerous faunal material, including malacological finds, as well as all sorts of metal finds: Anniboletti 2008b, 5, 7–8. The very fragmented pieces of metal, as well as the shells as tiny natural offerings, resemble what Sojc in this volume describes for a deposit at S. Anna in the fifth century BC.

[78] As to the issue of 'Roman' influence on the kind of dedications in sacred places between the fourth and the first centuries BC, see Glinister 2006; Stek 2015, esp. 12–14; Graham 2020b, 205–06; on the changes in the first centuries BC and AD, see e.g. Rüpke 2009; fully developed in the second century AD, see examples at Ostia in Rieger 2011.

[79] See Barfoed 2015, esp. 173–78, studying miniature pottery at Panhellenic (fewer items) and other (Peloponnesian) sanctuaries (more items). She interprets them as having a commemorative character beyond the mere 'votive', substituting full-sized cups, jugs, etc.

[80] Moser 2019, 79. See also Moser 2019, 66–81, esp. 79–81 regarding *arulae* in Italian sanctuaries of the Republican period; she calls the phenomenon of miniaturization and amassment 'democratization' (79): 'With each type of object, the reduction in size of the full-scale model is what allows a larger public closer access to the less inclusive aspects of communal, animal sacrifice.' She also emphasizes the 'individual experiential memories of age-old, communal practices' these objects transmit (80). See also Barfoed 2018; Pilz 2011 relating miniaturization to mnemonic operations.

[81] Rüpke (forthcoming).

[82] Knappett 2012; Kiernan 2009. Gosden 2005, 194 puts it this way: 'artifacts are produced by repeated sets of actions, but then themselves bring about "repeated sets of actions implemented by the type" (Clark 1978, 153).' He continues (196): 'Crucially, Gell criticizes the view that culture as whole dictates the practical or symbolic significance of artifacts.'

Meanings of Tiny Pottery Objects Related to the Production Process

The Making: Delicateness and Condensation

If we turn to the production process side, material features and technological aspects are manifold among the miniature pottery of Pompeii. They are made from various fabrics, which if they have larger-scale reference vessels either differ from or are the same as the fabrics of the larger siblings. Some are rough-shaped cups that cannot stand stably (VI.1.6–8; Fig. 4.11); others are well-formed vessels (Figs 4.5a, 4.11c, 4.12). They either imitate only approximately larger forms or represent the details of special shapes which can only be found in the miniaturized size.

In sum, the point of producing and creating a tiny pottery object can either be just about certain dimensions and a recognizable form, or it can be about the forming of an entire functional piece in smaller dimensions — including using the same fabric. Often, the tiny pots technologically imitate the larger ones, since they are, for example, also made on the wheel or use a fabric that is functionally identical to their larger siblings.[83]

This evidence shows that even if one layer of meaning is that of a miniature substitute for a life-size figure, being, or thing, this does not entail the functional uselessness of the tiny object. Although this kind of production process involves more effort, crudity of appearance and sloppiness in the making does not mean that they are of poor quality in the sense of neglect.[84] The value and meaning lies in other features of the piece, such as size, recognizability, content, shape, or technique. Still, the forming of a minute piece of pottery can mean an increased effort for the producer and heightens its value even if it is tiny and roughly made.[85]

The Carrying Capacities and Contents: Delicateness and Aesthetics

Independent of the numbers of the miniature vessels as objects at one place, they as individual pieces have one feature in common: they can hold only tiny amounts of contents. This is true for either religious or mundane contexts — that is, in the amount of offerings or of things like paint or perfume (see pp. 46–48). However, if content determines the size of the vessel, one could also argue that the gods, whether *Lares* or other deities, received only parts of something as a gift. People — in our case Pompeians — gave only a part of a yield, a share of the fruits to be expected over the year, a tithe (*aparche* or *dekate*) of their belongings.[86] The miniature size of the container was suitable for both aspects of the offering, making it clear that this is the share both sides agreed on and letting the share appear consistent, since an entire cup, plate, or jug was filled.

The value of the content and the share of an imagined or existent whole it represents determine the size of the miniaturized pottery, either in the accumulations at shared sacred spaces or in the foundational sacrifices, where they occur often only in a single piece. These meanings can only be created and transported because of the size of the containers in which they were produced.

Meanings of Tiny Pottery Objects Related to Consumption

Embodied Knowledge and Handling: Intensification and Focalization

In the case of miniature pottery from Pompeii, the miniatures largely relate to shapes, forms, and features that Pompeians used in full-scale objects (jar, jug, pitcher, goblet, plate, cup), with only small differences (e.g. parts such as handles or differences in fabric or techniques). Therefore, in both large and small dimensions, such shapes and fabrics were familiar to the Pompeians in their daily life. They were used as professionally applied tools and containers of craftsmen or as containers with medical or cosmetic applications. Until the Sullan *colonia* was established on what was Pompeii, tiny pottery

---

[83] Grasso 2004, 60–61. Miniature pottery from Campoverde at Satricum seems to confirm that the same workshops produced full-size and miniature vessels in the same fabric; see Kleibrink 1997–1998, 443–47.

[84] Knappett 2020, 174–75. The interpretation of tiny objects as cheap gifts is on purpose only mentioned in a footnote. Even though economical reasoning is an important driver for human decisions and actions, including religion, it falls short as the only reason for the production and employment of tiny objects; see also Ekroth 2003.

[85] See Stewart 2007, 38; Kohring 2011, § 17. By multiplying the labour invested into the production of the tiny pottery item, the higher investment is mirrored or adds to the significance of the product; the significance somehow also multiplies. See Ekroth 2003 on archaic Corinthian miniature pottery, to which she ascribes a more personal aspect to the offering instead of an economic explanation, following M. Shanks.

[86] Hughes 2018 argues with reference to material from Greek and Italian archaic to Hellenistic sacred places; see e.g. Pliny, *HN* XVIII.9: 'ac ne degustabant quidem nouas fruges aut uina, antequam sacerdotes primitias libassent.'

Figure 4.12. Accumulations of Hellenistic clay materials from Fondo Iozzino (<www.pompeiiinpictures.com>, Temples, Sanctuary Fondo Iozzino, part 2 © Jackie and Bob Dunn, by permission of the Ministero della Cultura — Parco Archeologico di Pompei, retrieved 15 May 2022).

was common in religious contexts as well. Their affordances differ from large pottery and require an adjustment in handling and behaviour. To handle downsized objects might be 'difficult, awkward or even impossible', as Kohring states.[87] A miniature thing (like an enlarged thing) might puzzle a user or beholder, since they have to relate form and function to size and their own bodies. They have to clarify its dimensions and, with it, its meaning in its context. However, when looking at the miniature pottery in Pompeii and the various contexts where they were extant, the puzzlement might have lasted only a millisecond, since one knew about its meaning and utilization and the object was easily 'at hand'.

An embodied knowledge of how to handle common pottery objects had to be adapted when it came to the miniature or miniaturized containers. Care and caution as well as focus and concentration were necessary to employ them in the intended action of offering or depositing them or, in the case of the *unguentaria*, to extract the substance in the right dose.

Relation of Sizes of Object and Beholder or User: Puzzlement

Closely related to the handiness of the miniature pottery Pompeians used for religious practices (in the Hellenistic or in Roman periods), one could also argue that the small object enlarges not only the beholder but more importantly the addressee, the deity. They are able to 'manipulate reality through abstraction'.[88] The case of the *Lares* is particular in one regard: since these deities of the families and households never reached life-size or larger, the miniaturized pottery maintains the correct relations between the dimensions of the container and offering and the addressees themselves.[89] The always smaller than life-size dimensions of these deities — a feature that applies not only to the *Lares* but all other deities venerated in the *lararia* in the houses, which could be explained as the particular closeness of these deities to daily life in the house — is reflected in the downsized pottery. It maintains the appropriate relation, since the gifts given in the tiny receptacles are as small as their receivers, the *Lares*.

These characteristics in the handling of the tiny pottery objects implies that on their pathway of being created and utilized, left and found again, their size made most sense in the moment the worshippers filled them and the vessel held the offering.

How Time Is Related to Size: Compression

An aspect that was not in focus here but could be read between the lines is the dimension of time that is internalized by and immanent to these miniature pottery pieces. In religious contexts, the marking-off of time and

---

[87] Kohring 2011, § 19. Bailey 2005, 42 uses the adjective 'uncanny'.

[88] Foxhall 2015, 3 referring to Bailey 2005, 32.

[89] On the statuettes of the *Lares* as part of the art production of the Late Republican period, see Hallett 2023.

space is a substantial part of rituals. With the different size resulting in a different handling of the tiny objects, time — as Bailey puts it — undergoes a 'compression', as mentioned above.[90] Time is compressed in these small cups, plates, or *coperchi*, since moving, filling, emptying, or handling them needs a shorter time span.[91] With the shrunken dimensions of the miniatures, the time for filling it, for picking it up, or for placing it somewhere also shrinks. In the moment when a person uses or employs a tiny pottery object in a religious act, normal relations are dissolved. In a foundational deposit, the miniaturized cups support focalizing time and space on the important action of sacralization.[92]

Somehow paradoxically, the amassment of such objects at sacred places expands or extends time, since it is the result of many repeated depositions over time. This, however, is true for objects of any size accumulating over time at sacred places. Especially in religious practices where people try to establish a communication with an 'ungraspable other', the option of a time warp — for example, back to situations of successful communication or into a future of a hopefully well-established contact — may be particularly appealing.

On both the production and the consumption side, human agents with their bodily abilities and limitations have or had to engage differently with tiny objects. The distances when handling them are shorter; movements have to be delicate, and minute motor activity skills are required.[93] Knappett pushes these implications of the interaction of human agents with tiny objects even beyond a pragmatic bodily aspect, since the more deliberate handling removes 'pragmatic qualities of the artefact [...] while the epistemic features are brought to the fore'.[94] With epistemically relevant operations, human beings add to the pragmatic features of their behaviour the dimension of niche construction, tapping into potentialities (e.g. of tools) so objects in their handling and arrangements have potential in the interplay with pragmatic aspects.

In the vocabulary of the German cultural anthropologist Hahn, these abilities and characteristics of the tiny objects could be rephrased as 'Eigensinn der Dinge', the obstinacy of things.[95] This means that they in their existence and affordances have an impact on our behaviour and perception of the world.

What does this interpretation of objects imply for the miniaturized objects, for tiny things, when they come into our field of vision? It is of course the reference to something bigger with (almost) the same form, features, maybe also the same first-hand function (*brocca* to *brocchetta*), which is an epistemically relevant operation. A miniaturization can abstract and intensify features (figurines as well as forms of vessels or tools) and can still be related in an epistemic, often also practical way, to the human body (as producer and user).

Chronologies: Why Numbers Change but Not the Size

Changes in how the miniature material is employed in religious contexts epitomize temporal shifts: changes in religious practices on the Italian Peninsula between the sixth to the fourth/third centuries BC, then the mid-Republican/Hellenistic periods to the first century BC, followed by the Roman Imperial period. In the Hellenistic period, the numbers are higher than in the Roman period, even if the tiny pottery was used continually until AD 79. People changed how they used the tiny pottery objects, since they can no longer be found in shared sacred spaces and tombs. Their employment in house-centred rituals might also be because the *lararia* became a prominent feature of household religion without an extensive usage of miniature pottery.[96]

As the material of offerings, votives, and dedications changes in these long centuries — broadly speaking, from clay and metal to stone with written messages — the relation of numbers of miniaturized to normally scaled pottery shifts to the latter. Instead of terracotta figurines, we find in the first centuries AD statuettes made from stone; terracotta *arulae* disappear from among the dedications or objects employed in ritual activities, as do terracotta body parts (the so-called anatomical votives). Both miniaturized and full-sized pottery decrease and from the late first century BC are no longer prevalent in the dedications to the gods (but of course are still nec-

---

[90] Bailey 2005, 32.

[91] Bailey 2005, 36. I do not follow Hughes 2018, 63 who 'associates tininess with times past'. See above, n. 10.

[92] I described the relation of the size of miniaturized objects and their meaning as 'condensed', referring to Knappett 2012, 103; see Rieger 2016.

[93] In contrast to monumentalized objects, which created distance and needed more than one person to handle them.

[94] Knappett 2011, 154, 180.

[95] Hahn 2015.

[96] Moser 2019, 66–81 and above, pp. 58–59.

essary and in use for the meals), whereas coins, stone objects (bases, statuettes), and inscriptions increase as offerings at sacred places.[97] The miniature pottery, as we saw in the case of Pompeii and its surroundings, continued to be used for household rituals.

How these changes in employing and using miniature pottery 'bring out the relationships between people and object world' would imply, according to the above-mentioned interpretations, that the focus and concentration, as well as puzzlement and compression, were no longer an important part in communication with the gods.[98] One could communicate more directly in inscriptions, but also in oral communication at festivals and in the continuing communal meals.

Conclusion

The above proposed interpretations of what tiny objects may have meant and 'wanted' are in line with Knappett (2011) and Kiernan (2009). They brought to the fore arguments of the dynamic creation of meanings which allow for understanding miniatures — whether pots, figurines, tools, or buildings — as polysemic and, I would add, polyvalent and even ambiguous.[99] They puzzle, they concentrate significance and focus attention, they condense characteristics and meanings, they compress time. These interpretations can be enriched and broadened when we include the approach of Gosden, who did not focus on miniaturization but on objects in their inter-artefactual relations, which refers to qualities, but considering also their quantities — their occurrences *en masse*.

When Gosden investigates what obligations objects impose on us and what role they play when they are available or appropriated to different cultural backgrounds (e.g. Roman pots in Britain), he argues that it is not always what we want to see in the objects, but that they have and 'act' along their own rules (and act from material to object and parts of objects and adaptations).[100]

He phrases the processes of adaptations and use between various materials and shapes 'transubstantiations', which can also transgress the borders between humans and objects (see e.g. the *fibulae* or pots that are handled). Here inter-artefactual and intercultural relations are also transgressed. Yet, for the question of what tiny objects want, transubstantiation and the transgression of an 'objectual border', if I may call it thus, are relevant ways to explain them, since they transubstantiate dimensions and redefine relations between body and object.

A tiny object requires a delicate treatment; miniature vessels can only keep or carry a tiny amount. However, the tiny things — if miniaturized and having reference in normal-scaled objects — have the potential to change the relations of human beings to their bodies. Miniatures internalize the human beings because their body is too big for the piece,[101] whereas monumental things externalize the body of a human being, because it feels tiny, incapable, lost in an oversized dress, at a monumental place, or in handling an instrument beyond the hand-held scale.[102]

In communication with the gods — whom people often imagined in the guise of humans — the shrunken sizes of containers can fulfil various purposes and have various meanings:

i) The tiny pottery object enlarges the bodily perception and epistemic approaches to the environment of the person handling the piece, and just as importantly, it enlarges the deity as addressee and recipient of the offering.

ii) The miniature vessel can also relate directly to a small-scale deity such as the *Lares*. The tiny objects from household or neighbourhood shrines suit the tiny dimensions of the *Lares*. They never 'grew up'. Here, the small dimensions of the offering (container) are adjusted to the addressees.

iii) The limited amount of contents (of whatever kind) the tiny pottery objects could carry or keep represents the share the deities received from people. The share of what people made their living from always fills the container — it is a 'whole', the entire amount of which is able to satisfy and please the deities.

---

[97] This is very generalized. Moreover, the places as such change, see Moser 2019; Stek 2013; 2015.

[98] Gosden 2005, 193–94.

[99] In cases where the tiny containers were used for offering, the ambiguity is obvious. The small size of the vessel represents the offering being a share of one's goods given to the gods; on the other hand, there is the aspect of 'only being a part of a larger whole', while on the other hand, they make the share of the content in relation to the small vessel look larger.

[100] Gosden 2005, 209.

---

[101] Bailey 2005, 42.

[102] Hughes 2018, 64. When dealing with miniaturized objects, the dimensions of the hand and the relation of the object to it are of foremost significance in terms of cognition, production, learning, usage — in how far precisely they could be studied further, see e.g. Graham 2020a. See also Petridou in this volume.

iv) The accumulation of tiny objects at sacred places represents the multiplicity of acts of communication with the deities. This is true also for normally sized objects. The tininess of *krateriskoi*, *kylikes*, *coppette*, or *arulae*, however, transmits the relational aspect of being related to a larger reference, the 'part-taking' which is an important aspect of religion as based on culturally embedded concepts such as deity, ritual, and religious practice.

v) The miniature containers which occur in single pieces in foundational rituals before the Roman Imperial period represent the moment and place in time and space in and on which the place changes character and is sacralized. The miniaturization can here be understood as an extreme focus on the event taking place.

After having shed light on categories, contexts, quantities, and qualities, we can come back to the core of religious communication. If people at Pompeii wanted to communicate with the gods beyond the plausibly perceivable world,[103] engaging and employing larger or smaller sizes of objects fulfils a clear purpose in this communication process. It is the concentration, focus, condensation, and puzzlement, as well as the play of ratios, dimensions, and expectations on the one (human) and the other (imagined divine) side, that is materialized in the tiny objects.

---

[103] Cf. Rüpke 2015, 348.

Works Cited

Allison, P. M. 2004. *Pompeian Households: An Analysis of the Material Culture*, Cotsen Institute of Archaeology Monographs, 42 (Los Angeles: University of California).

Anderson-Stojanović, V. R. 1987. 'The Chronology and Function of Ceramic Unguentaria', *American Journal of Archaeology*, 91: 105–22.

Anniboletti, L. 2007. 'Testimonianze preromane del culto domestico a Pompei: i compita vicinalia sulla facciata di abitazioni', *Fasti Online*, 83: 1–10.

——. 2008a. 'Aspetti del culto domestico di epoca tardo-sannitica: i sacelli sulle facciate di abitazioni pompeiane', in P. G. Guzzo and M. P. Guidobaldi (eds), *Nuove ricerche archeologiche nell'area vesuviana: scavi 2003–2006; atti del Convegno internazionale, Roma, 1–3 febbraio 2007*, Studi della Soprintendenza archeologica di Pompei, 25 (Rome: L'Erma di Bretschneider), pp. 209–22.

——. 2008b. 'Il sacello VIII 4, 24: un culto collegiale a Pompei', *Fasti Online*, 104: 1–9.

Bailey, D. W. 2005. *Prehistoric Figurines: Representation and Corporeality in the Neolithic* (London: Routledge).

Barfoed, S. 2015. 'The Significant Few. Miniature Pottery from the Sanctuary of Zeus at Olympia', *World Archaeology*, 47.1: 170–88 <https://doi.org/10.1080/00438243.2014.992077>.

——. 2018. 'The Use of Miniature Pottery in Archaic–Hellenistic Greek Sanctuaries. Considerations on Terminology and Ritual Practice', *Opuscula*, 11: 111–26 <https://doi.org/10.30549/opathrom-11-06>.

Berg, R. 2017. 'Toiletries and Taverns. Cosmetic Sets in Small Houses, *hospitia* and *lupanaria* at Pompeii', *Arctos*, 51: 13–39.

——. 2020. 'Locating the Use and Storage of Female Toiletry Items in Pompeian Houses', in A. Dardenay and N. Laubry (eds), *Anthropology of Roman Housing*, v, Antiquité et sciences humaines, 5 (Turnhout: Brepols), pp. 193–217.

Bon, S. E. and others. 1995. 'Research in "Insula" VI, 1 by the Anglo-American Pompeii Project, 1994–6', *Rivista di studi pompeiani*, 7: 153–57.

Bon, S. E. and others. 1997. 'The Context of the House of the Surgeon: Investigations in Insula VI, 1 at Pompeii', in S. E. Bon and R. Jones (eds), *Sequence and Space in Pompeii*, Oxbow Monographs, 77 (Oxford: Oxbow), pp. 32–49.

Bouzek, J. 2017. 'Koine of Early Iron Age Geometric Styles', in A. Mazarakis-Ainian, A. Alexandridou, and X. Charalambidou (eds), *Regional Stories: Towards a New Perception of the Early Greek World; Acts of an International Symposium in Honour of Professor Jan Bouzek* (Volos: University of Thessaly Press), pp. 41–53.

Bustamante-Álvarez, M. and others. 2017. 'Via degli Augustali VII, 4, 28: una fosa singular de mediados del siglo II a.C. en Pompeya', *Empúries*, 57: 85–118.

Canopoli, M. 2020. 'La ceramica miniaturistica di San Leucio', in P. Pensabene and A. D'Alessio (eds), *Arte e cultura nell'antica Canosa*, Estratto da Scienze dell'antichità, 18 (2012) (Rome: Scienze dell'antichità), pp. 233–43.

Caro, S. de. 1986. *Saggi nell'area del tempio di Apollo a Pompei: scavi stratigrafici di A. Maiuri nel 1913–32 e 1942–43*, Annali, Istituto Universario Orientale, Dipartimento di Studi del Mondo Classico e del Mediterraneo Antico, Sezione di Archeologia, 3 (Naples: Arte tipografica).

Coarelli, F. and others. 2005. 'Il progetto "Regio" VI: Campagna di scavo 2004', *Rivista di studi pompeiani*, 16: 166–207.

Cole, A. 2013. 'The Call of Things: A Critique of Object-Oriented Ontologies', *The Minnesota Review*, 80: 106–18 <https://doi.org/10.1215/00265667-2018414>.

Colombini, M. P. and others. 2009. 'An Etruscan Ointment from Chiusi (Tuscany, Italy): Its Chemical Characterization', *Journal of Archaeological Science*, 36.7: 1488–95 <https://doi.org/10.1016/j.jas.2009.02.011>.

Comella, A. 1981. 'Tipologia e diffusione dei complessi votivi in Italia in epoca medio- e tardo-repubblicana. Contributo alla storia dell'artigianato antico', *Mélanges de l'École française de Rome*, 93.2: 717–803 <https://doi.org/10.3406/mefr.1981.1297>.

Cool, H. M. E. 2016. *The Small Finds and Vessel Glass from Insula VI.1 Pompeii: Excavations 1995–2006* (Oxford: Archaeopress).

Cool, H. E. M. and D. G. Griffiths. 2015. 'The Miniature Vessels of Insula VI.1 Pompeii. New Evidence for Neighbourhood Cults', *Fasti Online*, 325: 1–16 <https://www.fastionline.org/docs/FOLDER-it-2015-325.pdf> [accessed 12 February 2023].

D'Alise, A. 2019. 'Ceramiche comuni dal santuario di Fondo Iozzino a Pompei', *Rivista di studi pompeiani*, 30: 197–204.

D'Ambrosio, A. 1993. 'Scavo nell'ex Fondo Iozzino', *Rivista di studi pompeiani*, 6: 219–21.

Dasen, V. and M. Vespa (eds). 2021. *Jouer dans l'antiquité classique: définition, transmission, réception* (Liège: Presses universitaires de Liège).

Draycott, J. and E.-J. Graham (eds). 2020. *Bodies of Evidence: Ancient Anatomical Votives; Past, Present and Future* (London: Routledge).

Duday, H., W. Van Andringa, and T. Creissen. 2019. 'La nécropole romaine de Porta Nocera à Pompéi', *Chronique des activités archéologiques de l'École française de Rome* <https://doi.org/10.4000/cefr.3937>.

Duhn, F. von and L. Jacobi. 1890. *Der griechische Tempel in Pompeji: Nebst einem Anhang; Über Schornsteinanlagen und eine Badeeinrichtung im Frauenbad der Stabianer Thermen in Pompeji* (Heidelberg: Winter).

Ekroth, G. 2003. 'Small Pots, Poor People? The Use and Function of Miniature Pottery as Votive Offerings in Archaic Sanctuaries in the Argolid and the Corinthia', in B. Schmaltz and M. Söldner (eds), *Griechische Keramik im kulturellen Kontext: Akten des Internationalen Vasen-Symposions in Kiel vom 24.–28.9.2001* (Münster: Scriptorium), pp. 35–37.

Elia, O. 1962. 'Culti familiari e privati della Campania. Arulae fittili pompeiane', in M. Renard (ed.), *Hommages à Albert Grenier*, II, Collection Latomus, 58 (Brussels: Berchem), pp. 559–66.

Ellis, S. J. R. and G. Devore. 2008. 'Uncovering Plebeian Pompeii: Broader Implications from Excavating a Forgotten Working-Class Neighbourhood', in P. G. Guzzo and M. P. Guidobaldi (eds), *Nuove ricerche archeologiche nell'area vesuviana (scavi 2003–2006): atti del Convegno internazionale, Roma, 1–3 febbraio 2007*, Studi della Soprintendenza archeologica di Pompei, 25 (Rome: L'Erma di Bretschneider), pp. 309–20.

Ellis, S. J. R. and others. 2012. 'The 2011 Field Season at I.1.1–10, Pompeii: Preliminary Report on the Excavations', *Fasti Online*, 262: 1–26 <https://www.fastionline.org/docs/FOLDER-it-2012-262.pdf> [accessed 12 February 2023].

Eschebach, H. and others. 1995. *Pompeji: Vom 7. Jahrhundert v. Chr. bis 79 n. Chr.*, Arbeiten zur Archäologie (Cologne: Böhlau).

Flohr, M. 2011. 'Reconsidering the Atrium House. Domestic Fullonicae at Pompeii', in E. Poehler, M. Flohr, and K. Cole (eds), *Pompeii: Art Industry and Infrastructure* (Oxford: Oxbow), pp. 88–102.

Flower, H. I. 2017. *The Dancing Lares and the Serpent in the Garden: Religion at the Roman Street Corner* (Princeton: Princeton University Press).

Foxhall, L. 2015. 'Introduction: Miniaturization', *World Archaeology*, 47.1: 1–5 <https://doi.org/10.1080/00438243.2015.997557>.

Gallo, A. 2012. 'Il santuario cantonale della Regio IX di Pompei (IX 1, 29). La decodificazione dei simboli', *Rivista di studi pompeiani*, 23: 39–60.

Gell, A. 1992. 'The Technology of Enchantment and the Enchantment of Technology', in A. Shelton and J. Coote (eds), *Anthropology, Art, and Aesthetics*, Oxford Studies in the Anthropology of Cultural Forms (Oxford: Clarendon), pp. 40–66.

——. 1998. *Art and Agency: An Anthropological Theory* (Oxford: Clarendon).

Gentili, M. D. 2005. 'Riflessioni sul fenomeno storico dei depositi votivi di tipo etrusco-lazialecampano', in A. Comella and S. Mele (eds), *Depositi votivi e culti dell'Italia antica dall'età arcaica a quella tardo-repubblicana: atti del convegno di studi, Perugia, 1–4 giugno 2000*, Bibliotheca archaeologica, 16 (Bari: Edipuglia), pp. 367–78.

Gibson, J. J. 1979. *The Ecological Approach to Visual Perception* (Boston: Houghton Mifflin).

Glinister, F. 2006. 'Reconsidering "Religious Romanization"', in C. E. Schultz and P. B. Harvey (eds), *Religion in Republican Italy*, Yale Classical Studies, 33 (Cambridge: Cambridge University Press), pp. 10–33.

Gosden, C. 2005. 'What Do Objects Want?', *Journal of Archaeological Method and Theory*, 12.3: 193–211 <https://doi.org/10.1007/s10816-005-6928-x>.

Graham, E.-J. 2020a. 'Hand in Hand: Rethinking Anatomical Votives as Material Things', in V. Gasparini and others (eds), *Lived Religion in the Ancient Mediterranean World: Approaching Religious Transformations from Archaeology, History and Classics* (Boston: De Gruyter), pp. 209–36.

——. 2020b. *Reassembling Roman Religion* (London: Routledge).

Grasso, L. 2004. *Ceramica miniaturistica da Pompei*, Quaderni di Ostraka, 9 (Naples: Loffredo).

Green, D. 2008. 'Sweet Spices in the Tomb: An Initial Study on the Use of Perfume in Jewish Burials', in L. Brink and D. Green (eds), *Commemorating the Dead: Texts and Artifacts in Context; Studies of Roman, Jewish and Christian Burials* (Berlin: De Gruyter), pp. 145–76.

Hahn, H. P. (ed.). 2015. *Vom Eigensinn der Dinge: Für eine neue Perspektive auf die Welt des Materiellen* (Berlin: Neofelis).

Hallett, C. H. 2023. '"Corinthian Bronzes": Miniature Masterpieces — Flagrant Forgeries', in J. Hopkins and S. McGill (eds), *Beyond Deceit: Valuing Forgery in Ancient Rome* (Oxford: Oxford University Press), pp. 44–92.

Hellström, P. 1965. *Labraunda: Swedish Excavations and Researches*, II.1: *Pottery of Classical and Later Date, Terracotta Lamps and Glass* (Lund: Gleerup).

Hicks, D. and M. C. Beaudry. 2010. 'Introduction: Material Culture Studies: A Reactionary View', in D. Hicks and M. C. Beaudry (eds), *The Oxford Handbook of Material Culture Studies* (Oxford: Oxford University Press), pp. 1–21.

Hodder, I. 2011. 'Human-Thing Entanglement: Towards an Integrated Archaeological Perspective', *Journal of the Royal Anthropological Institute*, 17.1: 154–77.

Hughes, J. 2018. 'Tiny and Fragmented Votive Offerings from Classical Antiquity', in S. R. Martin and S. M. Langin-Hooper (eds), *The Tiny and the Fragmented: Miniature, Broken, or Otherwise Incomplete Objects in the Ancient World* (Oxford: Oxford University Press), pp. 48–71.

Ingold, T. 2007. 'Materials against Materiality', *Archaeological Dialogues*, 14.1: 1–16 <https://doi.org/10.1017/S1380203807002127>.

Kastenmeier, P. 2007. *I luoghi del lavoro domestico nella casa pompeiana*, Studi della Soprintendenza archeologica di Pompei, 23 (Rome: L'Erma di Bretschneider).

Kiernan, P. 2009. *Miniature Votive Offerings in the North-West Provinces of the Roman Empire* (Wiesbaden: Harrassowitz).

Kleibrink, M. 1997–1998. 'The Miniature Votive Pottery Dedicated at the "Laghetto del Monsignore", Campoverde', *Palaeohistoria*, 39/40: 441–512.

Knappett, C. 2011. *An Archaeology of Interaction* (Oxford: Oxford University Press).

——. 2012. 'Meaning in Miniature. Semiotic Networks in Material Culture', in N. Johannsen, M. D. Jessen, and H. J. Jensen (eds), *Excavating the Mind: Cross-Sections through Culture, Cognition and Materiality* (Aarhus: Aarhus University Press), pp. 87–110.

——. 2020. 'Designing Things as "Poor" Substitutes', in L. Atzmon and P. Boradkar (eds), *Encountering Things: Design and Theories of Things* (London: Bloomsbury Academic), pp. 167–78.

Kohring, S. 2011. 'Bodily Skill and the Aesthetics of Miniaturisation', *Pallas*, 86: 31–50 <https://doi.org/10.4000/pallas.2079>.

Langin-Hooper, S. M. 2015. 'Fascination with the Tiny: Social Negotiation through Miniatures in Hellenistic Babylonia', *World Archaeology*, 47.1: 60–79 <https://doi.org/10.1080/00438243.2014.991803>.

Lanzi, D. 2019. 'Ceramica miniaturistica e ceramica d'uso comune dal santuario di Panetelle (Mondragone, Caserta)', *Poligrafia*, 1: 197–215.

Mack, J. 2007. *The Art of Small Things* (London: British Museum Press).

Mau, A. 1900. *Pompeji in Leben und Kunst* (Leipzig: Engelmann).

Mazois, F. 1824. *Les ruines de Pompéi*, 4 vols (Paris: Didot).

Meskell, L. 2015. 'A Society of Things: Animal Figurines and Material Scales at Neolithic Çatalhöyük', *World Archaeology*, 47.1: 6–19 <https://doi.org/10.1080/00438243.2014.991800>.

Miniero, P. and others. 1997. 'Il Santuario campano in località Privati presso Castellammare di Stabia Osservazioni preliminari', *Rivista di studi pompeiani*, 8: 11–56.

Mitchell, W. J. T. 2004. *What Do Pictures Want? The Lives and Loves of Images* (Chicago: University of Chicago Press).

Moser, C. 2019. *The Altars of Republican Rome and Latium: Sacrifice and the Materiality of Roman Religion* (Cambridge: Cambridge University Press).

Osanna, M. 2016. 'Gesto rituale e spazio sacro nella Pompei di età sannitica', in F. Fontana and E. Murgia (eds), *Sacrum facere: Atti del III Seminario di archeologia del sacro; lo spazio del 'sacro,' ambienti e gesti del rito; Trieste, 3–4 ottobre 2014*, Polymnia. Studi di archeologia, 7 (Trieste: Edizioni Università di Trieste), pp. 193–215.

——. 2021. 'Il Santuario di Fondo Iozzino: dai vecchi scavi alle nuove indagini', in M. Osanna (ed.), *Ricerche e scoperte a Pompei: in ricordo di Enzo Lippolis*, Studi e ricerche del Parco archeologico di Pompei, 45 (Rome: L'Erma di Bretschneider), pp. 195–210.

Pilz, O. 2011. 'The Uses of Small Things and the Semiotics of Greek Miniature Objects', *Pallas*, 86: 15–30 <https://doi.org/10.4000/pallas.2068>.

Pollock, S. and R. Bernbeck. 2010. 'An Archaeology of Categorization and Categories in Archaeology', *Paléorient*, 36.1: 37–47.

Ribera, A. and others. 2012. 'Pompeya 2011. El barrio de los perfumeros. Vía degli Augustali 26, 27 y 28', *Informes y trabajos*, 9: 383–409.

Ribeiro, A. 2016. 'Against Object Agency. A Counterreaction to Sørensen's "Hammers and Nails"', *Archaeological Dialogues*, 23.2: 229–35 <https://doi.org/10.1017/S1380203816000246>.

Rieger, A.-K. 2011. 'Wie persönlich kann ein Motiv sein? Eine archäologisch-historische Annäherung an Weihungen aus dem Magna-Mater-Heiligtum von Ostia', in W. Friese and I. Nielsen (eds), *Persönliche Frömmigkeit: Funktion und Bedeutung individueller Gotteskontakte im interdisziplinären Dialog; Akten der Tagung am Archäologischen Institut der Universität Hamburg (25.–27. November 2010)*, Hephaistos, 28 (Münster: Lit), pp. 146–65.

——. 2016. 'Waste Matters: Life Cycle and Agency of Pottery Employed in Greco-Roman Sacred Spaces', *Religion of the Roman Empire*, 2.3: 307–39 <https://doi.org/10.1628/219944616X14770583541481>.

——. (forthcoming). 'Pathways of Religious Experiences in the Urban Fabric of Roman Pompeii', in I. Bultrighini, C. Norman, and G. Woolf (eds), *Sanctuaries and Experiences: Knowledge, Practice and Space in the Ancient World; Proceedings of a Conference at the ICS University of London, April 2019*, Potsdamer altertumswissenschaftliche Beiträge (Stuttgart: Steiner).

Roselaar, S. T. 2011. 'Colonies and Processes of Integration in the Roman Republic', *Mélanges de l'École française de Rome*, 123.2: 527–55.

Rüpke, J. 2009. 'Dedications Accompanied by Inscriptions in the Roman Empire: Functions, Intentions, Modes of Communication', in J. P. Bodel and M. Kajava (eds), *Dediche sacre nel mondo greco-romano: diffusione, funzioni, tipologie = Religious Dedications in the Greco-Roman World: Distribution, Typology, Use; Institutum Romanum Finlandiae, American Academy in Rome, 19–20 aprile, 2006* (Rome: Quasar), pp. 31–41.

——. 2015. 'Religious Agency, Identity, and Communication: Reflections on History and Theory of Religion', *Religion*, 45.3: 344–66 <https://doi.org/10.1080/0048721X.2015.1024040>.

——. (forthcoming). 'Sacralization and Focalization: Agentic Perspectives on Sanctuaries', in I. Bultrighini, C. Norman, and G. Woolf (eds), *Sanctuaries and Experiences: Knowledge, Practice and Space in the Ancient World; Proceedings of a Conference at the ICS University of London, April 2019*, Potsdamer altertumswissenschaftliche Beiträge (Stuttgart: Steiner).

Schreiber, S. 2022. 'Die Praxis der Materialität. Zur Kontroverse nicht-menschlicher Handlungsfähigkeit (nicht nur) in den Archäologien', in T. L. Kienlin and R. Bussmann (eds), *Sozialität – Materialität – Praxis = Sociality – Materiality – Practice*, Cologne

Contributions to Archaeology and Cultural Studies = Universitätsforschungen zur prähistorischen Archäologie (Bonn: Habelt), pp. 337–74.

Schwartz, J. 2019. 'The Play's the Thing: Toys in Ancient Jewish Society — Visualizing through the Words of the Rabbis', *IMAGES*, 12: 7–19 <https://doi.org/10.1163/18718000-12340117>.

Senatore, M. R., M. Falco, and A. Meo. 2016. 'The Water Supply System of Ancient Pompeii (Southern Italy): From Resource to Geohazard', in A. Farid (ed.), *Geohazards Caused by Human Activity* (Rijeka: InTech), pp. 3–20.

Sigges, B. 2002. 'Vita cognita. Die Ausstattung pompejanischer Wohnhäuser mit Gefäßen und Geräten' (unpublished doctoral dissertation, University of Cologne).

Stek, T. D. 2013. 'Questions of Cult and Continuity in Late Republican Roman Italy: "Italic" or "Roman" Sanctuaries and the So-Called *pagus-vicus* System', in M. Jehne, B. Linke, and J. Rüpke (eds), *Religiöse Vielfalt und soziale Integration: Die Bedeutung der Religion für die kulturelle Identität und politische Stabilität im republikanischen Italien*, Studien zur alten Geschichte, 17 (Heidelberg: Antike), pp. 137–62.

——. 2015. 'Cult, Conquest and "Religious Romanization". The Impact of Rome on Cult Places and Religious Practices in Italy', in T. D. Stek and G.-J. Burgers (eds), *The Impact of Rome on Cult Places and Religious Practices in Ancient Italy*, Bulletin of the Institute of Classical Studies Supplement, 132 (London: Institute of Classical Studies), pp. 1–28.

——. 2017. 'The Impact of Roman Expansion and Colonization on Ancient Italy in the Republican Period. From Diffusionism to Networks of Opportunity', in G. D. Farney and G. J. Bradley (eds), *The Peoples of Ancient Italy* (Berlin: De Gruyter), pp. 269–94.

Stewart, S. 2007. *On Longing: Narratives of the Miniature, the Gigantic, the Souvenir, the Collection*, 10th edn (Durham, NC: Duke University Press).

Stockhammer, P. W. and H. P. Hahn (eds). 2015. *Lost in Things: Fragen an die Welt des Materiellen* (Tübingen: Waxmann).

Van Andringa, W. 2000. 'Autels de carrefour, organisation vicinale et rapports de voisinage à Pompéi', *Rivista di studi pompeiani*, 11: 47–86.

Van Andringa, W., H. Duday, and S. Lepetz. 2013. *Mourir à Pompéi: fouille d'un quartier funéraire de la nécropole romaine de Porta Nocera (2003–2007)*, Collection de l'École française de Rome, 468, 2 vols (Rome: École française de Rome).

Wardle, M. A. 1981. 'Musical Instruments in the Roman World', 2 vols (unpublished doctoral thesis, University of London, Institute of Archaeology).

Weiss, L. 2015. 'The Consumption of Religion in Roman Karanis', *Religion in the Roman Empire*, 1: 71–94.

Williamson, C. G. 2021. *Urban Rituals in Sacred Landscapes in Hellenistic Asia Minor*, Religions in the Graeco-Roman World, 196 (Leiden: Brill).

Witmore, C. 2014. 'Archaeology and the New Materialisms', *Journal of Contemporary Archaeology*, 1.2: 203–46 <https://doi.org/10.1558/jca.v1i2.16661>.

5. Are the Same Objects Desirable for People and for Gods? Material and Dimensional Interchangeability

Elisabeth Trinkl

This book is dedicated to the concept of material value with specific relation to aspects of dimension. Furthermore, we could also ask if the recognition of materiality and the evaluation of material value differ in various contexts — that is, if we can see significant differences for the use and understanding of materiality between the ritualistic/religious and the mundane world. Related to objects, we can ask if the same objects are desirable for people and for gods.

Archaeological objects are very often preserved just by chance. This 'lucky' situation for the modern world often stems from a misfortune for the ancients — loss, destruction, or another catastrophic event. Aside from that, there are types of occasions in which the intentional giving-away is an essential part; two contexts in particular are graves and sanctuaries. In these contexts, almost all kinds of objects can be deliberately deposited.[1] In both contexts, a similar disengagement from the everyday world occurs, making it impossible to continue using these objects.[2]

In this paper, we are only going to discuss depositions in sanctuaries, and we will focus on specific objects which have especially one property in common: they do not have the size and/or are not made of the material we would expect from their visual appearance. Before we embark into the definition of over- and undersized objects, we should investigate briefly the criteria for a dedication in general, i.e. who brings which object into a sanctuary and why.[3] In any case, the underlying purpose is the establishment of a human–divine relationship.

Do ut des: Ritual Exchange Practices

Objects of any kind can be a dedication, regardless of their material nature. Some objects are relatively permanent (ceramics, objects made of metal or stone, buildings), even though they may undergo change as a result of the consecration process. Other objects are in principle (often rapidly) perishable (e.g. food and organic materials in general),[4] or they disintegrate as part of the rite (e.g. incense, liquids in libations). Just as varied is the occasion for a dedication: it could be a wish, thanksgiving, a victory, or a recurring rite, to name only the most common occasions.[5] These are connected to corresponding prayers, possibly supplemented by other performative acts. Through the gift to the sanctuary, whatever the occasion, the human giver enters into direct contact with transcendent beings.[6] The offering of the gift hopes for a return gift from the deity; this return gift can be of a material or immaterial nature.[7] In order to prove this 'business' and to document longevity, votive offerings are provided with appropriate inscriptions.[8] Therefore, soon after writing was developed, we can already find appropriate inscriptions that call the giver and the receiver by name, as well as indicate expenditure (*chreos*) and the hoped-for return gift (*charis*). An exam-

---

[1] Osborne 2004.

[2] Reuse can also be specifically prevented by appropriate rites, e.g. cremation or ritually rendering consecrated objects useless.

[3] Rouse 1902; van Straten 1992; Boardman and others 2004.

[4] In addition, there are still immaterial parts of the rite, e.g. prayers and performances.

[5] On the connection of political and economic components to dedications, see Sassu 2010.

[6] Of course, it is not exclusively the votive offering itself that communicates with the deity, but also prayer and sacrifice: Kinderlen and Strocka 2005, 11. The smoke, enriched by fragrances, can be understood as a mediator: Naiden 2013.

[7] Antonacci 2005, 101–02; here lies the big difference to the exchange of gifts between elites.

[8] The inscriptions on votive offerings, however, do not appear to be the earliest Greek written documents; cf. Stähli 2014. In the Late Classical period, such dedicatory inscriptions were ultimately placed with particular prominence as building dedications by writing them directly on the architrave: Umholtz 2002.

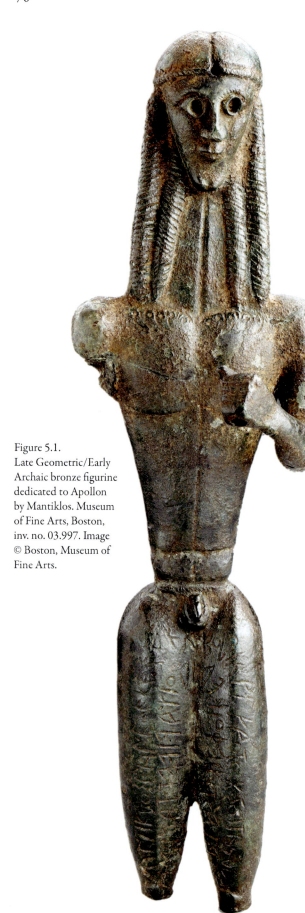

Figure 5.1.
Late Geometric/Early Archaic bronze figurine dedicated to Apollon by Mantiklos. Museum of Fine Arts, Boston, inv. no. 03.997. Image © Boston, Museum of Fine Arts.

ple is a bronze statuette that Mantiklos dedicated to Apollo around 700 BC (Fig. 5.1). The hexameter inscription running across both of the statuette's thighs reads: 'Mantiklos dedicated me to the far-shooting Lord of the Silver Bow, a tithe. You, Phoibos, give some pleasing favour in return' (*CEG* 326); the hoped-for return gift is concretely described as *charis*.[9] M. Erdman summarizes this exchange (*chreos/charis*) at the Source de la Douix as follows: 'the desired outcome was […] some sort of intangible value that only the deity could provide.'[10] A deity could not only refuse the counter-offering, but could even refuse the acceptance of an offering, as F. S. Naiden has shown.[11]

An important characteristic every gift in a sanctuary has is that it is detached from the living world; it is incorporated into the sacred realm from which it cannot be detached: this is the *ouk ekphora* principle of Greek sanctuaries.[12] Nevertheless, the object biography does not end with the consecration itself,[13] but the consecrated object can be subject to multilayered transformation processes (burning, exhibition, deposition, disposal, rotting, reuse of the material, etc.),[14] in which not only its appearance but also its consistency or materiality can fundamentally change. Although the interaction between the consecrator and the consecration itself no longer takes place, the functionality remains — since the primary function of the consecrated object is the consecration itself.

Donations, Gifts, and Votives: Shape and Material

The ritual centre in a Greek sanctuary is the cult place, independent of its immediate design, which will not be discussed here.[15] The pictorial centre is usually a cult image; it can be included in corresponding rites, such as ritual cleansing or decoration,[16] but it does not have to be. In principle, it is completely irrelevant what material

---

[9] Steiner 2003, 15.

[10] Erdman 2014, 98.

[11] Naiden 2013 especially emphasizes the 'active' part of the receiving deity. A rejection occurs especially in case of misconduct in the rite: Hes., *Op.* 724–26.

[12] Burkert 1977, 103.

[13] On the object biography, Gosden and Marshall 1999.

[14] For an overview of the various aspects of reusing votive offerings that are unattractive, broken, or simply in overabundance, see Lindenlauf 2006.

[15] Burkert 1977, 146–48.

[16] Burkert 1977, 148–54; Hölscher 2014.

the cult image is made of. In it, the deity and its image are merged. It is also not mandatory that it is an anthropomorphic image; it can also be an aniconic image. The list of 'images' or sacred stones that have fallen from heaven is long, but they are washed and adorned just like anthropomorphic images.[17] Therefore, neither the form nor the material is a determining element, at least with regard to the cult image.

This aspect is all the more relevant in the case of a gift donated to a sanctuary.[18] In the associated word group around *anatithemai*, which designates the consecration, material, occasion, and form are not addressed. What is important is that one places the consecration gift at an elevation;[19] one can automatically infer from this a certain mode of exhibiting the object.

The word group around *anatithemai*, which makes the mode of exhibition particularly clear, includes *katatithemai*; this 'laying down' corresponds not only to the circumstance in which we find most archaeological objects, but also to a frequently practised cult practice;[20] some meaning of display is nevertheless retained. In any case, the dedication itself is associated with the lasting memory of the dedication.[21] To ensure the sustainability of the dedication, it is therefore necessary to find a suitable location for the votive to guarantee sufficient visibility,[22] as well as — if possible — to increase the degree of recognition through size,[23] name inscription (Fig. 5.1),[24] or long life.[25]

When V. van Straten says a terracotta *pinax* measuring only a few centimetres 'may be the cheapest votive offering ever to have been hung in an ancient Greek sanctuary,'[26] he deliberately contrasts the *pinax* with the overabundance of expensive, large, and oversized votive offerings that can be inferred for many sanctuaries.[27] This assessment, however, seems to me not to take into account several groups of materials, such as wreaths or food, whose purchase value must have been far below the purchase value of the small *pinax* mentioned by van Straten, which is still decorated with a figural scene.[28]

In particular, the hanging of wreaths is a very well attested practice in Greek sanctuaries,[29] where the already mentioned elevated mode of display becomes all too clear; the purchase or the actual material value, however, remains relatively low. The demonstrative display of animal sacrifices can also be well understood. It is not only the numerous reliefs,[30] which themselves were consecrated as an offering in the sanctuary, that depict such an animal sacrifice or the preceding steps, such as procession and prayer, but also the deposited remains of the animal sacrifices themselves. *Bucrania* are almost ubiquitous as sculptural and artistic decoration and are so familiar to us that their original connection to ritual could almost be forgotten.[31] Animal heads made of stone or clay, decorated with *tainiai* and connected by garlands — both groups of objects that were in principle originally made of perishable material but are iconographically and literarily well documented — are a 'fossilized' memory of offered animal sacrifices.[32]

---

[17] Gaifman 2012.

[18] On multiformity in general and in summary on votives, see Haase 2002.

[19] Burkert 1977, 154–57; van Straten 1992, 248.

[20] However, the use is not limited to sacred contexts: Pakkanen 2015, 38.

[21] Kinderlen and Strocka 2005, 12.

[22] Van Straten 1992.

[23] Not only for reasons of representation should a votive offering be seen by users and visitors to a sanctuary; this circumstance naturally suits large-scale votive offerings. Compare to graves, cf. V. Vlachou 2017.

[24] On the name inscription of the statue dedicated by Mantiklos, see Day 1994, 39, 42; Stähli 2014, 122.

[25] A list of names of donors of melted-down votive gifts is placed in the sanctuary; this means that the names of donors are even linked to non-existent offerings in the sanctuary; van Straten 1992, 273–74.

[26] Van Straten 1992, 251.

[27] For the monumental discourse of the elites, cf. Guggisberg 2009.

[28] Liebieghaus, Frankfurt am Main, inv. no. Li 555; CVA Frankfurt am Main II, pl. 85.9. On the *pinax* is depicted a woman carrying a wool basket in front of her, perhaps a commemorative mark of an actual offering of wool, as we have inscribed evidence of from some sanctuaries: Brøns 2017, 71–72 pl. 13.

[29] Blech 1982, 269–312. Whether the ribbons, since they are used in large numbers not only at the tomb but also in the sanctuary, were actually such inexpensive gifts is discussed in more detail in light of the high price of textiles in Antiquity by Brøns 2017, tab. 12.

[30] Van Straten 1995.

[31] In connection with architectural decoration in Hellenism in Asia Minor, F. Rumscheid opines: 'Einleuchtend ist die allgemein akzeptierte Erklärung, daß es sich bei den Köpfen um die Darstellungen von Opfertieren handelt, die mit Binden geschmückt in Heiligtümern und anderswo angebracht waren.' He even considers the intentional mixture of sculptural and relief elements in the depiction of the bucranium: Rumscheid 1994, 276.

[32] The mediating play between painted and actual votive offerings can be well understood from the well-preserved altars of Pompeii: Rogers 2020.

Figure 5.2. Delos, Colossus of the Naxians.
Image from Giuliani (ed.) 2005, 15 Abb. 4.

In any case, votive offerings — regardless of material, shape, or size — were part of the furnishings of every sanctuary; in many cases they enriched the sanctuary not only materially but also ideally, in their being understood as contributing to the sanctuary's *kosmos*.[33] Let us imagine the Mantiklos Apollo next to the Colossus of the Naxians (Fig. 5.2) on Delos.[34] Both motifs are similar: a naked youthful man, probably identifiable as Apollo due to an attribute. Moreover, both include an inscription that explicitly identifies them as votive offerings.

From our present perspective,[35] both monuments stand out from comparable objects, each in one concrete way. The Colossus of the Naxians is the largest Greek *kouros* ever erected; the accompanying inscription, however, does not address the statue's monumentality, but emphasizes the material, *lithos*, which L. Giuliani thinks should be understood as local Naxian marble.[36] For us, this is an interesting point: the size of the sculpture, at least five times life-size, was literally 'unmissable' even for contemporaries, but in the inscription, it is the specificity of the material that is underlined. Why? It is not a costly imported material, but the local marble of Naxos, the origin of the consecrators; for the site of Delos, however, Naxian marble would have been an expensive and costly material. The small Mantiklos Apollo (Fig. 5.1) stands out today because it opens for us the series of scripture-bearing sculptures of Greek sculpture. What both the Mantiklos Apollo and the Colossus of the Naxians have in common is that their installation and exhibition in the *temenos* probably contributes to the *kosmos* of the sanctuary.

On the other hand, the terracottas documented in numerous sanctuaries, often in almost unmanageable numbers, bear an inscription only in absolutely exceptional cases. This indirectly proves that such an inscription is by no means a necessary criterion for the consecration. Their frequent deposition around the altar, however, points to an underlying ritual.[37] But these figurines certainly also contribute to the *kosmos* of the sanctuary. According to the Greek understanding, votive offerings that are often considered to be of little attractiveness, such as semi-finished products, objects that are partly left raw, or objects that have been rendered unusable intentionally, also fall into the same category.[38]

What does not apply to the statues and statuettes mentioned before, since they cannot be associated with a real functional component, must, however, be considered very carefully for other objects found in the sanctu-

---

33 Van Straten 1992, 268–69.

34 Archaeological Museum, Delos, inv. no. A334; Giuliani 2006. Franssen 2011, 101–04 discusses the attempt of noble families to locate and visualize their legitimacy in heroic prehistory, especially through oversized statues.

35 This is a modern perspective that can very quickly lose its significance with a new discovery.

36 Giuliani 2006. In addition to an inscription, the portrait of the donor can also clearly personalize the votive offering: Himmelmann 2001.

37 Von Hesberg 2007, 296–301: 'dass die Darbringung der Figuren zumindest seit geometrischer Zeit einen Vorgang darstellte, der dem Opfer am Altar komplementär entsprach und in ein Ritual eingebunden war.'

38 E.g. only roughly worked boat models in the sanctuary at Samos: Kyrieleis 1993, 112; unfinished architecture and inscriptions: Fouquet 2020. On deliberate damage, cf. Frielinghaus 2006; cf. also items that were made unusable by stacking or tying together, i.e. seven interlinked bracelets in Olympia: Philipp 1981, 231 no. 841 pl. 14. For unusable weapons in sanctuaries, cf. Baitinger 2011, 142–44.

ary — even if they are demonstrably a votive offering, as indicated, for example, by an inscription.[39] Vessels, tools, and such items do not only increase the possessions of the sanctuary and in many cases certainly contribute to the *kosmos* (see above), but they also find use in the rite or are themselves ultimately the object of the rite through their consecration. In order to be used in this way, certain criteria must be fulfilled: its outer form must allow its use, its dimensions must allow its handling, and the material from which it is made must be appropriately constituted.

For objects that primarily serve as cult utensils,[40] the material is therefore functionally predetermined. This also applies to the form; the function can be derived from the form, and the choice of material must be subordinate here. In my opinion, the *obeloi*, which eventually become a monetary unit, are a good example: the material must be heat resistant, and the spits must be long enough to be used easily.[41] Upon its transformation to coinage, the forms of device money degenerated to the so-called *Kümmerformen*, which were produced only in unusable forms.[42] A similar development can be seen in the case of tripods. Metal tripods are not only documented in 'normal format', however, but also in monumental and miniaturized forms. There are also literarily and archaeologically documented tripod dedications made of clay or even wood, which have lost their functionality not only because of their unsuitable dimensions but also because of the material used.[43]

Transference in Shape and Materiality

Before we now go into more detail on selected groups of materials that represent popular votive offerings, it is worth briefly pointing out that in connection with votive offerings, an intermedial transfer also takes place.

Inscriptions that name an object on the object itself as a votive offering represent a transfer from the spoken to the written word.[44] Through the visit to the sanctuary, the viewing of the exhibited objects, and the sound-reading of the inscriptions, a renewed transition from one medium to another takes place: the written word becomes a spoken word again.[45]

Similar to this transition from one medium to another, we can observe a kind of 'material transfer' in many places and on completely different objects. Although the form, which is most readily apparent in a votive offering, actually seems to prescribe a certain material, the concrete votive offering itself is made in a material deviating from it. Particularly in the case of works of art, the aim is a great closeness to nature or their apparently realistic reproduction (verisimilitude).[46] It does not matter that the material from which the work of art is made does not match the appearance of the finished object. In Antiquity, the process of artistic creation is closely linked to craftsmanship; this is also illustrated in mythology; for example, Pandora is made of clay by Hephaestus,[47] to cite just one mythological creation.

So, let us consider below selected groups of objects that are well attested as votive offerings in sanctuaries of different deities, but whose appearance — similar to Pandora — differs from the material they are made of,[48] or whose dimensions do not correspond to the commonplace.[49]

---

[39] A. Snodgrass distinguishes 'raw' (portable wealth) and 'converted' votives: Snodgrass 2006, 161–62.

[40] Day 1994, 44, sees a progression from cult inventory to votive offerings of the same form; the form is chosen because it represents an 'inherent value'.

[41] Luce 2011, 56: oversized *obeloi* are mentioned only once in inscriptions.

[42] For the discussion whether other miniaturized objects are to be counted as *Kümmerformen*, cf. Czech-Schneider 1998, 181–85.

[43] Czech-Schneider 2004; on, for example, miniature tripods made of clay and bronze at Amykleaion: Vlizos 2017, 89; on miniature bronze tripods from Olympia and miniature tripods of sheet bronze from Samos: Pilz 2011, figs 2–4; cf. n. 93.

[44] Oral performances are essential parts of the ritual; the written word perpetuates the unique event, cf. Day 1994, 41: 'Writing on the object is substituted for live performance.'

[45] Reading aloud results in a repetition of the original act, or at least in a ritual recharging: Day 1994, 41.

[46] This is true, to a certain extent, of the two sculptures mentioned above: the representation of the human body can be considered naturalistic, according to the contemporary specifications, even if the dimensions in both cases clearly deviate from it; the bronze used also deviates significantly from reality, cf. Bielfeldt 2014.

[47] Lather 2021, 104–08. Further examples would be the helping maidens of Hephaestus made of gold or the ivory statue with which Pygmalion fell in love.

[48] Body votives, the so-called *týpoi*, will not be discussed in detail here. With these votives, the situation is a little different than in the material groups presented here, but it is obvious that a 'material transfer' has occurred; the offering of the body part itself would hardly be in the sense of the donator. For an overview of so-called body votives, cf. van Straten 1981, 105–51; Hughes 2017; and Petridou in this volume.

[49] Literary and inscriptional evidence on oversized works and miniatures, as well as material transfer, compiled by Czech-Schneider 1998, 172–81, especially 178: '"Idee" des Objektes, die für einen

Figure 5.3. Ensemble of miniature vessels from Pheneos.
Image © University of Graz.

Dimension Transfer: Small-Scale Vessels

As shown above by the example of the two *kouroi*, which are based on the same shape, the actual dimensions often play a more subordinate role for the understanding of an object than we would have originally assumed.

Let us take at the outset an example from the excavations of the Institute of Classics of the University of Graz in cooperation with the Greek Administration of Antiquities at Pheneos in Arcadia:[50] clay vessels of strikingly small dimensions (Fig. 5.3). This group of materials is well represented in Pheneos in layers from sacred contexts dating to the Archaic and Classical periods. These vessels do not represent a specific characteristic of the site, however, but are particularly popular across almost the whole Peloponnese and some adjacent areas.[51] In the details, however, there is no uniform picture at the various sites:[52] the preferred forms vary as well as decoration and manufacturing technique; moreover, chronological trends and local preferences can also be observed.[53]

What the vast majority of the objects, which are generally grouped under miniature vessels, have in common is that they are tableware made of fired clay. In form (and also often in the decoration), they resemble vessels of functional size, but in this case, they are executed in a greatly reduced size; they are miniatures in the true sense.[54] However, a normal-sized model is not obligatory; this is shown, for example, by the groups of *krateriskoi* decorated with three female protomes from the Argolis,[55] as well as the mock vessels to be discussed below.

Apart from the discussion of individual find contexts, at the beginning of this century G. Ekroth in particular initiated the debate on the significance of miniature vessels.[56] Fundamental to our context are also the works of S. Barfoed, O. Pilz, and most recently E. Pemberton. Barfoed, who focuses especially on the Peloponnesian finds, has discussed several times recently the importance of the consecration of miniature vessels and postulates specific rites associated with them.[57] Pilz emphasizes the 'kommunikative Funktion' for the small-format objects, which have forfeited most of their functionality due to their miniaturization, so that the underlying thought ('cognitive level') becomes more important than the meaning or the value of the object itself.[58] Pemberton

---

imaginierten Gebrauch seitens der Götter durchaus ausreichend erscheint.' For a general overview, see Schattner and Zuchtriegel 2013.

[50] In general on Arcadia and its integration into the Peloponnese, cf. Nielsen and Roy 2009. For Pheneos, see Kissas and others 2017.

[51] A. Vlachou 2017, 258: 'Miniature vessels are commonly offered in all sites.' Miniature vessels also occur away from the Peloponnese in various contexts, but rarely in such high numbers as in the Peloponnese. Some sites with high numbers of pieces are located on the other side of the Gulf of Corinth, i.e. Perachora or in the chora of Delphi (Kirrha, Corycian Caves): Luce 2011, Abb. 14. On Chalkidike: Gimatzidis 2011. For Sicily, cf. Sojc in this volume. The small scale is not a sacral phenomenon of the first millennium, as the various miniaturized votive offerings from Crete show. In summit sanctuaries especially, they can be described as 'intrinsic elements of the cult': Tournavitou 2009, 229. Cf. also the discussion on miniature textiles below, as well as Sojc, this volume.

[52] Barfoed 2015a; 2015b.

[53] For an overview of the miniature vessels of the Peloponnese, see n. 51. At Pheneos, for example, closed vessel forms (hydria, jugs, amphorae) are currently clearly outnumbered. This also seems to be the case with normal-sized vessels.

[54] However, the strong reduction is not limited to the material pottery nor to tableware; other household utensils, weapons, or carts — in principle, almost all objects of daily life — are also attested in a strongly reduced form: Pilz 2011; see n. 89.

[55] There is much to suggest that all vessels of this form were made in the same workshop and thus represent a specific Argive characteristic: Ekroth 2013. However, there are similarities to the miniature *dinoi* with three bull protomes, for which 'normal-sized' examples in bronze, but mostly decorated with griffin protomes, are attested.

[56] Ekroth 2003.

[57] Most recently, Barfoed 2018. This approach is particularly supported by observations in which no 'normal-sized models' can be located for the vessel forms executed *en miniature*, e.g. the earliest group of miniature vessels at Tegea: Hammond 2005.

[58] Pilz 2011 sees not only the ritual environment reflected in the miniatures but also social role models; see also Pilz 2012.

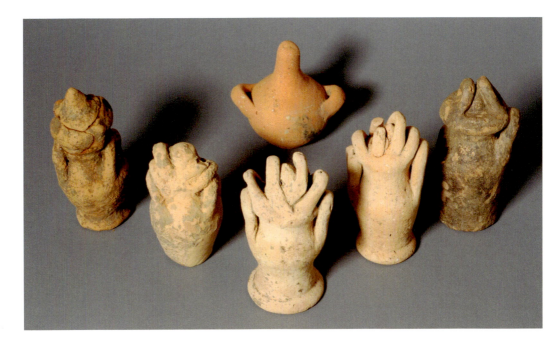

Figure 5.4. Mock vessels from Pheneos. Image © University of Graz.

also sees the significance of miniature vessels in 'a link between divine and human'.[59]

In the material group of small-format vessels, one group stands out in particular: so-called mock vessels.[60] In terms of quantity, these objects represent a very small group in the findings at Pheneos.[61] Their shapes are based on normal-sized vessels, but not to the same extent as the vast majority of other miniature vessels, which reproduce well-known vessel shapes. Two types of mock vessels are currently attested in Pheneos (Fig. 5.4): 1) vessels in the manner of a low *pyxis* with horizontal handles and a pointed lid, and 2) a slender amphora-like form with a pronounced neck and two vertical handles, which may be enriched by one or two additional pairs of handles.[62] Under normal conditions, a *pyxis* and an amphora represent containers whose primary function is to store their contents. What is striking about the latter two miniature forms, however, is that they precisely cannot serve as containers, because they are full ('solid') or the lid is not removable. They only pretend to be a vessel or container.[63] To make matters worse, in a sense, while a 'normal-sized' model can be assumed for the mock *pyxis*, such a model seems to be completely lacking for the 'amphora-like' form.[64] Here is a certain parallel to the previously mentioned *krateriskoi* with female protomes from the Argolis,[65] for which no normal-sized specimens are attested either. This raises a question of principle, not only for the sanctuary in Pheneos: Why would an object be dedicated to a sanctuary, when it has the form of a container but is constructed in such a way that this function cannot be fulfilled?[66]

For the miniature vessels, it may be possible to apply a similar explanatory model as that developed by H. von Hesberg for the mass-produced terracotta statuettes.[67]

---

[59] Pemberton 2020, 334. In grave complexes, vessels of the same shape are simultaneously present in normal format and miniaturized; consequently, it can be excluded that the miniature vessel is a substitute.

[60] Barfoed 2018, 116: 'token miniatures are the only category of miniature vessels that can truly be called non-functional.' This is where Foxhall's thesis particularly begins to take hold: 'while creating new meanings of their own, which potentially enrich and alter both the miniature itself and its prototype', Foxhall 2015, 1.

[61] At the famous Sanctuary of Hera in Argos there is only one singular piece, which C. Waldstein describes, 'it must be regarded as a mere freak of the potters' art, with no definite *raison d'être*'; Waldstein 1905, 101 fig. 41.

[62] Good comparisons were uncovered in the nearby Artemis Hemera sanctuary in Lousoi; Schauer 2001, 159 pls 18–19; Barfoed 2018, 116–17 fig. 5. The composition of several types of vessels is in principle not uncanonical, e.g. *kernoi*, cf. n. 89.

[63] The question is whether comparable arguments can be made for these mock vessels as we have for the miniaturized forms in Crete grouped under the term 'tokens': Knappett 2012.

[64] This gives the impression that a stack of vessels is reproduced here in a greatly reduced form, similar to how *kernoi* combine various individual elements. Multi-storeyed vessels and repetitive vessel parts placed side by side have been described by J. Bouzek as a characteristic of the Geometric period: Bouzek 2017, 52–53 fig. 11a.

[65] Cf. n. 55 above.

[66] Following on from this, one must finally ask whether this conspicuousness is characteristic of small-format objects.

[67] Von Hesberg 2007; cf. n. 37 above.

Figure 5.5. Dresses in miniature from the temple repositories in Knossos, replica. Image © University of Graz.

Figure 5.6. Relief table in miniature, Olympia, inv. no. T 202. Photo DAI, Athens, Neg.-Nr. D-DAI-ATH-1994-1374, photographer: Elmar Gehnen. © Ministry of Culture & Sports, Ephorate of Antiquities of Ilia, Hellenic Organization of Cultural Resources Development.

Through every individual object missing a specific intention, for example through a consecration inscription or a portrait with the terracottas, an identical consecration confirms, by every new cultic act, all previous cultic acts from a consecrator. The assumption, supported by some contexts, that the miniature vessels were usually consecrated in small groups rather than individually, would be compatible with this theory.[68] However, the Hesberg model cannot explain the small form.

Material Transfer: Textiles, Foodstuffs, and Wreaths

We previously have considered some votive offerings of unusual dimensions in the Greek sanctuaries; now let us examine a little more closely the material from which they were made. In the following, we will look at three selected examples of groups of objects where the shape and the material used do not at first seem to match.[69]

In the following cases, the material transfer becomes particularly clear, since the starting material of all three groups is organic and therefore rapidly perishable. Let us look at selected examples below that have fabric, food, and twigs as their starting materials.

Due to the complex manufacturing process, textiles in Antiquity generally had a certain material value, regardless of the material, decoration, or colour, although these factors could still contribute to an increased price. Robes and textile accessories also represent popular votive offerings in many sanctuaries of Greek gods and goddesses.[70] This is not specific to the first millennium; there are comparable dedications from the Aegean Bronze Age.[71]

In this context, some objects in the so-called temple deposits at Knossos represent a special feature. Among numerous examples of pottery, seals, shells, and especially 'snake goddesses' were also found two small robes as well as belts. Although the objects quite obviously represent textiles, they are, however, made in faience. A. Evans himself called the robes 'votive robes' (Fig. 5.5).[72] Even though they were found deposited, holes on the back indicate that they were originally intended to be hung, as

---

[68] From Achaea we know of flat clay plates on which are fixed miniature vessels: Kolia 2017, 106 tab. 38.3, cf. n. 81.

[69] The intentional reproduction of precious-metal votive offerings, e.g. made of clay, is often attributed to poorer strata of the population. The fact that the cheaper material used is often concealed under a metal covering seems to underline the attempt to reduce costs while retaining the more expensive visual impression: Kotitsa 2003. M. Vickers even suggests that the black-glazed clay pottery in particular deliberately imitated metal vessels, not only in appearance but also in form: Vickers 1998. This transfer of materials can finally even be observed in the cult image itself, if one thinks in particular

of acrolith statues: Häger-Weigel 1997.

[70] For dedicated textiles in inscriptions, see Brøns 2015; for the use of textiles in the sanctuaries in general, see Brøns 2017.

[71] For an overview, see Boloti 2017.

[72] For detailed information on the finds of the temple deposits, among which there are numerous other objects in reduced scale, according to the notes of A. Evans, see Panagiotaki 1993; especially on the robes and belts, Panagiotaki 1993, 59–62, 89–90; summarized by Panagiotaki 1999, 76–77.

Evans has also noted.[73] The display aspect that is characteristic of votive offerings in first-millennium sanctuaries is already evident here. In this exceptional case, perishable textiles are not only greatly reduced in size but also recreated in a durable material (faience). Their appearance corresponds to iconographic parallels; only the material used and the dimensions deviate from what we would expect.[74]

The second group of materials to be briefly addressed here is food. The offering of food, whether a slaughtered animal or other food (e.g. libation or cake), was an essential component of many cults.[75] Unless we have written or pictorial sources to fall back on, however, these perishable offerings are often difficult to trace in material culture, even if we know with certainty of their existence.[76]

For now, let us focus on one element of food offerings. The evidence for sacrificial cakes and breads is, at least terminologically, numerous: A. Brumsfield has compiled a rich list of differently shaped cakes prepared according to various recipes.[77] Many of the shapes mentioned in the written sources are attested, for example, in the Sanctuary of Demeter and Kore at the Acrocorinth, but they were formed of clay, as was the characteristic flat basket, *liknon*, in which they were carried.[78] The custom of dedicating bread and cakes, however, is not limited to the sanctuaries of Demeter and Kore, nor to Greece. It is complemented by the consecration of grains, as well as by all kinds of fruits and vegetables, eggs, cheeses, and other foods. Almost all foods have been found as replicas in clay from different regions,[79] or replicas are carried by a consecrated statuette.[80] Replicas of consecrated foods were also consecrated alongside a basket or table that is also replicated. Fruits and other food and their baskets are made of clay, like the previously mentioned *likna* from Corinth, while votive-like tables are made of clay (Fig. 5.6) or metal.[81] Again, these do not conform in either a naturalistic size or the actual material used. In this context, it becomes more urgent to ask whether the representation of such sacrificial ceremonies in particular means a substitute for the sacrifice itself or only its perpetuation after the sacrifice itself has passed, in the sense of a memorial or a repetitive thought.[82]

The third group of objects discussed here that were perishable in principle encompasses branches and wreaths;[83] they are securely, if not exclusively, associated with ritual acts. They are also mostly recognizable when they have undergone a material transfer. For example, wreaths made of gold that were exhibited in the sanctuary are attested, in some cases even revealing the foliage from which their models were made. A certain closeness to reality is sought (cf. above, likeness to nature).[84] Likewise, inventory lists mention wreaths made of precious metals.[85] A change was made from perishable to imperishable material, but their form was retained.

In this context, a geographical peculiarity is the miniature wreaths made of lead,[86] which are only attested

---

[73] Panagiotaki 1993, 59 fig. 3, B, D.

[74] Jones 2019, 58–59. A comparable transformation takes place with the so-called 'sacred knot', which is likely to be an artistically laid scarf: Alexiou 1967; Jones 2019, 281 figs 9.55–60. For the first millennium, costume accessories made of metal or other materials are often better attested than the textiles themselves. As with the aforementioned garments made of faience from Knossos, there are also examples of costume accessories that cannot have a functional character due to their dimensions or the material used; for example, brooches and needles made of lead or jewellery made of clay, to name just a few examples: Philipp 1981, 20; Boss 2000, 119–22; Baumbach 2004, 61 fig. 2.23.

[75] Rouse 1902; van Straten 1992; 1995.

[76] For example, for the altars in Olympia away from the altar of ashes, Pausanias (v.15.10) reports wheat grains soaked in honey, incense, olive branches, and wine. Völling sees at least for the altar of Artemis there the 'dinglichen Weihungen' replaced by these perishable consecrations; Völling 2002, 102.

[77] Brumsfield 1997, 169–71.

[78] Klinger 2021, 70–76.

[79] In rare cases, the cakes and even their components can be detected: Primavera and others 2019.

[80] E.g. Kinderlen and Strocka 2005, no. 25.56 f.; Klinger 2021, 76–83. Apparently, the sanctuaries produced these clay fruits at least partly themselves, as a model from the Sanctuary of Hera at Argos shows: Baumbach 2004, 91 fig. 4.39.

[81] Hausmann 1996, 6 no. 4 Taf. 1.4; Baumbach 2004, 91 fig. 4.40 (Argos); Krumme 2006 (Miletus); Filges 2015, 95 Abb. 12 (Priene). Cf. the plates from Aigeira, above, n. 68. A clay table *en miniature* was found in the Agamemnoneion in Mycenae: Cook 1953, 49 fig. 24 pl. 20. Among the *kernoi*, a similar combination of different groups of objects executed in unusual material and often of unusual size occurs; on the consecration of *kernoi* with applied miniature vessels, see Barfoed 2009, 165; Mitsopoulou 2011. Cf. also the handmade plaques with multiple small cups in Marmara (Achaea): Kolia 2017, 106 pl. 38.3.

[82] Van Straten 1992.

[83] For branches and wreaths on the altar, see Blech 1982, 449.

[84] Flowers and foliage depend on the occasion and owner of the cult: Blech 1982, 295–302. For carrying the wreaths in the cult, cf. Blech 1982, 302–12. The wreaths documented for the symposium and retied by M. Heilmeyer are a vivid representation; visually, there would have been little difference between wreaths made for the symposium and those made for a dedication: Heilmeyer 2002.

[85] Blech 1982, 299.

[86] Boss 2000, 112–15. For a list of find-spots, see Forsén 2017,

Figure 5.7. Wreaths made from lead from Pheneos. Image © University of Graz.

at Laconia and in a few neighbouring areas. Within the large group of Laconian lead motifs, wreaths even form the overwhelming majority in number. In terms of their material value, however, these small-format lead wreaths are probably at the other end of the scale compared to the gold wreaths mentioned above.[87] On the basis of the details, the lead wreaths themselves can be typologically differentiated, for example with pointed or round extensions (Fig. 5.7) or with stylized fruits. In my opinion, this again shows an attempt to establish a relationship to real wreaths made of various plants and fruits, despite the transfer of materials and dimensions. The material transfer is not limited to metal, however. Besides the metal replicas, miniature wreaths (spiked wreaths, resembling cogwheels) made of clay are documented.[88]

There are many other examples of material transfer in votive offerings, such as the models of buildings, ships, carriages, furniture, and so on, mostly in a reduced size.[89] Similar to the case of weapons made from non-weapon material, only of sheet metal, or *en miniature*,[90] it is also clear how the votive character is detached from functionality. In these cases, no one demands that dedicated weapons assume functionality according to their form, so why would we want to postulate that for other objects?

We can thus sum up that among the votive and sacrificial offerings we can delineate some groups that stand out due to their unexpected dimensions or atypical use of materials. We can speak of 'unexpected' when figurative images and representations (e.g. statues and statuettes) are not near-human in size.[91] Consequently, dimensions that exceed this framework, either much larger (monumentalization) or much smaller (miniaturization), are 'unexpected', although this is just as common, if not more common, than figures with life-size dimensions.[92] For the atypical use of materials, a parallel argumentation can be put forward. Starting from the humanly usable, objects must correspond not only with respect to their form (as well as dimensions) but also with respect to the material used. For votive and sacrificial offerings, however, this functionality is strongly shifted into the religious sphere. The actual material

---

144 n. 44; Kombothekra: Pilz 2020, 341. Besides wreaths, branches with leaves and fruits of different shapes have been found: Boss 2000, 115–17. Lead votives in general reflect characteristically Laconic cult components, some of which are also found in neighbouring regions: A. Vlachou 2017, 260.

[87] Antonacci 2005, 104: 'Because of their mass production, small size and cheapness, and wide variety, lead miniatures provided a particularly inexpensive and easy way to shape the character of the ritual, just as miniatures in other media did elsewhere.'

[88] On the Peloponnese and in the neighbouring regions, i.e. Aspis: Alexandridou 2012, 816 fig. 23; clay hoops with an undulating edge in Perachora: Baumbach 2004, 44–45. Due to the small format, the exact naming sometimes seems difficult: are they wreaths or the so-called *koulouria*, round breads? E. Kolia recently suggested an interpretation as a reduced *harpax*: Kolia 2017, 107 pl. 39.5. However, in my opinion these 'rings' lack the crucial detail for such a designation, namely the long handle.

[89] Pilz 2012, rightly emphasizes that these are not models in the sense of a prototype. The reduced format is often explained by their easier transportability; this argument is correct in principle (cf. the clay and wooden tripods, n. 93), but it falls somewhat short in view of some extremely valuable votive offerings transported over very long distances. On miniature ships, see Frielinghaus 2017, 26–28; Klinger 2021, 67–70; on carts, see Kolia 2011, 219 figs 28–29; Klinger 2021, 63–67. For an overview of dedicated miniature wheels, e.g. in the sanctuaries of Poseidon in Kalaureia and Helike, see Alexandridou 2013, 112–13.

[90] Rouse 1902, 116–17. Miniature weapons are mostly made of bronze, but are occasionally made of clay, especially shields. They also appear in sanctuaries that have not received dedications of real weapons: cf. Baitinger and Völling 2007, 201–02; Baitinger 2011, 159–60.

[91] For the relation of large-scale stone sculpture and small-scale coroplastics, cf. Schattner and Zuchtriegel 2013, 264–65.

[92] Whether this is monumentalization or miniaturization is, as Knappett showed, secondary; both have a strong inherent temporal compression that requires explanatory models outside the narrative otherwise used: Knappett 2012, 104.

used and its material properties often seem to recede into the background.[93]

In both processes, the purchase price changes, but it must be questioned whether this also changes the religious relevance. There is much to suggest, however, that objects are reinterpreted through their use in the ritual environment in such a way that the actual properties of the object (dimensions, material value) recede and are reassessed in favour of or through the rite.

Conclusion

The objects found in sanctuaries that have been discussed here, which can be classified as atypical and alien to life both in terms of the material used and/or the dimensions, seem to have been made primarily for use as votive offerings.[94] In this respect, the question arises whether it makes a difference to those dedicated objects whose traces of use clearly prove their detachment from everyday life. In the second case, there is a 'diminution' of the dedicator's material wealth, since the object passes from the possession of the dedicator into the possession of the deity or the sanctuary. Thus, the dedicator becomes 'materially poorer', but a permanent connection to the deity is established.[95] Precisely the same goal can be said for objects created explicitly for dedication, independent of their dimensions and material.

In principle, dimensions and material affect both the functionality of an object — if functionality is at all a relevant criterion in a ritual context — and the price of purchase and procurement. Therefore, the following strongly abbreviated explanatory model is often applied: offerings of smaller size and made of less expensive material must come from a clientele with less purchasing power, while precious material and monumentality indicate a wealthy clientele.

So, what makes an object a unique votive offering? It is easy to argue that high-priced votive offerings increase sacral assets, especially if they are made of recyclable material. Figurative and/or inscribed votive offerings can be connected to ideas of (self-)representation, and functional considerations are applicable in the case of various utensils.

From some textual sources, one can read that the material value, at least in the case of the sacrifice, is an essential value.[96] Why should this assessment be different for differently designed offerings and votives?[97] How, then, can small-format offerings, which are of course cheaper to purchase than larger or oversized objects, please the deity?[98] Here, a certain contradiction seems to arise.

Dedications in sets are documented in some places but are often difficult to prove.[99] A particularly prominent example is the cult bench of Kalapodi, where not only a large number of miniature vessels, but also needles, a statuette, and other objects were found *in situ*.[100] Thus, if a small-sized object is not to be considered as a single dedication but only as part of a group — a whole set — this may offer an explanation to some extent, because the larger number necessarily represents a higher

---

[93] A particularly illustrative example is handed down to us by Pausanias: Paus. IV.12.7–10: During the First Messenian War, the Delphic Pythia 'demands' for a victory one hundred tripods for the Sanctuary of Zeus on Ithome. While the Messenians donate tripods made of wood, the Spartans donate tripods made of clay, but in a much-reduced format, and through this offering they are finally victorious. Again, it is irrelevant that tripods — in order to keep their functional character — should actually be made of metal; cf. Czech-Schneider 2004.

[94] Osborne 2004, 2: 'The to-be-dedicated object may have been made precisely for this type of exchange, as figurines or miniatures are.'

[95] Erdman 2014, 98: 'actually an investment, so to speak, by the human participant. Through the loss of physical wealth that was then gained by the deity during deposition, the person who offered the object gained intangible value in the supernatural world instead.'

[96] Van Straten 1987, 167–68. Theophrastus and Menander, for example, describe that the Greeks were primarily concerned with the value of their sacrifice, more than the 'type'.

[97] If the same standard can be applied to sacrifice and votive offerings at all. In any case, a smaller number of regulations seems to have applied to the second, as C. M. Antonacci formulates for the Sanctuary of Helen and Menelaus at Therapne: 'dedicatory practice is less rule-bound than sacrifice, or than sacrifice is represented to be' (Antonacci 2005, 102). Nevertheless, 'as a form of the voluntary surrender of a valuable object to a god, dedication was functionally parallel to sacrifice' (Day 1994, 43). This is true in principle, but as we have already seen above, 'valuable' is not such a decisive criterion for the selection of a votive offering.

[98] On the basis of the previously outlined wealth of variants of votive offerings, the question must also be asked in principle whether there is a connection between a deity (supernatural entity) and a preferred type of votive offering consecrated in its sanctuary. This question is not only often difficult to answer, but one must proceed also with great care when comparing different places. However, such a discussion would go too far out of our context here.

[99] Consecrations in sets are attested for various objects made of different materials: miniature vessels, skewers, lead wreaths, anatomical votives, terracottas; cf. Salapata 2011, 3–4. Cf. the contributions of Rieger and of Sojc in this volume.

[100] Felsch 2013, 60–62; summarized by Barfoed 2018, 117–18 fig. 6.

material value. However, if we start from very small initial sums for each individual object, which is probably the case with miniature vessels as well as with most foodstuffs, even a large item or a set with numerous items can in no way match the expenditure involved in an oversized votive offering.

For the phenomenon that the material used deviates from the material to be assumed on the basis of the form or the appearance of the surface, the term 'skeuomorphism' was coined in the last century, regarding especially pottery.[101] This term does not have to be limited to ceramics, however, but can also be applied to the other above-mentioned (re-)creations in materials foreign to the object: for example, wreaths made of metal, food made of clay, or textile ribbons of stone. The fact that in these cases there is predominantly a transition from a less durable to a more durable material is probably connected with the idea of remembrance: for the underlying cultic act, this means that the connection between the human and the deity initiated by the cultic act is perpetuated, even if no new cultic act is performed. For this perpetuation, material fidelity is finally negligible. At the same time, these objects are often made with unusual dimensions.

So, although the 'use value' has been lost due to atypical dimensions (miniaturization/monumentalization), an unusual and impractical form, or non-functional use of materials, there remains 'exchange value' in the Greek sanctuary.[102] The dedication establishes a relationship with a supernatural entity, regardless of the size, shape, and material of the object dedicated into the sanctuary. That the omniscient gods attached less importance to the material than to the intention is already shown by the sacrificial fraud of Prometheus.[103] Neither the dimension nor the material is decisive; the establishment of a relationship is in the foreground — or in the case of Prometheus, angering the deity.

Especially in those sanctuaries which were played over centuries, changes in the cult practice are traceable in the material culture. Thus T. Völlig concludes that, despite the changed forms of expression of the cult at Olympia, 'der Glaube an die beeinflußbare Gunst der Götter sowie das Streben nach Anerkennung und Nachruhm unter den Menschen [...] unverändert lebendig geblieben'.[104]

Based on an established and repeatedly renewed relationship with the deity, an 'exchange practice' works in both directions.

Regarding the sanctuary at Delphi, one could infer from a passage in Pausanias a wish to 'influence' the deity. The population of Orneiai in the Argolis promised Apollo daily sacrifices and processions, if the god would assist them against the Sicyonians: 'they conquered the Sicyonians in battle. But finding the daily fulfilment of their vow a great expense and a still greater trouble, they devised the trick of dedicating to the god bronze figures representing a sacrifice and a procession.'[105] The promise was fulfilled despite certain economic measures and one-sided modifications; only the underlying material — a sacrificial animal becomes a bronze sculpture — was changed. In the Greek understanding of religion, the sacrificial animals now converted into bronze contribute as much to the relationship between the donator and the transcendent power, as well as to the perception of the ritual act in its presence or in its afterlife, as the originally promised sacrificial animals did.[106]

As these examples show, the intention of a dedication is more decisive than the material used. We learn nothing from Pausanias about the dimension of the bronze animals — one could also think of statues that are not close to life, i.e. reduced in size, as is documented in large numbers from many Greek sanctuaries. However, the statues represent not only the sacrifice, but also all the associated rites, which Pausanias summarizes under 'procession'. Not only representations of sacrificial animals but almost every type of object is also attested *en miniature*. They all have one primary purpose in common: they are supposed to function as mediators between man and a supernatural entity. In this respect, gifts with unusual form, whether monumentalized or miniaturized, represent not only no real exception; they but correspond to a satisfying religious practice for both sides (human and transcendent beings). All votive and sacrificial offerings, independent of their dimensions and material, thus represent, as G. Salapata succinctly puts it, a 'token of piety'.[107] They satisfy both man and god.

---

[101] M. Vickers sees here an overall social phenomenon that is not limited to the sacred environment: Vickers 1998.

[102] Luce 2011.

[103] Hes., *Theog.* 545–60.

[104] Völling 2002, 106.

[105] Paus. x.18.5; trans. Jones and Ormerod (from Czech-Schneider 2004).

[106] We can assume that the bronze sculptures were displayed appropriately prominently in the *temenos*.

[107] Salapata 2018.

Works Cited

Alexandridou, A. 2012. 'Le matériel votif archaïque', *Bulletin du correspondance hellénique*, 136/37.2: 815–17.
——. 2013. 'Archaic Pottery and Terracottas from the Sanctuary of Poseidon at Kalaureia', *Opuscula*, 6: 81–150.
Alexiou, S. 1967. 'Contribution to the Study of the Minoan "Sacred Knot"', in W. C. Brice (ed.), *Europa: Studien zur Geschichte und Epigraphik frühen Aegaeis; Festschrift für Ernst Grumach* (Berlin: De Gruyter), pp. 1–6.
Antonacci, C. M. 2005. 'Dedications and the Character of Cult', in R. Hägg and B. Alroth (eds), *Greek Sacrificial Ritual, Olympian and Chthonian*, Skrifter utgivna av Svenska institutet i Athen, 8.18 (Stockholm: Svenska institutet i Athen), pp. 99–112.
Baitinger, H. 2011. *Waffenweihungen in griechischen Heiligtümern* (Mainz: Verlag des Römisch-Germanischen Zentralmuseums).
Baitinger, H. and T. Völling. 2007. *Werkzeug und Gerät aus Olympia*, Olympische Forschungen, 32 (Berlin: De Gruyter).
Barfoed, S. 2009. 'An Archaic Votive Deposit from Nemea. Ritual Behavior in a Sacred Landscape' (unpublished master's thesis, University of Cincinnati).
——. 2015a. 'Cult in Context. The Ritual Significance of Miniature Pottery in Ancient Greek Sanctuaries from the Archaic to the Hellenistic Period' (unpublished doctoral thesis, University of Kent).
——. 2015b. 'The Significant Few. Miniature Pottery from the Sanctuary of Zeus at Olympia', *World Archaeology*, 47.1: 170–88.
——. 2018. 'The Use of Miniature Pottery in Archaic–Hellenistic Greek Sanctuaries. Considerations on Terminology and Ritual Practice', *Opscula*, 11: 111–26.
Baumbach, J. D. 2004. *The Significance of Votive Offerings in Selected Hera Sanctuaries in the Peloponnese, Ionia and Western Greece* (Oxford: Archaeopress).
Bielfeldt, R. 2014. 'Gegenwart und Vergegenwärtigung: Dynamische Dinge im Ausgang bei Homer', in R. Bielfeldt (ed.), *Ding und Mensch in der Antike: Gegenwart und Vergegenwärtigung* (Heidelberg: Winter), pp. 15–47.
Blech, M. 1982. *Studien zum Kranz bei den Griechen*, Religionsgeschichtliche Versuche und Vorarbeiten, 38 (Berlin: De Gruyter).
Boardman, J. and others. 2004. 'Dedications. Greek Dedications. II: Greek Votive Objects', in *Thesaurum cultus et rituum antiquorum*, I (Los Angeles: Paul Getty Museum), pp. 281–318.
Boloti, T. 2017. 'Offering of Cloth and/or Clothing to the Sanctuaries: A Case of Ritual Continuity from the 2nd to the 1st Millennium BCE in the Aegean?', in C. Brøns and M.-L. Nosch (eds), *Textiles and Cult in the Ancient Mediterranean* (Oxford: Oxbow), pp. 3–16.
Boss, M. 2000. *Lakonische Votivgaben aus Blei* (Würzburg: Königshausen und Neumann).
Bouzek, J. 2017. 'Koine of Early Iron Age Geometric Styles', in A. Mazarakis-Ainian, A. Alexandridou, and X. Charalambidou (eds), *Regional Stories: Towards a New Perception of the Early Greek World* (Volos: University of Thessaly Press), pp. 41–53.
Brøns, C. 2015. 'Textiles and Temple Inventories: Detecting an Invisible Votive Tradition in Greek Sanctuaries in the Second Half of the First Millennium BC', *Acta Hyperborea*, 14: 43–83.
——. 2017. *Gods and Garments: Textiles in Greek Sanctuaries from the 7th to the 1st Centuries BC*, Ancient Textiles, 28 (Oxford: Oxbow).
Brumsfield, A. 1997. 'Cakes in the Liknon: Votives from the Sanctuary of Demeter and Kore on Acrocorinth', *Hesperia*, 66: 147–72.
Burkert, W. 1977. *Griechische Religion der archaischen und klassischen Epoche* (Stuttgart: Kohlhammer).
Cook, J. M. 1953. 'Mycenae 1939–1952. Part III. The Agamemnoneion', *The Annual of the British School at Athens*, 48: 30–68.
Czech-Schneider, R. 1998. 'Anathemata. Weihgaben und Weihgabenpraxis und ihre Bedeutung für die Gesellschaft und Wirtschaft der frühen Griechen' (unpublished habilitation thesis, University of Münster).
——. 2004. 'Werkstoff und Format. Zur Bedeutung der dinglichen Erscheinungsformen von Weihgaben in der griechischen Kultpraxis', in J. Gebauer (ed.), *Bildergeschichte: Festschrift Klaus Stähler* (Möhnesee: Bibliopolis), pp. 99–110.
Day, J. W. 1994. 'Interactive Offerings: Early Greek Dedicatory Epigrams and Ritual', *Harvard Studies in Classical Philology*, 96: 27–74.
Ekroth, G. 2003. 'Small Pots, Poor People? The Use and Function of Miniature Pottery as Votive Offerings in Archaic Sanctuaries in the Argolid and the Corinthia', in B. Schmaltz and M. Söldner (eds), *Griechische Keramik im kulturellen Kontext: Akten des Internationalen Vasen-Symposions in Kiel vom 24. bis 28.9.2001* (Münster: Scriptorium), pp. 35–37.
——. 2013. 'Between Bronze and Clay. The Origin of an Argive, Archaic Votive Shape', in M.-C. Ferriès, M. P. Castiglioni, and F. Létoublon (eds), *Forgerons, élites et voyageurs d'Homère à nos jours: hommages en mémoire d'Isabelle Ratinaud-Lachkar* (Grenoble: Presses universitaires de Grenoble), pp. 63–77.
Erdman, K. M. 2014. 'Votives and Values: Communicating with the Supernatural', in A. Bokern (ed.), *Embodying Value? The Transformation of Objects in and from the Ancient World*, British Archaeological Reports, International Series, 2592 (Oxford: BAR), pp. 89–100.
Felsch, R. 2013. 'Zu einigen rituellen Deponierungen im Heiligtum von Artemis und Apollon bei Kalapodi in der antiken Phokis', in A. Schäfer and M. Witteyer (eds), *Rituelle Deponierungen in Heiligtümern der hellenistisch-römischen Welt: International Tagung Mainz 38.–30. April 2008* (Mainz: Generaldirektion Kulturelles Erbe Rheinland-Pfalz), pp. 53–67.

Filges, A. 2015. 'Ein Felsheiligtum im Stadtgebiet von Priene', in K. Sporn, S. Ladstätter, and M. Kerscher (eds), *Natur, Kult, Raum: Akten des internationalen Kolloquiums, Paris-Lodron-Universität Salzburg, 20.–22 Jänner 2012* (Vienna: Österreichisches Archäologisches Institut), pp. 81–109.

Forsén, B. 2017. 'Neue Funde aus dem Heiligtum der Artemis Lykoatis in Arkadien', in H. Frielinghaus and J. Stroszeck (eds), *Kulte und Heiligtümer in Griechenland* (Möhnesee: Bibliopolis), pp. 133–54.

Fouquet, J. 2020. 'Dekorative (Un)fertigkeit. Zum Prozess des Beschreibens auf einer Gruppe von spätarchaisch-frühklassischen Statuenbasen aus Athen', in N. Dietrich, J. Fouquet, and C. Reinhardt, *Schreiben auf statuarischen Monumenten*, Materiale Textkulturen, 29 (Berlin: De Gruyter), pp. 103–46.

Foxhall, L. 2015. 'Introduction: Miniaturization', *World Archaeology*, 47.1: 1–5.

Franssen, J. 2011. *Votiv und Repräsentation: Statuarische Weihungen archaischer Zeit aus Samos und Attika* (Heidelberg: Verlag Archäologie und Geschichte).

Frielinghaus, H. 2006. 'Deliberate Damage to Bronze Votives in Olympia during Archaic and Early Classical Times', in C. C. Mattusch, A. A. Donohue, and A. Brauer (eds), *Common Ground: Archaeology, Art, Science, and Humanities; Proceedings of the xvith International Congress of Classical Archaeology* (Oxford: Oxbow), pp. 36–38.

——. 2017. 'Schiffe im Votivkontext', in H. Frielinghaus, T. Schmidts, and V. Tsamakda (eds), *Schiffe und ihr Kontext: Darstellungen, Modelle, Bestandteile; Von der Bronzezeit bis zum Ende des Byzantinischen Reiches; Internationales Kolloquium 24.–25. Mai 2013 in Mainz* (Mainz: Verlag des Römisch-Germanischen Zentralmuseums), pp. 23–37.

Gaifman, M. 2012. *Aniconism in Greek Antiquity* (Oxford: Oxford University Press).

Gimatzidis, S. 2011. 'Feasting and Offering to the Gods in Early Greek Sanctuaries: Monumentalisation and Miniaturisation in Pottery', *Pallas*, 86: 75–96 <https://doi.org/10.4000/pallas.2099>.

Giuliani, L. (ed.). 2005. 'Der Koloss der Naxier', in L. Giuliani (ed.), *Meisterwerke der antiken Kunst* (Munich: Beck), pp. 12–27.

——. 2006. '"Aus demselben Stein bin ich": Zum Verständnis der Inschrift an der Basis des Naxier-Kolosses auf Delos', in A. Dostert and F. Lang (eds), *Mittel und Wege: Zur Bedeutung von Material und Technik in der Archäologie* (Möhnesee: Bibliopolis), pp. 101–12.

Gosden, C. and Y. Marshall. 1999. 'The Cultural Biography of Objects', *World Archaeology*, 31: 169–78.

Guggisberg, M. 2009. 'Größe als Gabe: Gedanken zum Format von "Prestigegütern" in frühen Kulturen der Mittelmeerwelt und ihrer Randzonen', in B. Hildebrandt and C. Veit (eds), *Der Wert der Dinge: Güter im Prestigediskurs* (Munich: Herbert Utz), pp. 103–41.

Haase, M. 2002. 'Votivkult', in H. Cancik and H. Schneider (eds), *Der neue Pauly: Enzyklopädie der Antike*, xii.2 (Stuttgart: Metzler), pp. 245–46.

Häger-Weigel, E. 1997. *Griechische Akrolith-Statuen des 5. und 4. Jhs. v. Chr.* (Berlin: Köster).

Hammond, L. 2005. 'Arcadian Miniature Pottery', in E. Østby (ed.), *Ancient Arcadia: Papers from the Third International Seminar on Ancient Arcadia, Held at the Norwegian Institute at Athens, 7–10 May 2002* (Bergen: Norwegian Institute at Athens), pp. 415–33.

Hausmann, U. 1996. *Hellenistische Keramik: Eine Brunnenfüllung nördlich von Bau C und Reliefkeramik verschiedener Fundplätze in Olympia*, Olympische Forschungen, 27 (Berlin: De Gruyter).

Heilmeyer, M. 2002. 'Kränze für das griechische Symposion in klassischer Zeit', in F. Zimmer (ed.), *Die griechische Klassik: Idee oder Wirklichkeit; Eine Ausstellung im Martin-Gropius-Bau, Berlin 1. März–2. Juni 2002 und in der Kunst- und Ausstellungshalle der Bundesrepublik Deutschland, Bonn 5. Juli–6. Oktober 2002* (Mainz: Von Zabern), pp. 296–99.

Hesberg, H. von. 2007. 'Votivseriation', in C. Frevel and H. von Hesberg (eds), *Kult und Kommunikation: Medien in Heiligtümern der Antike* (Wiesbaden: Reichert), pp. 279–309.

Himmelmann, N. 2001. *Die private Bildnisweihung bei den Griechen*, Nordrhein-Westfälische Akademie der Wissenschaften: Geisteswissenschaften. Vorträge, 373 (Wiesbaden: VS Verlag für Sozialwissenschaften).

Hölscher, F. 2014. 'Gottheit und Bild, Gottheit im Bild', in R. Bielfeldt (ed.), *Ding und Mensch in der Antike: Gegenwart und Vergegenwärtigung* (Heidelberg: Winter), pp. 239–56.

Hughes, J. 2017. *Votive Body Parts in Greek and Roman Religion* (Cambridge: Cambridge University Press).

Jones, B. 2019. *Ariadne's Threads: The Construction and Significance of Clothes in the Aegean Bronze Age* (Leuven: Peeters).

Kaplan, P. 2006. 'Dedications to Greek Sanctuaries by Foreign Kings in the Eighth through Sixth Centuries BCE', *Historia*, 55.2: 129–52.

Kinderlen, M. and V. M. Strocka (eds). 2005. *Die Götter beschenken: Antike Weihegaben aus der Antikensammlung der Staatlichen Museen zu Berlin* (Munich: Biering & Brinkmann).

Kissas, K. and others. 2017. 'Die Grabungskampagnen 2014 und 2015 in Archaia Pheneos', *Jahreshefte des Österreichischen Archäologischen Institutes in Wien*, 86: 149–73.

Klinger, S. 2021. *The Sanctuary of Demeter and Kore: Miscellaneous Finds of Terracotta*, Corinth, 18.8 (Princeton: American School of Classical Studies at Athens).

Knappett, C. 2012. 'Meaning in Miniature: Semiotic Networks in Material Culture', in N. Johannsen, H. J. Jensen, and M. D. Jessen (eds), *Excavating the Mind: Cross Sections through Culture, Cognition and Materiality* (Aarhus: Aarhus University Press), pp. 87–109.

Kolia, E. 2011. 'A Sanctuary of the Geometric Period in Ancient Helike, Achaea', *The Annual of the British School at Athens*, 106: 201–46.

——. 2017. 'The Archaic and Classical Sanctuary at Marmara in Aigeira', in H. Frielinghaus and J. Stroszeck (eds), *Kulte und Heiligtümer in Griechenland* (Möhnesee: Bibliopolis), pp. 97–117.

Kotitsa, Z. 2003. 'Verzinnte Keramik aus Makedonien: Wahrer Luxus oder billige Imitation?', in B. Schmaltz and M. Söldner (eds), *Griechische Keramik im kulturellen Kontext: Akten des Internationalen Vasen-Symposions in Kiel vom 24. bis 28.9.2001* (Münster: Scriptorium), pp. 70–73.

Krumme, M. 2006. 'Trapezomata – Bleimodell eines Tisches aus Milet', in R. Biering and others (eds), *Maiandros: Festschrift für Volkmar von Graeve* (Munich: Biering & Brinkmann), pp. 181–90.

Kyrieleis, H. 1993. 'The Heraion at Samos', in N. Marinatos and R. Hägg (eds), *Greek Sanctuaries: New Approaches* (London: Routledge), pp. 88–122.

Lather, A. 2021. *Materiality and Aesthetics in Archaic and Classical Poetry* (Edinburgh: Edinburgh University Press).

Lindenlauf, A. 2006. 'Recycling of Votive Offerings in Greek Sanctuaries. Epigraphical and Archaeological Evidence', in C. C. Mattusch, A. A. Donohue, and A. Brauer (eds), *Common Ground: Archaeology, Art, Science, and Humanities; Proceedings of the XVIth International Congress of Classical Archaeology* (Oxford: Oxbow), pp. 30–32.

Luce, J.-M. 2011. 'From Miniature Objects to Giant Ones: The Process of Defunctionalisation in Sanctuaries and Graves in Iron Age Greece', *Pallas*, 86: 53–73.

Mitsopoulou, C. 2011. 'The Eleusinian Processional Cult Vessel: Iconographic Evidence and Interpretation', in M. Haysom and J. E. Wallensten (eds), *Current Approaches to Religion in Ancient Greece: Papers Presented at a Symposium at the Swedish Institute at Athens, 17–19 April 2008*, Skrifter utgivna av Svenska institutet i Athen, 8.21 (Stockholm: Svenska institutet i Athen), pp. 190–226.

Naiden, F. S. 2013. *Smoke Signals for the Gods: Ancient Greek Sacrifice from the Archaic through Roman Periods* (Oxford: Oxford University Press).

Nielsen, T. and J. Roy. 2009. 'The Peloponnese', in K. A. Raaflaub and H. van Wees (eds), *A Companion to Archaic Greece* (Chichester: Wiley-Blackwell), pp. 255–72.

Osborne, R. 2004. 'Hoards, Votives, Offerings: The Archaeology of the Dedicated Object', *World Archaeology*, 36: 1–10.

Pakkanen, P. 2015. 'Depositing Cult. Considerations on What Makes a Cult Deposit', in P. Pakkanen and S. Bocher (eds), *Cult Material from Archaeological Deposits to Interpretation of Early Greek Religion*, Papers and Monographs of the Finnish Institute at Athens, 21 (Helsinki: Suomen Ateenan-instituutin), pp. 25–48.

Panagiotaki, M. 1993. 'The Temple Repositories of Knossos: New Information from the Unpublished Notes of Sir Arthur Evans', *The Annual of the British School at Athens*, 88: 49–91.

——. 1999. *The Central Palace Sanctuary at Knossos*, British School at Athens, Supplementary Volume, 31 (London: British School at Athens).

Pemberton, E. 2020. 'Small and Miniature Vases at Ancient Corinth', *Hesperia*, 89: 281–338.

Pilz, O. 2011. 'The Uses of Small Things and the Semiotics of Greek Miniature Objects', *Pallas*, 86: 15–30 <https://doi.org/10.4000/pallas.2068>.

——. 2012. 'Griechische Miniaturobjekte als kommunikative und indexikalische Zeichen', in A. Frings, A. Linsenmann, and S. Weber (eds), *Vergangenheiten auf der Spur: Indexikalische Semiotik in den historischen Kulturwissenschaften* (Bielefeld: transcript), pp. 149–71 <https://doi.org/10.14361/transcript.9783839421505.149>.

——. 2020. *Kulte und Heiligtümer in Elis und Triphylien: Untersuchungen zur Sakraltopographie der westlichen Peloponnes* (Berlin: De Gruyter).

Philipp, H. 1981. *Bronzeschmuck aus Olympia*, Olympische Forschungen, 13 (Berlin: De Gruyter).

Primavera, M. and others. 2019. 'Inside Sacrificial Cakes: Plant Components and Production Processes of Food Offerings at the Demeter and Persephone Sanctuary of Monte Papalucio (Oria, Southern Italy)', *Archaeological and Anthropological Sciences*, 11.4: 1273–87 <https://doi.org/10.3390/arts9020065>.

Rogers, D. 2020. 'The Hanging Garlands of Pompeii: Mimetic Acts of Ancient Lived Religion', *Arts*, 9.2: 65 <https://doi.org/10.3390/arts9020065>.

Rouse, W. H. D. 1902. *Greek Votive Offerings: An Essay in the History of Greek Religion* (Cambridge: Cambridge University Press).

Rumscheid, F. 1994. *Untersuchungen zur kleinasiatischen Bauornamentik des Hellenismus* (Mainz: Von Zabern).

Salapata, G. 2011. 'The More the Better? Votive Offerings in Sets', in A. Mackay (ed.), *ASCS 32 Selected Proceedings*, pp. 1–10 <http://ascs.org.au/news/ascs32/Salapata.pdf> [accessed 12 February 2023].

——. 2018. 'Tokens of Piety. Inexpensive Dedications as Functional and Symbolic Objects', *Opuscula*, 11: 97–109.

Sassu, R. 2010. 'Sanctuary and Economics. The Case of the Athenian Acropolis', *Mediterraneo antico*, 13: 247–62.

Schattner, T. and G. Zuchtriegel. 2013. 'Miniaturisierte Weihgaben: Probleme der Interpretation', in I. Gerlach and D. Raue (eds), *Sanktuar und Ritual: Heilige Plätze im archäologischen Befund*, Menschen, Kulturen, Traditionen, 10 (Rahden: Leidorf), pp. 259–65.

Schauer, C. 2001. 'Zur frühen Keramik aus dem Artemisheiligtum von Lousoi', in V. Mitsopoulos-Leon, C. Schauer, and W. Gauss (eds), *Forschungen in der Peloponnes: Akten des Symposions anlässlich der Feier '100 Jahre Österreichisches Archäologisches Institut Athen', Athen 5.3.–7.3.1998* (Athens: Österreichisches Archäologisches Institut), pp. 155–59.

Snodgrass, A. 2006. 'The Economics of Dedication at Greek Sanctuaries', in A. Snodgrass, *Archaeology and the Emergence of Ancient Greece and Related Topics (1965–2002)* (Edinburgh: Edinburgh University Press), pp. 258–68.

Stähli, A. 2014. 'Sprechende Gegenstände', in R. Bielfeldt (ed.), *Ding und Mensch in der Antike: Gegenwart und Vergegenwärtigung* (Heidelberg: Winter), pp. 113–41.

Steiner, D. T. 2003. *Images in Mind* (Princeton: Princeton University Press).

Straten, F. T. van. 1981. 'Gifts for the Gods', in H. S. Versnel (ed.), *Faith, Hope and Worship: Aspects of Religious Mentality in the Ancient World* (Leiden: Brill), pp. 65–151.

——. 1987. 'Greek Sacrificial Representations: Livestock Prices and Religious Mentality', in T. Linders and G. C. Nordquist (eds), *Gifts to the Gods: Proceedings of the Uppsala Symposium 1985*, Boreas: Uppsala Studies in Ancient Mediterranean and Near Eastern Civilizations, 15 (Stockholm: Almqvist & Wiksell), pp. 159–70.

——. 1992. 'Votives and Votaries in Greek Sanctuaries', in A. Schachter (ed.), *Le sanctuaire grec: huit exposés suivis de discussions* (Geneva: Fondation Hardt), pp. 247–90.

——. 1995. *Hiera kala: Images of Animal Sacrifice in Archaic and Classical Greece*, Religions in the Graeco-Roman World, 127 (New York: Brill).

Tournavitou, I. 2009. 'Does Size Matter? Miniature Pottery Vessels in Minoan Peak Sanctuaries', in A. L. D'Agata and A. Van de Moortel (eds), *Archaeologies of Cult: Essays on Ritual and Cult in Crete in Honor of Geraldine C. Gesell*, Hesperia Supplement, 42 (Princeton: American School of Classical Studies at Athens), pp. 213–21.

Umholtz, G. 2002. 'Architraval Arrogance? Dedicatory Inscriptions in Greek Architecture of the Classical Period', *Hesperia*, 71: 261–93.

Vickers, M. 1998. *Skeuomorphismus oder die Kunst, aus wenig viel zu machen*, Trierer Winckelmannsprogramme, 16 (Mainz: Von Zabern).

Vlachou, A. 2017. 'Ritual Practices in Early Iron Age and Early Archaic Peloponnese', in A. Mazarakis-Ainian, A. Alexandridou, and X. Charalambidou (eds), *Regional Stories: Toward a New Perspective of the Early Greek World* (Volos: University of Thessaly Press), pp. 249–78.

Vlachou, V. 2017. 'Pottery Made to Impress: Oversized Vessels for Funerary Rituals. A View from Geometric Attica and Beyond', in V. Vlachou and A. Gadolou (eds), *Τέρψις/Terpsis: Studies in Mediterranean Archaeology in Honour of Nota Kourou*, Études d'archéologie, 10 (Brussels: CReA-Patrimoine), pp. 191–207.

Vlizos, E. 2017. 'Das Heiligtum und seine Weihgaben. Bronzestatuetten aus dem Amyklaion', in H. Frielinghaus and J. Stroszeck (eds), *Kulte und Heiligtümer in Griechenland* (Möhnesee: Bibliopolis), pp. 71–95.

Völling, T. 2002. 'Weihungen in griechischen Heiligtümern am Beispiel des Artemisheiligtums von Kombothekra und des Zeusheiligtums von Olympia', in L. Zemmer-Plank (ed.), *Kult der Vorzeit in den Alpen*, I (Bozen: Verlagsanstalt Athesia), pp. 83–111.

Waldstein, C. 1905. *The Argive Heraeum*, II (Boston: Houghton).

MONUMENTALIZATION

6. Scaling Altars in the Etruscan Funerary Sphere

Diana Pavel

An array of altars relevant to analyses on the Etruscan funerary sphere has been discovered in connection to specific funerary constructions, particularly in association with either tumuli or chamber tombs.[1] These altars suggest the unfolding of specific rituals in honour of the recently deceased and in commemoration of the deified ancestors.[2] They show a great amount of variety in the creation of the spatial ceremonial settings, as well as in architectural type or size. The scale of these ritual objects can range between what could be, at a first glance, categorized as 'miniaturized' altars measuring only 23 cm high (Fosso Arlena) to what could be seen as 'monumentalized' structures reaching heights of up to 2 m (Grotta Porcina). The aim of this paper is to explore the interplay of dimensions between these altars and their corresponding spatial contexts, further reflecting how such vastly differentiated sizes could have impacted the social sphere of the worshippers and how they informed the bodily behaviour of the worshippers performing ritual actions at these altars.

The preservation of stone-built or rock-cut altars throughout Etruria represents the visible dimension of the phenomenon of altar-based rituals;[3] they are thus the main starting point for such an inquiry. The diversity of these altars has already been acknowledged through the proposal of a series of typologies based on their architectural types,[4] as well as based on their 'functionality',[5] which can further emphasize the complex phenomenon presented by these altars. It is not only through their material characteristics that they provide different parameters for the occurrence of rituals, but also through the creation of various spatial configurations associated with them. This leads to the specificity of the connection between the material and spatial parameters and the development of the socio-religious practices happening at the altar. These observations can also be applied to the altars associated with the funerary sphere.

Throughout Etruria, altars have been mainly linked to two different contexts, either to the sphere of the sanctuaries or to the funerary realm. However, an analysis with a focus on the spatial contextualization of altars shows that a definitive and strict differentiation of space between the two spheres, as well as its application onto the nature of the altar-based practices, cannot be acknowledged as such in the Etruscan world. This is particularly evidenced by the existence of sanctuaries within the necropoleis themselves or in their

---

[1] This article was written in the framework of the International Graduate School 'Resonant Self–World Relations in Ancient and Modern Socio-religious Practices', based at the Universities of Erfurt and Graz (IRT 2283).

[2] For overviews concerning the ancestor cult in Etruria, see in particular Camporeale 2009 and Prayon 2006.

[3] Acknowledging also the 'unseen' and unpreserved dimension of this phenomenon within the archaeological record, surrounding the altars made out of perishable materials.

[4] Menichelli 2009, 108–10 proposes ten architectonic types of Etruscan altars, namely the altars *ad antas*, stepped, rectangular, square, T-shaped, circular, rubble mounds, single block with circular base, single block with quadrangular base, and the terrace altar. See also Steingräber and Menichelli 2010.

[5] Steingräber 1982, 113–14 proposes three different types of altars, the 'Brandopferaltäre', the 'Grabopferaltäre und Opfertische/-platten', and the 'Durchbohrte Altäre und Altäre mit Opferschacht für chthonische Kulte'. Although I do not agree with such a strict differentiation that is based on the supposed predominance of one activity to be conducted at an altar and linked with the type of deity addressed at the altar, brought together under the criterion of 'functionality', and also considering the range of possible activities to be performed at an altar, these typologies do highlight the variety of altars discovered throughout Etruria.

Figure 6.1. Tomb of the Typhon, Monterozzi necropolis, Tarquinia. Painted facsimile (1911–1912) of Elio D'Alessandris with one of the renditions concerning the painting present on the altar. From the Collezione Acquerelli del Museo delle Antichità Etrusche e Italiche della Sapienza Università di Roma (no. 6354), reproduced by permission of the museum <https://web.uniroma1.it/polomuseale/node/6354> [accessed 12 February 2023].

close vicinity — 'santuari nelle necropoli' as they are called by G. Colonna,[6] or the 'extra-mural and extra-urban road sanctuaries with a funerary connection' described by I. Edlund.[7] These cases include, for example, the Cannicella sanctuary at Volsinii, which seems to have been integrated into the necropolis from its inception during the sixth century BC.[8] At Vulci, three small temples have also been found in an association with the necropoleis of Polledrara and Ponte Rotto, and at Chiusi, a small temple was integrated within the necropolis at Colle del Vescovo.[9] The religious complex at Montetosto, on the route from Caere to Pyrgi, is represented by a sanctuary situated in the adjacent area of a monumental tumulus measuring 60 m in diameter.[10]

In addition to the complexity brought forward by the spatial overlaps, another issue arises in the consideration of the otherworldly addressees associated with the altar-based practices happening in the 'funerary' sphere. In this regard, it is also plausible to assume that gods and goddesses with apotropaic or infernal attributes might have been the addressed recipients of such practices, and not limit the use of altars to the communication with the deified ancestors. This appears to be the case of the Tomb of the Typhon at the Monterozzi necropolis in Tarquinia. According to M. Cristofani, the inscription on the main pillar of the tomb — in front of which an altar was situated — suggests the possible existence of specific funerary rituals addressed to the god Tina.[11] Another very interesting inscription has been found on the walls of a passageway dug underneath the ramp going to the top of the Tumulus of the Crosses from the Banditaccia necropolis in Caere. It is assumed that funerary ceremonies took place on the top of this tumulus dated to the Orientalizing period.[12] The inscription presents the name of a series of deities, including the goddess Vei, who here receives the epiclesis *ati* ('mother'), the god Aita, and perhaps the god Tina.[13] Another very

---

[6] Colonna 1985, 116.

[7] Edlund 1987, 69–72.

[8] Roncalli 1987, 49.

[9] Colonna 1985, 116.

[10] Belelli Marchesini, Biella, and Michetti 2015.

[11] Cristofani 1969, 239.

[12] Bagnasco Gianni 2019, 17–18.

[13] It seems that the name of the god Tina appears as such within the first writing of the inscription, but this is changed at a later time through the addition of the morpheme *-sask-* to mean 'the place/

interesting epigraphic document in this regard is represented by the Lead Plaque of Magliano, dated to the fifth century BC, said to refer to a series of ritual practices that also took place at 'the monument of the deceased' and at a tomb of the Murina family.[14] According to L. B. van der Meer, the inscription might have stemmed from a sanctuary in the vicinity of a necropolis.[15] The addressed recipients of practices seem to include deities such as Suri, Ca(u)tha, Tin(a), Maris, and Lur, but also the ancestors.[16] This once again shows that a dichotomic approach might not have been perceived as such by the Etruscan communities of worshippers.[17]

Acknowledging therefore the complexity and diversity present in the archaeological record and proposing caution in clear associations of altars with contexts and addressed deities, the current paper will nonetheless follow the spatial criterion as a starting point for reflection in pursuit of the proposed themes. The altars discussed in the following present spatial connections to either tombs or to the more general context of the necropoleis, and such associations will be analysed, also in consideration of how these might have impacted the worshippers on a social level.

Spatial Configurations and the Scale of Altars

In order to focus on the scale of these altars in association with the funerary sphere, an important precondition is to analyse the spatial parameters that these altars are connected to. The scale of the altars, as well as their predetermined placement at the initiative of a social agent, were crucial in further influencing the unfolding and development of ritual practices, especially taking into account aspects such as visibility or accessibility. With regard to prehistoric monuments, F. Criado Boado suggests:

---

land beyond Tina' (Bagnasco Gianni 2019, 19).

[14] Van der Meer 2013, 337–38.

[15] Van der Meer 2013, 324.

[16] Van der Meer 2013, 337–38.

[17] Among other attested deities that seem to be mentioned in the context of tombs are also Suri (and possibly Vanth), as appears on a curse tablet from a tomb dated to the second half of the sixth century BC from Poggio Gaiella in Chiusi (Maras 2009, Cl sa.1), or Cavatha (appearing under the name *kavϑa*) on a vase from the San Cerbone necropolis in Populonia, dated to the first half of the fifth century (Maras 2009, Po do.1). These two deities, Suri and Cavatha, are generally recognized as having infernal attributes and also seem to be worshipped as such at the Southern Sanctuary of Pyrgi (Colonna 2006, 139–41).

The study of the location pattern of the monuments and their conditions of visibility, particularly of the visual catchments that they generate, and visibilisation, particularly how they are made out at a distance, will allow us to recognize, if they indeed exist, the regularities that show the will and intentional strategy to make a monument perceptible, underline its presence and provoke dramatic artificial effects in relation to it.[18]

This line of investigation will help to explore the desired effects imposed by the scale of the altars, in accordance with the spatial configurations and with how these altars could have been perceived within their contexts.

Taking into account the relation of these altars to their connecting or neighbouring tombs — particularly tumuli and chamber tombs — or in connection with the necropolis space itself, the diversity of spatial configurations allows for a differentiation to be made in this sense. The following overview does not aim to present an exhaustive approach, but rather focuses on a selection of relevant altars that allow for an ampler discussion concerning both the choice of scale and whether such decisions on behalf of the agents commissioning such constructions could be linked to specific spatial configurations.

A first spatial type refers to altars included within the tombs themselves, as exemplified by the altar of the Tomb of the Typhon from the Monterozzi necropolis, Tarquinia, dated to the second half of the third century BC (Fig. 6.1).[19] The altar, measuring 2.00 by 1.00 m and 1.50 m high, is positioned in the centre of the funerary chamber, and is placed in front of a painted pillar with an inscription said to describe funerary rituals and perhaps also specificities regarding the cult of the ancestors of the Pumpu family that owned the tomb.[20] The altar was located opposite the *dromos*, and it was therefore deliberately made visible from the entrance of the tomb. Another altar within the same spatial type was found in the Campana 1 Tomb of the Monte Abatone necropolis at Caere, dated to the third quarter of the seventh century BC. This altar, measuring 1.15 by 0.44 m and 1.13 m high, was cut out of the rock and placed in the main funerary chamber leading from the *dromos*, although this was obscured from view from the outside by being placed in the right corner of the room, at the entrance wall. In two other cases, an altar was included within one

---

[18] Criado Boado, Estévez, and Vázquez 2001, 169.

[19] The chronological dating of the tomb follows Steingräber 2006.

[20] Cristofani 1969; Morandi Tarabella 2004, 400.

of the lateral rooms from the *dromos*. In the Cima tomb, dated to the third quarter of the seventh century BC, an altar — preserved now only through its base — was centred and visible from the *dromos*, whereas in the Tomb of the Five Chairs (second half of the seventh century BC), an altar measuring 0.60 by 0.25 m and 0.40 m high was deliberately uncentred and hidden from view. Within this last tomb it seems that another possible altar was placed in the room to the right of the *dromos*, in a position replicating the one of the altar from the left room and, once again, being deliberately hidden from view. According to the data provided by F. Prayon, this structure measures 0.71 by 1.30 m and is 0.84 m high.[21]

The overall visibility of the altar in these cases was probably reduced during the occurrence of specific ceremonies within the tombs, given the usually small dimensions of these chambers and the frequently 'downsized' dimensions of the altars, to impose a certain bodily behaviour on the worshipper using it, such as bowing down. This type of spatial configuration might have led to creating a structuring of the audience between the members who had access inside the room and the others that might have been able to follow the ceremony only from the outside, from the *dromos*, without being actively engaged with the practices happening inside. Given the reduced number of people that might have had access to ceremonies at the altars sharing this spatial configuration, the embodied experience of such an audience would clearly be marked by the intrinsic nature of this closed space. This could have been further enhanced by other elements present in these rooms, such as the painted architectural elements distinguishable in the 'altar-room' of the Cima tomb.[22] The differentiation between those who could attend these ceremonies and those that did not would have been further marked by the fact that these edifices might have been closed after the initial burials, which would eliminate the possibility of accessing the altar without being permitted to do so by the ritual agents responsible for the funerary practices and for the potential commemoration ceremonies happening here. The closing of such tombs could also justify the lesser need to invest in 'monumental' altars that would require more time, cost, material, and labour-investment in order to be constructed, only for these to be abandoned after the funerary practices surrounding the burial of the deceased. The Tomb of the Five Chairs, for example, seems to present just one room, which contains only two sarcophagi, for the actual burial. Some tombs were reopened, however, as evidenced by those presenting multiple burial chambers, whereas others could have been reopened for commemorative practices. Therefore, both cases could suggest a long-term use of the altar. These altars might have also received individualized use; the reduced scale of these altars rather implies their use by one worshipper at a time, perhaps also establishing a more personal connection influenced by this smaller scale between this ritual object and the worshipper.[23]

A second type of spatial configuration of altars are those placed on top of tombs, either on top of tumuli or on top of chamber tombs, depending on the architectural predominance of one of the two types of funerary monuments in a particular chronological period or in a specific geographical area.[24] The positioning of altars on top of tombs seems to be quite a widespread phenomenon throughout the Etruscan territory, found in both southern and northern Etruria, as exemplified by the Etruscan tumulus on the Via San Jacopo in Pisa. The tumulus, dated to the seventh century BC, was surrounded by a series of stone *cippi* placed around its 30 m diameter, whereas the tomb itself seems to have presented a cenotaph of an aristocratic seafarer lost at sea.[25] The tumulus had a stone altar placed on its apex that seems to have presented relatively reduced dimensions in comparison to the diameter of the tumulus.[26] The impressive Cucumella tumulus at Vulci, dated to the seventh century BC and measuring 65 m in diameter and 18 m high,[27] also had a circular platform on top that has been interpreted as a potential altar.[28] Once again, this possible altar seems to have had rather reduced dimensions in comparison to the ample space offered by the top of the tumulus. These examples tend to show however the popularity of the placement of this kind of ritual objects on

---

21 Prayon 1975, 110 n. 608.

22 Steingräber 2009, 125.

23 Foxhall 2015, 3.

24 See, for example, the architectural evolution observable within the Banditaccia necropolis at Caere from the tumuli of the seventh and first half of the sixth centuries BC to the new tombs, the *tombe a dado* (cube tombs), of the second half of the sixth century BC onwards, as observable on the so-called Via dei Monti Ceriti or Via dei Monti della Tolfa.

25 Van der Meer 2011, 53–54.

26 See Bruni 1998, 106 for a short discussion on the altar and Bruni 1998, figs 26–28 for the relevant images of the discoveries on top of the tumulus; the dimensions of the partially demolished altar are not provided.

27 Steingräber 1981, 192.

28 Sgubini Moretti 1994, 32 n. 115.

top of the funerary construction, indicating the presence of ritual practices occurring in these delimited places. The Terrone tumulus from Blera, dated to the second half of the sixth century BC and measuring 16 m in diameter, presents an altar of impressive dimensions built on top. The altar is represented by a circular arrangement measuring 7.15 m in diameter, made out of two rings of blocks of tuff stone: an inner ring whose traces regarding the placement of stones seem to attest that it had at least two levels in height, and an outer ring whose blocks of stone might have presented mouldings.[29] An altar placed on top of a rectangular architectural complex, originally interpreted as a tomb and more recently as a cult complex constituted of banqueting halls,[30] was discovered in the Castro necropolis at Vulci. The altar had a rectangular shape and measured 12.8 m long and a possible 6.0 m wide and is dated (as is the complex itself) to the second half of the sixth century BC. The Grotta Pinta tomb from the Casetta necropolis, Blera, dated to the sixth century BC, also presents a very interesting example, as the surface of the rooftop, which was accessible through a set of stairs placed on the left side of the tomb, contains particular structures and spatial arrangements pertinent to ritual practices. These include two recesses for *cippi*, and a bench — perhaps a bench-altar — from which a drainage channel stems. The drainage channel, dug parallel to the stairs, further connected to the drainage system of the necropolis.[31] This could point to acts of libation or perhaps even animal sacrifices being performed here.

Most altars built on top of tombs represented imposing structures and had impressive dimensions, as is the case of the Terrone tumulus or of the Castro complex. In these cases, the relation between altars and space shows a mutual influence in the shapes and forms that the altars had taken in order to fit on top of these structures, which would of course influence the spatial parameters of the rituals taking place here. These oversized altars situated on top of these constructions intended to show a high degree of visibility meant not only for the attendees of specific practices conducted here, who might have attended from this upper level or from below, but also for passers-by, who could acknowledge the ceremonies happening here despite the visibility hindrance produced by viewing from ground level. The visibility of these altars would of course also depend on the height they were situated on, from the higher degree of visibility from ground level provided by the Terrone tumulus, whose total height is estimated at 4.5 m, to the rather invisible dimensions of the Cuccumella tumulus at Vulci, which measured up to 18 m high.[32] The accessibility of these places, provided by ramps (particularly in the case of tumuli) or by stairs dug into the rock on a lateral side of the tomb (specifically for the cube tombs), was on a general level quite restrictive, possibly reserved to members of the family or to the *gens* of the deceased. Still, not all altars on top of tombs presented such impressive sizes, as seems to be the case for the Grotta Pinta tomb or the Cuccumella tumulus. The scale of the altars would therefore primarily depend on the intentions of the commissioner of these projects and on the intended degree of visibility of practices conducted here. Some might have been deliberately obscured and might have attracted the attention of passers-by through the other senses (sounds, smoke, and so on), whereas others might have been specifically made visible as a mechanism to attract attention. Overall, this type of spatial parameters seems to suggest a wider intended attendance for these practices than might have been possible for rituals happening within the tombs themselves.

A third category regarding the spatial configuration of altars in connection with the funerary sphere is represented by altars placed outside tombs, in their close vicinity and in a rather strict relation to them. This is exemplified by an altar found in the Fosso Arlena necropolis dated to the end of the seventh or beginning of the sixth century BC. The altar was placed in front of a *fossa* tomb and a funerary stele, a complex that could have been easily accessible and visible within the necropolis, although the altar presents rather reduced dimensions at 0.23 by 0.37 m and 0.23 m high. A comparative example can be found at the Necropoli del Cavone di Monte li Santi in Narce, where an altar was placed in a central position within an open-air square to which at least three tombs were connected; furthermore, the altar was aligned with the entrance to one of the tombs, Tomba B.[33] The altar has a rectangular base measuring *c.* 1.20 m wide and a preserved height of 0.60 m.

The open space of the necropoleis would in theory allow for ample ceremonies to occur at the altars here while also providing sufficient space for different activities to be performed, particularly those that might need a larger amount of space, such as dancing. The prevalence of collective practices, however, should not be

---

[29] Ricciardi 1990, 151.
[30] Steingräber 1982, 107.
[31] Ricciardi 1987, 55.

[32] Steingräber 1981, 192.
[33] De Lucia Brolli and others 2016, 24–25.

taken for granted. Individualized uses of these altars for the deposition of offerings or the pouring of libations, for example, or for acts such as praying, might have been just as plausible, and this once again seems to be encouraged by the material affordances of the altars themselves. The small dimensions of the altar from the Fosso Arlena necropolis might further emphasize its use by one person at a time. Individualized practices at the altar might be further implied in accordance with the iconographic material, where depictions of individuals either stepping on the altar or bowing down in front of the altar and placing small offerings or pouring libations also occur. A fifth-century BC relief on a funerary stele from Marzabotto presents a female worshipper stepping on an altar and seemingly performing a libation,[34] whereas a fourth-century BC mirror engraving presents a satyr bowing down in front of an altar and placing an undetermined object into the fire of the altar.[35]

A fourth spatial configuration is represented by altars placed within specific complexes in connection with the necropoleis, differentiating itself from the former type through the specific markings delimiting the relevant space for practices from the general area of the necropolis. This is the case of the Grotta Porcina complex, dated to the first half of the sixth century BC. Within the necropolis and situated 85 m away from the Ruota di Grotta Porcina tumulus, an open-air area presents a stepped, structured space interpreted as a 'theatre-form structure' dug into the local rock and whose focus was a circular altar measuring 6.2 m in diameter and an estimated 2 m in height.[36] In the case of the Cima tumulus, the main tomb of which also contained an altar within the left room from the *dromos*, a special complex was found in its vicinity on the eastern side and in association with it. According to S. Steingräber, this potentially coeval area to the tumulus consisted of a special platform measuring *c.* 9.0 by 3.50 m, upon which a series of nine *cippi* were placed on the northern row and eight on the southern one. In the centre of the southern row, a circular indentation measuring *c.* 2.0 m in diameter was interpreted to suggest the presence of a circular altar here.[37]

These cases therefore reflect both a distinctively marked spatial separation within the area of the necropolis and an intentional selection of space to distinguish itself from the neighbouring funerary structures. Although the area of the altar is at a certain distance from the tomb itself, this does not mean that ceremonies in honour of the deceased or commemorating the ancestors only happened in these separate spaces, but only that these represented just one of the spatial arrangements where ceremonies of a funerary nature could have taken place. Both the Grotta Porcina and the Cima complexes most likely also presented spaces for the unfolding of ritual practices on top of the tumuli,[38] whereas in the case of the Cima tumulus, an altar is also placed within one of the tombs, as discussed above. This would therefore point to other reasons behind placing such a complex ceremonial space outside the tomb area — most likely in order to increase the number of participants present at these collective practices, since only a restricted number might have been able to access the altars either within the tombs or on top of them. The presence of these altar-connected complexes in the vicinity of the tumuli suggests the involvement of an elite family, which most probably also owned the tumulus in question, and its desire to strengthen the family bond, as well as showing through this expenditure the power and prestige of the family. In this sense, the impressive dimensions of these altars might have contributed by having such a desired effect on a social level.

In piecing together not only the dimensions of the altars but also the variety of spatial configurations associated with them, it seems that there is no recognizable pattern concerning the selection of scale of an altar and a certain type of spatial configuration. As a result, it can be implied that this selection might have remained a deliberate choice left to the initiative of the agents that commissioned the construction of such ritual objects in connection with the tombs. This would subsequently lead to differently conveyed messages impacting the socio-

---

[34] Colonna 1985, 44.

[35] *CSE* Vaticano I, no. 6.

[36] Other similar displays of stepped structures, although not presenting signs of an altar in their surroundings, can also be found in the *dromos* of the Avvolta tumulus in Tarquinia, which opens up in a square surrounded on three sides by a terraced structure comprised of two steps (Colonna 1993, 323–24), as well as at the Cuccumella tumulus in Vulci, where the rectangular vestibule to one of the tombs is surrounded by a series of three steps on the two long sides and seven steps on the side of the *dromos* (Colonna 1993, 328–31). These also might suggest the participation of a seated audience at funerary ritual taking place in these spatially designed areas. Whereas these two tumuli are dated to the seventh–sixth centuries BC, stepped structures seem to be found in Etruria in both funerary- and sanctuary-related contexts from this chronological horizon up until the Hellenistic period (Camporeale 2009, 229).

[37] Steingräber 2009, 128. Diameter reconstructed from the archaeological plan present in Steingräber 2009, fig. 31.

[38] Grotta Porcina: Steingräber 1981, 351; Cima: Steingräber 2009, 131.

religious practices developed at these altars, particularly regarding aspects such as accessibility and visibility on a social level and perhaps consequently also the perceived efficacy, or lack thereof, of the communication process with the otherworldly addressees enabled through the use of the altar.

The altars within tombs present a range of dimensions — from the smaller one included in the Tomb of the Five Chairs (0.40 m high) to the altar from the Tomb of the Typhon (1.50 m high) — suggesting that these did not all present downsized dimensions that might have been linked to symbolic purposes rather than functional uses. On the contrary, despite the smaller scale of these ritual objects, which was of course also influenced by the available space, their use might be suggested by the particular care to incorporate cavities, *cupellae*, or small channels on their upper surfaces, as at the Campana 1 Tomb. This shows that, when one tries to examine them through the perspective of miniatures, they were not rendered to present a clear loss of the original function of these objects.[39] The constant reburials visible in some of these tombs might also further attest to the use of the altars, as in the case of the Tomb of the Typhon. In this tomb, the sarcophagi of the deceased that were placed on the three-tiered benches surrounding the main burial chamber are dated from the middle of the second century BC to the first century BC,[40] attesting to the continued use of this tomb and perhaps of the altar itself.

At the same time, not all altars outside tombs or on top of tombs were oversized to provide a higher degree of visibility for large audiences and ample ceremonies, even if such practices seem to be attested. The Grotta Porcina altar represented the focus of socio-religious practices conducted here through the spatial configuration of the stepped structure surrounding it, but also through its impressive size (2.0 m high). The altar, therefore, might have been visible not only for a seated audience but also for more distant spectators, who might not have been in a position of authority to take part in such a formation but rather served as a standing audience. In this case and in the case of the altars of impressive dimensions situated on top of tombs (Terrone tumulus), which also might have been acknowledged from below, the visibility aspects were one of the main intended outcomes of the choices of agents initiating their construction. The Fosso Arlena altar, which overall presents even smaller dimensions than the one included in the Tomb of the Five Chairs, and the smaller altars placed on top of tombs, such as at the Grotta Pinta tomb or at the Cuccumella tumulus, seem to have deliberately been rather obscured from view given their dimensions, enhancing the aspects of seclusion and privacy of the practices conducted here.

Interplay of Scales: 'Miniaturizing' and 'Monumentalizing' the Altar

The previous section of the paper has focused on presenting a brief analysis of the different contexts with which the altars can be associated in the funerary realm and on showing the differences in scale that these altars seem to provide within each type of spatial configuration. There are, however, two main issues when discussing these altars. The first is the precarious archaeological preservation of some of these ritual objects, which leads to undeterminable estimates of their dimensions. The second issue is the lack of archaeological documentation in what concerns some of these altars; the dimensions of these altars are not always provided, and certain aspects, particularly their (preserved) heights, are frequently overlooked. In order to offer a more detailed analysis of the phenomena of 'miniaturization' and 'monumentalization' of altars, I have chosen three examples to use as reflection points, since they present cases of 'undersized' and 'oversized' altars that are better researched and that can therefore be used for a more fruitful investigation: the altars from the Fosso Arlena necropolis, from the Tomb of the Five Chairs, and from the stepped area of Grotta Porcina. This analysis will also lead to further reflections regarding the scale of the altars and their impact upon humans, particularly how these altars might have been perceived and what influences they might have had on the worshippers.

'Miniaturizing' the Altar: The Case Studies of Fosso Arlena and Tomb of the Five Chairs

At a distance of 5 km south of the city of Bolsena, an Etruscan settlement given the name of Civita sul Fosso d'Arlena was discovered, situated on top of one of the hills of the area. This settlement was surrounded by a defensive wall and presents traces of houses, as well as a temple dated to the fifth century BC.[41] The findings within the settlement suggest that it had been occupied

---

[39] See Foxhall 2015, 2.
[40] Cristofani 1969, 243.

[41] See Bloch 1955. For arguments against identifying this structure as a temple, but rather as a domestic architectural complex, see Tamburini 2013, 164–65.

from the seventh century BC up until the fourth century BC.[42] In the vicinity of the settlement to the south-east, the necropolis of Fosso d'Arlena is present on one of the adjacent hills, with its earliest burials also dated in correspondence to the city to the seventh century BC. Chamber tombs seem to be predominant within the necropolis, the majority built between the seventh and the sixth centuries BC. The funerary inventory of the uncovered tombs seems to attest to a predominance of locally produced objects, particularly *impasto* and *bucchero* vases.[43] Among these discoveries within the necropolis, a small altar present in front of a *fossa* tomb was found.[44] The *fossa* tomb was, however, ransacked and at the moment of discovery presented only traces of bucchero and *impasto* fragments.[45] Between the altar and the tomb, a stele was present, now damaged and split into two parts. The altar would have been highly accessible, given its position outside in the necropolis and visible by attracting attention through the stele, with the orientation of the altar following the position of the tomb.

The altar is dated to the end of the seventh or beginning of the sixth century BC, and it is represented by a rectangular block of sandstone measuring 0.23 by 0.37 m and 0.23 m high. On its upper surface, the altar presents three central *cupellae* that are linked with small channels going to the back. Accompanying these is a series of smaller *cupellae* placed on the outer sides of the upper surface of the altar, with four towards the front side and two towards the back side.[46] On the front side of the altar, two ovoidal recesses are sculpted within the altar. The characteristics of the altar, particularly the presence of the *cupellae* on its upper side, have been interpreted as allowing two different kinds of activities to be performed. The central *cupellae* have been associated with the pouring of liquids, liquid that would then flow through the small, adjoining drainage channels towards the back side of the altar onto the ground and towards the tomb, respectively; the smaller *cupellae* on the outer side of the upper surface of the altar would be used for solid offerings.[47] The two recesses on the front side of the altar have been interpreted differently by researchers, with G. Colonna suggesting that the two recesses replicate the mobility characteristic of a portable wooden altar,[48] whereas R. Bloch and A. Pfiffig see the two shapes as a depiction of the gates connected to the underworld.[49]

On the right side of the altar, there are two inscriptions, with different styles of writing that seem to attest to two different chronological periods. The oldest inscription, dated to the end of the seventh or beginning of the sixth century BC, from right to left reads *aratiia*[---], whereas the more recent one, dated to the second half of the sixth century BC, from left to right reads *far(ϑ)*.[50] The two inscriptions have been analysed by G. Colonna, who proposes the connection of the word *aratiia* [---] with the male name Arat(h) in genitive form, that was possibly followed by the gentilicial name of the person, now lost;[51] the later inscription of *farϑ* has been associated with the Latin Genius, referring to the 'progenitor' or ancestor of the family. The addition of the second inscription has been interpreted as a rededication addressed to the deceased, who had at this moment received the attribute of ancestor of the family.[52] A second translation and interpretation of the inscription is brought forward by D. F. Maras, suggesting that the text could refer instead to the *numen* of the god Rath, although acknowledging the differentiation in the writing styles between the two words.[53] The engraving of this second inscription at least half a century later after the initial one suggests the continuity of practices conducted in this area and in connection with the tomb of this individual that, according to one interpretation of the inscription, would (still) come to be commemorated as the ancestor of the family at least two generations after his entombment. The archaeological evidence might point therefore to a continuity of practices at this 'undersized' altar, which continued its function in enabling communication with otherworldly addressees for at least half a century after its construction. Moreover, the secondary inscription added to the altar might suggest an intentional act of perpetuation and an attempt to fix the otherworldly recipient addressed here, with

---

[42] Steingräber 1982, 297.

[43] Bloch 1955, 52.

[44] Bloch 1955, fig. 3; Pfiffig 1975, fig. 27.

[45] Pfiffig 1975, 78; Bloch 1955, 64.

[46] Bloch 1955, 64.

[47] Bloch 1955, 64.

[48] Colonna 1985, 33.

[49] Bloch 1955, 64: 'Sur sa face antérieure sont dessinées en creux deux portes, surmontées l'une d'un arc, l'autre d'un linteau, qui figurent peut-être les portes de l'Hadès.' Cf. Pfiffig 1975, 78.

[50] Colonna 1985, 33.

[51] Colonna 1985, 33.

[52] Colonna 1985, 33.

[53] For the inscription to be read instead as *flarx*[---] *ratiuuϑ* [---]: Maras 2009, 443–44, Vs in.1.

6. SCALING ALTARS IN THE ETRUSCAN FUNERARY SPHERE 95

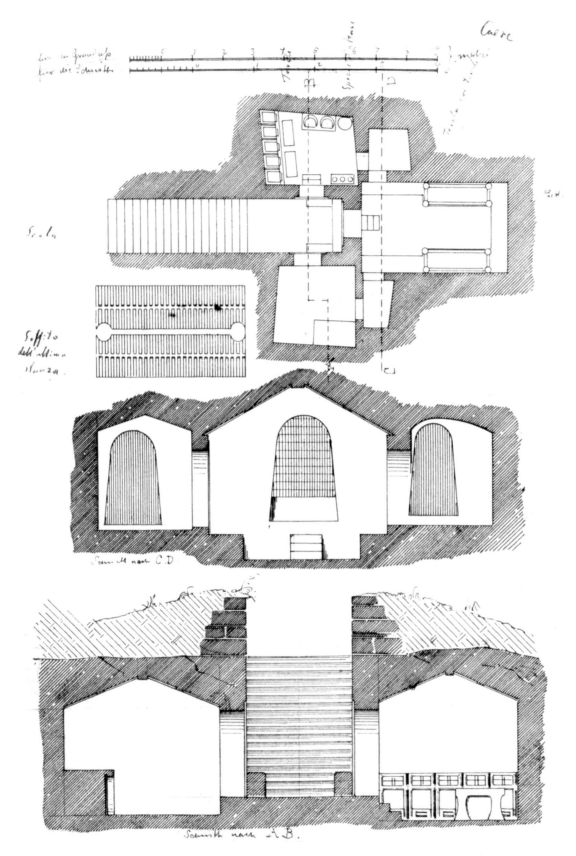

Figure 6.2. Plan of the Tomb of the Five Chairs, Banditaccia necropolis, Caere. Reproduction of a nineteenth-century drawing in possession of the German Archaeological Institute at Rome (J. Ciganovic, Neg. D-DAI-ROM 74.410R), reproduced with permission.

the deceased buried in the tomb now receiving the specific status of 'progenitor' of the family. The 'undersized' dimension of the altar does not detract therefore from its function.

In the discussion of 'undersized' altars, the comparable example of the Tomb of the Five Chairs offers a very interesting case for analysis. The Tomb of the Five Chairs, found within the Banditaccia necropolis at Caere, represents the only tomb within a tumulus that must have originally been more than 20 m in diameter and that was situated to the west of the Via Sepolcrale Principale and across from Strada Nuova. The tomb is dated to the third quarter of the seventh century BC, and it receives its name from the discovery of five statuettes placed on rock-cut chairs or thrones within one of the chambers. The tomb itself (Fig. 6.2) was accessible from a large, shared courtyard through a stepped *dromos* that led to two lateral chambers and to the main burial chamber where two funeral beds were carved out of the rock and placed on each side of the room. A bench was also running alongside the walls of the room. The lateral chambers that opened from the *dromos* are connected through small passageways to two corner chambers that lead further into the main burial chamber. The left lateral chamber is of significant interest, since it presents a unique arrangement of 'miniaturized furniture' symbolically placed for ritual practices, to include an altar.[54]

The altar is dated, as is the tomb itself, to the third quarter of the seventh century BC. The altar is carved out of the local rock and is represented by a single block with a quadrangular base. On its upper surface it presents three *cupellae* that can be associated with practices of libations or used for the deposition of offerings, including foods. The altar is 0.60 m long and 0.25 m wide, with a height of 0.40 m. The altar is located within the room on the left from the *dromos* and is situated in the south-east corner of the room, on the right side of the chamber entrance. Due to its corner position, the altar would have not been visible from outside the room, neither from the *dromos* nor from the corner chamber. The access route was most probably conducted through the *dromos*, although, as mentioned before, the room was also secondarily accessible through a passageway from the corner chamber linked to the main burial chamber. As placed within the room, the orientation of the altar would have been towards the south.

The special furnishings of the room itself seem to indicate particular funerary rituals conducted here or perhaps rather a symbolic representation of a cult instead of actual funerary practices.[55] The altar can be connected to the specific placement of five terracotta figurines of 0.50 m in height seated on five thrones present in the room. The thrones were placed in an orderly manner alongside the western wall; they were carved out of the local rock and each had a backrest with a cruciform decoration, armrests, and a footstool. Out of the five terracotta figurines, only three are still preserved, two of which can be found at the British Museum and one at the Capitoline Museum. All figurines are depicted performing the same gesture: their left arm is covered by the chequered tunic, except the hand, which is placed with the palm down onto the lap, and their right arm is stretched forward with the hand held upwards. In front of these terracotta figurines, there were two tables, perhaps meant to evoke a funerary banquet.[56] These statuettes, reconstructed to suggest the representations of three male and two female figures, have been widely interpreted as depicting the ancestors of the family and portrayed in order to welcome the recently deceased couple into the afterlife by sharing a common banquet,[57] with the couple perhaps symbolically represented by two round thrones with backrests placed on the northern side of the room.[58] Next to these thrones, placed atop a small platform, a cylindrical basket was also displayed in the north-east corner of the room. This was also carved out of rock and its upper part, today partially missing, must have had a decorative motif. If the room had a symbolic value, depicting a scene of a banquet happening at the reunion of the recently deceased and their ancestors in the afterlife, instead of allowing the undertaking of funerary ceremonies inside, then perhaps there is a complementary approach between this room and the room opposite, the one on the right side of the *dromos*. Here, there is only one structure present, a so-called 'table' carved out of the tuff stone, currently damaged, that could have been accessible during the funerary ceremony or afterwards for the deposition of offerings destined for the deceased couple.[59] Within this room, the structure seems to be placed in the south-eastern corner, suggest-

---

[54] Steingräber 1997, 101.

[55] Steingräber 1997, 102.

[56] Steingräber 1997, 101.

[57] Tuck 1994, 620. Steingräber 2016, 107 interprets their gestures to depict the figures as 'in the act of pouring libations and eating together with the tomb-founding couple buried on the stone beds in the back chamber'.

[58] Camporeale 2009, 226.

[59] Prayon 2006, 33.

ing not only similarities between its position to that of the altar, but also in regards to the intent to hide it from view, as it is just barely visible from the *dromos* and obscured from the corner room. All these might point to the fact that this structure should be seen as an altar as well, enabling the communication with the otherworldly recipients through the deposition of offerings, and perhaps in a complementary approach to the previously discussed room, this might have allowed collective funerary practices to occur here. According to F. Prayon, this structure measures 0.71 by 1.30 m and is 0.84 m high.[60]

A few reflections can be pursued, building on the dimensions of these altars and considering the contexts that these altars have been found in. Firstly, these altars as 'undersized' structures do create exertion on the human body and influence the body of the worshippers to behave in a specific way. Secondly, it is doubtful to ascertain whether the reduced dimensions of an altar might have affected its functionality and might have transformed it into a miniaturized version instead, with a loss of its original role. The Fosso Arlena altar, despite its small dimensions, seems to have been used in the communication with the otherworldly deities, as the inscriptions seem to point to and reinforce such a process. Moreover, the addition of the newer inscription onto the altar at least half a century after the previous one highlights the desire on the part of a human agent to strengthen this connection with the otherworldly recipients addressed in the ritual practices. At the same time, in the case of the Tomb of the Five Chairs, it is not the reduced dimensions of the altar in itself that might suggest its 'miniaturized' status. It is rather the context — namely, the entirety of the room itself where the altar was found — that might indicate in this particular case a rather symbolic meaning offered to the altar to enable a process of communication, perhaps this time left to the agency of the couple buried within the tomb.

'Monumentalizing' the Altar: The Case Study of Grotta Porcina

Grotta Porcina represents one of the necropoleis situated near the ancient Etruscan settlement of Blera, adjacent to the road connecting the city of Blera with that of Norchia. Its beginnings are dated to the first half of the sixth century BC; during the Roman times of the third century BC, it became connected to the Via Clodia built throughout inner Etruria. The necropolis seems to have been in use also in Roman times, up to the first century BC. One of the most impressive monuments of this necropolis is a large tumulus, the so-called Grande Ruota or Ruota di Grotta Porcina (Fig. 6.3), which has a diameter of 28 m and a height of 3.5 m. It is decorated on its upper side with a tripartite cornice. The tumulus was carved out of the local tuff rock and is connected to the adjacent cliff through a bridge from the northern side with a length of 3 m, also carved out of the rock, thereby enabling access to the top of the tumulus, most probably for the undertaking of funerary ceremonies.[61] Within the tumulus, the tomb is constituted out of three rooms that have been damaged due to their reuse in time.[62] At a distance of 85 m away from the tumulus, there is a specially delimited open-air cult area neighbouring the tumulus and most likely directly linked to it. Within this open-air cult area, an altar, dated to the sixth century BC, seems to have been the central element of specific funerary practices conducted here.

There was a specific structuring of the space surrounding the altar as the focal point of this stepped area dug out of the local rock and measuring 12 by 15 m (Fig. 6.4). The altar was, however, not placed in a central position within this structure, but slightly to the north-east of the terraced area. The stepped rectangular area that surrounded the altar seems to have had at least three steps for the seated spectators of the ceremony, thereby limiting the possible audience in attendance. As an open-air altar, this was most probably accessible from all sides, but the structuring of the place suggests that the seated spectators were supposed to witness a specific performance rather than being perhaps able to play an active role in the unfolding of the ritual practices. Regarding visibility, the complex manner and rich effort put into emphasizing the altar as the focal point from all angles within the structure is notable, as well as its impressive dimensions, and the existence of the steps as seats for visitors would provide unrestricted visibility for all attending the ceremonies. From the western side and partially from the northern side of the seating structure, the adjacent tumulus was also visible in the background.[63]

Despite a lack of information concerning the continuity of use of the structures, the open-air cult area must have been defined throughout the centuries by its connection to the necropolis and maintained an important status, with at least two different religious structures

---

[60] Prayon 1975, 110 n. 608.

[61] *Documentazione*, 1.

[62] *Documentazione*, 1.

[63] See Colonna 1993, 333.

built at a later time around it. In the proximity of the stepped area and of the tumulus, a small temple with a single *cella* was built around 500 BC and destroyed by a fire in the third century BC.[64] Another structure of the first century BC, a small funerary *aedicula*, was built here in the vicinity of the altar,[65] suggesting the continued importance of the area throughout the centuries.

The altar itself was completely cut out of the local tuff rock. It is unfortunately partially damaged nowadays, with only its circular base remaining. The base has a diameter of 6.2 m and an estimated original height of 2 m. It presents traces of decorative elements, since the lower part of an animal frieze can still be seen in the mouldings of the altar — supposedly a procession of quadrupeds, including *felinae, bovinae, equidae*, and alternating with vegetal elements.[66] This procession also continues onto the access ramp. The altar had an inclined bridge of access (1.6–1.8 m wide) from the eastern side and outside the terraced area, suggesting, along with the impressive size of the altar itself, that it was possibly also used as a ramp of access for sacrificial animals. The sacrifice of animals is further suggested by the existence of a descending groove on the south-western side, interpreted as a drain for the blood of slaughtered animals.[67]

The circular form and the access ramp of the altar have been interpreted to evoke the characteristics of the tumulus itself, with the altar functioning as a 'substitute' for the tumulus.[68] Such a hypothesis creates a very interesting example highlighting the interplay of scales between the several elements of relevance here. The altar through its impressive dimensions might suggest that it is 'monumentalized', making it highly visible within the stepped complex and perhaps even outside it and from the area of the necropolis, most likely catering to the needs of a collective audience participating in practices conducted in this space. At the same time, if the similarities brought forward by the shape of the altar with that of the tumulus, by the bridges of access of the two, and by the possibility of conducting practices on top of both structures, imply that the altar was built in order to replicate the tumulus, it can be suggested that the altar represents then a 'miniaturized' version of the tumulus, regardless of its imposing dimensions. In this case also, its 'miniaturization' does not interfere with its role as enabling the communication with the deities addressed here through specific practices. Whether the altar was perceived as a miniaturized tumulus by the Etruscan communities of worshippers is difficult to assess, but the care put into the selected placement of the area to include the visibility of the tumulus in the background of the altar points to a specific motivation of the human agents in associating the two structures and bringing their connection together in a visible manner during the occurrence of altar-based practices.

Altars, Scales, and the Human Body

From presenting an overview of the scale of altars and their spatial configurations in relation to the funerary sphere and delving deeper into providing specific examples of 'miniaturized' and 'monumentalized' altars, a few reflections can be further introduced considering the scale of these altars and the effects this interplay might have produced on the human body of the worshippers.

To start with, it is interesting to consider to what extent this highly visible dimension of altars throughout Etruria, specifically linked to the preservation of stone-built or rock-cut altars, shows the monumental facet of these ritual objects. In this regard, the 'experiential qualities' of monumentality that they provide, qualities such as durability, visibility, and commemoration, can be acknowledged.[69] The commemoration function of a monument can be intrinsically linked due to its Latin terminology, since the noun *monumentum* stems from the verb *moneo*, 'to remind of, to bring to the notice of, to warn'; thus, 'its etymological root emphasizes that the monument's primary function is to evoke a particular response through the viewer's memory'.[70] Altars can be identified as ritual objects of commemoration practices due to their function as structures allowing communication between humans and otherworldly addressees. The durability of these altars is given by the selected material of construction used in the building of these monuments. The most probably intentional motivations on behalf of the human agents to confer durability and visibility to such objects can of course be linked to the social sphere, an attempt to provide prestige and reinforce the authority of the agents themselves. The 'monumentality' of these altars, as envisioned by the original commission-

---

[64] Steingräber 1981, 351.
[65] Steingräber 1981, 351.
[66] Colonna 1993, 331.
[67] Steingräber 1981, 350.
[68] Colonna 1993, 334–36.

[69] Meyers 2012, 14; see also Scarre 2011.
[70] Meyers 2012, 7.

Figure 6.3. The Grande Ruota tumulus located within the Grotta Porcina necropolis. Photographer: Carlo Finocchietti, reproduced with permission. Online access at the following link: <https://blogcamminarenellastoria.wordpress.com/2021/01/20/larea-archeologica-etrusca-di-grotta-porcina/> [accessed 12 February 2023].

Figure 6.4. The circular altar within the stepped area from the Grotta Porcina necropolis. Photographer: Carlo Finocchietti, reproduced with permission. Online access at the following link: <https://blogcamminarenellastoria.wordpress.com/2021/01/20/larea-archeologica-etrusca-di-grotta-porcina/> [accessed 12 February 2023].

ers, represents therefore a material outlet for the continuity of socio-religious practices.

More than these characteristics, however, it is also interesting to consider J. Osborne's perspective on the topic of monumentality. He claims:

> Monumentality is something more than the shape, or size or visibility, or permanence of the monument — though these variables absolutely carry their own significance. Monumentality lies in the meaning created by the relationship that is negotiated between object and person, and between object and the surrounding constellation of values and symbols in a culture.[71]

Following this relational approach, the care in the building, decorating, as well as in maintaining both the 'oversized' altars as well as the ones characterized by smaller dimensions, implies the importance conferred upon the formation and development of altar-based practices. The case of the Fosso Arlena altar is particularly relevant in this regard, since throughout its most probable use it was deemed necessary to receive a new inscription, which suggests the intentionality behind the continuity of practices to be conducted here and perhaps a re-establishment of the connection between worshipper, altar, and worshipped ancestor. Altars from the wider archaeological record show signs of having been used for long periods of time, and they must have been therefore maintained by specific persons involved in the pro-

---

[71] Osborne 2014, 13.

cess. Within the funerary realm, and in the case of altars connected to specific tombs, this role could have been undertaken by the members of the family and the successors carrying the tradition throughout generations, maintaining the established socio-religious practices at the altar and with further possibilities of innovation.

Another important aspect to be taken into account is the influence that the material affordances of these altars exert on the embodied experience of the worshippers performing individualized acts of worship at the altar or as part of a larger group or community coming together and enacting elaborate rituals. The scale and type of these altars, as well as the spatial configurations associated with them, also impact the human body in itself, since the smaller scale of the altars would suggest a need to kneel or bow down not only in order to perform an action, such as pouring a libation or placing an offering, but also in order to touch the altar, to observe the sculptural elements, or to read the engraved inscriptions. Such influences on the human body are also visible in the iconographic record in scenes that include depictions of altars, particularly in the engraved mirrors that show scenes of kneeling onto the altar, bowing down in front of the altar, or even stepping onto the altar itself.[72] The smaller scale of some altars provides a differentiated experience than the one supported by the oversized altars, one that encourages an individualized use and that perhaps enhances the sensory experience of the worshipper, who is not only supposed to see the altar but also to touch it. The other senses must have also been accentuated by the closeness of the worshipper to the altar and to the sensory activities brought forward during the use of the altar, such as the use of incense. This of course also depends on who had the authority to access or use these altars, particularly in regard to those placed on top of tombs or within tombs.

The oversized altars that form part of the archaeological record provided the possibility to be stepped on during their use, as seems to be the case at the Grotta Porcina necropolis or at the Castro necropolis. Given their visibility from afar, this could have actually created a physical distance between the material and the worshipper; ritual practices happening at the altar of the Grotta Porcina were rather meant to be seen from a distance, from the seated audience of the stepped ceremonial area. The same could be hypothesized about the oversized altars placed on top of tombs, where the people who might not have had access to participate in the ceremonies could have watched or rather acknowledged the occurrence of such practices from below. This would have further impacted the embodied experience of the attendees of the socio-religious practices happening here, as well as creating differentiations on the social scale and bringing forward 'notions of belonging or exclusion'.[73]

---

[72] Kneeling: *CSE* Schweiz I, no. 31; bowing: *CSE* Vaticano I, no. 6; stepping: *CSE* DDR I, no. 45.

[73] Huet 2015, 151.

Works Cited

Bagnasco Gianni, G. 2019. 'Notes on Etruscan Cosmology: The Case of the Tumulus of the Crosses at Cerveteri', in G. Magli and others (eds), *Archaeoastronomy in the Roman World* (Cham: Springer), pp. 17–34.

Belelli Marchesini, B., M. C. Biella, and L. Michetti. 2015. *Il Santuario di Montetosto sulla Via Caere-Pyrgi* (Rome: Officina edizioni).

Bloch, R. 1955. 'Découverte d'un habitat étrusque archaïque sur le territoire volsinien', *Mélanges d'archéologie et d'histoire*, 67: 47–68.

Bruni, S. 1998. *Pisa Etrusca: anatomia di una città scomparsa* (Milan: Longanesi).

Camporeale, G. 2009. 'The Deified Deceased in Etruscan Culture', in S. Bell and H. Nagy (eds), *New Perspectives on Etruria and Early Rome: In Honour of Richard Daniel de Puma* (Wisconsin: University of Wisconsin Press), pp. 220–50.

Colonna, G. (ed.). 1985. *Santuari d'Etruria* (Milan: Electa).

——. 1993. 'Strutture teatriformi in Etruria', in *Spectacles sportifs et scéniques dans le monde étrusco-italique: actes de la table ronde de Rome* (Rome: École française de Rome), pp. 321–47.

——. 2006. 'Sacred Architecture and the Religion of the Etruscans', in N. Thomson de Grummond and E. Simon (eds), *The Religion of the Etruscans* (Austin: University of Texas Press), pp. 132–68.

Criado Boado, F., M. Santos Estévez, and V. Villoch Vázquez. 2001. 'Forms of Ceremonial Landscapes in Iberia from the Neolithic to Bronze Age. Essay on an Archaeology of Perception', in P. Biehl, F. Bertemes, and H. Meller (eds), *The Archaeology of Cult and Religion* (Budapest: Archaeolingua), pp. 169–78.

Cristofani, M. 1969. 'La tomba del "Tifone": cultura e società di Tarquinia in età tardo', *Atti della Accademia nazionale dei Lincei*, 14.4: 213–56.

De Lucia Brolli, M. A. and others. 2016. 'Nuovi dati sulla necropoli del Cavone di Monte Li Santi a Narce (Scavo 2015)', *Bollettino di archeologia*, 7: 1–72.

Documentazione per il Ministero per i beni e le attività culturali e per il turismo: schede del sito archeologico, Grotta Porcina, Comune di Vetralla, Provincia di Viterbo.

Edlund, I. 1987. *The Gods and the Place: The Location and Function of Sanctuaries in the Countryside of Etruria and Magna Graecia (700–400 B.C.)*, Skrifter utgivna av Svenska institutet i Rom, Series in 4°, 43 (Stockholm: Svenska institutet i Rom).

Foxhall, L. 2015. 'Introduction: Miniaturization', *World Archaeology*, 47.1: 1–5.

Huet, V. 2015. 'Watching Rituals', in R. Raja and J. Rüpke (eds), *A Companion to the Archaeology of Religion in the Ancient World* (Chichester: Wiley-Blackwell), pp. 144–54.

Maras, D. F. 2009. *Il dono votivo: gli dei e il sacro nelle iscrizioni etrusche di culto* (Pisa: Fabrizio Serra).

Meer, L. B. van der. 2011. *Etrusco ritu: Case Studies in Etruscan Ritual Behaviour* (Leuven: Peeters).

——. 2013. 'The Lead Plaque of Magliano', in C. Chiaramonte Trerè, G. Bagnasco Gianni, and F. Chiesa (eds), *Interpretando l'antico: scritti di archeologia offerti a Maria Bonghi Jovino*, Quaderni di Acme, 134 (Milan: Cisalpino), pp. 323–42.

Menichelli, S. 2009. 'Etruscan Altars from the 7th to the 4th Centuries B.C.: Typology, Function, Cult', *Etruscan Studies*, 12: 99–129.

Meyers, G. 2012. 'Introduction. The Experience of Monumentality in Etruscan and Early Roman Architecture', in M. Thomas and G. Meyers (eds), *Monumentality in Etruscan and Early Roman Architecture: Ideology and Innovation* (Austin: University of Texas Press), pp. 1–20.

Morandi Tarabella, M. 2004. *Prosopographia etrusca*, I.1: *Etruria meridionale*, Studia archaeologica, 135 (Rome: L'Erma di Bretschneider).

Osborne, J. F. 2014. 'Monuments and Monumentality', in J. F. Osborne (ed.), *Approaching Monumentality in Archaeology* (Albany: State University of New York Press), pp. 1–22.

Pfiffig, A. 1975. *Religio etrusca* (Graz: Akademische Druck- und Verlagsanstalt).

Prayon, F. 1975. *Frühetruskische Grab- und Hausarchitektur*, Mitteilungen des Deutschen Archäologischen Instituts, Römische Abteilung, 22 (Heidelberg: Kerle).

——. 2006. *Die Etrusker: Jenseitsvorstellungen und Ahnenkult* (Mainz: Von Zabern).

Ricciardi, L. 1987. 'Recenti scoperte a Blera e nel suo territorio', *Antiqua*, 12.5–6: 42–68.

——. 1990. 'Blera (Viterbo). Le necropoli rupestri della Casetta e del Terrone', *Bollettino d'archeologia*, 5/6: 147–54.

Roncalli, F. 1987. 'Le strutture del santuario e le tecniche edilizie', in *Santuario e culto nella necropoli di Cannicella: relazioni e interventi nel convegno del 1984*, Annali della Fondazione per il museo 'Claudio Faina', 3 (Orvieto: Porziuncola), pp. 47–60.

Scarre, C. 2011. 'Monumentality', in T. Insoll (ed.), *The Oxford Handbook of the Archaeology of Ritual and Religion* (Oxford: Oxford University Press), pp. 9–23.

Sgubini Moretti, A. M. 1994. 'Ricerche archeologiche a Vulci: 1985–1990', in M. Martelli (ed.), *Tyrrhenoi Philotechnoi: atti della giornata di studio organizzata dalla Facoltà di Conservazione dei Beni Culturali dell'Università degli Studi della Tuscia in occasione della mostra 'Il mondo degli Etruschi'; Testimonianze dai Musei di Berlino e dell'Europa orientale, Viterbo, 13 ottobre 1990* (Rome: Gruppo Editoriale Internazionale), pp. 9–50.

Steingräber, S. 1981. *Etrurien: Städte, Heiligtümer, Nekropolen* (Munich: Hirmer).

——. 1982. 'Überlegungen zu etruskischen Altären', in H. Blanck and S. Steingräber (eds), *Miscellanea archaeologica: Tobias Dohrn dedicata* (Rome: Giorgio Bretschneider), pp. 103–16.

——. 1997. 'Le culte des morts et les monuments de pierre des nécropoles étrusques', in F. Gaultier and D. Briquel (eds), *Les plus religieux des hommes: état de la recherche sur la religion étrusque; actes du colloque international* (Paris: La documentation française), pp. 97–116.

——. 2006. *Abundance of Life: Etruscan Wall Painting* (Los Angeles: Getty Publications).

——. 2009. 'The Cima Tumulus at San Giuliano – An Aristocratic Tomb and Monument for the Cult of the Ancestors of the Late Orientalizing Period', in M. Gleba and H. Becker (eds), *Votives, Places and Rituals in Etruscan Religion: Studies in Honor of Jean MacIntosh Turfa* (Leiden: Brill), pp. 123–33.

——. 2016. 'Architecture of the Tombs', in N. Thomson de Grummond and L. Pieraccini (eds), *Caere*, Cities of the Etruscans, 1 (Austin: University of Texas Press), pp. 97–112.

Steingräber, S. and S. Menichelli. 2010. 'Etruscan Altars in Sanctuaries and Necropoleis of the Orientalizing, Archaic and Classical Periods', in L. B. van der Meer (ed.), *Material Aspects of Etruscan Religion: Proceedings of the International Colloquium; Leiden, 29–30 May 2008* (Leuven: Peeters), pp. 51–74.

Tamburini, P. 2013. 'Culti e luoghi di culto nella Val di Lago Volsiniese', in G. M. Della Fina and E. Pellegrini (eds), *Da Orvieto a Bolsena: un percorso tra Etruschi e Romani* (Ospedaletto: Pacini), pp. 148–66.

Tuck, A. 1994. 'The Etruscan Seated Banquet: Villanovan Ritual and Etruscan Iconography', *American Journal of Archaeology*, 98.4: 617–28.

7. Urban Monumentality and Religion

Jörg Rüpke

This chapter examines the characteristic features of religion as they developed in urban conditions and the reactions to them. The focus is on monumentality as a defining characteristic of urbanity, even if monumentality itself precedes urbanity. Monumentality of practices, of architecture, and of the city itself is shown to have a major impact on religious practices and processes of differentiation. Such changes also include conceptual developments. Monumentality of religious architecture is sometimes justified and profiled by the monumentality of its inhabitants or owners, gods in monumentalized form. In such a form, the elusive gods are fixed in urban space and thus related to urban space and actors, that is, subjected to new forms of control. Without being explicitly comparative, the analysis covers the beginnings of urban history and their developments into early empires and their cities into the first millennium AD.

Monuments and Monumentality

Whether looking for 'urban', 'iconic', or 'material religion', it is the monumental forms of religious architecture that come to mind.[1] Huge mosques, tall halls of Buddhist temples, towering temples, and medieval or recent cathedrals are employed as icons of cities as much as of religious groups. This is not a new strategy, however, as exemplified by gigantic building projects making the 'new Islamic city' in central Asia, contesting the primacy of Rome's St Peter in contemporary Lagos, or affirming Amritsar as a Sikh rather than Hindu city.[2] The phenomenon of extravagant architecture or imagery goes back to earlier periods of urbanization in most regions, albeit not in every city but in places such as Tikal, Constantinople, Chang'an, Rome, Memphis, and Uruk. And yet, monumental forms were and are not restricted to urban space. Nor is religion. We need to analyse the intersections of urbanism and religion as historically contingent developments. This does not exclude that there are typical co-occurrences, patterns of intersection, affordances of religious action, monumental forms, and urbanity that contribute to explain the frequency of the historical constellations.

Methodologically, I treat monumentality as a human possibility and cultural category. I take it as a subfield of materiality, but the focus is on the material as an artefact. The specific monumental character is produced by upscaling, by producing or arranging things that are considerably bigger and thereby indicate a functional difference.[3] It is thus a practice of transcendence.[4] Technologically, this is typically a collective enterprise, but it presupposes individuals' initiatives, plans, and leadership.[5] We might speculate that individual appropriation frequently takes the form of miniaturization. On the other end of a continuous scale,[6] miniatures often represent large things in smaller forms — cattle rather than sheep, divine statues rather than human effigies. This is open to the test.[7]

---

[1] I am grateful to the audience at Eisenach, Germany, for the intensive discussion. Special thanks go to Georgia Petridou, Susanne Rau, and Katharina Rieger for their thorough reading and many useful criticisms and hints. Work on this chapter has been supported by the German Science Foundation (DFG) in the framework of the International Research Training Group 'Resonant Self–World Relations in Ancient and Modern Socio-religious Practices', based at the Universities of Erfurt and Graz (IRT 2283) and in the framework of the Kolleg-Forschungsgruppe 'Religion and Urbanity: Reciprocal Formations' at the Max Weber Centre of the University of Erfurt (FOR 2779). Taylor Gerald Fitzgerald meticulously copy-edited the text.

[2] Islamic cities: Moser 2013; Lagos: cf. Garbin 2012; Amritsar: cf. Behal 2021. In general, van de Port and Meyer 2018.

[3] On this difference, see Brysbaert 2018.

[4] Cf. Meyer 2020, 19.

[5] Watkins 2020, 26; Sørensen 2020, 71.

[6] See Roberts (ed.) 2016.

[7] I remember that my first material memorial object (*Andenken, Stehrumchen*) was a miniature of the cathedral of Cologne.

If our perspective on material things of whatever size is relational, the meanwhile established conceptual distinction between monument and monumentality is crucial. Monumentality, then, is 'an ongoing, constantly renegotiated *relationship* between things and person'.[8] If monumentality is a quality of the relationship, it is reasonable to not only start from larger-than-life things but also from larger-than-life object-related action. If habitual size and ultimately the body is the standard for the first, everyday life is the measuring rod for the latter. I follow the suggestion of Thomas that 'monumentalising life could refer to the process by which aspects of everyday, unconsidered practice were made visible and memorable by bringing to notice things that would otherwise be passed over'.[9] In the production of larger structures, larger social groups are mobilized or rather constituted. And vice versa, 'monuments emerge from monumentality, that is, from the ways through which abstractions and meanings and specific material realities are reunited'.[10] Levenson speaks of 'intended', 'perceived', and 'received' (i.e. successfully transmitted) monumentality.[11] As has been pointed out for northern European late Neolithic societies, such material realities need not take the form of henges or long barrows but might also be flint mines or horizontal spaces barely visible from afar.[12]

Monumentality, as delineated so far, has further spatial and temporal aspects. Monumental objects and actions need considerable space. Such space might be communal, nested space, that is, space of enhanced quality in the middle of (or at least, within) the common space of that social formation that includes the agents. Monumental space might also form an interface between two or more groups (or wide-ranging individuals), a shared space at the margins of everyone's comfort zone (even if a border wall might have two very different 'faces'), or an overlap of or a hub between various networks; border sanctuaries between Greek and Roman *poleis* or *civitates*, i.e., polities and territories, might be mentioned here.[13] Neolithic monumentality typically reached out beyond the settlement, transformed and constituted a landscape and asserted claims to it.[14]

Such a process developed over time. The same holds true for later societies and the palimpsest character of overlapping landscapes thus created.[15] Monuments could form in incremental fashion, step by step.

Durability, therefore, is not the only temporal quality of monumentality. Monuments — as suggested by the Latin term *monumentum*, although this term (followed by many European languages) primarily referred to tombstones and other memorials not necessarily of large size — are constituted by monumental practice;[16] it is on this that the energetic size of monuments might be measured.[17] The very process of a monumental construction would be a period of above-average cooperation and an exceptional division of labour that might even take on a festive character. Full-time engagement demands an exemption from other burdens, perhaps even from being fed.[18] Only initiators relying on advanced state formation would be able to replace such labour input by forced labour of slaves, captives, or prisoners. Monuments were being built before this. Segmentary societies reached higher degrees of complexity as a precondition for and through engaging in monumentalizing projects. Mobilization of a large number of people, enabled by increased sedentism,[19] created opportunities to strengthen social cohesion as well as further differentiation; the size of the monument, therefore, might have been the effect rather than the aim of maximal mobilization and could develop over time, as we shall see shortly with the monumental pillars of Göbekli Tepe.[20] As stated before, monumentality started before urbanization.

Such memories might influence further use of the monument, a second-order monumentality performed and experienced in secondary (and maybe quickly changing) uses and ascriptions of meaning. The tombs of the late Iron Age settlement near Frienstedt at the western outskirts of today's Erfurt were oriented towards a Bronze Age tumulus.[21] Even the construction of later, tertiary, memorials to remember earlier monumental achievements — a 'monument' proper — might result in festive experiences,[22] remarkable not least for the

---

[8] Osborne 2014, 3; see also Levenson 2019, 23.
[9] Thomas 2020, 295.
[10] Valera 2020, 240.
[11] Levenson 2019, 24.
[12] See Gebauer and others 2020b; especially Teather 2020, 15.
[13] See de Polignac 1995.
[14] See e.g. Gebauer 2020.

[15] Falconer and Redman 2009, 9.
[16] Meyers 2012, 7–8.
[17] See Hageneuer and Schmidt 2019.
[18] Sørensen 2020, 78.
[19] For the costs, Duru 2018.
[20] On maximal mobilization, cf. Duru 2018, 71–72.
[21] Schmidt 2018, 43.
[22] For Mesopotamia, Harmanşah 2013, 103.

extraordinary consumption of meat.²³ Musealized iconic remnants of such structures, often the result of archaeological research, or just small tables and texts might thus make a monumental past visible in contemporary cities or the wider landscape.²⁴

Monumentality, undeniably, is related to power structures, in all stages of its life.²⁵ The relationship is not straightforward. If leadership roles are presupposed as much as they are furthered in contemporary projects of monumentalization, it is a heterarchical structure that emerges, different scales of prestige and power that cannot be offset against each other and do not adhere to the same hierarchy.²⁶ The prestige is object-related and by no means easily transformed into permanent institutions of ascribed political authority. It might be challenged by the next monumental project. Successive Roman generals and their families each left monumental temples.²⁷ Monumentalization is an indication of an ongoing contest rather than its result.²⁸ It should not go unnoticed that the actual use of monuments was (and is) often astonishingly short-lived in comparison to the potentials of the materials used;²⁹ monumentality is a risky and expensive strategy in the face of societal change. Nero's *domus aurea* in Rome and Ceaucescu's largest parliamentary building in Bucharest were examples for that.

Emphasis needs to be on the relational aspect anew. Monuments are agents as much as expressions of monumentality. A question that quickly arises is: Who did it? Yet, it is the monument that produces the question, producing rather than presupposing what seems to be 're-presented', e.g., the authority ascribed even to the absent inhabitants of royal palaces or, for example, 'palace cities' (*gongcheng*) in Chinese cities, established in Bronze Age China and prefigured in Palongcheng in the second millennium BC.³⁰ From a synchronic perspective, the monument might be seen as a 'moral' or 'juridical person', a very big mask (*persona*) for what must be a very big 'person'. In concrete constellations, the monument or the assemblage of which it is a significant part might have very different affordances: creating a common focus for observers from outside or forcing people into a close, intimate social distance,³¹ even if they belong to competing factions as in an ancient or modern sports arena. For fluid territorial societies or feeble long-distance networks in particular,³² the enduring temporalities of past, present, and future produced by the monument and the related monumental practices might be of utter importance for stabilizing social assemblages of humans.

'In the beginning was the house' was the first sentence of my historical account of ancient Mediterranean religion,³³ and I dare to generalize this even beyond the original scope. It might not be accidental that it is the house that provides a — historically, perhaps *the* — most frequent object of monumentalization. If the body is the measuring rod (and likely to be an object of monumentalization itself in gigantic statuary), it is the agency of the house that is scaled up. The house does not only provide space and shelter but identity and continuity beyond individual death for its inhabitants. The lens offered by the concept of 'house society' has proved the explanatory power of supposing such a view as existing in the minds of the historical agents.³⁴ It is such effects of a structure and of related activities like narratives that must have been sought in establishing 'history houses' at Çatalhöyük,³⁵ as well as many forms of larger monuments, whether long houses or long barrows, if not henges and encircling walls at other places; Chinese settlements displayed such walls from the sixth millennium onwards.³⁶

I suggest interpreting practices of monumentality also as ritual activities, drawing on a definition of ritual as an action made non-quotidian, set apart by self-reflective practices, that is, by ritualization.³⁷ In such a perspective, the construction, use, and repair work on monuments — even if seemingly of different pragmatic concerns — do not only share their material focus (which is

---

23 See Sørensen 2020, 79.

24 For a critique of a neoliberalist reduction of such pasts to a 'cultural urbanism' as a mere backdrop to creativity and a basis of marketing in a 'global urbanism', see e.g. Courage 2013; Ilchenko 2020.

25 See Bußmann 2019, 102, on today's pharaonic monumentality.

26 For the concept, Ehrenreich, Crumley, and Levy (eds) 1995.

27 Rüpke 2012, 141–44.

28 Sørensen 2020, 71.

29 See Falconer and Redman 2009.

30 Steinhardt 2019, 14 and 20; Steinhardt 1999.

31 See Hall 1976.

32 'Super-communities', Teather 2020, 25.

33 Rüpke 2018, 24.

34 House society: Gillespie 2000, 476; cf. Watkins 2020, 21 (Çatalhöyük); Naglak 2021 (Iron Age Gabii).

35 Clare and others 2018; Hodder 2018a; 2018b.

36 Steinhardt 2019, 5; a monumental stone at Shimao, Shenmu on the Yellow River around 2000–1700 BC (ibid., 10).

37 Rüpke 2021b, 24–30; see also Thomas 2020, 293: 'enhanced attentiveness to the significance of things and actions.'

a trivial assertion). Memories are linked, actions might be mimetic, even if possibly reformatted by an evolving monumental assemblage. The latter might be characterized by 'mere' conservation, 'mere' repetition such as multiplication, or 'mere' enlargements, to list only those options that seem to indicate a certain lack of fantasy. The monumentality of Stonehenge consisted as much of its size as of the extremely laborious movement of the blue stones from afar, which was recalled by subsequent architectural modifications and their respective changes in ritual.[38] The frequent rebuilding of wooden Roman theatres from the third to the mid-first centuries BC, usually seen as a measure of political control by denying a permanent space for assembling to the Roman populace,[39] might also be seen as the first (and their dismantling as the last) phase of the ludic ritual performed in the built-up structure, involving large numbers of citizens as agents or spectators of these processes, in a way typical of the audience at the Olympic Games.

As with pilgrimages, the rituals of the phase in between building or repair work could also involve many others, as spectators and users even from very different and distant places. As such ritual movements created monumental spaces themselves — evidently of ephemeral character. Even small objects might be at the centre of such activities, as demonstrated by many processions in ancient Mediterranean cities, for example, the divine symbols carried on litters at Rome.[40] From a ritual perspective, it is the change of scale rather than its direction that is primary, miniaturization being more frequently scrutinized by scholars of religion.[41] In contrast, archaeologists have tended to focus on the huge and monumental when studying religion.

The complex temporality of monuments as mentioned before evolves out of such practices. The period of construction, typically narrated as a founding event and indicating a founding figure, is the past remembered and celebrated in a present of refiguring social relations on supposedly past and traditional lines. Memories of such celebrations accrue, might even be monumentalized, for instance as permanent rather than just ephemeral triumphal arches at Rome and elsewhere in the Roman world, thus creating a museum. These reshape the representation and ultimately the contents of earlier memories, thus creating a new point of departure for imagining the future. It is the intensive incorporation of, and investment in, the monument as part of the ritual setting and practice that I suggest conceptualizing as a process of sacralization.[42]

And religion? If, for the purpose of creating a comparative analytical category capturing phenomena in societies of very different degrees of complexity,[43] religion is defined as risky first- or second-order communication with non-unquestionably plausible actors beyond the situation, monumentality and religious change are intertwined.[44] I am not so much referring to the 'cosmological acquisitions' of long voyages reaching far out into an environment brought under control, nor am I referring to the cosmological associations implemented by means of aligning monuments with, for example, salient landscape features or abstract cardinal points, or of associating them with either death or the supernatural as such.[45]

My interest in the following is on the relationality of religions and architectural practices and signs, that is, on the mutual constitution of both rather than on the enhancement of referential values and of the expressiveness of monuments. As indicated before, I argue that big houses create big dwellers. Temples, which are often called 'houses' like human residences,[46] house statues, but conceptually they are not built for that purpose. In many instances, the statues follow later, in order to indicate what the houses signify. The primary human strategy can be seen in the monumental practices related to celestial phenomena. By housing or at least anchoring them, the sun and moon as visible agents in a landscape are aligned with societal practices. This is part of the scaling up of human (and a specific group of humans') agency, scaling up what is reachable, influenceable, monumentalizable, in the Neolithic and Bronze Ages and, *mutatis mutandis*, later. An 'imaginal',[47] a mental image, is behind the objects and informed by the objects. It is productive in the highly selective processes of monu-

---

[38] For the workload involved in building monumental tomb chambers, see Furholt and Müller 2011, 19.

[39] Beacham 1991; Sear 2006.

[40] Rüpke 2007, 94; Luginbühl 2015; Stavrianopoulou 2015; Estienne 2014; Latham 2016.

[41] Cf. Smith 1978.

[42] Rüpke 2020.

[43] For complexity as the most important comparative scale, Berreman 1978, 50.

[44] Rüpke 2021a.

[45] Helms 1988; Sheridan and Schulting 2020, 208; Gebauer and others 2020a, 1. See also Pavel in this volume.

[46] Liverani 2006, 60; Rüpke 2018, 64; the body metaphor is thus hardly satisfactory, yet see Warden 2012.

[47] Corbin 1986, 265.

mentalization. A multiplicity of gods is seen as demanding multiple temples and vice versa. The same seems to have been true of those more individualized ancestors or different groups of ancestors that were no longer (or for the time being) seen as keen to be put together into a shared tomb.

Monumentality and the City

Associating the city with monumentality is not a new move. In Richard Childe's foundational essay and his invention of an 'urban revolution', the new stage of civilization, cities, are not only characterized by a considerably larger number of people living in a high density and the food surplus that allows this.[48] It is 'specialization of labour' that allows for such processes, which is reflected in an urban population composed of correspondingly differentiated 'classes'.[49] It is this division of labour and the large-scale and forcible extraction of the agricultural surplus that is the core of Childe's vision of the early city, condensed in the image of the centralized, towering temple: 'Truly monumental public buildings not only distinguish each known city from any village but also symbolize the concentration of the social surplus.'[50] A ruling class, the invention of systems of writing and accounting, science, art, long-distance trade, and the working of imported raw materials by 'specialist craftsmen' as full citizens are necessary correlates of this urban revolution according to Childe.[51] As James Osborne rightly points out, this focus on power and its representation was both consequential and limiting for subsequent research on monumentality.[52] The same holds true for the fields of Urban History and History of Religion.

Reflection on monumentality invites us to critically reassess the role of monumentality in processes of urbanization. We must start with a twofold historical statement. First, monumentality predates cities. The massive stone structure at Göbekli Tepe from the Pre-Pottery-Neolithic period between the tenth and the ninth millennia might have formed the centre of a settlement instead of being a rallying point of nomadic hunters and gatherers.[53] It is impossible to reconstruct the imaginations entertained by the initiators and their many successors, but the 'imaginal' certainly embraced festive occasions that included talking about the dead and narratives triggered by the images of the T-shaped pillars.[54] Maltesian 'temples', complex sequences of partly buried and dark rooms, were likewise places of feasting and intensive experiences some five millennia later, monumentalizing ecologically critical points of an insular landscape.[55] Northern European monumental tombs, henges, or ditched circles (from the sixth millennium onwards) preceded cities by millennia.[56]

Secondly, neither monumentalization nor urbanism were continuous or linear developments. As stated before, the monuments as lived in were short-lived, and the same holds true for many large settlements and early cities. Göbekli Tepe and many comparable places were given up at the end of the PPN (Pre-Pottery-Neolithic) phase, as was the 'Jericho' of Tel-Sultan; the extended but never monumentalized settlement of Çatalhöyük disintegrated by the early sixth millennium.[57]

Yet cities and monumentality are closely associated. Again, it is helpful to invoke the relational and procedural character of monumentality. Cities, too, are processes rather than finished products.[58] They mediate between urban and rural producers and consumers — both of which are located on both sides.[59] They are fragile social constellations looking for material, architectural stabilization. But they are also societies whose success is based on a diversity that contests any such monumental homogenization.[60] Thus, any monument is at the time of its creation as well as over its lifetime, its biography, the object of very different agents and agencies and is a subject that transforms such different monumentalities. The Temple of Jerusalem offers a good example: it was built at a central, towering location, monumentalized by huge animal sacrifices, destroyed and repaired, and subject to massive Herodian innovations before its nearly complete

---

48 Childe 1950, 4 and 9–10 as traits no. 1 and no. 2.

49 Childe 1950, 7 and 11, trait 3.

50 Childe 1950, 12, trait 4, illustrated with a 'reconstruction of the White Temple, standing on an artificial platform at Erech [Uruk]', Childe 1950, fig. 14. On the building's character as a temple, see Crawford 2015, 39.

51 Childe 1950, 12–16, traits 5–10.

52 Osborne 2014, 5.

---

53 Schyle 2016; Clare and others 2018; Hodder 2018a; 2020; Jeunesse 2020; Lang and others 2013; Peters and others 2014.

54 But see Kinzel and Clare 2020, 35.

55 Kolb 2014, 160–63; Parkinson and others 2020.

56 Overviews: Furholt and Müller 2011; Furholt 2011; Müller and others 2020.

57 Özdöl-Kutlu and others 2015.

58 Wynne-Jones and Fleisher 2014, 136.

59 See Parkins (ed.) 1997.

60 Jacobs 1970.

annihilation and conversion by the Romans and later Muslim repurposing.⁶¹

Such monumentality could take very different forms. In principle, mass movements of people in sufficiently open spaces might perform and bolster such a society — for instance, a teeming marketplace. Merely limited bodily interaction might not suffice, given its ephemeral character and the complexity of the society at stake. Architecture articulating the exceptional size of the space — in comparison to all the other marketplaces in the system of settlements involved — might accrue. The enhancement of facades by individual houses facing such a place might illustrate a process of slow and socially diffused monumentalization, whether at the Roman Forum or central European marketplaces such as those at Prague or Krakow.⁶² The articulation of streets by colonnades and (often less numerous) thoroughfares or of built-up areas might follow similar processes of visible mobilization of a large number of people and resources, even distributed over decades or centuries, as with Roman city walls or medieval European cathedrals. Even in advanced stages of state formation and politically ranked societies as exemplified by early Greek *poleis*, 'the urbanization of the landscape [...] was a complex, active process stemming from, and in turn encouraging, a series of deliberate and conscious decisions undertaken by, and ultimately affecting, a wide variety of different social and political levels throughout the community'.⁶³ The resulting monumentality of the settlement, experienced by its inhabitants and its visitors (that is, its external users), is probably even more pervasive than the acropolis temple highlighted by Childe. Undeniably, we must return to the latter, too.

In my discussion so far, I have deliberately postponed the monument typically dominating the discussion of monumentality and the city: the 'city wall'. Undeniably, the wall, whether in the form of an earthen rampart or a much later stone wall, is an early type of monument. PPN Jericho had one, even if our idea of its function — to defend from water? — as well as the size of the contemporary settlement is highly debated.⁶⁴ In agreement with Chinese as well as extra-Chinese traditions of research, a recent survey of Chinese architecture bluntly states: 'Urbanism in China begins by the sixth millennium BCE [...] with a wall the defining feature of a Chinese city'.⁶⁵ The Chinese character *cheng* denotes 'city' as well as 'wall'. Yet large enclosures are known from Neolithic societies that could hardly be called urban. They might have been monumental arenas of political spectacles that were enclosed by ditches and palisades.⁶⁶ In other instances, highly visible structures might have been part of an appropriation of landscape rather than primarily a provision for condensed social interaction, as the concept of 'fortified hills' has brought to the fore;⁶⁷ actual use (for instance of *Kreisgraben* sites) also might have changed substantially over the lifetime of such arrangements.⁶⁸

A comparative study of 'early civilizations' points to a dichotomy of an 'Old World' stress on walls (and implicitly boundaries) against a 'New World' widespread lack of them (and implicitly a stress on centres).⁶⁹ Yet, the phenomenological approach to this type of defence mechanism and resource investment lacks a relational perspective on monumentality, a perspective that includes the addressees as well as agents of such constructions: 'Elite enclaves, temples, and administrative centres were often enclosed by formidable walls [...] Walled structures were therefore symbols of power and exclusivity as well as secure areas.'⁷⁰ The exclusionist and defensive purpose has often been inverted in sociological analyses of power. In such a perspective, the wall is captured by the image of the trap, people are subjected to the intensive exertion of power after having been caged into river valleys.⁷¹ From the point of view of those struggling for power, walls seemed to have been used as (nearly) perfect instruments of controlling movements and social interaction.

A critical reading of walls is ever more relevant today,⁷² but even such a skewed image does not capture the full experience. Walls have gates, often articulated ones, that might be frequently open, allowing people to cross through the walls. Walls might promise security

---

61 The bibliography is extensive: Drijvers 2013; Fuss 2012; Purkis 2017; Wharton 2013; Ahmad 2012; Lassner 2017; Galor and Bloedhorn 2015; Lipschits 2013; Daschke 2010; Albertz 2020.

62 Szende 2022.

63 Fitzsimons 2014, 244, drawing on George L. Cowgill.

64 Anati 2020.

65 Steinhardt 2019, 8.

66 Rüpke 2006, 37–38; for the evidence, see above.

67 E.g. Sanches and Vale 2020; Valera 2020.

68 Furholt and Müller 2011.

69 On centres, cf. Trigger 2003, 141.

70 Trigger 2003, 133.

71 Mann 1986, see 99, but cf. 131, where he stresses the defensive character of the walls.

72 See Horváth, Benţa, and Conrod 2019a; 2019b; Szakolczai 2019.

in many regards, including to those outside: a place of refuge, a place of deposit, and more. Last but not least, they might result from huge collaborative efforts and are reliable indicators of power and prestige, often a highly visible display.[73]

In such a perspective, walls are part of the 'urban imaginary',[74] or, more briefly, of what might be called, in a long and variegated conceptual history, 'urbanity'.[75] For the purpose of my analysis, I define urbanity (again partly based on Jacobs's 1970 analysis of urban economies) as an awareness of the quality of a settlement as a place of internal diversity in tension with a strong centralizing or homogenizing impetus, typically represented by those in power. Thus, urban aspirations, the wish to engage in and be part of such a settlement, embraces images, fears, and hopes with very different inclinations between those two poles in the individual actors.[76] Nevertheless, they are typically unified by a shared feeling of a strong difference to the non-urban and the similarity to other places of urbanity, yet again in tension with many individuals' interest in the openness, the connectivity of the place for economic or family purposes. The reflexiveness of such ambivalent urbanity is not just related to a mental concept. What I call urbanity is 'created and continuously transformed on the one side by the overlapping circulations of people, goods, ideas, and ways of life, and on the other side by the stabilizing practices of the city's administrative powers and its infrastructure'.[77] This social experience is, as Magoni and others rightly observe, not restricted to those dwelling within the city, but it is based on the interactions with the materiality of the city.

Why (at least frequently) walls? At this point the concept of 'imageability' becomes handy.[78] What is sufficiently conspicuous to represent the urban experiences in narratives and discourse when talking about one's own traveling or introducing one's own place of origin to outsiders? What offers sufficient iconic qualities to give the settlement such imageability? What may have been built or repaired or defended in emergency situations by one's own or one's household's hands? What most shapes everyday movements both spatially and temporally (e.g. by nightly closure)? I suppose that it is this intersection

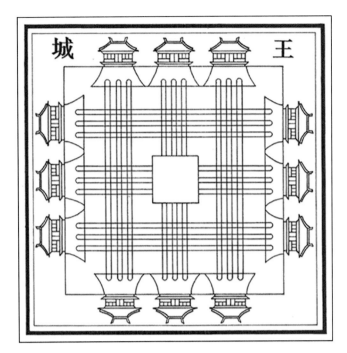

Figure 7.1. Kaogongji from the Song-era Xindingsanlitu, source: <https://commons.wikimedia.org/wiki/File:Chengzhou_Diagram.jpg> [accessed 12 February 2023]. Public domain.

of monumental presence and monumental practice that has given prominence to walls as indexes and symbols of urbanity. Historically and, as we have seen, in global comparison, both urbanity and walls are independent. Walls are neither necessary nor sufficient, in the same way that all other parameters invoked for definitions of the urban are neither necessary nor sufficient. Instead, it is the discursively constructed and often monumentally practised urbanity that renders a place so special to be a 'city' by (perhaps thus developing) local taxonomies. Walling and walls have just frequently been part of that.

The City as a Monument

Statistically, my stress on the distributed agency of monumentality and urbanity seems to clash with a widespread fact in urban history: many cities are founded on the initiative of regional or (even more frequently) imperial rulers. Many texts engaging in constructing urban imaginaries present themselves as guides to city foundations or are historically based on models established in such practices, from ancient Mesopotamia to East Asia. A palace, a temple, and a wall form typical ingredients; it is not diversity that is stressed but clear hierarchies and, if necessary, the segmentary control of a larger populace.

---

[73] Padilla Peralta 2020.
[74] Magoni and others 2014, 168.
[75] Rau 2020.
[76] Keith 2014; Burchardt and Westendorp 2018; Harris 2021.
[77] Magoni and others 2014, 168.
[78] Fisher 2014, 201, following K. Lynch.

The section on Zhou rituals (Zhouli) in the *Kaogong Ji*, for instance, offers direction for the building of a 'ruler's city' (*wangcheng*) as early as the first half of the first millennium BC (Fig. 7.1).[79] Here, it is a large palace with intersecting major thoroughfares that defined the image of a city.

In the Shang period, the ruling dynasty moved the capital around by founding a new capital for every single ruler.[80] A millennium before, the Sumerian King List imagined a somewhat comparable practice. It denied the possibility of multiple ruling cities (and kings) at the same time. Instead, it postulated a permanent change of that city that held the quality of royal capital, one capital at a time.[81] At Rome from Julius Caesar onwards,[82] successive rulers monumentalized adjacent but well-differentiated *fora*, urban multi-purpose places in the very city centre. For millennia, the act of founding cities was and is a major instrument in controlling territories and displaying the resources (often in a competitive and sometimes even threatening way) of a ruler, from Mesopotamian through Greek and Roman 'colonies', Chinese and Mesoamerican subcentres, and medieval Indian or European new cities to imperialist appropriations all over the world.[83]

How does that fit with the model of urbanization as a bottom-up monumentalizing practice developed in the previous section? Rather than identifying a discrepancy, I suggest reading the 'imperial' practice as a confirmation of the enormous success ascribed to both practices, urbanity as well as monumentality. Now, city-building as such has advanced to a monumental practice. The urban assemblage is interpreted as a single monument, which, admittedly, needs a bit of internal order. Of course, a coherent rationality should replace the coincidences of the historical emergence as suggested by handbooks across cultures, from the aforementioned *Kaogong Ji* to Vitruvius's *On Architecture*. Again, we need to apply a relational approach to such monumentality and take the full life cycle of the monument into account, as well as the agents and agencies involved.

Often it is already-urban populations that are mobilized and moved, such as the tens of thousands already living in Shang capitals.[84] They probably were thus offered the possibility to escape the opaque complexity of the multiple layers of existing cityscapes by appropriating unspoiled soil (however fictitious that might have been). In early medieval Europe, urban specialists moved around with the king from *Pfalz* to *Pfalz*, thus constituting ephemeral, temporary cities, as did East African inter-lacustrine specialists; clan chiefs along with the king of the territory thus constituted and were controlled by short-lived cities.[85] Founding new houses would include major festivals not as frequently witnessed in traditions of permanent repair work of existing housing structures; erecting monumental architecture would thus be part of one's own social performance and not just remembrance or backdrop to new, less object-related acts of monumentality. Emerging orders were replaced or rather anticipated by top-down planning (at least to a degree certainly much exaggerated in descriptive *and* prescriptive documents). Employing members of totalitarian organizations like the military might seem contradictory but would in fact offer those the promises of urbanity while retaining a high level of control, at times to the disappointment of both expectations. In the end, urban monumentality was as ambivalent as other forms of monumentality: it could express civic pride or oppressive rulership, lively competition or monopoly. Walls could separate wards and thus segment people horizontally in Indus urbanism as much as skyscrapers could enable the rich to escape the smell of the crowd in late nineteenth-century Chicago.[86]

Urbanity and Monumental Religion

How has the monumentality of urbanity — that is, the inherent material, performative, and conceptual monumentality of the urban shaped not least by religious practices and considerations, as discussed above, and the specific forms and instigations for monumentality present in urban settlements — shaped religious practices and ideas? In this final section, some observations will be brought together, each again on the basis of evidence from just a few sites which are, however, suggestive of more widely shared developments and allow us to better define abstract processes and local paths. Despite easily

---

79 Steinhardt 2019, 20; in detail, Steinhardt 1999.
80 Steinhardt 1999, 14–16.
81 Van de Mieroop 2016, 46; Crawford 2015, 47–48.
82 See Raja and Rüpke 2021.
83 See, e.g., Coquery-Vidrovitch and Almeida-Topor 1996.

84 Steinhardt 2019, 16.
85 See Coquery-Vidrovitch 1991.
86 Indus urbanism: Sinopoli 2015, 324; Chicago skyscrapers: Urry 2013, 351.

quotable ample evidence, logically, the 'observation' in its generalized form attains the status of a hypothesis.

The upscaling of certain activities and infrastructures in processes of urbanization in all its variants — big houses here, walls or marketplaces there, water and wastewater nearly everywhere — is paralleled in religious ritual practices. Organizers of specific ritual performances seem to have been informed by an urban ideal to include everybody or at least every relevant body (freeborn, male, elders, citizens proper, depending on local cultures) in its procedures. Major festivals demanded space for massive copresence, either in the form of an assembly or in organized movement, such as a procession, or at least the successive visiting of a shared place. Such space might have been sought within or outside of walls; it might have been empty space carved out of the continuous building up of a city in the form of huge places or as specific architecture optimizing at least visual and acoustic access at staged rituals, such as walled temple arenas looking onto a raised stage or circuses and (amphi)theatres allowing attendees to look down on performances.

Houses as dominating forms of habitation were a preferred location for monumentality in pre-urban settings, expressing and creating social differences and aspirations for one or another form of power. This is continued and even emphasized in the limited space of urban settlements. Such an urban way of living and seeing difference seems to have contributed to an emphasis on houses as typical places for the presence of divine figures. The difference to human accommodation could be marked by either miniaturization ('house altars', niches) or monumentalization and the development of (slightly) different architectural forms, 'shrines' or 'temples'.[87] Building non-house forms of sacralizable space accommodated other forms of monumentalization, to stress the difference, for instance, in pyramidal form within urban space (as at Mexico or Rome) or in the form of urban green spaces, such as parks. Empty spaces needed demarcation by monumentalization in particular, whether this was included in built-up religious space or places between domestic architecture. In the relational perspective on monumentality employed here, we can see that monumental architecture invited even beyond its construction a permanent, typically rhythmical interaction in monumentalized ritual form. Big buildings were at least annually marked by big rituals.

Big buildings, too, entailed big gods. The ascription of divine power could follow and shape the ascription of power to the leaders of monumentalizing projects. Likewise, the heterarchy visible in contemporary or even competing projects could have been reflected in the typically unorganized character of polytheistic world-views. This might have supported the heterarchy and overlapping 'competences' of the many locally and situationally produced divinities characteristic of polytheistic practice.[88] The multiplicity and permanence of different sacralized spaces in a social space characterized by diversity on multiple scales seems to have gone together with the nurturing of a likewise fluid and often heterarchical polytheism built on the implicit idea of the co-presence of differently articulated divine figures, related by kinship, cooperation, or division of labour.

Often, such gods were not just present via their houses but monumentalized in statuary form, too. Beyond the availability of technical knowledge and the organized labour of artisanship, larger-than-human figures also monumentalized economic achievements and urban power and self-esteem expressed in the luxury goods of long-distance trade.[89] Lapis lazuli and precious metals, marble and valuable stones, ivory, or precious textiles were the stuff out of which goddesses and gods were made, monumentalizing everyday practices and building collective and individual prestige on its implementation and continuation.

It is no wonder that the repeated and habitualized association of religious communication with built-up places and associated objects like statues and other forms of images also bound religious reflection to objects. The sharpest religious conflicts seem to have arisen and been pursued over such objects and places, not just in the fight over dominance in appropriation or interpretation of certain places like the Holy Sepulchre in Jerusalem or the Golden Shrine in Amritsar but also in the formation of iconoclastic movements and their delocalizing and above all de-monumentalizing agenda.[90]

Last, but not least, we return to city walls. The monumental borderline of city walls around a certain space or between parts of a larger urban space seems to have trig-

---

[87] For Mayan cities, see Magoni and others 2014, 161.

[88] Rüpke 2022.

[89] See Wengrow 1998; 2010.

[90] Belting 2016; Birk, Kristensen, and Poulsen 2014; Estienne and others 2014; Jaccottet (ed.) 2021; Nissinen and Carter 2009; Assmann 1990; 2001; von Graevenitz, Rieger, and Thürlemann (eds) 2001; Woyke 2005; Frankfurter 2008; Groneberg and Spieckermann (eds) 2007; Golinski and Radermacher (eds) 2019.

gered a more conscious reflection about the location of ritual spaces in relation to such walls. This could stress the protecting function of divine addressees inside ('city gods', often in central or elevated positions like an acropolis) as in many Mesopotamian or Greek or Italian cities. It could also trigger the intentional location of sanctuaries outside of the border lines, ideologically stressing a rural–urban continuum, as in the case of many Chinese cities or sanctuaries of Greek *poleis*. The Roman architect Vitruvius developed theories about the fitting locations for gods of war and fire.[91] This border and its necessary interruptions in the form of gates afforded ritual stress of these 'anomalies' of the continuous line — or rather the necessary permeability and importance of routes of exchange. Not least the fact that, in many instances, urban space and a continuous local population continued into 'suburbs' beyond the walls tended to de-emphasize walls or to stress segmentary identities rather than a dichotomic urban–rural one.

Looking beyond Monumentality

Religious monumentality did not trigger urban monumentality, nor vice versa. What we see in this attempt at a global perspective on monumentality as a relational practice is the co-monumentalization of both religion and urbanity. Nevertheless, more specific forms of the interaction between religious and urban practices and reflections are detectable or at least hypothesizable — as many historical periods do not allow us to approach what people knew or intended. Religious place-making not only shaped urban maps but also might have set precedents for the spatial projection and subsequent use or consumption of functionally different services; the same can be said for their combination in multi-purpose religious spaces, as is clearly defined in Israelite or Chinese temple yards. Evidently, such intersections are historically contingent developments. It is also true, however, that typical co-occurrences of practices of monumentality and affordances of monumental form exist. The relational approach taken in this chapter, which constantly reflects the triangle of actors, monumentalized and monumentalizing practices, and objects (sometimes even miniaturized), has proven fruitful. It has helped us to see the social and material conditions and results of both religious and urban practices. Such an analytic approach shares a major problem of monumental practices, too. Practically and sometimes deliberately, they obscure everyday non-monumental or even consciously miniaturized objects (statuettes, stones, representations of food, etc.), frequently aiming at invisibility rather than prominence. It is these different scales that constitute the very basis for the impact of the monumental. It is the closeness and intertwining of these scales that may be a characteristic of the permanent making of the urban and that may also enable invisibility and hiding as urban and religious practices.

---

[91] Vitr., *De arch.* 1.7.1–2.

Works Cited

Ahmad, A. 2012. 'The Ottoman Model in Jerusalem: The Common Capital of All Religions', *The Journal of Rotterdam Islamic and Social Sciences*, 3.1: 1–25 <https://doi.org/10.2478/jriss-2013-0006>.

Albertz, R. 2020. 'How Jerusalem's Temple Was Aligned to Moses' Tabernacle: About the Historical Power of an Invented Myth', in L. Niesioloski-Spanò and E. Pfoh (eds), *Biblical Narratives, Archaeology and Historicity: Essays in Honour of Thomas L. Thompson* (London: T & T Clark), pp. 198–209.

Anati, E. 2020. 'Rethinking Jericho and the Birth of the World Earliest Town', *Expressions*, 30: 10–19.

Assmann, J. 1990. 'Die Macht der Bilder: Rahmenbedingungen ikonischen Handelns im alten Ägypten', *Visible Religion*, 7: 1–20.

——. 2001. 'Bildverstrickung: Vom Sinn des Bilderverbots im biblischen Monotheismus', in G. von Graevenitz, S. Rieger, and F. Thürlemann (eds), *Die Unvermeindlichkeit der Bilder* (Tübingen: Gunter Narr), pp. 59–76.

Beacham, R. C. 1991. *The Roman Theatre and its Audience* (Cambridge, MA: Harvard University Press).

Behal, R. 2021. 'Religion, Religiosity and the Urban World: Everyday Lives of People in Amritsar City, Punjab, India', in S. Rau and J. Rüpke (eds), *Religion and Urbanity Online* (Berlin: De Gruyter) <https://doi.org/10.1515/urbrel.17467644>.

Belting, H. 2016. 'Iconic Presence. Images in Religious Traditions', *Material Religion*, 12.2: 235–37 <https://doi.org/10.1080/17432200.2016.1172769>.

Berreman, G. D. 1978. 'Scale and Social Relations. Thoughts and Three Examples', in F. Barth (ed.), *Scale and Social Organization* (Oslo: Universitetsforlaget), pp. 41–77.

Birk, S., T. M. Kristensen, and B. Poulsen (eds). 2014. *Using Images in Late Antiquity* (Oxford: Oxbow).

Brysbaert, A. 2018. 'Constructing Monuments, Perceiving Monumentality. Introduction', in A. Brysbaert and others (eds), *Constructing Monuments, Perceiving Monumentality & the Economics of Building: Theoretical and Methodical Approaches to the Built Environment* (Leiden: Sidestone), pp. 21–47.

Burchardt, M. and M. Westendorp. 2018. 'The Im-materiality of Urban Religion: Towards an Ethnography of Urban Religious Aspirations', *Culture and Religion*, 19.2: 160–76 <https://doi.org/10.1080/14755610.2018.1444656>.

Bußmann, R. 2019. 'Monumentality in Context – a Reply from Egyptology', in F. Buccellati and others (eds), *Size Matters: Understanding Monumentality across Ancient Civilizations* (Bielefeld: transcript), pp. 99–104 <https://doi.org/10.14361/9783839445389-007?>.

Childe, V. G. 1950. 'The Urban Revolution', *Town Planning Review*, 21.1: 3–17.

Clare, L. and others. 2018. 'Establishing Identities in the Proto-Neolithic: "History Making" at Göbekli Tepe from the Late Tenth Millennium cal BCE', in I. Hodder (ed.), *Religion, History, and Place in the Origin of Settled Life* (Boulder: University Press of Colorado), pp. 115–36 <https://doi.org/10.2307/j.ctv3c0thf.9>.

Coquery-Vidrovitch, C. 1991. 'The Process of Urbanization in Africa (From the Origins to the Beginning of Independence)', *African Studies Review*, 34.1: 1–98.

Coquery-Vidrovitch, C. and H. Almeida-Topor (eds). 1996. *La ville européenne outre-mers: un modèle conquérant? (XVe – XXe siècles)*, Collections de l'Université des Sciences Humaines de Strasbourg (Paris: L'Harmattan).

Corbin, H. 1986. *Temple and Contemplation*, Islamic Texts and Contexts (London: KPI & Islamic Publications).

Courage, C. 2013. 'The Global Phenomenon of Tactical Urbanism as an Indicator of New Forms of Citizenship', *Engage*, 32: 88–97.

Crawford, H. 2015. *Ur: The City of the Moon God* (London: Bloomsbury Academic).

Daschke, D. 2010. *City of Ruins: Mourning the Destruction of Jerusalem through Jewish Apocalypse*, Biblical Interpretation Series, 99 (Leiden: Brill).

de Polignac, F. 1995. *Cults, Territory, and the Origins of the Greek City-State* (Chicago: University of Chicago Press).

Drijvers, J. W. 2013. 'Transformation of a City. The Christianization of Jerusalem in the Fourth Century', in R. Alston, O. M. Van Nijf, and C. G. Williamson (eds), *Cults, Creeds and Identities in the Greek City after the Classical Age* (Leuven: Peeters), pp. 309–29.

Duru, G. 2018. 'Sedentism and Solitude: Exploring the Impact of Private Space on Social Cohesion in the Neolithic', in I. Hodder (ed.), *Religion, History, and Place in the Origin of Settled Life* (Boulder: University Press of Colorado), pp. 162–85 <https://doi.org/10.2307/j.ctv3c0thf.11>.

Ehrenreich, R. M., C. L. Crumley, and J. E. Levy (eds). 1995. *Heterarchy and the Analysis of Complex Societies*, Archaeological Papers of the American Anthropological Association, 6 (Arlington: American Anthropological Association).

Estienne, S. 2014. 'Aurea pompa venit: Présences divines dans les processions romaines', in S. Estienne and others (eds), *Figures de dieux: construire le divin en images* (Rennes: Presses universitaires de Rennes), pp. 337–49.

Estienne, S. and others (eds). 2014. *Figures de dieux: construire le divin en images* (Rennes: Presses universitaires de Rennes).

Falconer, S. E. and C. L. Redman. 2009. 'The Archaeology of Early States and their Landscapes', in S. E. Falconer and C. L. Redman (eds), *Polities and Power: Archaeological Perspectives on the Landscape of Early States* (Tucson: University of Arizona Press), pp. 1–10.

Fisher, K. D. 2014. 'Making the First Cities on Cyprus: Urbanism and Social Change in the Late Bronze Age', in A. T. Creekmore III and K. D. Fisher (eds), *Making Ancient Cities: Space and Place in Early Urban Societies* (Cambridge: Cambridge University Press), pp. 181–219.

Fitzsimons, R. D. 2014. 'Urbanization and the Emergence of the Greek *polis*: The Case of Azoria, Crete', in A. T. Creekmore III and K. D. Fisher (eds), *Making Ancient Cities: Space and Place in Early Urban Societies* (Cambridge: Cambridge University Press), pp. 220–56.

Frankfurter, D. 2008. 'Iconoclasm and Christianization in Late Antique Egypt: Christian Treatments of Space and Image', in J. Hahn, S. Emmel, and U. Gotter (eds), *From Temple to Church: Destruction and Renewal of Local Cultic Topography in Late Antiquity* (Leiden: Brill), pp. 135–59.

Furholt, M. 2011. 'Materielle Kultur und räumliche Strukturen sozialer Identität im 4. und 3. Jt. v. Chr. in Mitteleuropa: Eine methodische Skizze', in S. Hansen, and J. Müller (eds), *Sozialarchäologische Perspektiven: Gesellschaftlicher Wandel 5000–1500 v. Chr. zwischen Atlantik und Kaukasus* (Mainz: Von Zabern), pp. 243–67.

Furholt, M. and J. Müller. 2011. 'The Earliest Monuments in Europe – Architecture and Social Structures (5000–3000 cal BC)', in M. Furholt, F. Lüth, and J. Müller (eds), *Megaliths and Identities: Early Monuments and Neolithic Societies from the Atlantic to the Baltic; 3rd European Megalithic Studies Group Meeting, 13th–15th of May 2010 at Kiel University* (Bonn: Habelt), pp. 15–32.

Fuss, M. 2012. *Die Konstruktion der Heiligen Stadt Jerusalem: Der Umgang mit Jerusalem in Judentum, Christentum und Islam*, Stuttgarter biblische Beiträge, 68 (Stuttgart: Katholisches Bibelwerk).

Galor, K. and H. Bloedhorn. 2015. *The Archaeology of Jerusalem: From the Origins to the Ottomans* (New Haven: Yale University Press).

Garbin, D. 2012. 'Introduction: Believing in the City', *Culture and Religion*, 13.4: 401–04 <https://doi.org/10.1080/14755610.2012.751789>.

Gebauer, A. B. 2020. 'Group Benefits? The Story of a Cluster of Megalithic Monuments in Danish Funnel Beaker Society', in A. B. Gebauer and others (eds), *Monumentalising Life in the Neolithic: Narratives of Change and Continuity* (Oxford: Oxbow), pp. 217–25.

Gebauer, A. B. and others. 2020a. 'Introduction', in A. B. Gebauer and others (eds), *Monumentalising Life in the Neolithic: Narratives of Change and Continuity* (Oxford: Oxbow), pp. 1–5.

——. (eds). 2020b. *Monumentalising Life in the Neolithic: Narratives of Change and Continuity* (Oxford: Oxbow).

Gillespie, S. D. 2000. 'Rethinking Ancient Maya Social Organization: Replacing "Lineage" with "House"', *American Anthropologist*, 102.3: 467–84.

Golinski, H. G. and M. Radermacher (eds). 2019. *Bild, Macht, Religion: Kunst zwischen Verehrung, Verbot und Vernichtung* (Bochum: Kunstmuseum Bochum).

Graevenitz, G. von, S. Rieger, and F. Thürlemann (eds). 2001. *Die Unvermeidlichkeit der Bilder*, Literatur und Anthropologie, 7 (Tübingen: Gunter Narr).

Groneberg, B. and H. Spieckermann (eds). 2007. *Die Welt der Götterbilder*, Beihefte zur Zeitschrift für die alttestamentliche Wissenschaft, 376 (Berlin: De Gruyter).

Hageneuer, S. and S. C. Schmidt. 2019. 'Monumentality by Numbers', in S. Hageneuer and others (eds), *Size Matters: Understanding Monumentality Across Ancient Civilizations* (Bielefeld: transcript), pp. 291–308 <https://doi.org/10.14361/9783839445389-017>.

Hall, E. T. 1976. *Die Sprache des Raumes*, repr. 1966 (Düsseldorf: Schwann).

Harmanşah, Ö. 2013. *Cities and the Shaping of Memory in the Ancient Near East* (Cambridge: Cambridge University Press).

Harris, R. 2021. *How Cities Matter* (Cambridge: Cambridge University Press) <https://doi.org/10.1017/9781108782432>.

Helms, M. W. 1988. *Ulysses' Sail: An Ethnographic Odyssey of Power, Knowledge, and Geographical Distance* (Princeton: Princeton University Press).

Hodder, I. 2018a. 'Introduction: Two Forms of History Making in the Neolithic of the Middle East', in I. Hodder (ed.), *Religion, History, and Place in the Origin of Settled Life* (Boulder: University Press of Colorado), pp. 3–32 <https://doi.org/10.2307/j.ctv3c0thf.5>.

——. (ed.). 2018b. *Religion, History, and Place in the Origin of Settled Life* (Boulder: University Press of Colorado).

——. 2020. 'From Communal to Segmentary: An Alternative View of Neolithic "Monuments" in the Middle East. Comments on Chapters 2 and 3', in A. B. Gebauer and others (eds), *Monumentalising Life in the Neolithic: Narratives of Change and Continuity* (Oxford: Oxbow), pp. 49–51.

Horváth, Á., M. I. Benţa, and J. E. D. Conrod. 2019a. 'Introduction. On the Political Anthropology of Walling', in Á. Horváth, M. I. Benţa, and J. E. D. Conrod (eds), *Walling, Boundaries and Liminality: A Political Anthropology of Transformations* (London: Routledge), pp. 1–8.

——. (eds). 2019b. *Walling, Boundaries and Liminality: A Political Anthropology of Transformations*, Contemporary Liminality, 7 (London: Routledge).

Ilchenko, M. 2020. 'Working with the Past, Re-discovering Cities of Central and Eastern Europe: Cultural Urbanism and New Representations of Modernist Urban Areas', *Eurasian Geography and Economics*, 61.6: 763–93 <https://doi.org/10.1080/15387216.2020.1785907>.

Jaccottet, A.-F. (ed.). 2021. *Rituels en image, images de rituel: iconographie, histoire des religions, archéologie* (Bern: Lang).

Jacobs, J. 1970. *The Economy of Cities* (New York: Vintage).

Jeunesse, C. 2020. 'Elite Houses or Specialised Buildings? Some Comments about the Special Buildings of Göbekli Tepe in Relation to Chapters 2 and 3', in A. B. Gebauer and others (eds), *Monumentalising Life in the Neolithic: Narratives of Change and Continuity* (Oxford: Oxbow), pp. 53–56.

Keith, M. 2014. *The Great Migration: Urban Aspirations* (Washington, DC: World Bank).

Kinzel, M. and L. Clare. 2020. 'Monumental – Compared to What? A Perspective from Göbekli Tepe', in A. B. Gebauer and others (eds), *Monumentalising Life in the Neolithic: Narratives of Change and Continuity* (Oxford: Oxbow), pp. 29–48.

Kolb, M. J. 2014. 'Monumentality among the Mediterranean Isles', in J. F. Osborne (ed.), *Approaching Monumentality in Archaeology* (Albany: State University of New York Press), pp. 153–80.

Lang, C. and others. 2013. 'Gazelle Behaviour and Human Presence at Early Neolithic Göbekli Tepe, South-East Anatolia', *World Archaeology*, 45: 410–29 <https://doi.org/10.1080/00438243.2013.820648>.

Lassner, J. 2017. *Medieval Jerusalem: Forging an Islamic City in Spaces Sacred to Christians and Jews* (Ann Arbor: University of Michigan Press).

Latham, J. A. 2016. *Performance, Memory, and Processions in Ancient Rome: The Pompa Circensis from the Republic to Late Antiquity* (Cambridge: Cambridge University Press).

Levenson, F. 2019. 'Monuments and Monumentality – Different Perspectives', in F. Buccellati and others (eds), *Size Matters: Understanding Monumentality across Ancient Civilizations* (Bielefeld: transcript), pp. 17–40 <https://doi.org/10.14361/9783839445389-003>.

Lipschits, O. 2013. *The Fall and Rise of Jerusalem: Judah under Babylonian Rule* (Winona Lake: Eisenbrauns).

Liverani, M. 2006. *Uruk: The First City* (London: Equinox).

Luginbühl, T. 2015. 'Ritual Activities, Processions and Pilgrimages', in R. Raja and J. Rüpke (eds), *A Companion to the Archaeology of Religion in the Ancient World* (Malden: Wiley), pp. 41–59.

Magoni, A. and others. 2014. 'The Production of Space and Identity at Classic-Period Chunchucmil, Yucatán, Mexico', in A. T. Creekmore III and K. D. Fisher (eds), *Making Ancient Cities: Space and Place in Early Urban Societies* (Cambridge: Cambridge University Press), pp. 145–80.

Mann, M. 1986. *The Sources of Social Power: A History of Power from the Beginning to A.D. 1760*, I: *The Sources of Social Power* (Cambridge: Cambridge University Press).

Meyer, B. 2020. 'Religion as Mediation', *Entangled Religions*, 11.3 <https://doi.org/10.13154/er.11.2020.8444>.

Meyers, G. E. 2012. 'Introduction: The Experience of Monumentality in Etruscan and Early Roman Architecture', in M. L. Thomas and G. E. Meyers (eds), *Monumentality in Etruscan and Early Roman Architecture: Ideology and Innovation* (Austin: University of Texas Press), pp. 1–20.

Moser, S. 2013. 'New Cities in the Muslim World: The Cultural Politics of Planning an "Islamic" City', in P. Hopkins, L. Kong, and E. Olson (eds), *Religion and Place: Landscape, Politics and Piety* (Wiesbaden: Springer), pp. 39–55.

Müller, J. and others. 2020. 'Narratives of 3rd-Millennium Transformations: New Biographies of Neolithic Societies, Landscapes and Monuments', in A. B. Gebauer and others (eds), *Monumentalising Life in the Neolithic: Narratives of Change and Continuity* (Oxford: Oxbow), pp. 115–24.

Naglak, M. 2021. 'House, Rhythm, and Ritual at Gabii, Latium', *Religion and Urbanity Online* <https://doi.org/10.1515/urbrel.14935350>.

Nissinen, M. and C. E. Carter (eds). 2009. *Images and Prophecy in the Ancient Eastern Mediterranean* (Göttingen: Vandenhoeck & Ruprecht).

Osborne, J. F. 2014. 'Monuments and Monumentality', in J. F. Osborne (ed.), *Approaching Monumentality in Archaeology* (Albany: State University of New York Press), pp. 1–19.

Özdöl-Kutlu, S. and others. 2015. 'The End of the Neolithic Settlement: Çatalhöyük and its Neighbours', in I. Hodder and A. Marciniak (eds), *Assembling Çatalhöyük* (Leeds: Maney), pp. 179–95.

Padilla Peralta, D. 2020. *Divine Institutions: Religions and Community in the Middle Roman Republic* (Princeton: Princeton University Press).

Parkins, H. M. (ed.). 1997. *Roman Urbanism: Beyond the Consumer City* (London: Routledge).

Parkinson, E. and others. 2020. 'Storied Structures, Sustainability and Resilience in Late Neolithic Malta: Excavations at Santa Verna, Gozo', in A. B. Gebauer and others (eds), *Monumentalising Life in the Neolithic: Narratives of Change and Continuity* (Oxford: Oxbow), pp. 229–38.

Peters, J. and others. 2014. 'Göbekli Tepe: Agriculture and Domestication', in C. Smith (ed.), *Encyclopedia of Global Archaeology* (New York: Springer), pp 3065–68 <https://doi.org/10.1007/978-1-4419-0465-2_2226>.

Port, M. van de and B. Meyer. 2018. 'Heritage Dynamics: Politics of Authentication, Aesthetics of Persuasion and the Cultural Production of the Real', in B. Meyer and M. van de Port (eds), *Sense and Essence: Heritage and the Cultural Production of the Real* (New York: Berghahn), pp. 1–40.

Purkis, W. J. 2017. 'Jerusalem, 1000–1400: Every People under Heaven', *Material Religion*, 13.4: 552–54 <https://doi.org/10.1080/17432200.2017.1377450>.

Raja, R. and J. Rüpke. 2021. 'Creating Memories in and of Urban Rome: The Forum Iulium', in T. A. Hass and R. Raja (eds), *Caesar's Past and Posterity's Caesar* (Turnhout: Brepols), pp. 53–66.

Rau, S. 2020. 'Urbanity (Urbanitas, Urbanität, Urbanité, Urbanità, Urbanidad...): An Essay', in S. Rau and J. Rüpke (eds), *Religion and Urbanity Online* (Berlin: De Gruyter) <https://doi.org/10.1515/urbrel.11276000>.

Roberts, J. L. (ed.). 2016. *Scale*, Terra Foundation Essays (Chicago: Terra Foundation for the Arts).

Rüpke, J. 2006. *Zeit und Fest: Eine Kulturgeschichte des Kalenders* (Munich: Beck).

——. 2007. *Religion of the Romans*, trans. R. Gordon (Cambridge: Polity).

——. 2012. *Religiöse Erinnerungskulturen: Formen der Geschichtsschreibung in der römischen Antike* (Darmstadt: Wissenschaftliche Buchgesellschaft).

——. 2018. *Pantheon: A New History of Roman Religion* (Princeton: Princeton University Press).

——. 2020. 'Ritual Objects and Strategies of Sacralization within Religious Communication', in M. Stürzebecher and C. D. Bergmann (eds), *Ritual Objects in Ritual Contexts* (Jena: Bussert & Stadeler), pp. 200–13.

——. 2021a. *Religion and its History: A Critical Inquiry* (London: Routledge).

——. 2021b. *Ritual als Resonanzerfahrung*, Religionswissenschaft heute, 15 (Stuttgart: Kohlhammer).

——. 2022. 'Gods in the City', in C. Bonnet. and others (eds), *Naming and Mapping the Gods in the Ancient Mediterranean* (Berlin: De Gruyter), pp. 891–910.

Sanches, M. de Jesus and A. M. Vale. 2020. 'Connecting Stories of the Neolithic in North-Eastern Portugal: Walled Enclosures and their Relationships with the Genealogy of the Landscape', in A. B. Gebauer and others (eds), *Monumentalising Life in the Neolithic: Narratives of Change and Continuity* (Oxford: Oxbow), pp. 251–62.

Schmidt, C. G. 2018. *Vorbild Feind? Der mitteldeutsche Fundplatz Frienstedt: Germanische Elite unter römischem Einfluss* (Kiel: Universitätsbibliothek Kiel) <https://macau.uni-kiel.de/receive/diss_mods_00023264?lang=en?> [accessed 24 February 2023].

Schyle, D. 2016. 'Zur Interpretation des Göbekli Tepe: Heiligtum oder Dorf?', in T. Kerig, K. Nowak, and G. Roth (eds), *Alles was zählt: Festschrift für Andreas Zimmermann* (Bonn: Habelt).

Sear, F. 2006. *Roman Theatres: An Architectural Study* (Oxford: Oxford University Press).

Sheridan, A. and R. Schulting. 2020. 'Making Sense of Scottish Neolithic Funerary Monuments: Tracing Trajectories and Understanding their Rationale', in A. B. Gebauer and others (eds), *Monumentalising Life in the Neolithic: Narratives of Change and Continuity* (Oxford: Oxbow), pp. 195–215.

Sinopoli, C. M. 2015. 'Ancient South Asian Cities in their Regions', in N. Yoffee (ed.), *The Cambridge World History*, III: *Early Cities in Comparative Perspective, 4000 BCE–1200 CE* (Cambridge: Cambridge University Press), pp. 319–42.

Smith, J. Z. 1978. *Map Is Not Territory: Studies in the History of Religion*, Studies in Judaism in Late Antiquity, 23 (Leiden: Brill).

Sørensen, L. 2020. 'Monuments and Social Stratification within the Early Funnel Beaker Culture in South Scandinavia', in A. B. Gebauer and others (eds), *Monumentalising Life in the Neolithic: Narratives of Change and Continuity* (Oxford: Oxbow), pp. 71–85.

Stavrianopoulou, E. 2015. 'The Archaeology of Processions', in R. Raja and J. Rüpke (eds), *A Companion to the Archaeology of Religion in the Ancient World* (Malden: Wiley), pp. 349–60.

Steinhardt, N. S. 1999. *Chinese Imperial City Planning* (Honolulu: University of Hawaii Press).

——. 2019. *Chinese Architecture: A History* (Princeton: Princeton University Press).

Szakolczai, A. 2019. 'The Meaning and Meaninglessness of Building Walls', in Á. Horváth, M. I. Bența, and J. E. D. Conrod (eds), *Walling, Boundaries and Liminality: A Political Anthropology of Transformations* (London: Routledge), pp. 35–53.

Szende, K. 2022. 'From Model to Rival? Competition or Complementarity in Bishops' Seats in East Central Europe', *Religion and Urbanity Online* <https://doi.org/10.1515/urbrel.13901342>.

Teather, A. M. 2020. 'Neolithic Monumentality for the 21st Century', in A. B. Gebauer and others (eds), *Monumentalising Life in the Neolithic: Narratives of Change and Continuity* (Oxford: Oxbow), pp. 9–16.

Thomas, J. 2020. 'The Lives of Monuments and Monumentalising Life', in A. B. Gebauer and others (eds), *Monumentalising Life in the Neolithic: Narratives of Change and Continuity* (Oxford: Oxbow), pp. 287–97.

Trigger, B. G. 2003. *Understanding Early Civilizations: A Comparative Study* (Cambridge: Cambridge University Press).

Urry, J. 2013. 'City Life and the Senses', in G. Bridge and S. Watson (eds), *The New Blackwell Companion to the City* (Malden: Wiley-Blackwell), pp. 347–56.

Valera, A. C. 2020. 'Ephemeral and Cosmological Monumentality: The "Strange" Ditched Enclosures of Chalcolithic South Portugal', in A. B. Gebauer and others (eds), *Monumentalising Life in the Neolithic: Narratives of Change and Continuity* (Oxford: Oxbow), pp. 239–50.

Van de Mieroop, M. 2016. *A History of the Ancient Near East, ca. 3000–323 BC*, 3rd edn (Chichester: Wiley-Blackwell).

Warden, P. G. 2012. 'Monumental Embodiment: Somatic Symbolism and the Tuscan Temple', in M. L. Thomas and G. E. Meyers (eds), *Monumentality in Etruscan and Early Roman Architecture: Ideology and Innovation* (Austin: University of Texas Press), pp. 82–110.

Watkins, T. 2020. 'Monumentality in Neolithic Southwest Asia: Making Memory in Time and Space', in A. B. Gebauer and others (eds), *Monumentalising Life in the Neolithic: Narratives of Change and Continuity* (Oxford: Oxbow), pp. 19–28.

Wengrow, D. 1998. '"The Changing Face of Clay": Continuity and Change in the Transition from Village to Urban Life in the Near East', *Antiquity*, 72: 783–95.

——. 2010. *What Makes Civilization? The Ancient Near East and the Future of the West* (Oxford: Oxford University Press).

Wharton, A. J. 2013. 'Jerusalem's Zions', *Material Religion*, 9.2: 218–43 <https://doi.org/10.2752/175183413X13703410896050>.

Woyke, J. 2005. *Götter, 'Götzen', Götterbilder: Aspekte einer paulinischen 'Theologie der Religion'*, Beihefte zur Zeitschrift für neutestamentliche Wissenschaft – und die Kunde der älteren Kirche, 132 (Berlin: De Gruyter).

Wynne-Jones, S. and J. Fleisher. 2014. 'Swahili Urban Spaces of the Eastern African Coast', in A. T. Creekmore III and K. D. Fisher (eds), *Making Ancient Cities: Space and Place in Early Urban Societies* (Cambridge: Cambridge University Press), pp. 111–44.

8. Perceptions of Changing Religious Landscapes in Augustan Rome

Devmini Malka Wijeratne

Introduction

Augustus finding Rome a city of bricks and leaving it a city of marble is one of the more known facts associated with him. In addition to building imposing and recognizable structures such as the Temple of Apollo Palatinus, the Forum of Augustus, and his own Mausoleum, the *Res gestae* states that he also renovated eighty-two temples over the course of the period he was politically active.[1] While it cannot be said that he rebuilt temples more than he built new ones, this was certainly true of the period leading up to Mark Antony's defeat in 31 BC. A key aspect of Augustus's reign was the extent to which he connected himself to *Mos maiorum* and the various values, traditions, and rituals encompassed by this the concept. There are several examples of Augustus's more overt displays of his connection to *Mos maiorum*, however, in the case of these renovations, this connection — or rather, his respect for it — was demonstrated through the very act of renovating the temples and thereby allowing the continuation of these traditions and rituals. There was of course, a definite political motive behind this connection: this was Augustus's attempt to set himself apart from his enemies, particularly Mark Antony, whom he painted as being overly indulgent and therefore not adhering to (Augustus's interpretation of) the values of *Mos maiorum*.

The temples Augustus renovated — though they were most likely of a smaller scale than the more famous structures from Augustus's career — would still have been considered monuments by the communities that had previously used them for several generations. Since their key purpose was to act as a space within which traditions and rituals could be practised, the communities would already have associated the temples with *Mos maiorum* and also with the continued observation of traditions and rituals which they would have participated in to some degree for most of their lives. It could be argued that, when he renovated the temples, Augustus drew attention back to this meaning and reinstated the importance of continuing and maintaining the practices of *Mos maiorum*. It could also be argued, that by refocusing attention on the temples, Augustus was able to intensify the level of meaning attached to the temples and the practices observed within them, thereby possibly turning what was once a simple regular practice into something intrinsically connected to the very essence of what it was to be 'Roman', as well as something that ensured the success of Rome and all those who lived in the city. This in turn allowed him to take advantage of the added political element of contrasting himself against his enemies, connecting the decline of the temples with the neglect of *Mos maiorum* and therefore the neglect of Rome's fortune and Roman identity. Augustus therefore was presented as the sole individual dedicated to ensuring the resurgence of the concept. By renovating the temples, Augustus was able to employ existing monuments to present his political message. In short, the renovations were a physical manifestation of his message of how he planned to rebuild and reinstate the values, traditions, and rituals of the past. This paper will explore how these temples worked as monuments by taking various definitions of what a monument represents and demonstrating how the temples, and Augustus's actions fit — or in some cases do not fit — these definitions.

The Extent of the Decline

There is very little evidence pointing to the level of decline in the temples when Augustus began renovating them. We also have little evidence of which temples Augustus was specifically involved in. If we take into consideration that Augustus's aim was to alter the meaning associated with the temples, it can then be concluded

---

[1] *R. Gest. div. Aug.* 20.4.

that the temples were standing structures that were still employed within the communities in which they stood. On the other hand, if they were completely destroyed, they may have been in use until the destruction occurred. We can surmise as much from the following passages.

In this passage from the *Res gestae*, it is implied that Augustus simply helped to repair damages or that he helped rebuild any temples that were destroyed suddenly and unexpectedly.

> Capitolium et Pompeium theatrum utrumque opus impensa grandi refeci sine ulla inscriptione nominis mei. [...]. Forum Iulium et basilicam quae fuit inter aedem Castoris et aedem Saturni, coepta profligataque opera a patre meo, perfeci et eandem basilicam consumptam incendio, ampliato eius solo [...]. Duo et octoginta templa deum in urbe consul sextum ex auctoritate senatus refeci nullo praetermisso quod eo tempore refici debebat.
>
> (The Capitolium and the theatre of Pompey both works involving great expense, I rebuilt without any inscription of my own name [...] I completed the Julian Forum and the basilica which was between the temple of Castor and the temple of Saturn, works begun and far advanced by my father, and when the same basilica was destroyed by fire I began its reconstruction on a large site [...] In my sixth consulship, in accordance with a decree of the senate, I rebuilt in the city eighty-two temples of the gods, omitting none which at the time stood in need of repair.)[2]

Likewise, this passage from Suetonius cites age and unfortunate circumstance as the reason why the temples required renovations in the first place. He further implies, however, that Augustus helped embellish temples that may have not needed as much repair:

> Aedes sacras uetustate conlapsas aut incendio absumptas refecit easque et ceteras opulentissimis donis adornauit, ut qui in cellam Capitolini Iouis sedecim milia pondo auri gemmasque ac margaritas quingenties sestertium una donatione contulerit.
>
> (He rebuilt sacred buildings that had collapsed from age and or had been destroyed by fire, and beautified both them and all the others with the most splendid gifts, for example depositing in the chamber of Capitoline Jupiter as a single donation 16,000 pounds of gold as well as pearls and precious stones worth 500,000,000 sesterces.)[3]

Similarly, these passages from *The Life of Atticus* and Livy's *History of Rome* both describe the derelict state of the Temple of Jupiter Feretrius.

---

2 *R. Gest. div. Aug.* 20.1–5 (trans. Shipley 1924).
3 Suet., *Aug.* 30 (trans. Wardle 2014).

> ex quo accidit, cum aedis Iovis Feretrii in Capitolio, ab Romulo constituta, vetustate atque incuria detecta prolaberetur, ut Attici admonitu Caesar eam reficiendam curaret.
>
> (Hence it was, that when the Temple of Jupiter Feretrius, built in the Capitol by Romulus, was unroofed and falling down through age and neglect, Caesar, on the suggestion of Atticus took care that it should be repaired.)[4]

> hoc ego cum Augustum Caesarem, templorum omnium conditorem aut restitutorem, ingressum aedem Feretri Iovis, quam vetustate dilapsam refecit, se ipsum in thorace linteo scriptum legisse audissem, prope sacrilegium ratus sum Cosso spoliorum suorum Caesarem, ipsius templi auctorem, subtrahere testem.
>
> (Augustus Caesar, the founder and restorer of all the temples, rebuilt the temple of Jupiter Feretrius, which had fallen to ruin through age, and I once heard him say that after entering it he read that inscription on the linen cuirass with his own eyes. After that I felt it would be almost sacrilege to withhold from Cossus the evidence as to his spoils given by the Caesar who restored that very temple.)[5]

The state of decline described in these passages could be used as an indicator of the condition of the eighty-two temples Augustus renovated. The constant shifts of power over the course of the civil war meant that some individuals were beginning to construct new temples, while others were beginning to neglect theirs.[6] Maintenance of these temples would have largely depended on private funds, which, as a result of the civil wars, would have been largely dwindling.[7] It is possible that these were in a similar, if not worse, state of decline than the Temple of Jupiter Feretrius.

Furthermore, the reference to Augustus as the founder and restorer of all temples could again imply that the temples of Rome had been in a more noticeable state of decline once Augustus began his ascent to power. Ruin and decay were not limited to the temples of Rome but had become a recognizable part of the landscape for the citizens of Rome, which was having a detrimental impact on Rome's reputation as a capital city.[8] It is possible that Augustus's emphasis on the importance of

---

4 Nep., *Att.* xx.3, trans. Watson 1824.
5 Liv. iv.20.7, trans. Roberts 1912.
6 Cooley 2009, 195.
7 Wallace-Hadrill 2005, 78.
8 Zanker 1988, 19 and 154–55; Suet., *Aug.* 28.

preserving the supposedly once-great traditions of Rome forced the inhabitants of the city to view this decay as an indicator of their own failure to maintain these traditions, which — they were being convinced — had been a vital aspect of Rome's success.[9] Overall, it could be said that the level of decline was at a stage where Augustus could have made a statement with his actions rather than merely appearing to fix what was broken.

The Temples as Monuments

The main definition of monuments used throughout this paper will be the Latin root of the term *monēre*, meaning to remind. As has already been stated, the temples would already have stood as a reminder of *Mos maiorum* simply because the temples were used for the purpose of carrying out the various traditions and rituals encompassed within the concept. Augustus, through his renovations, took this a step further and brought this association to the forefront of how the temples were seen. They were no longer simply spaces within which traditions and rituals were practised but the means by which individuals and communities were able to observe practices that made up a significant aspect of their identity, as well as the means by which they could serve their respective communities and Rome itself. In other words, whatever meaning was already placed on the temples was greatly intensified with the attention the renovations brought; Augustus brought greater visibility and placed more importance on the everyday. Continuing from this, another interpretation that fits with Augustus's actions is Osborne's definition of monumentality, in which he describes monuments as being 'an ongoing, constantly renegotiated relationship between thing and person between the monument and the person experiencing the monument'.[10] It can be argued that the renovations equal the renegotiation of the relationship between individuals and communities and their temples. As mentioned and as it will be argued, this renegotiation resulted in a more intense interpretation of what the temples stood for.

Resembling the idea of monuments serving as a reminder is Colangelo's interpretation of monuments as mass media.[11] While Colangelo's points are mainly in relation to modern, more technologically advanced monuments, it can be argued that the temples Augustus renovated were very much a form of mass media because the scale and centrality of the temples in their respective communities would certainly have created awareness of Augustus and his political message. On the other hand, the temples were only viewed by those within the community, and there are several more imposing and clear examples of Augustan architecture being employed as media. The following paper will agree to a large extent with Colangelo's argument that monuments inform the people that interact with them, of themselves, the place they are in and others around them, and also influence how they understand themselves 'individually and collectively'.[12] A more obvious definition, or rather purpose, of the monuments would replicate DeMarrais, Butter, and Earle's interpretation of monumental buildings as things that 'associate a group with a place and represent the power and authority of its leaders [...] often expressing relatively unambiguous messages of power'.[13] In this instance, the definition is only partly true. While the paper will argue that the intent of the renovations was to associate a group with a place, it will also consider the challenge posed by Osborne towards De Marrais's definition when he argues that the interpretation did not always match the intent of the individual or regime that constructed — or in this case renovated — a monument.[14] In the case of these temples, there is, of course, the added complication that we may never truly know what Augustus's intentions were, nor will we ever know how the people of Rome perceived and interpreted these intentions. Nevertheless, based on the sources available and on Augustus's lasting legacy, his intentions and reactions to these intentions can be surmised.

---

[9] Augustus, in his propaganda, argued that the supposed neglect of the ancestral traditions or *Mos maiorum* in the Late Republic by his enemies directly correlated with the general state of uncertainty and unhappiness within Rome at the time. A key form of propaganda during the Augustan Age was the construction or, in this case, reconstruction of various temple buildings, through which he demonstrated the contributions he was making to the preservation of *Mos maiorum*. The significance of *Mos maiorum* is discussed further in the section on *monēre* of this article, while the importance of construction is discussed in the section on statements of power and monuments as mass media.

[10] Osborne 2014, 3.

[11] Colangelo 2020.

[12] Colangelo 2020.

[13] DeMarrais, Castillo Butters, and Earle 1996, 18; see also Caraher 2014 and Notroff, Dietrich, and Schmidt 2014.

[14] Osborne 2014, 6.

Monēre

In this section, the paper will take on the Latin root of the term 'monuments' and will explore a few examples of what Augustus sought to remind the people of through the renovation of the temples. The examples explored here will be the reminder of *Mos maiorum*, Augustus's ideal portrayal of *Mos maiorum*, and the shortcomings of his rivals.

Reminders of *Mos maiorum*

As mentioned, there are several examples of Augustus's more obvious associations with *Mos maiorum*, where his image and his name, as well as the values, traditions, and rituals he was promoting, decorated the walls of the structures he built. In the case of these renovations, however, neither he, nor his connection to *Mos maiorum* were overtly depicted on the renovations — as far as we are aware. In fact, the temples were not reconstructed under his name; rather, they were renovated under the names of the community leaders or whoever oversaw the renovations.[15] Augustus simply provided the funds and the encouragement required for them to be carried out. It can be argued that while there was no overt display of a connection to *Mos maiorum*, his respect and reverence for the concept was evident in his action of preserving the temples. The renovations alone could be considered a demonstration of *Mos maiorum* (or his interpretation of it) because by doing this he was quite literally preserving Rome's past and enabling the traditions and rituals practised within the temples to continue. Furthermore, he was also showing reverence for the ancestors of that community who had possibly made use of the temples for several generations prior to the start of Augustus's reign.[16]

The Portrayal of *Mos maiorum*

The temples, as well as the meaning assigned to them by the communities that used them, would already to some extent have involved *Mos maiorum* and the traditions and rituals practised within them, simply because they were places where these were practised. The very existence of the temples and the fact that they were worn down would suggest that the practice of traditions and rituals were already very important to the people of Rome. Additionally, there was also an underlying knowledge that the gods needed to be pleased in order to obtain what a certain individual or community wanted. Cicero alludes to this in *De legibus*:

> Sit igitur hoc iam a principio persuasum ciuibus, dominos esse omnium rerum ac moderatores deos, eaque quae gerantur eorum geri iudicio ac numine, [...] et qualis quisque sit, quid agat, quid in se admittat, qua mente, qua pietate colat religiones, intueri, piorumque et impiorum habere rationem.
>
> (The gods are lords and managers of all things, and whatever happens, happens by their judgement and will [...] that they observe what sort of human being each person is, what each does, what each permits him — or herself, in what state of mind and with what sort of piety each observes religious customs.)[17]

While this is Cicero's own opinion, it does suggest that a good relationship with the gods was important to the people of Rome and that they did their best to ensure that this relationship was maintained. Likewise, the reference to religious customs would suggest that the rituals existing within Rome were carried out with the purpose of establishing a favourable relationship with the gods. In other words, the importance of continuing traditions and rituals and of maintaining a good relationship with the gods was not new to the people of Rome.

Augustus, on the other hand, took this a step further. What was once possibly more a relationship between an individual and a single or many gods was now portrayed as a relationship that ensured the success of Rome as a whole and as a relationship that depended on perfection to remain positive. Chaniotis points out that the gods of the Greek and Roman world obeyed the laws of space and time, and therefore could never be in more than one place at any given time.[18] It was believed, therefore, that they simply visited the temples which caught their attention and that they needed an incentive to come there.[19] Their attention was garnered through a variety of visual signals — among other things — especially the appearance of the temple and the altar.[20] The decline of the temples that Augustus renovated did not necessarily mean

---

15 *R. Gest. div. Aug.* 20.1–5; Cass. Dio LIII.2.4–6, LVI.40.4–5.

16 For further information on how Augustus established himself as the prime example of his own definition of *Mos maiorum*, see Zanker 1988, 156–62.

17 Cic., *Leg.* II.15, trans. Zetzel 1999.

18 Chaniotis 2011, 265.

19 Chaniotis 2011; Rüpke 2010, 191–93.

20 Chaniotis 2011, 265.

that the traditions and rituals practised within them were also neglected. However, Augustus's message of *Mos maiorum* presented an ideal which the people of Rome had to adhere to if they expected Rome's greatness to be maintained. The decline of the temples in local communities, according to Augustus's message, would by extension have meant that the rituals carried out within these temples no longer met a standard that would attract the attention of the gods. Ovid, who was born at the very start of Augustus's career and who was therefore exposed to Augustus's message on *Mos maiorum* for most of his life, hints at a message of perfection — or rather, a need for perfection — in the *Fasti*:

> nos quoque templa iuvant, quamvis antiqua probemus, | aurea: maiestas convenit ipsa deo. | laudamus veteres, sed nostris utimur annis: | mos tamen est aeque dingus uterque coli.
>
> (We too are tickled by golden temples, though we approve of the ancient ones: such majesty befits a god. We praise the past, but use the present years; yet both customs are worthy to be kept.)[21]

Again, while Ovid was a poet and was mostly writing to entertain, he was closely tied to Augustus, and the latter's influence is evident in the majority of Ovid's writing. It is therefore possible that Ovid was not the only individual who believed that the gods required a level of perfection. This belief was possibly the result of Augustus's influence, and the idea of an ideal or perfection was possibly a key part of his political message. It can therefore be surmised that, by drawing attention to decline, Augustus was also drawing attention to the idea that the more derelict state of the temples may prompt the gods to ignore the rituals being held in their honour, thus threatening the success of not only the individuals and communities that performed these practices but of Rome itself. Ovid was not alone in these sentiments, however, nor were these sentiments apparently new. In *The City of God*, Augustine quotes Varro, stating that Varro 'feared that the gods would be driven out, not by enemy attack but by the indifference of the Roman people'.[22]

The Shortcomings of Augustus's Rivals

By aiding their renovation, Augustus was presenting himself as an individual willing to help the people in maintaining this relationship, thereby ensuring that Rome continued to celebrate the successes it had been enjoying. Furthermore, through the renovations, Augustus maintained and provided a symbolic form of the traditions that would ensure that they would not be forgotten.[23] Augustus simultaneously scapegoated his enemies and framed them as the reason why the decline occurred in the first place.

It is possible that there was already an air of resentment towards the amount of money being invested in the various wars and being diverted away from the people of Rome. For instance, this passage from Cicero implies that the nobility of Rome had failed in maintaining the ancient traditions and rituals of Rome:

> Sed neglegentia nobilitatis augurii disciplina omissa veritas auspiciorum spreta est, species tantum retenta; itaque maximae rei publicae partes, in is bella quibus rei publicae salus continetur, nullis auspiciis administrantur, [...]. At vero apud maiores tanta religionis vis fuit, ut quidam imperatores etiam se ipsos dis inmortalibus capite velato verbis certis pro re publica devoverent.
>
> (But owing to the carelessness of our nobility the augural lore has been forgotten, and the reality of the auspices has fallen into contempt, only the outward show being retained; and in consequence highly important departments of public administration, and in particular the conduct of wars upon which the safety of the state depends, are carried on without any auspices at all [...] But among our ancestors religion was so powerful that some commanders actually offered themselves as victims to the immortal gods on behalf of the state, veiling their heads and formally vowing themselves to death.)[24]

While Cicero may be exaggerating the circumstances, Augustus certainly did contrast himself against his enemies, painting himself as a pious and humble leader.[25] His enemies, on the other hand, were presented as overindulgent and selfish, as demonstrated by this passage from the *Fasti*:

---

21 Ov., *Fast.* I. 223–26, trans. Frazer 1931.

22 Zanker 1988, 102, paraphrasing Aug., *Civ.* III.

23 Assmann 2006, 17. By providing customs with a symbolic form, the memory of these customs is less likely to be forgotten over time. As this paper will explore in the section on place and community, this was very much Augustus's intention. See also the section on statements of power and monuments as mass media.

24 Cic., *Nat. D.* II.9–10, trans. Wallace-Hadrill 1997, 13.

25 For more on Cicero's views on religion, see Rüpke 2012, 186–204.

pluris opes nunc sunt quam prisci temporis annis, | dum populous pauper, dum nova Roma fuit, | dum casa Martigenam capiebat parva Quirinum.

(Wealth is more valued now than in the years of old, when the people were poor, when Rome was new, when a small hut sufficed to lodge Quirinus, son of Mars.)

at postquam fortuna loci caput extulit huius | et tetigit summo vertice Roma deos, | creverunt et opes et opum furiosa cupido, | et, cum possideant plurima, plura petunt.

(But ever since the Fortune of this place has raised her head on high, and Rome with her crest has touched the topmost gods, riches have grown and with them the frantic lust of wealth, and they who have the most possessions still crave for more.)[26]

By renovating the temples, it could be argued that one of Augustus's goals was to draw attention to the supposed failures of his enemies, framing their neglect of Rome and their indulgences in luxury and their own political ambitions as what caused the temples and therefore generations of traditions and rituals to decline. The temples, therefore, now not only stood as a reminder of the people's personal connection with their traditions and rituals and their relationship with the gods, but they also stood as a reminder of Augustus himself and how he differed from his enemies. Additionally, what could once have been a more intimate practice that only impacted a certain individual or, at most, their immediate community was now presented as a practice that went far beyond a single individual and impacted the very framework on which Rome was built.

Sense of Place and Community

Continuing from the arguments of DeMarrais, Colangelo, and Wu, I will argue that a key reason why Augustus's message was so successfully conveyed through the monumentalization of the temples, was because the temples — prior to their renovation — were already acting as means through which the people felt a sense of self, place, and community.[27] As Agnew argues, for a sense of national identity to exist, a common memory needs to be created and shared among people who would otherwise have little to nothing in common.[28] Monuments, as Assmann observes, like rituals and other customs, could be seen as 'memory aids' that allow individuals to belong to a particular community and to share, learn, and remember the culture of this community.[29] Monuments could then be seen, in this context, as a means through which common memory and history is created, conveyed, and experienced, and this may well have been what Augustus was attempting to achieve.

The common memory created and shared in this instance would have been the concept of *Mos maiorum* — more specifically, the ideas on tradition and ritual that the concept encapsulated. While the words of Varro and Cicero demonstrate that the concept and its customs were already established in Roman culture, the very existence of the temples would also suggest this. Nevertheless, at the same time, Cicero wrote about the decline in these customs, and the derelict state of the temples would imply that they were in a state of disuse, which in turn would mean that the customs were less practised and were slowly being forgotten. In other words, even if *Mos maiorum* had been a vital aspect of life for the generations that built the temples, enough time had passed for the generation of the Augustan Age to have forgotten exactly how important it had been to previous generations. They only had Augustus's own interpretation of its importance to go by. As argued previously, the supposed poor practice of the old customs provided the public with an explanation for the turmoil of the years preceding the renovations that had caused such detriment to their own quality of life. Since Augustus provided a convenient solution to this apparent problem, it is possible that, regardless of whether or not the customs were important in generations past, the people needed his help and simply accepted his interpretations of *Mos maiorum* as fact. It could be argued that this interpretation of the importance of *Mos maiorum* was a counterfactual element added to the common or cultural memory.[30]

---

[26] Ov., *Fast*. 1.197–99 and 209–12, trans. Frazer 1931.

[27] DeMarrais, Castillo Butters, and Earle 1996; Colangelo 2020; Wu 2005.

[28] Agnew 1998, 229.

[29] Assmann 2006, 4.

[30] Assmann 2006, 16. Assmann argues that 'all rituals of connective memory contain a counterfactual element. They all involve introducing into the present something distant and alien for which there is no room in everyday life and which therefore has to be ritually imagined at regular intervals in order to maintain a context that is threatened by disintegration and oblivion'. In this case, *Mos maiorum* and its importance in Rome can be considered the 'distant and alien' thing that needed to be 'ritually imagined'. This warped perception on the importance of *Mos maiorum* would have served to further establish Augustus as the saviour of ancient customs and in

When Augustus began highlighting tradition and ritual as a significant aspect of Roman identity that set Rome apart from the rest of the empire, the communities' association of the temples with identity was heightened further, going from simply being an aspect of their identity to a crucial characteristic and in turn becoming a marker for where they stood in relation to the world around them. The task of carrying out rituals and traditions, or rather, continuing them, did not just have an impact on how one individual or a community placed themselves or viewed themselves in relation to the wider community or world around them. There were in fact, several particularities surrounding the performance of rituals and traditions which could have impacted the way in which a community saw an individual, or how a community itself was seen. As Bourdieu argues, a custom has a hold on an individual because each individual has the ability of 'acting as a judge of others and of himself'.[31] In this instance, the head of a family would be provided with the task of ensuring that the ritual traditions practised from generations before them were continued in the same manner and with the same standard. The success of these rituals would in turn impact the success of the individual's family and his own standing and authority within it. Additionally, the success of the ritual and the family would in turn reflect on the individuals' capabilities and influence how much they were respected by other families in their immediate community.[32] On the other hand, a failure to carry on rituals that had been successfully carried out by previous generations, through external factors such as economic hardships and the lack of an appropriate sacred space, could have resulted in the individual feeling alienated as his ability to carry out his main responsibilities would have been stripped away. Leading on from Bourdieu's argument, therefore, the rituals carried on within these temples would, to individuals of various Roman communities, have been a custom that decided their place within that community.

It can be argued that Augustus, by renovating the temples, ensured that such alienation and neglect of traditions did not occur. On the other hand, it can also be argued that he achieved the converse; he simultaneously heightened the stakes for individuals and communities and their respective reputations by heightening the importance of carrying out and carrying on these traditions and rituals in a suitable manner. By doing something as simple as renovating the temples, Augustus managed to intensify the way in which individuals viewed the temples as a means through which they identified themselves against the backdrop of their community, the city of Rome, and the empire itself.

Statements of Power and Monuments as Mass Media

If we take DeMarrais's definition of a monument and compare it to the temples Augustus renovated, they could, on the surface, appear to be a prime example of the description DeMarrais provides. In Augustus's involvement in the renovations of these temples that had potentially stood for several generations before the start of his career, it could be argued that he was essentially weaving a part of himself into the existing Roman landscape and establishing his presence and ever-growing power throughout the city, making it seem as if his career had already been established for much longer than it actually had. It could be further argued that he was presenting his own position to be as established alongside the buildings he was renovating and that he was presenting the idea that his legacy would last for as long as the structures he built and helped renovate.

Additionally, as was already discussed in the previous section, there was a definite message about himself as a politician and as a leader that Augustus was attempting to convey through the renovations. This message was that he was a selfless individual who genuinely revered the traditions and rituals practised by various communities in Rome and wanted to show respect for the generations who had maintained these traditions in the past by allowing this maintenance to be continued.[33] Additionally, he presented himself as believing that even the most minor of traditions and the communities that practised them played an intrinsic part in Rome's success, thereby making the communities with which he associated himself feel important. Finally, and most importantly, in addition to his power, the absence of his name and image on these buildings and there being little evidence of his direct involvement in the renovations would have presented an image of Augustus as a pious man who was not driven by political ambitions, but by his respect for Rome and *Mos maiorum*.

It would appear that he was quite successful in carving out this image for himself. Cassius Dio for instance, seems to have been convinced by Augustus's seemingly

---

turn to have established his reputation as a leader who provided relief for the people of Rome through the maintenance of old customs.

31 Bourdieu 2010, 16–22.

32 Bourdieu 2010, 16–22.

33 Zanker 1988, 153–56. See also: Scheid 2005, 175–97.

selfless image when he commends both Augustus and Agrippa for their refusal to take credit for the restoration of the temples and for rejecting the ability to use these buildings for their own self-promotion:[34]

καὶ τὰ μὲν ἱερὰ τὰ Αἰγύπτια οὐκ ἐσεδέξατο εἴσω τοῦ πωμηρίου, τῶν δὲ δὴ ναῶν πρόνοιαν ἐποιήσατο: τοὺς μὲν γὰρ ὑπ᾽ ἰδιωτῶν τινων γεγενημένους τοῖς τε παισὶν αὐτῶν καὶ τοῖς ἐκγόνοις, εἴγε τινὲς περιῆσαν, ἐπισκευάσαι ἐκέλευσε, τοὺς δὲ λοιποὺς αὐτὸς ἀνεκτήσατο. οὐ μέντοι καὶ τὴν δόξαν τῆς οἰκοδομήσεως σφῶν ἐσφετερίσατο, ἀλλ᾽ ἀπέδωκεν αὐτοῖς τοῖς κατασκευάσασιν αὐτούς. [...] εὐδοκιμῶν τε οὖν ἐπὶ τούτοις καὶ ἐπαινούμενος ἐπεθύμησε καὶ ἑτέραν τινὰ μεγαλοψυχίαν διαδείξασθαι, ὅπως καὶ ἐκ τοῦ τοιούτου μᾶλλον τιμηθείη, καὶ παρ᾽ ἑκόντων δὴ τῶν ἀνθρώπων τὴν μοναρχίαν βεβαιώσασθαι τοῦ μὴ δοκεῖν ἄκοντας αὐτοὺς βεβιάσθαι.

(As for religious matters, he did not allow the Egyptian rites to be celebrated inside the pomerium, but made provision for the temples; those which had been built by private individuals he ordered their sons and descendants, if any survived, to repair, and the rest he restored himself. He did not, however, appropriate to himself the credit for their erection, but allowed it to go as before to the original builders [...] When, now, he obtained approbation and praise for this act, he desired to exhibit another instance of magnanimity, that by such policy he might be honoured all the more and might have his sovereignty voluntarily confirmed by the people, so as to avoid the appearance of having forced them against their will.)[35]

τά τε ἑαυτοῦ χρήματα σωφρόνως ἐπαύξων ἐς τὴν δημοσίαν χρείαν ἀνήλισκεν, καὶ τῶν κοινῶν ὡς ἰδίων κηδόμενος ὡς ἀλλοτρίων ἀπείχετο. καὶ πάντα μὲν τὰ ἔργα τὰ πεπονηκότα ἐπισκευάσας οὐδενὸς τῶν ποιησάντων αὐτὰ τὴν δόξαν ἀπεστέρησε: πολλὰ δὲ καὶ ἐκ καινῆς, τὰ μὲν ἐπὶ τῷ ἑαυτοῦ ὀνόματι τὰ δὲ καὶ ἐφ᾽ ἑτέρων, τὰ μὲν αὐτὸς κατεσκεύασε τὰ δὲ ἐκείνοις οἰκοδομῆσαι ἐπέτρεψε, τὸ τῷ κοινῷ χρήσιμον διὰ πάντων ἰδών, ἀλλ᾽ οὐ τῆς ἐπ᾽ αὐτοῖς εὐκλείας ἰδίᾳ τισι φθονήσας.

(His own wealth, which enhanced by sober living, he spent for the public needs; with the public funds he was as careful as if they were his own but would not touch them as belonging to others. He repaired all the public works that had suffered injury but deprived none of the original builders of the glory of their founding. He also erected may new buildings, some in his own name and some in others', or else permitted these others to erect them, constantly having an eye to the public good, but grudging no one the private fame attaching to these services.)[36]

Since Cassius Dio was writing over a century later, it would be safe to say that the people of Rome who lived through Augustus's career were equally convinced by the image he provided. It is possible that although the temples displayed no overt connection to Augustus, the communities were still aware of his involvement in the renovation of their temples. They would also have been aware of Augustus's power and influence and would also have been familiar with his more imposing monuments in the centre of Rome. That he interacted with these smaller communities in Rome and aided them in maintaining their public spaces and traditions and rituals without taking any credit for his efforts may have made them feel obligated to show him support. They may have been further reminded of this obligation, of Augustus's interaction and his help, whenever they entered and employed the temples he helped renovate. Such feelings of obligation could in turn have helped Augustus garner support for himself in a time when ever-increasing tensions with Mark Antony meant another war was inevitable.

It is also important to realize that it was not only Augustus's character being curated at this time. The renovation of the temples also coincided with major renovation projects carried out by many of his followers, most notably Agrippa.[37] These renovations focused not just on religious sites but also on facilities that were crucial in improving the overall quality of life within Rome. Such projects included the building of aqueducts, clearing the heavily polluted canals, and providing sources of fresh water (fountains) throughout the city.[38] With Augustus's supporters following his example and improving the city, they, collectively, represented a political group that, unlike the politicians of the Late Republic, were actively attempting to help the people of Rome. Augustus was therefore not the sole individual who had managed to obtain the approval of the Roman people; instead, he and all those who supported him were held in high esteem by the people of Rome. Furthermore, the public's ability to experience the temples (and other public buildings) began not when the construction finished but when it first began. Firstly and most obviously, the con-

---

34 Gowing 2016, 127–28.

35 Cass. Dio LIII.2.4–6, trans. Cary 1954.

36 Cass. Dio LVI.40.4–5, trans. Cary 1954.

37 For further reading of the contributions made by Augustus and his followers to transformation of Rome, see Favro 2005, 110–20.

38 Zanker 1988, 139.

struction would have created several new jobs and therefore greater sources of income for the public.³⁹ Likewise, Zanker points out, the public would have watched the city being built and simultaneously seen the promised positive change being realized. The noise of construction, the flow of ideas, and the experience of seeing the city transformed before them would inevitably have created an atmosphere of great anticipation and even hopefulness for what the future would bring. Following the completion of the temples, the area surrounding it would have seen much social interaction,⁴⁰ during which the temples and other public buildings, the transformation of the city, and the people transforming the city would have been discussed. It would have created great enthusiasm for the leadership of Augustus and his followers. In this instance, the renovated temples were advertisements of Augustus's image even before they were completed.

As Osborne points out, however, the intention of the monument's builder did not always match how the monuments were then interpreted by those who interacted with them.⁴¹ Additionally, it is also important to realize that, in the case of Augustus, we will never know what his true intentions were when he called for the renovation of these temples. It is possible that the buildings simply needed to be maintained, and Augustus, having a position of power and the financial means to do so, ensured that the maintenance took place. Additionally, it can be argued that whenever Augustus attempted to display his power through a monument, it was far from a mere implication. In the case of these temples, he distanced himself from any overt involvement in the renovations, so could these renovated temples then be considered statements of power or forms of mass media? It is likely, in this instance, that rather than aiming for the temples to stand as a testament of his power, Augustus aimed for them to stand as a testament of his character and his good intentions towards the people of Rome. It is possible that by refusing to claim credit or provide any official titles for himself, Augustus believed that the titles would be willingly given to him by the people of Rome as an acknowledgement of the renovation of the temples. Such intentions are implied in the previous passages by Cassius Dio and the following passages from the *Res gestae*:

Dictaturam et apsenti et praesenti mihi delatam et a populo et a senatu, M. Marcello et L. Arruntio consulibus non recepi. [...] Consulatum quoque tum annuum et perpetuum mihi delatam non recepi.

(Even though the post of dictator was conferred upon me both when I was absent and when I was present by both people and senate in the consulship of Marcus Marcellus and Lucius Arruntius [22 BC], I did not accept it [...] when the consulship too was conferred upon me at that time for a year and in perpetuity, I did not accept it.)⁴²

Yet, it may be that the people of Rome did not interpret Augustus's intentions on their own. Perhaps his portrayal of himself as a leader wanting no credit was successful, and he had to provide gentle reminders that he was the man responsible for the renovated state of their temples and their ability to continue traditional practices and rituals; some good examples of such reminders are the very passages from the *Res gestae* at the beginning of this article. Augustus very clearly names himself as the renovator of numerous temples in Rome, despite stating in those same passages that he refused to inscribe his name on those buildings. This therefore points to the conclusion that the people of Rome would not have been permitted to be wholly unaware of Augustus's involvement in the renovation and that subtle reminders existed in several unknown forms that ensured his part was not forgotten over time.

Moreover, Augustus was offered various titles throughout his career, resulting in him first becoming emperor and then, towards the end of his career, being referred to as a god. Whichever way the people of Rome interpreted the new meaning with which Augustus imbued the temples, they certainly accepted him as their leader and most certainly respected and supported him throughout his career. Therefore, while Augustus's intent in renovating the temples goes against DeMarrais's idea of monuments as statements of power, it does not wholly match Osborne's idea that the interpretation of a monument did not always match the builders' intended message. Augustus's intent was most likely more a statement of his character than his power. Furthermore, while not everyone may have known of his involvement in helping maintain the temples and *Mos maiorum*, they were certainly aware of him and of the more obvious depictions of his power, his character, and message elsewhere in Rome. They were convinced by this message and did support him.

---

³⁹ Childe 1950, 12.
⁴⁰ Childe 1950, 16.
⁴¹ Osborne 2014, 7; see also Agnew 1998, 236.

⁴² *R. Gest. div. Aug.* 5.3.

Conclusion

There are several grand and imposing examples of Augustan architecture which would fit in an overall definition of a monument and monumentality. The renovated temples, although far smaller and among the less significant constructions of the Augustan Age, were nevertheless monuments to the communities that used them. The temples would have played a very central role in their lives and in the lives of the generations before them. I would therefore argue that although the larger structures of the Augustan Age were undeniably the most recognizable monuments and means of mass media of that age, the smaller reconstructed temples were also monuments and mass media in their own right. This is because the *res publica* probably interacted with these temples more than they would have with the much larger temples Augustus built. The larger temples — which they were undoubtedly familiar with — presented the all-powerful leader of the Roman Empire; the smaller temples represented their connection to this leader and served as a reminder of the service he granted them. It could be argued that while these temples lacked the pomp and grandeur of Augustus's larger temples, they had a more effective and relatable message of his character that left a more significant impression on the people of Rome and that allowed him and his deeds to be remembered for generations to come.

Works Cited

Agnew, J. 1998. 'The Impossible Capital: Monumental Rome under Liberal and Fascist Regimes, 1870–1943', *Geografiska Annaler: Series B, Human Geography*, 80.4: 229–40.

Assmann, J. 2006. *Religion and Cultural Memory: Ten Studies*, Cultural Memory in the Present (Stanford: Stanford University Press).

Bourdieu, P. 2010. *Outline of a Theory of Practice*, Cambridge Studies in Social and Cultural Anthropology, 16, original edition published in 1972 (Cambridge: Cambridge University Press).

Caraher, W. 2014. 'Patronage and Reception in the Monumental Architecture of Early Christian Greece', in J. Osborne (ed.), *Approaching Monumentality in Archaeology*, IEMA Proceedings, 3 (Albany: State University of New York Press), pp. 39–57.

Cary, E. 1954. *Dio's Roman History*, VI (London: Heinemann).

Chaniotis, A. 2011. 'Emotional Community through Ritual. Initiates, Citizens and Pilgrims as Emotional Communities in the Greek World', in A. Chaniotis (ed.), *Ritual Dynamics in the Ancient Mediterranean: Agency, Emotion, Gender, Representation* (Stuttgart: Steiner), pp. 264–90.

Childe, V. G. 1950. 'The Urban Revolution', *The Town Planning Review*, 21.1: 3–17.

Colangelo, D. 2020. *The Building as Screen: A History, Theory, and Practice of Massive Media* (Amsterdam: Amsterdam University Press).

Cooley, E. A. 2009. *Res gestae Divi Augusti: Text, Translation and Commentary* (Cambridge: Cambridge University Press).

DeMarrais, E., L. Castillo Butters, and T. Earle. 1996. 'Ideology, Materialization, and Power Strategies', *Current Anthropology*, 37: 15–31.

Favro, D. 2005. 'Making Rome a World City', in K. Galinsky (ed.), *The Cambridge Companion to the Age of Augustus* (Cambridge: Cambridge University Press), pp. 234–63.

Gowing, A. 2016. 'Cassius Dio and the City of Rome', in J. Madien and C. Lange (eds), *Cassius Dio: Greek Intellectual and Roman Politician* (Leiden: Brill), pp. 117–36.

Notroff, J., O. Dietrich, and K. Schmidt. 2014. 'Building Monuments, Creating Communities: Early Monumental Architecture and Pre-Pottery Neolithic Göbekli Tepe', in J. Osborne (ed.), *Approaching Monumentality in Archaeology*, IEMA Proceedings, 3 (Albany: State University of New York Press), pp. 83–105.

Osborne, J. F. (ed.). 2014. *Approaching Monumentality in Archaeology*, IEMA Proceedings, 3 (Albany: State University of New York Press).

Rüpke, J. 2010. 'Representation or Presence? Picturing the Divine in Ancient Rome', *Archiv für Religionsgeschichte*, 12.1: 181–96.

——. 2012. *Religion in Republican Rome: Rationalization and Ritual Change* (Philadelphia: University of Pennsylvania Press).

Scheid, J. 2005. 'Augustus and Roman Religion: Continuity, Conservatism and Innovation', in K. Galinsky (ed.), *The Cambridge Companion to the Age of Augustus* (Cambridge: Cambridge University Press), pp. 175–97.

Wallace-Hadrill, A. 1997. '*Mutatio morum*: The Idea of a Cultural Revolution', in I. Habinek and A. Schiesaro (eds), *The Roman Cultural Revolution* (Cambridge: Cambridge University Press), pp. 3–22.

——. 2005. '*Mutatas formas*: The Augustan Transformation of Roman Knowledge', in K. Galinsky (ed.), *The Cambridge Companion to the Age of Augustus* (Cambridge: Cambridge University Press), pp. 55–85.

Wu, H. 2005. *Remaking Beijing: Tiananmen Square and the Creation of a Political Space* (London: Reaktion).

Zanker, P. 1988. *The Power of Images in the Age of Augustus* (Ann Arbor: University of Michigan Press).

9. The King and the Population as Protagonists of the Oath: Intermediatory Semantics in Ancient Near Eastern Treaties

Elena Malagoli

The goal of this paper is to show how the figure of the king in the context of the ancient Near East acted as an intermediary for two different groups: one is his people and the other one is the gods. In order to do so, I will analyse passages from treaties — especially from *CTH* 51, which is considered unique in its nature — and other documents, such as prayers and songs. The focus of this paper will thus be on the Hittite and Mittanian socio-political context resulting from the peculiarity of the treaty signed by these two polities. I will try to answer three questions: Why did the king act as an intermediary between his people and his pantheon? How was this intermediation employed? And what was the condition that made such a situation possible?

CTH 51 is the so-called 'Mittani treaty'. It is a peace treaty between two important polities of the second-millennium Near East, the Hittite and the Mittani kingdoms, and it was signed during a time of major political change. Mittani rose to power in the Middle to Late Bronze Age, and the exact factors that led to its genesis are still debated. Unfortunately, we first need to address the problem of chronology. The sixteenth century BC is sparsely documented and has often been referred to as a 'Dark Age'. There is not yet a fixed chronology for this area, because of the lack of data allowing us to place specific events in a specific time beyond any reasonable doubt;[1] approximation is thus needed. This leads to many speculations on the chronology of the second millennium which, as things stand, cannot be definitive. Nonetheless, the Mittani treaty can be traced back to around the mid-fourteenth century BC, thanks to comparative data on its central figures.

Before digging into the main topic, let us define the historical scenario. During this time period, there were three major political powers on the ancient Near Eastern chessboard: Egypt's XVIII dynasty (Akhenaten and Tutankhamun are especially relevant); the Hittite Empire, led by Suppiluliuma I; and Mittani, a polity located in the Khabur Basin.

During the Middle and Late Bronze Age, expansionism to the detriment of smaller polities was very common, and new tendencies towards the formation of empires were on the rise. During the sixteenth century, in the very heart of the Anatolian plateau, the Hittite kingdom quickly expanded to encompass most of central Anatolia, becoming an empire during the reign of Suppiluliuma I. The extent of its power was such that we have records of treaties and skirmishes with Egypt, one of the superstars of the political landscape. The other superstar was Mittani, a polity a little less understood than Ḫatti and Egypt due to lack of primary sources. We know about its existence and importance thanks to the records provided by its contemporaries, such as Ḫatti, Egypt, and Kassite Babylon. We know, for example, that it was so significant that a series of royal marriages were arranged between Mittanian princesses and Egyptian pharaohs. The practice of royal marriage is a clear indicator of Mittani's status, since it indicated political alliances and agreements among nations. At one point, Mittani was so politically relevant that it was able to make considerable demands during the negotiation for the marriage of Tušratta's daughter to Amenhotep III.[2]

Like many others in its time, Mittani was organized as a palace-based society, where local kings ruled under the Mittanian hegemony. Along its western borders were Alalaḫ and Ugarit, while at the eastern edge was the kingdom of Arraphe. The northern limit was Lake Van and the southern one was the city of Terqa, but there also were collectively governed settlements in

---

[1] Beckman 2000, 19–21.

[2] This is known as the 'Mittanian letter', catalogued as *EA* 24; Moran 1992, 63–71. In other sources, the marriage is between Artatama I's daughter and Amenhotep II/Thutmosis IV; cf. Wilhelm 1989, 28–29.

the Euphrates Valley.³ Therefore, the spatial extent of this polity was very large, and its north-western border steadily approached the Hittite one, causing territorial tensions between the two powers.

This brings us to the bone of contention that led to *CTH* 51. Mittani political history during the fourteenth century was scourged by fights for succession that triggered perfect conditions for Hittite expansionism. The death of King Artašumara threw the country into political chaos, and Tušratta, who was not in the line of succession, ascended to the throne. This situation legitimized the Hittite King Suppiluliuma in launching an assault into the Mittanian territories against the new usurper. In doing so, a war was added to the political chaos. During the war between the Hittites and Mittani, Tušratta was murdered, and his son Šattiwaza came to the throne. Still facing the problem of his father's usurpation, Šattiwaza was not a strong enough king to retain power, and Šuttarna III, a descendent of the late king, forced him to flee the country. Here is where things get complicated: at the beginning of the war, Suppiluliuma seemed to endorse the party of Šuttarna III but ended up forming an alliance with Šattiwaza, thus producing the famous 'Mittanian treaty'. So, what made Suppiluliuma change his mind about the usurpation? There are no certainties, but Assyria probably played a role in his decision. In fact, Šuttarna III, once seated on Mittani's throne, allied with Assyria, a kingdom that would become a huge political power in the next hundred years. Suppiluliuma was afraid of this alliance because it could produce a tremendous power bloc on his eastern border. Therefore, when Šattiwaza asked him for help, Suppiluliuma chose to endorse him.⁴ These are the political circumstances that led to *CTH* 51, where Suppiluliuma acknowledges Šattiwaza as the rightful king of Mittani and agrees to help him reclaim his throne: they therefore establish the treaty, which regulates the duties of both parts.

This treaty is a fine example of diplomacy in the Late Bronze Age, and it is particularly interesting because it shows how the diplomatic machine worked when two major powers were involved. Even if Mittani was brought to its knees by the wars, it was still 'internationally' regarded — and we take the liberty of using the anachronistic term 'international' here — as one of the big polities. This made its status very peculiar, especially when compared to the other and more usual protagonists of the treaties. In the Hittite collection, there are two main types of treaties: the subordinate type and the equal type. The first is characterized by the dominance of the Hittite kingdom, which benefits from the best deal at the expense of the other party (see for example *CTH* 49 and *CTH* 53); the second is characterized by the equal status of the two participants, as seen in the treaty *CTH* 91 between Ḫatti and Egypt.⁵ *CHT* 51, however, has been called a 'pseudo-equal' treaty,⁶ since it is not a subordinate type of treaty but neither is it a completely equal treaty.

The Mittani kingdom suffered major land losses and the actual power of its king was severely compromised, but despite all this, Mittani was an important kingdom that could not be treated as a simple subordinate.⁷ This is why *CTH* 51 is a pseudo-equal treaty. The role of the participants is quite balanced, and both are required to follow a specific behaviour in order to not break the treaty. This does not happen in the subordinate treaties, where the Hittite king had many advantages and could be spared many duties.⁸

The treaty thus provides fertile ground to better understand not only the role of the polities involved but also and especially the role of the kings who took the oath — an oath that would bind them to its terms. The protagonists are crucial to this inquiry: much attention has been given to the polities, and there is no doubt they are relevant, but what I would like to point out is the role of the single king, because ultimately it is he who takes the oath. In doing so, he involves the entirety of his community.

If we take a closer look at the structure of an ancient Near Eastern treaty, we see some stable elements that rarely vary: the preamble (where the participants introduce themselves), the historical introduction, the normative section, the list of divine witnesses, and the curses and blessings.⁹ The importance of the list of divine witnesses is due to a treaty's similarity to an oath, which was a widespread tool during this period. An oath was used to bind the participants to specific behaviour; if they did not comply, they would face the gods' punishment. As can be seen in many international treaties of the Bronze Age, the participants are not merely the kings who take the oath; they act for their entire people, who

---

3 Otto 2014, 35; von Dassow 2014, 14.
4 Bryce 2005, 184–85; Llop 2011, 596–97.

5 Devecchi 2015, 22–25; Beckman 1996, 2.
6 Devecchi 2015, 24.
7 Bryce 2005, 161–84.
8 Devecchi 2015, 15–16.
9 Devecchi 2015, 32; Beckman 1996, 2–3.

are also affected by the terms stipulated. Here we come to the core of this inquiry. When the oath was taken, its effectiveness extended beyond the kings to their subjects and even to the next generations.[10] An example of this is given in *CTH* 51, which reads:

> In the future the Hittites and the Mittannians [shall not look upon one another] with a malevolent eye. The Hittites shall not do evil to the Mittannians; [the Mittannians] shall not do evil to the Hittites. When the King of Hatti goes to war, the king of [the land] of Mittanni [shall attack] any enemy of [Hatti]. As someone is the enemy of the land of Mittanni, [he shall be] the enemy [of Hatti. The friend] of the King of Hatti [shall be] the friend of the king of the land [of Mittanni].[11]

In this scenario, both kings (Hittite and Mittanian) are acting as intermediaries, meaning that when they take the oath, they take it not by or for themselves, but on behalf of all their people. It is worth noticing that the kings could be spared the gods' punishment, but this was not true for the population. The question is, therefore, who are exactly 'the people'?

Let us start by saying that when we refer to the Hittite or the Mittanian population, we loosely refer to the people who lived and acted in these territories and were considered as part of the polity. Therefore, we also need to answer the following question: What were the circumstances that allow the king to act as an intermediary for his people?

To answer, it is fruitful to better analyse the structure and the meaning of the oath, but I will first briefly deal with the question of who the people are, since it is at the same time simple and difficult to answer. We have many documents from the ancient Near East but — and this is the unfortunate fate of many ancient societies — they mainly deal with the higher classes. The archives that have been excavated in the last 150 years belonged to palaces or temples, and they paint a picture of life in the city at best. What was happening in the outskirts of the cities, the countryside, or the faraway mountains is still up for debate. This is not meant to discourage an inquiry, however, as there are many things we do know.

When discussing ancient Near Eastern societies, it is important to keep in mind that we are talking about a vast territory with several social structures. Still, I would like to pinpoint some features that can be helpful to paint a general picture. For most of the ancient Near East, the primary difference is between the city and the *outside*. The outside does not mean just the outskirts or the countryside where farming took place, but also the steppes and the mountains where the nomadic and semi-nomadic people lived. This last category included bandits as well as herders and stock-owners who constantly moved with their herd. Socially speaking, they were not viewed favourably by the people living in the city, who refer to them as smelly and uncivilized.[12] Yet, in Hittite society, those cattle and sheep were still regarded as belonging to the Hittite crown, as is indicated by treaties which demanded their return to Hittite territory if they were to be found in a neighbouring independent state. This means that even if there were cultural differences, these people (and their goods) were considered as belonging to a larger society that included people living in the city, land- and stock-owners, and the herdsmen who took care of the animals (and who were usually at the lowest level of the social hierarchy).[13]

Thus, when the king addressed the entirety of his people, what he meant is something particularly broad and not so clearly defined as we would expect it today. This does not mean that it was completely unregulated; during the time of Hammurabi and among the Hittites as well, there is evidence that Hittite society was divided into groups and that lawful punishments were regulated accordingly.[14] For the purpose of the treaties, though, this differentiation was not necessarily important, especially during international agreements. In this context, 'the people' would ideally refer to all the king's subjects.

I mentioned that the oath is a very ancient tool, one that in the ancient Near East can be traced back to the Assyrian *kārums*, the markets of the early second millennium.[15] The oath's basic structure remained virtually the same throughout the Bronze Age: it consists of a statement pronounced (or written) by someone in the presence of the gods, who act as witnesses and guarantors of what has been stated. In addition, there could be specific punishments issued by the gods if it was broken. Therefore, the oath was widely employed and particularly efficient at binding its participants to specific tasks, such as telling the truth, as well as legally articulating peace treaties.

---

[10] Devecchi 2015, 17.

[11] Trans. Beckman 1996, 41.

[12] See, for example, Beckman 2013, 204 on the famous 'marriage of Martu'.

[13] Bryce 2002, 83, 276 n. 23.

[14] Bryce 2002, 29–30, 51–52; Biga 2006, 108–09; Liverani 2011, 351.

[15] Veenhof and Eidem 2008, 102–05, 228–29; Bryce 2005, 21–24.

The function of the oath would thus be to bind, or, as Agamben would say, 'to keep together/to preserve'. This practice does not found nor establish anything; its purpose is to validate the statement and to guarantee its efficacy.[16] It is also notable that the semantic elements used to describe the treaty (and therefore the oath) in this particular context — such as *isḫiul-* and *lingai* in Hittite, and *riksu/rikiltu* and *māmītu* or *nīš ili* in Akkadian — all loosely translate to the concept of binding or tying together.[17]

If we further break up the oath's components, the crucial role of the individuals taking it also becomes clear. The protagonists willingly agree to bind themselves in doing (or not doing) something, and they accept the consequences if they do not keep their word. This kind of responsibility is at the very base of the communication that takes place between the human participants and the gods. This is another topic that would be fruitful to investigate, but the lack of space forces me to pass over it. I would like to point out, though, that this communication needs to be understood in terms of its participants' agencies in a religious context, not just a political one.[18] This kind of communication is fragile, in a way, and it needs to be reinforced by actions (such as the periodic public reading of the treaty in front of the statue of the god). All these elements — the statement, the witnessing of the gods, the shared symbolic system, and the actions — make possible the efficacy of the oath.

Keeping in mind the purpose of the oath, we move to the evolution of the king's role in the ancient Near East, which is a key element in order to answer our initial questions as to why and how the king acted as an intermediary between his people and his pantheon and what the conditions were that made such a situation possible. It is important to remember that the kind of people's representation that we experience today was not the norm during the Bronze Age. If we think about a modern leader who makes decisions for its people (as the prime minister or the president of a country could do today) that would be far from the role of an ancient Near Eastern king. I will now take a closer look at the role of the king in this specific context.

In the Early Dynastic Period (shortened to 'EDP', *c.* 2900–2300 BC), the power of the king was already on the rise. When today we use the word 'king' — or, as I already did in this paper, the adjective 'international' — it truly is anachronistic. The kings of the city of Uruk or the city of Lagaš were very different from Charlemagne or King Louis XIV of France. Nonetheless, it would be fruitless to forge new words for every change in meaning that is not relevant to this inquiry. These kings were leaders of city-states during a shift in the dynamics of power. This shift involved the transition of powers from the temple to the palace. During the Early Dynastic Period (*c.* 2900–2300 BC), the city temple was not just a place where divine activities occurred, as we would expect today, but was also a place for economics and politics. It hosted different spaces: for the gods and the priests, for gatherings of the believers, for storing food and supplies, and for economic and administrative activities such as shops and archives. It is in the Early Dynastic Period that the temple started to give way to the palace.

The transition from temple to palace is difficult to break down, mostly because of the lack of direct evidence. It is interesting to note how many cities started to adopt a different kind of managerial power at the end of the third millennium. We can see the emergence of classes of elite families:

> Whereas Early Bronze II polities focused on maintaining a balance between collective needs and private ambitions, instituting leveling mechanisms to prevent the dissolution of social solidarity [...] Early Bronze III towns communicate the attempt to concentrate social power in fewer hands — whether of individual aggrandizers or of kin-based units (such as the House, as suggested by Chesson in 2003). The power of these individuals or families was maintained and legitimized as a manifestation of the corporate will by means of ritual sanction and feasting (e.g., at temples), and by the recruiting of collective labor to carry out monumental construction, which in turn served as tangible evidence of the power of the city and its elites. Palaces represented the attempt of those elites to establish a permanent locus for the stockpiling and redistribution of staple products. Despite the attrition of leveling mechanisms established in the Early Bronze II (such as a uniform material culture), Early Bronze III leaders could maintain a sense of common purpose based on collective urban identity.[19]

The change that we witness revolves around the palace gaining more military, administrative, and economic powers that often overlapped with those of the temple. Slowly, the temple gained an ideological dominance and the palace an operational one. Why this bifurcation of functions happened at all, we cannot know, but the presence of laic transactions is already attested in the EDP

---

[16] Agamben 2008, 5–7.
[17] Devecchi 2015, 11–12; Beckman 1996, 1–2.
[18] For the use of 'communication', cf. Rüpke 2015.

[19] Greenberg 2014, 43.

IIIa, with the selling of non-temple land to private owners. The transition from temple-city to palace-city was obviously slow, and the palace needed to keep a relationship with the temple in order to legitimate its power. Therefore, the royal family had the right to carry out specific tasks (tax collection, legislative power, etc.) because it mirrored the divine family that resided in the temple. This was possible also because the very idea of 'temple' or 'palace' was a little blurrier than what we might perceive today. Organizationally speaking, the domestic house, the temple, and the palace were all considered structures called 'houses'. These structures were similar to each other in the sense that they all were productive and administrative entities of society. It should be clear now why there was little difference among 'the house of Person' and 'the house (the temple) of God' or 'the house (the palace) of the king'. The difference is blurred, if there even was a difference. The palace would then be a 'big house' (Sumerian for 'palace' would be *é-gal*, where *é* translates to 'house'), in every possible way. It is a bigger house where the residents, or the family, is a more important one: they are the royal family. This sets the scene also for an economic and tributary dependence based on importance. Therefore, if the palace had an operational importance, then the temple had an ideological importance. The link between the residents of the temple (the godly family) and those of the palace is a mirrored structure based on relevance. Nonetheless, there was no supremacy of one over the other: the temple and the palace had different functions, but they needed to validate each other.[20]

To better understand the scale of the transition, it is interesting to look at the words for 'king' — or, better said, for what is usually translated as 'king'. The words are *en*, '(great) priest'; *ensi*, 'farmer (of the god)'; or *lugal*, 'great man'.[21] As can be seen by these words, the semantic borders are a little blurry and can encompass different meanings. Just as the temple's authority and responsibilities were progressively shared with the palace, so did the same transition occur between priests and kings. The royal family became increasingly more relevant in the structure of society, but for its role to be effective, the king needed a strong relationship with the gods. He could be in charge so long as his relationship with the gods was considered righteous by his society. From this perspective, the role of the king was a religious one too,

because he needed to maintain the favour of the gods for his land and people to be prosperous. This context also allowed the possibility for a usurper to be legitimized by the gods. If the usurper was able to gain control and take on the role of king, ideologically that meant he was chosen by the gods and was therefore a righteous leader. It is in this time period that the conquests start to gain a role in the king narrative.[22]

At the very beginning of the Akkadian Empire, the king was a heroic figure and a military leader, as demonstrated by the kings Sargon and Naram-sin. This type of kings and their kingdoms were characterized by unprecedented territorial expansion and wars for supremacy. Therefore, early on the image of the king was closely related to his military victories, his strength on the battlefield, and his unrivalled authority. This narrative reached its extreme with Naram-sin, who declared himself 'god on earth'.[23]

It is not an easy task to trace the emergence of the king in the ancient Near East, because when the first texts appeared, the concept of the king as a leader was already established. According to the Sumerian King List, originally composed at the end of the third millennium BC, kingship descended from heaven and was given by the gods not to an individual, nor to a family, a tribe, or a territory, but to a city, so it was transferred from one city to another in succession. After the mythical flood (through which the god Enlil planned to destroy humankind), the reason given for the change of dynasty was either that the city was 'smitten with weapons' or that its 'term of office was abolished'. Both cases had the same consequence, namely 'its kingship was carried to' a new city. Still, very early, some cities retain a special role. For example, the role the city of Nippur held was not acknowledged in the Sumerian King List, and yet control over Nippur (where the temple of the god Enlil was) was seen as a sign of the legitimacy of a king's claim to be the rightful ruler of the whole of Babylonia.[24]

In the late 1970s, Frankfort stated:

> We must note, in the first place, that the original articulation of the Mesopotamian society was local rather than tribal. In other words, habitat rather than kinship defined one's social affiliation. However, the elders, who dealt with current affairs, seem to have been not only influential members of the community but heads of

---

[20] Liverani 2011, 141–44.

[21] For the various translations, see Liverani 2011, 154–55; Finer 1999, 114–15.

[22] Liverani 2011, 115–16, 161–64.

[23] Biga and Capomacchia 2008, 151–54; Liverani 2011, 193–201, 210–11.

[24] Roaf 2013, 333.

families, for they are designated in Sumerian by the word *abba* ('father'). In the elders we seem therefore to have a connecting link between Primitive Democracy and the primordial organization of society in family and clans. But while a social order based on kinship does not, as a rule, contain features which prevent it from spreading over large areas, Primitive Democracy was unsuitable for such expansion, because it carried with it the autonomy of each separate locality and entirely lacked organs through which to exercise conjoint authority. Moreover, it entailed some of the disadvantages of freedom. Often it must have been difficult to get the assembly to act, since voting and submission by all to the will of the majority were unknown. The issues were clarified through general discussion — 'asking one another' as the Babylonians expressed it. Communal actions required unanimity, and this could be reached only by means of persuasion. Hence, the need for action and leadership fostered a parasitical growth of personal power which ultimately destroyed the original system of government.[25]

The idea of a 'Primitive Democracy', as intended by Jacobsen (1943), is difficult to sustain, especially in the absence of explicit textual evidence. In the Late Bronze Age, there is already evidence of formalized relations between states — as attested by several different sources such as treaties, letters, and so on — and this worked both inside and outside the state.[26] In this sense, there is nothing 'primitive' about it, but at the same time it is very likely that the context in which the idea of 'king' arose in the ancient Near East was that of large family groups. It is thus possible that the transition from *leaders of a group of people* to *divinely anointed kings* occurred in a pre-historical time. Between these two broad categories, there is that of the military leader, which is far more commonly attested and can be identified in historical sources. A successful military campaign could increase the crown's possessions through the spoils of war, including movable property, cattle and other livestock, and prisoners of war, for whom sizable ransoms might be paid. The high sums recorded by the archives may indicate that this was a major goal of ancient Near Eastern warfare and that prestige goods were important in delivering the message of what a successful king should do or be.[27] What really matters about these militaristic features is that they are related to a single individual: the idea of a 'hero' is closely linked to military might, which in this time period is related to physical strength and ability to conquer land. This kind of king is the one who stands out among his peers, who is capable of such deeds that he can be subject to deification.

Let us take a step back, however, because the deification of the king is a relatively recent feature. As already stated, it occurred for the first time with Naram-sin (2254–2218 BC), who declared himself 'god on earth'.[28] The features of the early kings in the ancient Near East were almost universally the same. These included being chosen by the gods, being pious, being militarily successful, being physically unblemished, and being male, and they were closely linked to a geographical dimension.[29] During the first Babylonian Dynasty (*c.* 1800–1500 BC), political and cultural changes ensured that the king was not only or primarily a military leader and a heroic figure subject to deification, but he was now also a father figure to his people; from this, the trope of the 'good shepherd' was introduced. This change in perception is not completely new, since it has roots in the administrative role taken on by the king in the Early Dynastic Period, but there are some pivotal additions to it that lead to the change I want to point out.

It is useful to think about ancient Near Eastern societies in terms of units: the smallest unit is the family, with its hierarchical roles: the head of the family, the extended relatives, etc. Another unit is the royal family, which can be considered bigger from an ideological point of view (see the term *lu-gal* for king). Building on this there are the gods, specifically the divine family who resides in the temple and who serves as a blueprint for the all the rest. All these units organically interact with each other in a continuum that encompasses nature, gods, people, the environment, etc. In the same pattern as the family, the gods look upon their people (who are usually identified as the individuals belonging to a specific geographical area) in the same way the head of the family looks upon its kin. This is the reason why the transition from the narrative of the king as a primarily military leader to the king as a father figure was possible. In a broader sense, when the king took on the role of father figure towards his people, another unit can be identified. In this way, the community fell ideologically under a larger umbrella, one that could be called the 'children of the king'. It is in this context that the symbolic fatherhood of the king is expressed.

---

25 Frankfort 1978, 215–16.
26 Liverani 2001, 2–3.
27 Sallaberger 2013, 237–38.

28 Biga and Capomacchia 2008, 151–54; Liverani 2011, 193–201, 210–11.
29 Roaf 2013, 332–34, 354.

This symbolic fatherhood has two main symbols: the sun and the good shepherd. In 2016, Karlsson summarized them, focusing attention on 'the Mesopotamian "ideology of protection", derived in analogy from various social relations'.[30] The image of the sun and that of the father are thus interchangeable, since both are paternalistic in nature. In this regard, Šamaš's attribute of 'the just ruler' can be compared to the function of a father to his people, a relationship typical of a patrimonial state. In the same way, as shepherds, the Assyrian kings tend to forgive people who are linked to cattle (which can be understood as a form of patrimony). It is interesting to note that the Assyrian king referred to himself as a 'universal shepherd'. In both cases — as the sun and as the shepherd — the king's responsibilities are to provide and protect. Building on this, the king's role to sustain peace and security and provide abundance was not limited to Assyria but had a global dimension: in this updated and benevolent role, these kings served as shepherds for the whole world and for all humanity. The Mesopotamian kings presented themselves as good shepherds highlighting their ethical responsibility. Therefore, their kinship was not about power but about responsibility. This was exemplified by the self-sacrifice of Dumuzi (another god associated with the shepherd) in the story of Inanna's descent. In summary, the imagery of the king as sun and shepherd were paternalistic, signifying royal benevolence and the distribution of resources to the people under his care. It is also worth noticing a feature that regards the foreign lands: these lands gave tribute, and in exchange they received from the king in the city the ideological goods of order, justice, and protection: this was done through the image of the king taking the role of the good shepherd over the foreigner as well.

The sovereign is thus compared to a shepherd (Sumerian *sipa*; Akkadian *rē'ûm*). At the beginning of the second millennium, Šamaš was the shepherd who helped shaping the royal person. In his hymn, the relationship between justice, the right behaviour, the sun, the shepherd, and divination is very close: indeed, gods wrote their decisions on the liver of a lamb. 'Above, you lead all who dwell on earth in the right path. Shepherd of the regions below, pastor of the regions above. You, Sun, are the regulator of the light of the universe'.[31] As the sun that constantly and routinely circles the Earth, Šamaš is the most striking element of dynamic order. For this reason, he is reckoned to be the guardian and watchman of creation; he is the one who is in charge, so that the universe — in the same manner as the sun — continues to move in its proper course. Šamaš is thus supposed to guide people back into their proper course and to revoke the evil judgement against them. These remarks could be extended to the king, as it is exactly what he does when proclaiming a *mîšarum*, or the extinguishing of debts: the correction of unfair situations. As a good shepherd, the king goes in search of his lost flock and sets them back on the right path. This royal image was extremely resilient in the Near East, as we can see in the name of year 2 of Abī-Ešuḫ, who commemorates the *mîšarum* proclaimed by the king upon his accession:[32]

> Year: Abi-eshuh, the king, the beloved shepherd of Anum and Enlil, who looked toward Sumer and Akkad with a loyal eye, led aright the feet of the people, established [...], good will and reconciliation in his land, caused order (nì-gi-na) and redress (nì-si-sá) to exist and made the land to prosper.[33]

As shown, the idea of the king as someone in charge for his people was not new. Yet there is an economic difference between the concept of the king as the sun and the king as the good shepherd. During the Early Dynastic Period, a new economic-administrative system of salaries produced debts that were basically impossible to pay back. In this scenario, the royal power rose as a point of reference of balance for society, since the king had the power to remove the debts' interest rates. As already mentioned, this practice was then called *mîšarum*, usually translated as 'clean slate',[34] and it became more and more widespread, attaching to the figure of the king the image of the saviour of his people. This shift is of major importance to this inquiry, because now the king is not just a hero-warrior, but increasingly becomes the good and just administrator. It goes even further: now the centre of the attention of the king is his people.

This, of course, does not mean that the king was not an intermediary between the gods and the people before this shift in his role. What I would like to highlight is that the new fatherly role that he assumes strengthens this intermediary role and legitimizes the king in applying practices such as the *mîšarum*. This practice is particularly telling because it stands at the crossroads of many things that the king had to do in order to build the narrative of good king. First of all, the *mîšarum* was a driving force

---

30 Karlsson 2016, 181–82.
31 Trans. Reiner 1985, 71.
32 Charpin 2013, 73–75.
33 Trans. Charpin 2013, 74.
34 Hudson 2000, 140–44; Steinkeller 1981, 120–40.

to establish the king as the one who has the power to make things right, not just morally but also economically. Secondly, it consolidated his role as leader by a more centralized system and helped bring together his state from a financial point of view. Even though the *mîšarum* practice was introduced because of a spiralling lack of control over the assets of the state, it still ensured a form of control. Moreover, this practice put the kings in a non-competitive stance with the temple, since it was the jurisdiction of the palace to take care of taxes and incomes.

Let us thus return to the idea of the good shepherd. The 'shepherd' probably originated among the Amorites, who practised pastoralism above all, but the key point here is the new idea of a king who looks with care and concern over the needs of his people. The population, like a herd with no shepherd, is not able to survive on its own. This is the new approach that the king has towards his people, which emerges from a paternalistic attitude rooted in the ancient Near Eastern idea of 'family'.

As already mentioned, the family was the core unit in ancient Near Eastern society. The available data suggests that from tribal and nomadic groups arose an urban society based on the idea of family.[35] Slowly, this family became less and less extended, so that the figure of the father as head of the family gained relevance. This shift in the perception of the family must be read alongside the urban society that arose simultaneously. The people living in the city were utterly different from the nomadic or semi-nomadic people of the steppes or of the countryside, and it is the kind of family referring to the people living in the city that I refer to when I mention 'the family'.

The features of the societies of the steppes are difficult to clearly identify, because what we know is often mediated by the tales of the people of the cities. A famous example is the 'Marriage of Martu', a tale from the early second millennium in which a goddess contemplating marriage to Martu, the eponymous deity of the West Semitic Amorites, is cautioned by her companion concerning the nature of his people. The text describes them as nomadic, untrustworthy, bad-smelling, unruly, and ungodly, and Martu's companion then asks if she is certain she is willing to marry one of them.[36] The differences between the people living in the city and those living outside of the city are very clear, and they are so many that doubt is cast on the marriage itself. This is just an example to show how the family was becoming increasingly nuclear: it was no longer the community that took care of the needs of the poorest, the orphans, and the widows. Now it was the king. Usually, this kind of care was expressed through the forgiveness of debts. This act was meant to re-establish justice and to bring back a 'natural' and 'normal' situation that had been falling apart. In doing so, the king portrayed himself as the just ruler, the one who brought justice back on behalf of his people. It is also worth mentioning that, in this period, we see the emergence of the law codes (with Hammurabi's as the most famous one) and a renewed interest in legal justice; a justice that, nonetheless, always needed to be validated by the gods.[37] I mention the law codes because, ideologically speaking, they are a tool closely related to the treaty, since it is a juridical tool validated by a divine entity.

This new relationship between the king and his people is obviously propagandistic in nature. Nonetheless, from the time of the first Babylonian dynasty onward we find a renewed close connection between the two: the king is responsible for the people, and the people rely on the king for different things, from the prices of the goods to the penal system.

This relationship becomes clearer by looking at the texts. Let us return to *CTH* 51 and to the way the king introduces himself. He says: 'Suppiluliuma, Great King, Hero, King of Hatti, Beloved of the Storm-god.'[38] The same epithets can be observed virtually unchanged in other treaties, such as *CTH* 62: '[Thus says] My Majesty, Mursili, [Great King, King of Hatti], Hero, Beloved of the Storm-god; [son of] Suppiluliuma, [Great King, King of Hatti, Hero]';[39] or *CTH* 76: 'Thus says My Majesty, Muwattalli, Great King, [King] of Hatti, Beloved of the Storm-god of Lightning; son of Mursili, Great King, Hero';[40] or *CTH* 105: '[Thus says Tabarna, Tudhaliya], Great King, [King of] Hatti, Hero, Beloved of the Sun-goddess of Arinna; [son of Hattusili, Great King, King] of Hatti, Hero: [grandson of] Mursili, Great [King], King of Hatti, Hero; [descendant] of Tudhaliya, [Great King, King] of Hatti, Hero'.[41] In these examples, the Hittite kings introduce themselves in the public and diplomatic context of the treaties. There are different aspects to consider: in *CTH* 51, we see that the first to appear is the king's name, Suppiluliuma; then there are his appellatives, that deal with all the features of his role. He is the 'Great King' and the 'King of Ḫatti',

---

35 Frankfort 1978, 215–16.
36 Beckman 2013, 204.
37 Biga 2006, 79–80; Liverani 2011, 281–88.
38 Trans. Beckman 1996, 38; see also Devecchi 2015, 243.
39 Trans. Beckman 1996, 55; see also Devecchi 2015, 212.
40 Trans. Beckman 1996, 82; see also Devecchi 2015, 152.
41 Trans. Beckman 1996, 99; see also Devecchi 2015, 227.

where 'king' is the translation of *lugal*, even though there is debate on its actual meaning. It is a term widely spread diachronically and synchronically throughout the ancient Near East, but it seems to have referred to powerful kings who implemented their hegemonic policy and intensified their war activity, possibly indicating an independent ruler.[42] But here it is important to remember the shift in the perception of the king, who is now also a father figure. Then he is a 'hero/warrior', UR.SAG;[43] he is the champion among and for his people. Lastly, he is 'Beloved of the Storm-god', ᴰUTU-ši, so that his relationship with the divine and the legitimation that derives from it are always clear when the treaty is read.

What these introductions indicate is a predominantly social feature of the role of the king. He is not just a king, he is a great king, the most successful one, the one who takes care of his people. He is not just a man, he is a hero among men, where these men are his people. He is also the king of Ḫatti, which gives space and dimension to the place and people we are addressing. And, finally, he is the beloved of the Storm-god, the head of the pantheon who presides over justice. The king repeatedly presents himself with these epithets throughout *CTH* 51, and this is not surprising. This kind of introduction is often used in the treaties (especially 'Great King', 'King of Ḫatti', and 'Hero') and it acts as the calling card of the Hittite king.

Let us now consider *CTH* 91, the treaty stipulated between Ḫatti and Egypt, which reads:

> I have now established good brotherhood and good peace between us forever, in order likewise to establish good peace and good brotherhood in [the relations] of Egypt with Ḫatti forever. [...] Ramses, Beloved of Amon, Great King, King of Egypt, is doing this in order to bring about the relationship which [the Sun-god] and the Storm-god established for Egypt with Ḫatti in accordance with their relationship from the beginning of time, so that for eternity he might [not permit] the making of war between [them]. [...] And Ramses, Beloved of Amon, Great King, King of Egypt, for all time shall not open hostilities against Ḫatti in order to take anything from it. And Ḫattusili, Great King, King of Ḫatti, for all time, shall not open hostilities against Egypt in order to take [anything] from it. The eternal regulation which the Sun-god and the Storm-god made for Egypt with Ḫatti is intended peace and brotherhood and to prohibit hostilities between them.[44]

Despite some differences, the similarities are impressive. *CTH* 91 is particularly interesting because this treaty is considered the only one between equals, and the epithets that the Hittite king uses to introduce himself are essentially the same used in the other treaties, saying: 'Ḫattusili, Great King, King of Ḫatti, Hero'.[45] In this specific treaty, the epithet 'beloved of the Storm-god' does not appear, but the Storm-god is mentioned (alongside the Egyptian Sun-god) to seal the good relationship between the two kings and thus between the two populations. This is an example of how the gods satisfy the unique role of witnesses that they have in the treaty context.

In the passages mentioned above, the Hittite king is one of the protagonists of the oath, and he is able to take it on behalf of his whole population because of his special status. He is the champion, but he is also the one who takes care of the people by mediating with the gods, so that the kingdom can be peaceful and prosperous. This role of mediator is carried on by all the ancient Near Eastern kings, but for the Hittite king, the role is even more dominant due to the peculiar position that he occupies in his society. He is not just a king but also a priest responsible for the cult of the main deities of the Hittites. Therefore, he is not just in charge of his empire (benefitting from such a position); he also has responsibilities towards his land and his people. If he does something wrong that upsets the gods, the whole population suffers the consequences.[46]

Let us consider the so-called 'Muršili's prayer', regarding an outbreak of plague:

> O gods, [my] lords! A plague broke out in Ḫatti, and Ḫatti has been severely damaged by the plague. And since for twenty years now in Ḫatti people have been dying, the affair of Tudḫaliya the Younger, son of Tudḫaliya, started to weigh on [me]. I inquired about it to the god through an oracle, and the affair of Tudḫaliya was confirmed by the deity. Since Tudḫaliya the Younger was their lord in Ḫatti, the princes, the noblemen, the commanders of the thousands, the officers, [the corporals(?)] of Ḫatti and all [the infantry] and chariotry of Ḫatti swore an oath to him. My father also swore an oath to him. [But when my father] wronged Tudḫaliya, all [the princes, the noblemen], the commanders of the thousands, and the officers of Ḫatti [went over] to my father. The deities by whom the oath was sworn [seized] Tudḫaliya and they killed [Tudḫaliya]. Furthermore, they killed those of his brothers [who stood by] him. [...] they sent to Alasiya (Cyprus) and [...]. And [since Tudḫaliya the Younger]

---

42 Liverani 2011, 153–54; Finer 1999, 114–15.
43 Huehnergard 2011, 528.
44 Trans. Beckman 1996, 92.

45 Devecchi 2015, 264–69; Beckman 1996, 90–95.
46 Gilan 2011, 277–81; Collins 2007, 159.

was their [lord], they [...] to him [...]. [...] and the lords transgressed the oath.[47]

When the plague ravaged the Hittite kingdom, there was no doubt that it was brought by an angry god. Thus, it was King Muršili II's duty to deal with it.[48] In his prayer to the assembly of the gods and goddesses, it is clear that he had to mediate with the gods for the sake of all the population, and that a broken oath — which was said to be the cause of that specific plague — was a serious enough issue to enrage the gods.

There are several interesting facts about this passage. The first is the role of the new king, who, even without doing anything wrong himself, needs to approach the wrath of the gods on behalf of all. The second is the transgression that triggered the punishment, that is, the broken oath and the wrong behaviour. The third is the wrath of the gods itself, which indicates the amount of power these deities were perceived to have over the environment and daily life. Lastly, there are the consequences of the broken oath, as it is clear that even if only the king or a small number of people did something wrong, the outcome affects the entire Hittite population.

It is also worth noticing that the broken oath is the cause of the plague not because the gods were called upon when the oath was taken, but for a more general reason: we could consider the oath as somehow sacred. It is a tool that works not just between humans, but also between gods, and between gods and humans. The role that the gods have is to witness something, and this happens in a context with structured features. If what has been witnessed is compromised, the gods intervene as they should, precisely because they are bound by the oath. In this context, the oath is the structure that binds both the gods and the kings to deal with its effects. It is not unsurprising that the king needs to intervene between gods and humans to rectify things; I have mentioned this role many times already. But it is still interesting to notice how this occurred, by which means, and under which circumstances.

I have described how the Hittite king is a priest and is at the top of the hierarchy as well. What might appear to be two separate forms of power — the kingship and the priesthood — are very much entangled in this context. This is not surprising in this time period, because there was nothing like a secularized form of power. All kinds of legitimation came from the gods, or generally from a transcendent power. It would be impossible to truly separate the ideological power (the religion) from the political power (the kingship) using Michael Mann's IEMP system.[49] In the ancient Near East and in Ḫatti more specifically, these sources of power enhanced each other and could not really function alone. Therefore, the Hittite king acted simultaneously as king and as priest, as religion was so deeply rooted in daily life that it could not be ignored. This must always be acknowledged, otherwise one could experience the gods' wrath, which would affect everyone, as seen in Muršili's prayer about the plague.[50]

The Hurro-Hittite *Song of Hedammu* reads:

[Ea] king of wisdom spoke among the gods. The god [...] began to say: 'Why are you (*plural*) destroying [mankind]? They will not give sacrifices to the gods. They will not burn cedar as incense to you. [If] you (*plural*) destroy mankind, they will no longer [worship] the gods. No one will offer [bread] or libations to you (*plural*) any longer. Even Teššub, Kummiya's heroic king, will [himself] proceed to grasp the plow. It will come about that even Ishtar and Hebat will themselves grind at the millstones.'[51]

The king had to address the gods because they were omnipresent and closely linked to humans in every sphere of life. One of the key features of the Hittite religion was its attention to the well-being and fertility of the land, which were guaranteed through divine intervention. This intervention ensured that the harvest, the livestock, and the consequent general prosperity of the population were maintained. The prominent figure in such a context was the king, who was the main interlocutor with the divinities, who were the highest step in the hierarchy of the universe. In the passage from the *Song of Hedammu*, the relationship between parts (human and deities) is particularly clear: the Hittite world was a continuum where humans and divinities were interdependent and were part of a system that included everything, from the plants and the animals from which sustenance is derived, to the gods who guaranteed its growth and prosperity. In this way, the gods were not so dissimilar to men and needed to be maintained through offerings and oblations. If they were not fed, cared for, and ingratiated, they had the capacity to compromise the basic processes of nature or the health of people by sending famine, plagues, wars, etc.[52]

---

[47] Trans. Singer 2002, 61–62.

[48] Collins 2007, 51–52.

[49] Mann 1986, 22–28.

[50] Collins 2007, 157–58.

[51] Trans. Bachvarova 2005, 55, who slightly modified Hoffner 1998, 52.

[52] Beckman 1989, 99–101.

Divinities permeated the world to such an extent that we refer to the Hittite pantheon as an extreme form of polytheism, in which everything (even substances such as fire or silver) had its divine resident. From a chronological point of view, the Attic gods were predominant in the first phase but, with the consolidation of the Hittite power, the pantheon was enriched with other divinities, including the towns' gods or entities belonging to kingdoms conquered by Ḫatti. This accumulation also happened because it was possible to 'kidnap' a divinity simply by removing its statue or effigy from the temple and taking it elsewhere. This guaranteed that the conquered peoples could not ask for the intervention of their own divinity and ensured therefore that the conquest that occurred endured. An important characteristic is that, in this area, the deities kept their name, although they were identical in functions: this produced a large community of deities connected to storms, the sun, or other weather conditions.

It is unclear if these deities were considered the same ones with a different name, or if they were just gods with common traits. We also cannot be sure if, when introduced into the Hittite pantheon, there might have been a slight uneasiness about identifying them outright with known gods, as one might get them wrong, despite their apparent equivalence. What is certain is that their names were preserved in their original form, making the Hittite pantheon a heterogeneous agglomeration of deities; this was something that the Hittites were particularly proud of. The process of accumulation was so intense that it formed a community of divinities whose names refer to different linguistic and geographical origins. The reasons behind this high level of accumulation are not completely clear, but it might be due in part to a resistance to syncretization. For example, many Hittite towns maintained individual storm-gods and refused to identify their local deities as manifestations of a single national figure.[53]

The Hittites' unfiltered reception of deities from all regions of their expanding realm had its advantages. It provided a high degree of political, social, and cultural tolerance; it served to demonstrate how far and over how many peoples the Hittites' conquests extended; and it demonstrated that the Hittites' policy was not merely to tolerate but also to absorb and assimilate elements of the cultures and societies of the peoples who made up the Hittites' realm. The lack of an official religious doctrine or of any form of theological dogma enshrined in sacred texts (like the Bible or the Qur'an) ensured that there were no obstacles to the reception of foreign cults and deities from anywhere the Hittites wished to take them, whether for political or other reasons.[54]

This situation slightly changed in the thirteenth century BC, when an attempt to systematize the pantheon occurred. Many gods were grouped into *kaluti*, or 'circles', of males and females, as can be seen in Yazilikaya's bas-reliefs. It is significant that, although the iconography makes most of these gods immediately recognizable as long-standing members of the Hittite pantheon, their hieroglyphic labels give their names in Hurrian. Syncretization had finally been carried out, even if it seems not to have expanded beyond the highest spheres of the pantheon.[55]

To summarize, the relationship that these gods had with Near Eastern kings (and the Hittite kings in particular) is clearly articulated, but even in different contexts and cultures they shared some features. What is particularly interesting about the Hittite king (which is slightly different from the other kings of the ancient Near East) is that he was the representative of the gods before his people and, since he occupied the highest priestly role, he also performed many rituals himself, sometimes accompanied by the whole royal family. He was responsible for the shrines and temples because they were the houses of the gods. If the gods were pleased by the worship (that had to accord to a strict series of rules, such as dressing and feeding the statue of the gods), then they would have granted the king longevity, offspring, and power, and therefore, in a domino effect, the whole Hittite population would have been prosperous.[56]

In this context, the role of the rituals is crucial, because they are the predominant way whereby the king acts out his responsibilities towards gods and people. In his paper, Amir Gilan quotes Catherine Bell and Stanley Tambiah on the ritual:

> In these rituals, writes Bell (1997, pp. 108–09), people make offerings to a god with the practical and straightforward expectation of receiving something in return — whether it be as concrete as a good harvest and a long life or as abstract as grace and redemption [...]; one gives in order to receive in return (*do ut des*). Direct offerings may be given to praise, please, and placate divine power, or they may involve an explicit exchange by which human beings provide sustenance to divine powers in return to divine contributions to human well-being. However, a Hittite festival had a political dimension as well, in that,

---

53 Beckman 1989, 99; Bryce 2002, 135–36; Collins 2007, 173–74.

54 Bryce 2002, 136.

55 Beckman 1989, 99; Trémouille 2008, 286–87.

56 Polvani 2008, 252; Beckman 1989, 100–03.

quoting Bell again (1997, p. 128) it 'constructs, displays and promotes the power of political institutions...' It does this, to use Stanley Tambiah's famous ritual definition, in that it 'symbolically and/or iconically represents the cosmos and at the same time indexically legitimates and realizes social hierarchies' (1979, p. 153).[57]

The prayers are one of the tools that the king employed to communicate first hand with the gods. Muwatalli's prayer (*CTH* 381) offers a glimpse of how this exactly occurred:

> Thus says *tabarna* Muwatalli, Great King, king of Hatti, son of Mursili, Great King, king of Hatti, the hero: If some problem burdens a man('s conscience), he makes a plea to the gods. He places on the roof, facing the Sun, two covered wickerwork tables: He places one table for the Sun-goddess of Arinna, and for the male gods one table. On them there are: 35 thick breads of a handful of moist flour, a thin bowl of honey mixed with fine oil, a full pot of fat-bread, a full bowl of groats, thirty pitchers of wine. And when he prepares these, the king goes up to the roof and he bows before the Sun-god of Heaven.[58]

As seen in these lines, the prayers were accompanied by a ceremony or a ritual carried out by the king. Muwatalli continues to address the whole pantheon:

> He says as follows: Sun-god of Heaven and Sun-goddess of Arinna, my lady, Queen, my lady, queen of Hatti, Storm-god, king of Heaven, my lord, Hebat Queen, my lady, Storm-god of Hatti, king of Heaven, lord of Hatti, my lord, Storm-god of Ziplanda, my lord, beloved son of the Storm-god, lord of the Land of Hatti, Seri and Hurri (B: Seri, the bull who is champion in Hattusa, the land), all the male gods and the female gods, all the mountains and the rivers of the Land of Hatti, my lords. Divine lords — Sun-goddess of Arinna, my lady, and all the gods of the Land of Hatti, my lords — *whose priest I am, who have conferred upon me, from among all others, the rulership over Hatti*.[59]

What I would like to again point out is how the king refers to himself in this context. He is the priest of all the gods, and those gods bestowed upon him the rulership of Ḫatti. He thus has a dual role, because just as he acts on behalf of his people when he takes an oath, he does the same on behalf of the gods when he performs a ritual or wins a battle for them. He is the one who can speak for them, due to his special status of king and priest, and in doing so he also re-establishes the hierarchies of power. The intermediary semantic works both ways, as the king acts as the intermediary on behalf of his people and on behalf of all the gods.[60]

Let us move to *CTH* 385.10, which reads:

> She [the sun-goddess of Arinna] gave them a battle-ready, valiant spear saying: 'May the hostile foreign lands perish by the hand of the labarna, and let them take goods, silver and gold to Hattusa and Arinna, the cities of the gods!' May the land of Hatti graze abundantly(?) in the hand of the labarna and the tawannanna, and may it expand! [...] May the land of the labarna and his tawannanna succeed, and may it thrive and prosper![61]

In this passage, we see how the gods allow the *labarna*, the king, to do tasks on their behalf, because the spoils that the king will loot will go to the temples of the gods in the cities of Ḫatti and Arinna and will ultimately belong to the gods. Nonetheless, the one who is in charge and is responsible for looting and bringing spoils to the gods is the king, the one who guarantees it.

If the reason why he can act on behalf of his people is endorsed by the fatherly status that the king assumes in the ancient Near East as 'the good shepherd', he can act on behalf of the gods because he is the one that the gods choose to be their mediator with mankind. And this is why it is his duty to ensure that mankind treats the gods properly. The Annals of Ḫattušili I (*CTH* 4) reads:

> I the great king, tabarna, took the hands of the female slaves from the millstone, and the hands of the male slaves from the sickles. I freed them from *šaḫḫan* and *luzzi*. I ungirded their belts. I released them to my lady the sun goddess of Arinna in perpetuity.[62]

Here, the king frees captives so that they can devote more time to serving the gods. As Bachvarova points out, the gods being neglected and in need of care is a trope in Hittite narratives.[63] If the gods are neglected, bad things may happen to the population, such as the fall of their city, plagues, or natural disasters, so that is a situation that must be taken care of. And the one who needs to do it is the king, because he is the mediator between gods and people. We come across a situation that can be summarized like this: the population needs to take care of the gods, so that the gods can act on the world, and the king needs to ensure this flow of work between the parts.

---

57 Gilan 2011, 281.
58 Trans. Singer 2002, 86.
59 Trans. Singer 2002, 86–84, emphasis mine.
60 Collins 2007, 163.
61 Trans. Singer 2002, 26.
62 Trans. Bachvarova 2005, 52.
63 Bachvarova 2005, 55.

If we now look back at *CTH* 51, we see the importance of the king's role in the oath that he takes:

> A duplicate of this tablet is deposited before the Sun-goddess of Arinna, since the Sun-goddess of Arinna governs kingship and queenship. And in the land of Mittanni a duplicate is deposited before the Storm-god, Lord of the kurinnu of Kahat. It shall be read repeatedly, for ever and ever, before the king of the land of Mittanni and before the Hurrians. Whoever, before the Storm-god, Lord of the kurinnu of Kahat, alters this tablet, or sets it in a secret location — if he breaks it, if he changes the words of the text of the tablet — in regard to this treaty we have summoned the gods of secrets and the gods who are guarantors of the oath. They shall stand and listen and be witnesses.[64]

The passage goes on to address all the gods who must witness this particular treaty. Here, we can see how the two kings, Suppiluliuma and Šattiwaza, make the oath and call upon the gods ('we have summoned the gods') but that the consequences of this action affect all the population, both Hittite and Mittanian:

> They (the gods) shall stand and listen and be witnesses to these words of the treaty. If you, Prince Shattiwaza and you Hurrians do not observe the words of this treaty, the gods, lords of the oath, shall destroy you [and] you Hurrians, together with your land, your wives, and your possessions. [...] you, together with any other wife whom you might take (in place of my daughter), and you Hurrians, together with your wives, your sons, and your land, shall thus have no progeny. [...] And you, Shattiwaza — these oath gods shall snap you off like a reed, together with your land, because of not delivering goodness and recovery(?) among the Hurrians — you(!) shall be eradicated. [...] You, Shattiwaza, and the Hurrians shall be the enemies of the Thousand Gods. They shall defeat you. [...] If you, Prince Shattiwaza, and you Hurrians observe this treaty and oath, these gods shall protect you, Shattiwaza, together with your wife, [daughter of the king] of Hatti, hers sons and grandsons, and you Hurrians, together with your wives and sons, and [together with your land].[65]

It is key to keep in mind that, even if the one who speaks in these lines is Suppiluliuma, the king of the Hittites, this treaty was signed by Šattiwaza as well, and we then see the Mittanian king acting as an intermediary for his people too. With the treaty and because of the special status that kings had in the ancient Near East as the interlocutors of the gods, the king acts on one hand on behalf of the gods — he is the only one who can address them — and on the other hand on behalf of his people — he takes the oath for them as well, and they become the target of blessings and curses.

It is important to remember that, when swearing the oath, the king holds a specific position: he is the protagonist. In the passage about the deposition, we can see how it was meant to seal the treaty and to give importance to what was happening. This should not mislead us into thinking that the gods are the protagonists: they are still the divine witnesses to the treaty, as clearly stated by the sentence 'They shall stand and listen and be witnesses'. Their role, one of utmost importance, is to be there to support what the king is doing. And he is allowed to act because of his role as intermediary between the people and the gods.

To finally answer the questions asked at the beginning of this paper, it can be said that the king can act as intermediary for his people because the changes in the perception of his role (such as the 'good shepherd') reinforce this feature. A consequence of this is that he is now allowed to speak for them as a father figure. It is important to remember that the main role that he had before this transition, that of the leader, already allowed him to speak for his people, but now the power that he holds is even more legitimized and given a moral aspect. Moreover, the intermediary role of the king is not limited to his relationship with his people; he can act as intermediary for the gods as well, because of the special position he holds in the ancient Near East, which is precisely the mediator between humanity and the gods. This role is particularly stressed for Hittite kingship, since he is also the most important priest of the clergy.

This intermediary feature was mainly employed in public and social contexts, such as treaties and prayers or rituals. This allowed the king to build a dialogue with every sphere of potential influence, especially with the clergy. The symbiotic relation that emerges between the palace and the temple is reflected in the relationship between kings and priests: it can be assumed that there was tension between their exercises of power, but this tension was negotiated and mediated through several strategies. For the Hittite kings, it was being head of the clergy; for the Babylonian kings it was a close relationship with the temple and the legitimization of the role of king that the temple provided.

The information gathered from oaths, treaties, prayers, and songs provide an exceptional look into the role of a king standing at the intersection of people and gods. It clarifies the strategies through which these kings reaffirmed themselves at this specific crossroad, and it also clarifies how they were able to maintain this role as the protagonist of their society.

---

64 Trans. Beckman 1996, 42; see also Devecchi 2015, 250.
65 Trans. Beckman 1996, 43–44; see also Devecchi 2015, 251–52.

Works Cited

Agamben, G. 2008. *Il sacramento del linguaggio* (Bari: Laterza).
Bachvarova, M. 2005. 'Relations between God and Man in the Hurro-Hittite Song of Release', *Journal of the American Oriental Society*, 125.1: 45–58.
Beckman, G. 1989. 'The Religion of the Hittites', *The Biblical Archaeologist*, 52.2–3: 98–108.
——. 1996. *Hittite Diplomatic Texts* (Atlanta: Society of Biblical Scholars).
——. 2000. 'Hittite Chronology', *Akkadica*, 119–20: 19–32.
——. 2013. 'Foreigners in the Ancient Near East', *Journal of the American Oriental Society*, 133.2: 203–16.
Biga, M. G. 2006. 'La Mesopotamia e la Siria nel Medio Bronzo', in S. De Martino (ed.), *Storia d'Europa e del Mediterraneo*, I (Rome: Salerno Editrice), pp. 63–131.
Biga, M. G. and A. M. Capomacchia. 2008. *Il politeismo vicino-orientale* (Rome: Libreria dello stato).
Bryce, T. 2002. *Life and Society in the Hittite World* (Oxford: Oxford University Press).
——. 2005. *The Kingdom of the Hittites* (Oxford: Oxford University Press).
Charpin, D. 2013. '"I Am the Sun of Babylon": Solar Aspects of Royal Power in Old Babylonian Mesopotamia', in J. A. Hill, P. Jones, and A. J. Morales (eds), *Experiencing Power, Generating Authority: Cosmos, Politics, and the Ideology of Kingship in Ancient Egypt and Mesopotamia* (Philadelphia: University of Pennsylvania Press), pp. 65–96.
Collins, B. J. 2007. *The Hittites and their World* (Atlanta: Society of Biblical Literature).
Dassow, E. von. 2014. 'Levantine Polities under Mittanian Hegemony', in E. Cancik-Kirschbaum, N. Brisch, and J. Eidem (eds), *Constituent, Confederate, and Conquered Space* (Berlin: De Gruyter), pp. 11–32.
Devecchi, E. 2015. *Trattati internazionali ittiti* (Brescia: Paideia).
Finer, S. E. 1999. *The History of Government from the Earliest Times*, I: *Ancient Monarchies and Empires* (Oxford: Oxford University Press).
Frankfort, H. 1978. *Kingship and the Gods: A Study of Ancient Near Eastern Religion as the Integration of Society and Nature*, repr. of 1948 edn (Chicago: University of Chicago Press).
Gilan, A. 2011. 'Hittite Religious Rituals and the Ideology of Kingship', *Religion Compass*, 5.7: 276–85.
Greenberg, R. 2014. 'No Collapse: Transmutations of Early Bronze Age Urbanism in the Southern Levant', in F. Höflmayer (ed.), *The Late Third Millennium in the Ancient Near East* (Chicago: Oriental Institute of the University of Chicago), pp. 31–58.
Hoffner, H. A. Jr. 1998. *Hittite Myths*, 2nd edn (Atlanta: Scholar).
Hudson, M. 2000. 'How Interest Rates Were Set, 2500 BC–1000 AD: *Máš*, *tokos* and *fœnus* as Metaphors for Interest Accruals', *Journal of the Economic and Social History of the Orient*, 43.2: 132–61.
Huehnergard, J. 2011. *A Grammar of Akkadian* (Winona Lake: Eisenbrauns).
Jacobsen, T. 1943. 'Primitive Democracy in Ancient Mesopotamia', *Journal of Near Eastern Studies*, 2.3: 159–72.
Karlsson, M. 2016. *Relations of Power in Early Neo-Assyrian State Ideology* (Boston: De Gruyter).
Liverani, M. 2001. *International Relations in the Ancient Near East, 1600–1100 BC* (Basingstoke: Palgrave).
——. 2011. *Antico Oriente: storia società economia*, rev. edn (Bari: Laterza).
Llop, J. 2011. 'The Creation of the Middle Assyrian Provinces', *Journal of the American Oriental Society*, 131.4: 591–603.
Mann, M. 1986. *The Sources of Social Power*, I: *A History of Power from the Beginning to A.D. 1760* (Cambridge: Cambridge University Press).
Moran, W. L. 1992. *The Amarna Letters* (Baltimore: Johns Hopkins University Press).
Otto, A. 2014. 'The Organisation of Residential Space in the Mittani Kingdom as a Mirror of Different Models of Governance', in E. Cancik-Kirschbaum, N. Brisch, and J. Eidem (eds), *Constituent, Confederate, and Conquered Space* (Berlin: De Gruyter), pp. 33–60.
Polvani, A. M. 2008. 'Capitolo VII', in M. G. Biga and A. M. Capomacchia (eds), *Il politeismo vicino-orientale* (Rome: Libreria dello stato), pp. 243–78.
Reiner, E. 1985. *Your Thwarts in Pieces your Mooring Rope Cut: Poetry from Babylonia and Assyria*, Michigan Studies in the Humanities, 5 (Ann Arbor: Horace H. Rackham School of Graduate Studies at the University of Michigan).
Roaf, M. 2013. 'Mesopotamian Kings and the Built Environment', in J. A. Hill, P. Jones, and A. J. Morales (eds), *Experiencing Power, Generating Authority: Cosmos, Politics, and the Ideology of Kingship in Ancient Egypt and Mesopotamia* (Philadelphia: University of Pennsylvania Press), pp. 331–59.
Rüpke, J. 2015. 'Religious Agency, Identity, and Communication: Reflections on History and Theory of Religion', *Religion*, 45.3: 344–66.
Sallaberger, W. 2013. 'The Management of the Royal Treasure: Palace Archives and Palatial Economy in the Ancient Near East', in J. A. Hill, P. Jones, and A. J. Morales (eds), *Experiencing Power, Generating Authority: Cosmos, Politics, and the Ideology of Kingship in Ancient Egypt and Mesopotamia* (Philadelphia: University of Pennsylvania Press), pp. 219–56.
Singer, I. 2002. *Hittite Prayers* (Atlanta: Society of Biblical Literature).

Steinkeller, P. 1981. 'The Renting of Fields in Early Mesopotamia and the Development of the Concept of "Interest" in Sumerian', *Journal of the Economic and Social History of the Orient*, 24.2: 113–45.

Trémouille, M.-C. 2008. 'La presenza dei Hurriti in alta Mesopotamia, Anatolia e Siria nel II millennio', in M. G. Biga and A. M. Capomacchia (eds), *Il politeismo vicino-orientale* (Rome: Libreria dello stato), pp. 279–314.

Veenhof, K. and J. Eidem. 2008. *Mesopotamia: The Old Assyrian Period* (Fribourg: Academic Press).

Wilhelm, G. 1989. *The Hurrians* (Warminster: Aris & Phillips).

DOMESTIC SPACE

10. Small, Versatile, Numinous: Pagan-Mythological Statuettes at the End of Antiquity

Ine Jacobs

Introduction

The number of publications concerned with the fate and reception of pagan-mythological statuary in the last centuries of Antiquity and beyond is increasing rapidly. Site-specific and regional catalogues of statues and statue fragments have been supplemented with studies on reception, many of them focusing on negative reactions.[1] Destruction and so-called 'mutilation' are indeed prevalent in the written sources and have drawn more attention in the archaeological record. At the same time, the find context of many statues makes it clear that they survived throughout the centuries. The logical conclusion therefore is that negative approaches were never omnipresent in a Christianized era and that at least some people, families, and entire urban populations saw continued use in selected objects. Whereas initial studies preferred ongoing paganism as explanation, secular motivations have in the meantime gained precedence in the scholarly discourse.

All this can be applied to smaller statuettes as well, many of which were found in the houses of elite members of society and which are commonly interpreted as expressions of culture and education but rarely as vessels of numinous power. Our current caution towards cult practices in Late Antiquity (themselves only rarely defined), has made us shy away from religion altogether. We seem to have consciously or unconsciously reduced 'religion' to 'worship'; either there is evidence for worship or pagan-mythological imagery is decorative, allegorical, or neutral in nature. Especially in the presence of data that clearly signals 'Christian', we feel the need to reconcile this 'Christian' data with other evidence by resorting to 'secular' explanations. It should be stressed from the beginning, however, that we do not necessarily understand what factors made someone self-identify as Christian, Jewish, or 'pagan', and what material culture is associated with that identification. If we follow current understandings of religion as the myriad ways of inducing experiences of supernatural power and rendering the extraordinary 'sensible', some of them easily recognizable and definable while others are less so, a re-evaluation of much of the material evidence for Late Antiquity is in order.[2]

The purpose of this paper is to reassess the potential role of pagan-mythological marble statuettes in religious communications at the end of Antiquity. I will start this paper with an assessment of our evidence for statuettes in Late Antiquity, followed by a discussion of basic but often overlooked and highly important methodological considerations. After, I will briefly describe two contexts in which pagan-mythological statuettes were still on display in the first half of the seventh century: the House of the Painted Inscription (Casa dell'iscrizione dipinta) at Hierapolis (western Turkey) and the colonnaded main street of Sagalassos (south-western Turkey). In both contexts, the statuettes were preserved by multiple generations of viewers and users long after many other statuettes had already disappeared. In attempting to understand what these statuettes were doing so late in time, in a final section I broaden my view to contemporary practices involving 3D depictions of human forms, from the very small to the large, and to practices involving pagan-mythological imagery more broadly.

Statuettes in Late Antiquity

Statuettes are small-scale copies of the human body, often closely related to life-sized statues, with similar or identical attributes and also proportions. 'Pagan-mythological' statuettes represent either divinities, some belonging to

---

[1] For instance, Sauer 2003; Kristensen 2013; popularized further in Nixey 2017.

[2] I follow the understanding of religion as proposed for instance in (2005) 'Editorial Statement', *Material Religion*, 1.1: 4–8.

the Graeco-Roman pantheon and some of eastern origin, or protagonists in stories we today broadly refer to as mythology.³ Most examples preserved are in marble, although there must have still been metal examples as well (see below). They were produced for many centuries with a final peak in the fourth and early fifth centuries, which is associated with the late antique villa boom.⁴ The latest examples are thought to have been carved in the fifth century.⁵ Some of these later products depict the protagonist in a more comprehensive narrative scene, complete with foliage or accompanying fauna, as for instance the Statuette of Ganymede found at the House of the Greek Charioteers in Carthage, the Statuette of a hunting Diana found at Saint-Georges-de-Montagne, or the more inward-looking Amor and Psyche group at Hierapolis, which is discussed below. Others remained, however, as isolated figures, seated or standing, with the gaze directed towards the viewer. This was probably the case also with all statuettes in the second case study of this paper. Examples of statuettes in late antique contexts have been found in virtually all Mediterranean regions and as far away as Britain.⁶

Most statuettes with known find contexts come from private houses. In a few cases they formed part of private *lararia*, with well-studied examples in the Panayia Domus in Corinth or the famous *lararium* or *Iseum* with neighbouring *Mithraeum* found on the Esquiline Hill.⁷ Panayiotis Panayides has made a convincing argument for the presence of a suite of rooms functioning as *lararium* in the House of Theseus in Nea Paphos from the late fourth century onwards, with the statues remaining there until the late sixth.⁸ Many more statuettes were found in private indoor reception halls, banqueting rooms, gardens, and domestic fountains.⁹ They would have been better proportioned for such settings than their larger cousins found in public buildings or in open spaces. For instance, the Amor and Psyche group found at the House of the Painted Inscription at Hierapolis was well suited for the marble-paved *exedra* room in which it likely stood in the last phase of occupation. In addition, a smaller number of statuettes comes from public sanctuaries, like the Shrine of Liber Pater at Cosa and the Sanctuary of Magna Mater in Ostia that are briefly discussed below.¹⁰ Still other statuettes were retrieved in public settings, often fountains and bath buildings.¹¹ At Sagalassos, the statuette assemblage was used in the final phase of a colonnaded street.

Larger late antique assemblages, domestic or otherwise, were generally composed of elements of diverse date, origin, iconography, and size. In late antique villas, late antique statuettes moreover are found mingled with much older statuary, either family heirlooms or antiques taken from elsewhere.¹² The assemblage found on the street of Sagalassos had been produced at various dates: the statuettes had been taken from other locations, were of diverse subject matter, and varied in size. They were combined in the second quarter of the sixth century to serve a new purpose, about two hundred years after the youngest of the statuettes had been produced. The Amor and Psyche group at the House of the Painted Inscription at Hierapolis has been dated to the fourth century and probably had been used elsewhere before its introduction in the house, which is thought to have been built in the fifth century.¹³

---

3   I prefer 'pagan-mythological' over 'mythological', as used for instance in Stirling 2005 (see p. 3 for a definition), and over the commonly used term 'ideal statuary', which cloaks the content of the statues.

4   See e.g. Hannestad (2007a, 292, 299; 2007b, 197), who makes the connection between late statuary production and the late antique villas in the Mediterranean.

5   Stirling 2005, 110–12. Hannestad (1994, 117–44; 2007a–b) and Bergmann (1999) treat most of the known collections of late antique statuettes.

6   Stirling 2005, 132–36 discusses the transport from east to west.

7   Corinth: Stirling 2008; Rome: Visconti 1885; Ensoli Vittozzi 1993.

8   Panayides 2016; Panayides (forthcoming).

9   Stirling 2016, 270. Stirling 2005 is a fundamental work for late antique pagan and mythological small-scale statuary discovered in private houses all over the Mediterranean. Stirling (2007) compares evidence from Gaul and Spain, and Stirling (2008, 132–36) focuses on domestic statuary found in Greece.

10   Statuary finds in public sanctuary contexts include the Sanctuary of Magna Mater in Ostia (Boin 2013) and the Shrine of Liber Pater in Cosa (Collins-Clinton 1977).

11   Bartman (1992, 42) mentions statuettes found in the Trajanic Baths of Cyrene and the Roman theatre at Capua, as well as the Julian and South Basilicas of the Roman forum at Corinth. In addition, fifteen statuettes were found in the theatre of Corinth (Sturgeon 2004, 17). Other public locations in which statuettes were still on display into the seventh century include the Imperial Baths at Sagalassos (Mägele 2009, v.1.3), the fountain near the stadium at Ephesus (Jobst 1986), and the colonnaded street at Pompeiopolis (Tulunay 2005; Jacobs and Stirling 2017, 223–24).

12   Stirling 2005, 219–24; 2017, 270–74. For the eclectic composition of assemblages in earlier sanctuaries, see Kaufmann-Heinimann 1998, 191.

13   Canazza 2019, 538, 567–68 for the Amor and Psyche group; Zaccaria Ruggiu 2019b, 127–28 for the chronology of the house.

10. SMALL, VERSATILE, NUMINOUS

Following Bartmann and Stirling, I define 'statuette' here loosely, as statues in the round that are below life-sized.[14] The smallest are just over 10 cm, whereas many were around 75–80 cm high and around 45–55 kg in weight. In other publications, very small items are often indicated by the term 'figurine', thus distinguishing them from larger imitations of the human or animal form based on size.[15] On the one hand, statuettes of different size are often found together or in combination with other statuary, including life-sized statuary, tondos, busts, and table legs, to which they are closely related in size and their three-dimensional nature. In fact, many of the statuettes of so-called Good Shepherds were in fact carved as table legs.[16] It is therefore impossible to make an *a priori* division based on size alone. Indeed, as I will argue below, the statuettes on display in the later centuries of Antiquity fulfilled roles similar to those of larger statues. On the other hand, there are certainly differences in affordances between items of different size. The smallest statuettes had the possibility to enter into different gestural relationships, being far easier to manipulate and also to move around and about. Larger objects, though still easily moveable with two pair of hands, were less suitable for intimate engagements and were more visible, even when displayed in residential settings with controlled access limited to family members and chosen guests. All statuary that stayed significantly under life-sized may of course have been conceived of as being more controllable by human agents than, say, life-sized statues.

Literary and iconographic sources for continuing gestural relationships with at least the smallest statuettes in Late Antiquity are sparse but do exist. The option is mentioned in literary sources, including Ammianus Marcellinus's fourth-century account of Asclepiades, who always carried a statuette of Dea Caelestis with him.[17] Zosimus, at the end of the fourth century, wrote

Figure 10.1. Portrait bust holding a statuette of the Aphrodite of Aphrodisias, from the Atrium House, Aphrodisias (inv. no. 1986-1). Geyre, Aphrodisias Museum. Fourth century (?). Photo courtesy of Aphrodisias Excavations.

how the priest Nestorius placed a statuette of Achilles underneath the cult statue of Athena Parthenos to ensure a transfer of power from one onto the other and thus preserve the city from an earthquake.[18] In the Atrium House at Aphrodisias, excavations uncovered a probably fourth-century portrait bust of a priest cradling a statuette of Aphrodite of Aphrodisias in his left arm (Fig. 10.1).[19]

Such small and easy-to-handle statuettes turn up in later sources as well. Malalas, in the sixth century, described a statue of Constantine in gilded wood, holding in his right hand the Tyche of Constantinople, which in Malalas's time supposedly was still processed through the streets of Constantinople on the anniversary of the city's inauguration.[20] Similar engagements

---

14 Bartman 1992, 2–3. Later in this paper, I use 'figurines' to refer to small-scale terracotta imitations of human and animal forms. A distinction based on material has the merit of differentiating based on availability: terracotta figurines would have been easier to produce, cheaper, and thus available to a wider audience, whereas marble, metal, ivory statuettes, and so on were either in the possession of more wealthy individuals or, as in a few cases described here, public assets. Yet, I acknowledge that this distinction has its own problems and, like the distinction based on size, needs to be recognized for what it is: an etic categorization established for reasons of convenience.

15 See e.g. Elsner 2020, 133.

16 Feuser 2013, 155–61, 257–71 cat. nos 133–62.

17 Amm. Marc. XII.13 (AD 362).

---

18 Zos. IV.18.2–4.

19 Stirling 2005, 120–21; Brody 2007, 24–25.

20 Ioh. Mal. 322: 'He had another statue made of himself in gilded wood, bearing in its right hand the tyche of the city, itself gilded, which he called Anthousa. He ordered that on the same day as the Anniversary race-meeting this wooden statue should be brought

Figure 10.2. Barberini diptych. Paris, Louvre. Sixth century. Photo by Marie-Lan Nguyen 2011, Public Domain <https://commons.wikimedia.org/w/index.php?curid=507486> [accessed 12 February 2023].

are depicted on late antique iconographic sources into the sixth century: on the left vertical panel of the Barberini diptych, a male figure in military attire — identified either as consul, a soldier, or a general of the Byzantine armies — is on his way to the scene in the central panel (Fig. 10.2).[21] In his hands he holds a female statuette of a winged Victory, goddess of triumph. The statuette is standing on one foot, the other raised in the air. Her clothes are almost transparent. She holds a laurel wreath with a central jewel, intended for the horsemen in the central panel, who has been identified with Emperor Anastasius and more recently with Emperor Justinian.[22] Emperors are of course often associated with Victories; indeed, on the central panel of the Barberini diptych itself, another Victory, this time standing on a globe, is crowning the emperor, even though the deeply undercut wreath has disappeared. The Victory on the left panel is undeniably the representation of a small statuette, however, as underlined by the high and richly decorated base. Dulbreuck suggested it may be a consular attribute, like the *sparsio* bag visible at the figure's feet, as the other example of such a statuette appears on the right hand of Caesar Constantius Gallus, consul for the year 354, from the *Chronography of 354*.[23] Even if this is the case, this does not make it a powerless attribute — on the contrary, such an attribute only makes sense if its presence is thought to be numinous in some way or another. The mentioning of the Tyche statuette in Malalas and especially the appearance of the Victory statuette on the Barberini diptych are important because they take us away from the sphere of pagan religion into a less easily definable religious realm, where statuettes were considered useful to emperors and high magistrates who, definitely by the sixth century, self-identified as Christian. We will return to this matter later on in this article.

---

in, escorted by the soldiers wearing cloaks and boots, all holding candles; the carriage should march around the turning post and reach the pit opposite the imperial kathisma, and the emperor of the time should rise and make obeisance as he gazed at this statue of Constantine and the Tyche of the city. This custom has been maintained up to the present day.' (Trans. Jeffreys, Jeffreys, and Scott 1986).

21 Delbrück 1929, 192 no. 48.

22 Anastasius: Delbrück 1929, 192 no. 48 for a description of the panel with the Victoria statuette; Justinian: Cutler 1998, 336.

23 Another such statuette appears in the *Calendar of 354*, where a Victory is carried by Caesar Constantius Gallus. Unlike the statuette on the Barberini diptych, this figure is positioned on top of a very flat surface resting on Constantius's right hand. See Delbrück 1929, pl. 20.

Statuettes in the Archaeological Record of Late Antiquity

There are many factors influencing the quality and quantity of the archaeological evidence, which in its turn naturally impacts scholarly interpretation. These factors may seem obvious to archaeologist readers, but as they are rarely explicitly acknowledged in publications of statuettes and especially because they have major bearings on our interpretation of the evidence, I consider it essential to outline two of them here: the importance of find contexts and the mirage of continuity, both of which are particularly pertinent for examining the later life of statuary in general.

Even if it is very hard or even impossible to answer *why* statues were treated in a particular manner based on archaeological evidence alone, their find circumstances should make it possible to at least examine *under what circumstances* they entered the archaeological record, as well as *when* that even took place. Yet, find contexts of statuettes have not always been recorded or published in such detail that we can with certainty speak on these issues. For most statuettes, secure find contexts are lacking altogether. Many statuettes in museum collections today only have an alleged origin or can only roughly be assigned to a site. When a more precise find-spot is known, their sometimes-fragmentary condition indicates that they were moved around, perhaps as the result of salvage and recycling operations. In the case studies discussed later in this article, later occupants of the sites certainly displaced fragments, though leaving enough in place to reach a reliable reconstruction.

Moreover, statuettes, as the most prized objects of excavations and study, which are at the same time both precious and easy to move, have often been the first objects to be freed from the earth and thus to have been separated from associated artefacts and ecofacts. For instance, associations with particular types of ceramics, lamps, or — very popular in all kinds of contexts into the seventh century — low-value bronze coins, have simply not been noticed and definitely not been published. Consequently, our understanding of the formation process of the archaeological record also often remains limited.

Dating the end of engagement with statuary is also particularly difficult. Often, the date given is based on associated pottery, lamps, and especially coins and their date of minting. There are, however, several issues when using coins in this manner. For instance, coins dating to the late fourth and early fifth centuries — the period that most sanctuaries are thought to have gone out of use — appear to have been in use for very long periods of time.[24] The (violent?) end of activity at the Shrine of Liber Pater at Cosa could thus only very loosely be dated: 108 small bronze coins dating to the fourth and fifth centuries were found; the latest datable coin, of Honorius, was minted between 410 and 423 but with additional issues that could go as late as the reign of Valentinian III (425–455). They only allow for an already broad *terminus post quem*, made even broader by the fact that many coins are heavily worn, thus suggesting that they ended up in this location quite some time after the date of minting.[25] For older excavations, establishing an end date becomes even more difficult, as associated objects were not registered and the only datable evidence is associated inscriptions. For instance, Douglas Boin has pulled together the evidence for continued display of statuary in the Sanctuary of Magna Mater in Ostia. A total of thirty items was found, including imperial portraits, reliefs, almost life-sized statues, and a bronze 0.70 m high statuette of Venus, in perfect condition. Boin largely avoids the question of how long the items would have remained on display, concluding at the end that the Venus statuette was there 'even at the start of the fifth century'. Although there is no explicit evidence for visits to the area or further engagement with the statuary present, there is also no reason why they could not have continued throughout the fifth century and even beyond.[26]

Find contexts that have been registered in more detail are those where statues had already been gathered and disposed of, often in basins, cisterns, sewers, or wells. Even here the archaeological context is not always registered to such an extent or is simply not informative enough to shed light on the motives for deposition. In most cases, it is impossible to make a distinction between items that were disposed of because they had been damaged beyond repair and those that were taken down for changes in taste or religious reasons. The issue is further compounded by the growing evidence for the display of broken statues in Late Antiquity. For instance, in the colonnaded street at Sagalassos, the central figure of a group of the Three Graces was put on display by herself.[27] Of course, the gathering and disposal of statuary for recycling or during a clean-up operation also erases many if not all traces of earlier engagements. Of most use are the contexts where there is no doubt that deposition occurred because of strong sentiments; one such case of which will be presented below. But as has been demonstrated by Anghel, such depositions are much rarer than generally thought.[28] In short, even in contexts of disposal, it is very hard to draw conclusions about particular motivations.

All these uncertainties or simply the absence of information concerning find context have, quite understandably, led scholars to focus their inquiries on questions of production, workshops, and transport. Investigations of exact appearance and lineage of especially marble statuettes far outnumber those dealing with usage by and engagements with humans. We sometimes forget that many of the statuettes published in catalogues or excavation reports were around for several centuries, or, what is more pertinent, for dozens of generations. Some of the statuettes at Sagalassos, for instance, were probably produced in the second century, meaning that they were in circulation for half a millennium. We cannot assume that the people who gathered them in the street in the second quarter of the sixth century looked at them or engaged with them in the same manner as when they were purchased for the first time. The often-numerous architectural interventions in domestic contexts up until the moment of destruction meant that house owners had to make conscious decisions on what to do with their statuettes as well. Therefore, although the propagation of statuettes has been connected to the villa boom of the fourth and early fifth centuries, the motivations of the original patron(s) to purchase or gather them may have been complemented or supplanted by other sentiments. Likewise, new generations may have engaged with these items in very different ways. In other words, even if the impression in archaeological time is one of continuity, we have to acknowledge that in human time, the reception and usage of these objects were in constant flux.

Engaging with continuity and curation is very difficult, even more so than examining physical changes often interpreted as damage and violence. Although the exact interpretation of the latter is frequently out of reach, outward changes to a statue at least indicate a changed perception in a relatively straightforward man-

---

[24] Sanders 2003, 387; 2004, 172–74.

[25] Collins-Clinton 1977, 15–16. Based on the fragmentation of some of the statues, the excavators suggested that they had been attacked and smashed on purpose, after which the area was abandoned and eventually collapsed.

[26] Boin 2013, 256–57, with bibliography. Boin (2013, 263–65) moreover points to the evidence for continued curation in Ostia and nearby Rome in the fifth and even the sixth centuries.

[27] Jacobs and Stirling 2017, 212.

[28] Anghel 2011.

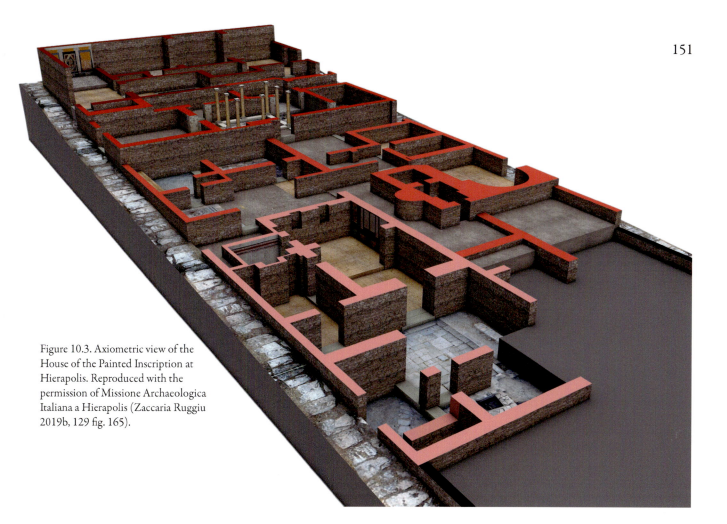

Figure 10.3. Axiometric view of the House of the Painted Inscription at Hierapolis. Reproduced with the permission of Missione Archaeologica Italiana a Hierapolis (Zaccaria Ruggiu 2019b, 129 fig. 165).

ner. Outward changes at first sight seem to be more frequent with larger scale statues than statuettes, with, for instance, only one example of a statuette marked with a cross.[29] Mutilation to genitalia is better known and studied for larger statues. It is not unknown for smaller items, however, as is suggested by the abraded breasts of a naked torso belonging to a statuette of originally *c.* 12 cm high found at Sagalassos.[30] Some of the differences may indeed be the result of dissimilar levels of scholarly attention rather than divergent perception in the past. Contexts like the Sanctuary of Demeter and Persephone in Cyrene confirm in any case that no differentiation based on size was made when statues were attacked and their facial features mutilated.[31]

Equating the absence of any outward change with the absence of change altogether may be very tempting, but as many statues and statuettes remained visible presences for lengthy periods of time and were therefore part of constantly changing and evolving settings and society, this assumption is a fallacy.[32] If we want to understand what our statuettes were doing in the first half of the seventh century, looking at contemporary practices and society is much more pertinent than examining the villa culture of AD 400 or analysing iconographic attributes established in a period that culturally, socially, and religiously was very different from AD 600.[33]

Statuettes in Context at the End of Antiquity

In both settings discussed below, statuettes were clearly still functional components of domestic or public life in the sixth to mid-seventh centuries. This is about two to three hundred years after the late antique villa boom

---

[29] Kristensen 2012, fig. 1 cat. no. B9.

[30] SA-2010-CG-202-254. The preserved fragment was found in an erosional-collapse layer.

[31] White 2006, 196–97.

[32] This is underlined by the growing number of studies acknowledging this for large-scale monuments like the rider statue of Marcus Aurelius in Rome or the bronze horse rider of Constantinople, e.g. Kinney 2002; Boeck 2021.

[33] Even though it is possible that the originally intended identification of specific statuettes (equalling again their modern iconographic identity) was preserved throughout multiple generations, this cannot and should not be taken for granted. Sixth- and seventh-century populations may have identified their statues in ways that would have been inconceivable to their predecessors as well as to modern researchers.

is thought to have taken place, two hundred years after the period that most temples are thought to have closed for public worship, and at least half a century beyond the period that Christianity is thought to have gained a stronger hold on all aspects of society.[34]

The first case study is the House of the Painted Inscription at Hierapolis, a wealthy residence just to the north-west of the theatre in the heart of the city centre. Excavations here uncovered a house block ('Insula 104') made up of several elite residences that came into being in the fifth century and remained functional into the mid-seventh century when they were destroyed in an earthquake (Fig. 10.3).[35] The House of the Painted Inscription was named after the extraordinary find of the penitential Prayer of Manasseh, painted potentially at the start of the sixth century in red and purple paints on a white background in a brick-paved room at the very back of the house.[36] Although the exact function of the room remains uncertain, the location of the text at eye level on all four walls of the space indicates that it was intended to be recited (or sung) with the door of the room closed. The location of this prayer room at the back of the house may be explained by the fact that it was a later addition to the residential suite, but it also suggests privacy and intimacy, which is further confirmed by the fact that the only entrance was through a narrow door from the neighbouring room.

By contrast, an Amor and Psyche group (with a height of 54 cm) was apparently still present in the much more accessible areas of the house (Fig. 10.4). Fragments of the group were found in the entrance to the house (room 38), others in two *exedrae* (rooms 41 and 42) opening off the neighbouring courtyard, all in collapse layers from the mid-seventh century.[37] The dispersal of fragments to other rooms is connected to mid-Byzantine interventions, which were apparently largely aimed at recovering still-useful building materials. As the heaviest fragment, the base with the lower legs, was found on the floor of room 41, it is likely that this was the group's original location of display.[38] The luxurious marble floor

Figure 10.4. Amor and Psyche from the House of the Painted Inscription at Hierapolis after partial restoration. Fourth century. Reproduced with the permission of Missione Archaeologica Italiana a Hierapolis (Zaccaria Ruggiu 2019b, 103 fig. 120).

and wall decoration of the room would have been a suitable setting for statuary. The marble 'opus sectile' panels of the floor are interrupted in the centre by the later insertion of a squarish onyx panel, which would have been one potential and very central location of display. Though invisible from the main door, the *exedra* was still located close to the house entrance and would have been visible to all visitors. The display of a pagan-mythological theme here happened openly. Moreover, it coincided with strong religious Christian feelings.

The second context, the main colonnaded street at Sagalassos (south-western Turkey) is rarer in that the statuettes were found in a public context. In the second quarter of the sixth century, the building crew in charge of the renovation of the street integrated at least eight statue brackets into the newly built piers flanking the paved road. There was a minimum of three statuettes on display along the eastern border of the street: an Apollo (Fig. 10.5), a Hygieia, and a Hygieia with Hypnos (Fig. 10.6). An unknown, smaller statuette was mounted on top of a small console near the agora gate staircase. Along the western side of the street, a third statuette of Hygieia stood on top of a console near a crossroads;

---

34 For Sagalassos, see Talloen 2019, 187–95.

35 Zaccaria Ruggiu 2019a.

36 Zaccaria Ruggiu 2019b, 123–26. For the prayer, see D'Andria and others 2006; Ritti 2019; Brocca 2019 with further references. For a summary of the internal and external dating evidence, see Ritti 2019, 678–79.

37 Zaccaria Ruggiu 2019b, 102–03, 114; Canazza 2019, 567–68 with further references.

38 Zaccaria Ruggiu 2019b, 111–15.

Figure 10.5. Fragments of a statuette of Apollo found on the colonnaded street at Sagalassos. Ağlasun, Sagalassos Excavation House depots. Late second century. Photo by author.

Figure 10.6. Statuette of Hygeia with Hypnos from the excavations of the colonnaded street at Sagalassos, after restoration. Burdur Museum. AD 250–260 or later. Photo courtesy of the Sagalassos Archaeological Project.

an Aphrodite was present about halfway down the street near a street fountain; a central figure of a group once representing the Three Graces stood more to the north; and possibly a much smaller statuette, depicting Aphrodite, stood on a smaller console near the agora gate staircase. There is no reason to assume that the statuettes were already on display in an earlier phase of the street. Even if they were not introduced during the last grand-scale sixth-century renovation phase, they were carefully curated at the time. They remained staring out over the heads of passers-by until the entire city was severely damaged by an earthquake around AD 620. Some of the statues apparently even survived this seismic event and only toppled down at a later unknown moment in time.[39] There can be little doubt that the population of Sagalassos in the sixth and seventh centuries self-identified as Christian. In the street itself, there was ample reference to Christianity: multiple crosses and prayers had been scratched onto columns and a pavement slab, and some architectural fragments lying in the street carried crosses in relief.[40]

Occupation in the city continued after the earthquake and the street was partially cleared of larger debris to facilitate the continuation of traffic to occupied areas south of the centre. The fallen statuettes were moved as well. For instance, all metal implements were missing, which could have happened at this moment in time. Overall, however, there is not much evidence that the population paid these statuary parts much attention. The only exception was the naked torso of an Aphrodite statuette, preserved from shoulders to navel, with the

---

[39] For more information on the stratigraphic position of the statuettes, see Jacobs and Stirling 2017, 217–19.

[40] Jacobs and Waelkens 2014, 248.

Figure 10.7. Torso of Aphrodite from the excavations of the colonnaded street at Sagalassos, after conservation. Ağlasun, Sagalassos Excavation House depots. Second century (?). Photo courtesy of the Sagalassos Archaeological Project.

upper buttocks just visible (Fig. 10.7). This fragment was discovered in more exceptional circumstances. It had been thrown into a disused street fountain, on top of an already present pile of rubbish. Moreover, it had been covered by a large and heavy column base, which had been lifted from the street border just next to the fountain especially for this purpose (Fig. 10.8). The weight of the base indicates that several people were involved in this operation. The fact that they were able to use a column base for this purpose clearly puts the date of the events after the early seventh-century earthquake, which caused the colonnade and columns to fall onto the street pavement. A naked torso fragment potentially once belonging to a subsidiary *putto* was also discovered in a nearby post-earthquake rubbish dump. Like the rest of the Aphrodite statuette and some of its companions, it must have been lying on top of the street pavement after the earthquake. Unlike most other fragments, this one was also picked up and thrown onto a rubbish pile, where it was covered with more rubbish.

Secular Statuettes, Numinous Statuettes

The archaeological context of the naked torsos, in particular that of the female torso in the street fountain, makes it clear that seventh-century perception of these statue parts differed from contemporary thoughts on other statuary fragments lying in the immediate area.

Although archaeological evidence is the result of human action and therefore not necessarily consistent or easy to categorize, the particular treatment of the naked torso in any case contradicts the idea that it was seen merely as decoration or cultural artefact. It is furthermore unlikely that it was merely considered morally offensive. This would have led to discard, as had already happened elsewhere to so many other naked statues, including Aphrodites.[41] Instead, the Aphrodite torso fulfils both prerequisites of religious deposition as put forward by Silviu Anghel in his study of buried statues of deities: (1) it was buried and removed from the surface, and (2) it was not simply thrown away or reused.[42] The sealing in the fountain basin therefore suggests that someone believed the torso possessed dangerous qualities that needed to be constrained and neutralized. Literary sources on the alluring powers of Aphrodite have been discussed on several occasions.[43] Moreover, multiple late antique literary sources also suggest a connection between burial and the binding of the power of a deity or demon.[44]

The archaeological record here therefore suggests a reaction fuelled by negative emotions, anger or fear or both. This stands in stark contrast with the current *communis opinio* on small-scale statuettes found in late antique domestic settings or the public domain that are thought to have been purchased and displayed by for aesthetic reasons, as moral *exempla*, or as expressions of status, rank, and education by both pagans and Christians (or Jews).[45] Although the evolution of thought on the functioning of statuettes is complex, Lea Stirling's sweeping 2005 overview of late antique statuettes has been especially defining. Stirling composed her overview in opposition to scholars recognizing cult whenever they

---

[41] At the Vedius Gymnasium at Ephesus, for instance, nude statues had already been removed by the early fifth century, Auinger and Rathmayr 2007, 243–48; Auinger 2011, 71–76.

[42] Anghel 2011, 5. Depositions in a Christian context are very rare. Most known depositions are closely connected with traditional pagan cult. Anghel acknowledges only one 'Christian' example, which, interestingly, is also very late (postdating the Byzantine reconquest of Carthage in AD 533) and, moreover, could also be identified as an Aphrodite, found buried in eleven fragments underneath the mosaic floor of a basilica (Anghel 2011, 235). For the find situation see Alexander, Ben Abed-Ben Khader, and Métraux 1996, 367 figs 17g–h; Kristensen 2013, 32).

[43] See for instance Lepelley 1994, 5; Stirling 2005, 157–58; Kristensen 2013, 222–28.

[44] Anghel 2011, 261–65.

[45] Gazda 1981, 168–70, 177; Stirling 2005, 26–27, 153–55; Hannestad 2007a, 273–74 all point to the importance of *paideia* for the creation of statuary collections.

Figure 10.8. Street fountain with column base, underneath which the Aphrodite torso was found. Photo by author.

came across pagan-mythological statuettes. Instead, she argued that high-status house owners, all of whom had enjoyed the classicizing education system or *paideia*, realized that references to pagan mythology could serve various purposes but also that the depictions themselves did not channel power or hold power.[46] Like pagan and mythological motifs on other media, including mosaics, paintings, silverware, curtains, and tapestries, they are thought to at best *reflect* ideas of plenty and good fortune in the house rather than to have *acted* and actively contributed to it. Stirling therefore assumed 'that mythological statuary is decorative unless further evidence of pagan worship exists'.[47]

In particular when there is material evidence for Christian presence in the house, this is considered to be an all-decisive factor in defining the decorative nature of statuary.[48] Amor and Psyche groups — like that at Hierapolis, for instance — are known from earlier centuries of Late Antiquity as well and for more than two hundred years apparently comfortably sat in Christian households. To name but one other example, excavations of the House of the Valerii in Rome, which appears to have been sacked by Alaric's troops in 410, uncovered in the atrium a statuette of Cupid and Psyche. Other finds included silver liturgical vessels with Christian inscriptions and symbols.[49] Both texts and inscriptions suggest that the Valerii self-identified as Christian by the early fifth century. Therefore, it was concluded that '[i]n this scenario, the ideal statuary is best interpreted in a decorative sense'.[50] As both our case studies were without any doubt situated in a Christian milieu, according to this line of thinking we should not even bother asking the question about numinous potential.

There are two main problems with this interpretative framework. Firstly, the long survival of pagan-mythological subjects in elite houses has been connected to the control elite house owners exercised over their property — they got to tell who accessed which areas of the

---

[46] Stirling 2005, 138–64.

[47] Stirling 2005, 22. She lists the following indicators for pagan worship (p. 224): 'clear reference to elements of pagan practice, such as votive offerings, priests, or sacrifice; evidence of actual sacrifice near the statuary; an identifiable shrine; or presence of Eastern mystery divinities.'

[48] Stirling 2005, 26. There are issues with equating the presence of material culture with Christian iconography to Christian self-identification as well. Defining the religious self-identification

of houseowners based on their material culture is a notoriously difficult exercise.

[49] Brenk 1999.

[50] Stirling 2005, 26.

house and who did not.⁵¹ It is assumed that in the more private spaces, statuary was protected from the less predictable and superstitious masses who may not have been able to make appropriate distinctions between powerless and powerful.⁵² Stirling explicitly cites this as the reason why statuettes are found foremost in the more intimate suites, whereas for instance portrait statues would be also on display in more accessible courtyards.⁵³ However, this argument is more difficult to use for the group of Amor and Psyche at Hierapolis, which although not immediately visible from the house entrance, was not confined to an intimate space either — as opposed to the prayer. It would have been visible and accessible to visitors. The assemblage at Sagalassos cannot be fitted into the reasoning above either, as it would have been visible to and within reach of everyone living in the city as well as to visitors from outside. Tying preservation and usage solely to levels of education therefore does not work in these circumstances. Instead, we need to look for an explanation that would also take the wider populations of cities into account.

Admittedly, it has been argued, including by me, that for much of Late Antiquity, there was a public complement to elite *paideia*. Building on Robert Markus's division of late antique society into three spheres — the 'profane', the 'sacred', and the 'secular'⁵⁴ — it is thought that the 'secularization' of institutions and objects, externalized as the removal of offensive ritual aspects and physical attributes, made it possible to assimilate multiple classical elements into a Christian society and to further profit from them in many different ways. The notion of the secular has been used as an explanation for the continuation of New Year celebrations and civic games.⁵⁵ Texts featuring gods and mythological creatures could be used by Christians as well because they had been 'secularized', and became 'simple cultural inheritance'.⁵⁶ The same 'secularized' subjects remained a source of inspiration far into the sixth century for silversmiths, mosaicists, painters, and so on.⁵⁷ In the same way as late fourth-century edicts stressed the artfulness of statues and suggested they should be appreciated for their beauty,⁵⁸ the notion appears to apply to statuary in the public domain as well. Statues that had not received veneration supposedly could transition into the secular sphere without much fuss, where they were regarded as general cultural heritage, references to a rich past, and elements of decoration and representation.⁵⁹

It has to be said that Markus understood 'secular' habits and contexts as 'capable of being linked either with damnation or salvation, depending on the ultimate purposes to which it is harnessed'.⁶⁰ Later scholars took the idea and pushed the secularization of late antique society further. The increased focus on issues of aesthetics, cultural significance, self-representation, antiquarianism, and so on,⁶¹ eventually stripped the texts and objects involved from religious potential altogether.⁶² Probably based on a modern perception of a secular world, in the modern mind they have become powerless and passive reflectors of a changed late antique society, which may not have been what Markus originally intended when he discussed his views on the secular in Late Antiquity.

Yet, there is a second problem with the *paideia*-secular framework. The notion of the secular is thought to have been valid mainly until the start of the sixth century, whereupon its relevance declined with the increasing influence of a more ascetic Christian tradition over activities within society, including charity, justice, building projects, urban calendars, politics, and so on. This supposedly led to a growing desecularization, with Christianity getting a grip on ever-more aspects of everyday life or rejecting them altogether.⁶³ As also stressed earlier in this paper, engagements with statuettes were not necessarily unchanging. The motivations to acquire statuettes in the fourth or fifth century (or earlier) may

---

51 Stirling 2005, 139–48.

52 See e.g. Mango 1963; Saradi-Mendelovici 1990, 50, 55. The notion is pervasive in scholarship of the period.

53 Stirling 2016, 270, 289.

54 Markus 1986; 2006, 11–13.

55 Markus 1990, 107–09.

56 Lepelley 2010, 489.

57 Liebeschuetz 1995; Leader-Newby 2004.

58 *Cod. Theod.* XVI.10.8 (382), XVI.10.15 (399).

59 Lepelley 2001.

60 Markus 1986, 85.

61 On antiquarianism, see Bassett 2004, 101 (Kedrenos on the statues in the Zeuxippos baths), 115–16 (the Lausos collection); Machado 2009.

62 Machado 2009, 354 concludes that Christian intellectuals could endeavour to understand pagan rituals and myths whilst staying 'religiously neutral'. The statues discovered in the Sanctuary of Magna Mater at Ostia have been suggested to possess 'a unique social and cultural significance for those who lived and worked in later Ostia' (Boin 2013, 267).

63 Markus 1990, 16; Van Dam 2007, 361. Statuary collections elsewhere were supposedly being removed from both private houses and public buildings in cities of the same region. See Jacobs 2016, 112 for examples from western Asia Minor.

have been very different from the reasons for preserving them for multiple generations. And indeed, if we consider contemporary, i.e. sixth- and seventh-century, practices more broadly, there are plenty of indications for a society that considered representations of divinities, Christian and non-Christian, to be numinous.

First of all, small-scale figurines in other materials, mostly terracotta but with a couple of examples in bronze as well, were still (or again) being produced into the sixth and seventh centuries in for instance northern Egypt as well as in Sagalassos itself.[64] The frequent interpretation of such figurines as 'holdovers from a "pagan" era' has also here long curtailed attempts to understand their functioning in contemporary society.[65] David Frankfurter's in-depth study on female figurines in late antique Egypt, taking into account their find locations and using comparative materials, has argued for usage both in votive practices in church settings and in more varied religious communication in the domestic sphere, probably centred on a small altar or within a domestic shrine for which the evidence is, however, scanty. In Sagalassos, ceramic workshops produced small-scale zoomorphic and anthropomorphic figurines, mostly of riders on horseback, with a total height of some 12 cm.[66] Production continued at least until the first half of the sixth century, and they remained in use into the seventh, judging from their retrieval from debris of the early seventh-century earthquake as well as from floor deposits laid out after the seismic shock.[67] Find-spots indicate that they were present in commercial and in domestic contexts as well as in the local churches. A usage parallel to that suggested by Frankfurter for Egypt can be proposed, with ceramic miniatures being presented to the church as votive or communicative media and evoking different engagements outside of the church context. Both in late antique Egypt and late antique Sagalassos (and environs), the use of figurines was apparently both perfectly admissible and perceived of as an act conjuring and guiding power.

The occurrence of these figurines underlines that three-dimensional representations of the human form continued to be perceived as having beneficial power by wide layers of society. Like the continued use of small-scale marble statuettes, there are no textual references to these figurines, and the archaeological record needs to be allowed to speak for itself for us to begin to understand what these objects were thought to achieve for contemporary populations. They certainly withstand attempts to label them as either Christian or pagan. In fact, like with the last usage of our statuettes, that categorization is probably the wrong question to ask altogether.[68]

Of course, terracotta figurines differ not only in material but also in size from the statuettes in our two case studies. Their smaller size and weight would have made it easier to engage with them in personal and intimate relationships. But to consider them as entirely unconnected and irrelevant for marble human representations would be a fallacy.[69] I have already referred to sixth-century sources on gestural relations with portable marble and metal statuettes above. Moreover, other historical sources of the sixth century confirm that the perception of power associated with three-dimensional human depictions ranged from the very small to the life-sized, if not larger. This is perhaps demonstrated best by the metric inscription on a base for a statue of Emperor Justinian, found at the eastern site of Cyrrhus. The text refers to imperial munificence, i.e., the emperor apparently had the walls of the site restored. It ends with the statement 'To [honour] the splendour of your virtues, the city carries your image, Emperor, as a defence against evil'.[70] What the evil referred to in the inscription entailed, we are not told, but the statue itself was considered a deterrent.[71] Similar attestations are known best from the later *Parastaseis syntomoi chronikai* and the

---

[64] Marsengill 2014, 91 mentions two fourth- or fifth-century statuettes of St Peter, one of St Paul, and one of another possible apostle, as well as one seventh-century statuette of a pilgrim or saint.

[65] Frankfurter 2015, 192.

[66] Talloen 2011, 593–96; Jacobs and Waelkens 2017, 184–86.

[67] Remains of riders and their horses produced at Sagalassos were also discovered at Seleuceia Sidera (Pisidia), see Laflı 1998.

[68] Lichtenberger 2017 questions the use of the labels 'pagan' and 'Jewish' in relation to figurines and oil lamps produced by a workshop active probably in the second half of the third century and early fourth in Beit Nattif.

[69] There is an academic tendency to treat types of small-scale human representation separately, with stone, metal, and certainly terracotta items looked at by different specialists. It may very well be that the material of these objects was much less important in the past than it has become in academic research. We for instance find bricolage assemblages of varying types and material in household shrines in Pompeii (Boyce 1937). The present academic mode of categorization reflects post-antique art-historical aesthetic hierarchies (marble and bronze over terracotta) and an interest in statuettes as primarily *objets d'art*, but not necessarily ancient reality.

[70] LSA-2636 (translated by Ulrich Gehn). For the base, see also Alpi 2011.

[71] This itself is part of a much wider phenomenon whereby the imperial image is considered to have protective power, see for instance Jones 2011; 2016.

Patria of Constantinople, in which we find statues capable of doing harm or of protecting their surroundings or the city as a whole.[72] Late antique literary evidence for 'talismanic' usage of statues has been gathered a few years back by Luke Lavan.[73] This evidence offers further confirmation that statues of emperors, as well as Victory and Tyche, are perceived to be numinous, to have efficacious power in and of themselves. They respond to needs and concerns for which Christianity offered no alternative.[74] Unconnected to the Christian god and his saints, they belong to a distinct realm of power, one that has roots in the pagan past but for which the characterization 'pagan' is not helpful; these statues do not reflect beliefs identical to those of previous generations and going back for centuries. That would not make sense within the framework of overall Christian households and settlements. A fundamental flaw of the 'pagan survival' paradigm is its implicit insistence on the priority of immaterial beliefs, which are assumed to exist in a coherent condition independent of their material manifestation. Belief here overrides practice and material form, so that statues are reduced to representations that are almost as passive as those in the *paideia*-secular framework. Over the course of the centuries, these effigies had developed into contemporary tools considered useful also by people self-identifying as Christians. Like with the figurines above, attempts to label such statues themselves as either Christian or pagan is reductive and beside the point.

What then happens if we rethink the numinous potential of the statuettes in Hierapolis and Sagalassos? The Amor and Psyche group at Hierapolis belonged to a wide range of sensual imagery depicting mythological lovers. Such imagery had once been omnipresent in the home in the form of statuary, on mosaics, silverware, lamps, etc.[75] Susanne Muth has argued that the details of many of such scenes on mosaics contradict the idea that these were intended to convey the education of the house owners, as they do not focus on central elements in mythological stories. The real interests and concerns of the house owners are revealed by the choice to depict sexual encounters of mythological heroes or the interaction between mythological lovers. They are sometimes surrounded by an entire cortege, children, nursemaids, dogs, in a reflection of the real-life household. On mosaics, such imagery is known to have continued far into the sixth century with examples like the mosaic of Achilles and Briseis in Madaba.[76] Textile wall hangings as well suggest the continued popularity of this thematic until the end of Antiquity.

The popularity of such depictions therefore betrays the house owners' hopes and desires in relation to sexuality and marital relations and, by extension, family prosperity. If we remember that the group of Amor and Psyche was on display in a heavily decorated open *exedra*, potentially on a socle in the centre of the space, and combine this with the perceived protective power of statuary as mentioned in contemporary literary sources, the most logical conclusion is that the group was there to give clear direction to such sentiments. The Prayer of Manasseh no doubt was applied to direct the household hopes and fears as well, but as a penitential prayer aimed at confessing one's sins and asking for forgiveness, its purpose was very different from that of the naked lovers in the other wing of the house. On the whole, the Christian god, its angels, and saints were addressed for manifold needs but are less known to deal with matters of sexuality and marital bliss. The disparity between these two domains of life is only underlined further by the contrast between the simple setting of the prayer room and the luxurious marble framing of the statuette.

As already said, the assemblage at Sagalassos is diverse, and searching for programmatic unity is pointless. Yet, it remains likely that the statuettes were brought together in the first quarter of the sixth century with some reason in mind. In theory, it is possible that this is all the builders of the street could get their hands on in this period, or that these statuettes fitted together relatively well in size.[77] This is, however, a very minimalistic approach. In the past I have regarded this display as a public counterpart to the cultural motivations driving statuary display and preservation in private houses and have argued that the statuettes were installed on top of consoles by referring to the socio-political necessity of providing a city with an impressive and prestigious entrance into its

---

72 Cameron and Herrin 1984; Berger 2013. See the overviews on powerful statuary in Mango 1963; James 1996.

73 Lavan 2011.

74 On this notion of parallel realms of power in Late Antiquity, see Jacobs (forthcoming).

75 Muth 2001.

76 Dunbabin 2018, 368, 369 fig. 8.

77 In other public settings, the statuettes are disproportionally small for their find context. This may offer an indication that life-sized statues this far into Late Antiquity were low in number, whereas statuettes had led a more sheltered life inside elite residences for several centuries before being moved to the public domain (Jacobs 2016, 100–01, 105–08). In the street at Sagalassos, most statuettes may have been relatively well proportioned (Jacobs and Stirling 2017, 224).

centre, i.e., for decoration purposes.⁷⁸ I have also pushed the evidence further by suggesting that the Hygeia statuettes, maybe even the Grace and the Aphrodite, had been physically altered and reinterpreted as Muses and were added to the Apollo statuette in an attempt by the city to display culture and intellectual activity.⁷⁹

Alternatively, the statuettes were not altered or reinterpreted when they were put on top of their consoles. The presence of three Hygieias, the personification of health, and Apollo, who also had healing and purification among his powers, would suggest a particular stress on health and healing. It is interesting to note that, when the Antonine Nymphaeum of the Upper Agora of Sagalassos was given its final statuary decoration, this also revolved around curative powers: it included a statue of Asclepius, his mother Coronis, Hygieia, and a plinth for a male statue, probably again an Apollo.⁸⁰ The date of the ensemble in the *Nymphaeum* cannot be ascertained, but it is very likely that it can be attributed to the sixth century. As has been said, the composition of the collection on the colonnaded street has been assigned to the second quarter of the sixth century. Especially if we assume that these statues were still conceived of as powerful and influential, it is tempting to connect this predilection with health to the arrival of the bubonic plague. The additional naked female statues of Aphrodite and one Grace could be evocations of healthy bodies, unmarked by buboes. In the *Nymphaeum* display, a naked male youth was present, possibly for similar reasons, together with (rather fitting in this line of interpretation), a statue of Nemesis. Such statuary displays would then have been composed for similar reasons as that given by the city of Cyrrhus for their erection of a statue of Justinian: for reasons of protection.

The Apollo with Muses hypothesis mentioned above also depends on a whole series of assumptions and unknowns, yet (as far as I know) no one has objected to it, which probably says more about our own secular society than the sixth and seventh centuries. I imagine that the more numinous scenario for many will be more difficult to accept as a possibility. Admittedly, I have very little evidence for it, but it would be in line with contemporary engagements with terracotta figurines in the same city, it would mirror contemporary apotropaic usage of other statuary, and would also be reinforced by the eventual strong reaction to the Aphrodite torso after the seventh-century earthquake — it is easy to imagine that with protection having failed miserably, more negative feelings surfaced.⁸¹ Rather than arguing that this perception of power was a novelty in the seventh century, I therefore suggest that it had been very much present when the statuary collection was put together a hundred years earlier, no matter what the exact motivations of the sixth-century population were.

Conclusions

I started this article with a brief overview of research on statuettes in Late Antiquity. We know much more about production and iconographic models than we do about the reasons or even the dates that statuettes went out of use. Their multiple and developing roles throughout often several centuries remain virtually unexplored. It is important to acknowledge how patchy our information on some of these aspects is, as this scarcity has pushed us towards sweeping generalizations that are thought to hold true for vast geographic areas and lengthy periods of time, but that are not necessarily supported by the archaeological evidence of individual case studies.

I have tried to lay bare the fundamental problem that the modern-day axiom on the usage of small-scale statuettes as, broadly defined, secular objects of culture, learning, and prestige, is not an empirically proven fact. It is based on a selection of fourth- and fifth-century literary sources on statuary and in particular on modern-day assumptions about the secularized nature of fourth- and fifth-century society. It is also based on a false dichotomy between decoration and cult. It is not constructed from the material evidence and its find contexts. Many of these are not of very high quality, but as excavations become ever better and more detailed (or more detail is published), it may be necessary to re-evaluate this idea and stop applying it as a one-size-fits-all explanation for the usage of statuettes throughout Late Antiquity.

The House of the Painted Inscription at Hierapolis and the colonnaded street at Sagalassos are both recent excavations in which statuettes remained valued parts of the household and the larger cityscape, respectively, into the seventh century. I have argued that the statuettes

---

⁷⁸ Jacobs 2016, 113–15.

⁷⁹ Jacobs and Stirling 2017, 212–14.

⁸⁰ Waelkens and others 1997, 136–62; Mägele 2005; Jacobs 2010, 274–75; 2019, 31–32.

⁸¹ Even though Anghel's corpus mostly predates the Sagalassos deposition by almost three centuries and is very different in composition and interpretation, it remains interesting to note that none of the statues discussed in this publication had been merely decorative in character during their life (Anghel 2011, 242–44).

here were present, generations after their creation, not or no longer because of decorative reasons or for reasons of prestige, but because they were viewed as being numinous, i.e., they still functioned as conduits of hopes and desires for households and were expected to offer protection to entire cities until the very end of Antiquity. This opinion was shared by all layers of society, and we can find supporting evidence in contemporary literary and epigraphic sources as well as in contemporary practices involving terracotta figurines. Such numinous potential cannot and should not be equated with worship, nor should it be considered as the survival of paganism. The statuettes discussed were part of a world that we would nowadays describe as Christian, but that apparently remained inhabited by manifold superhuman and supernatural powers with assigned roles and powers.

Interestingly, these statuettes were treated in much the same way as their larger cousins. They may have had different affordances and they may have been chosen for a particular location because of their size, but when it comes to numinous power, there are no indications that any distinction was made.

Works Cited

Alexander, M. A., A. Ben Abed-Ben Khader, and G. P. R. Métraux. 1996. 'The Corpus of Mosaics of Tunisia: Carthage Project, 1992–1994', *Dumbarton Oaks Papers*, 50: 361–68.

Alpi, F. 2011. 'Base de statue de Justinien ornée d'une inscription métrique', *Syria*, 88: 342–43.

Anghel, S. 2011. 'Burying the Gods: Depositing Statues in Late Antiquity' (unpublished doctoral thesis, Columbia University).

Auinger, J. 2011. 'The Sculptural Decoration of Ephesian Bath Buildings in Late Antiquity', in O. Dally and C. Ratté (eds), *Archaeology and the Cities of Asia Minor in Late Antiquity*, Kelsey Museum Publication, 6 (Ann Arbor: Kelsey Museum of Archaeology), pp. 67–80.

Auinger, J. and E. Rathmayr. 2007. 'Zur spätantiken Statuenausstattung der Thermen und Nymphäen in Ephesos', in F. Bauer and C. Witschel (eds), *Statuen in der Spätantike: Akten des internationalen Workshops in München am 11. und 12. Juni 2004*, Kunst im ersten Jahrtausend. Reihe B: Studien und Perspektiven, 23 (Wiesbaden: Reichert), pp. 237–69.

Bartman, E. 1992. *Ancient Sculptural Copies in Miniature*, Columbia Studies in the Classical Tradition, 19 (Leiden: Brill).

Bassett, S. 2004. *The Urban Image of Late Antique Constantinople* (Cambridge: Cambridge University Press).

Berger, A. 2013. *Accounts of Medieval Constantinople: The Patria* (Cambridge, MA: Harvard University Press).

Bergmann, M. 1999. *Chiragan, Aphrodisias, Konstantinopel: Zur mythologischen Skulptur der Spätantike*, Palilia, 7 (Wiesbaden: Reichert).

Boeck, E. N. 2021. *The Bronze Horseman of Justinian in Constantinople: The Cross-Cultural Biography of a Mediterranean Monument* (Cambridge: Cambridge University Press).

Boin, D. 2013. 'A Late Antique Statuary Collection at Ostia's Sanctuary of Magna Mater: A Case-Study in Late Roman Religion and Tradition', *Papers of the British School at Rome*, 81: 247–77.

Boyce, G. K. 1937. *Corpus of the Lararia of Pompeii*, Memoirs of the American Academy in Rome, 14 (Rome: American Academy in Rome).

Brenk, B. 1999. 'La cristianizzazione della Domus dei Valerii sul Celio', in W. V. Harris (ed.), *Transformations of Urbs Roma in Late Antiquity*, Journal of Roman Archaeology Supplements, 33 (Providence: Journal of Roman Archaeology).

Brent Plate, S. and others. 2005. 'Editorial Statement', *Material Religion*, 1.1: 4–8.

Brody, L. R. 2007. *The Aphrodite of Aphrodisias*, Aphrodisias, 3 (Mainz: Von Zabern).

Brocca, N. 2019. 'La *Preghiera di Manasse* nella tradizione delle Chiese cristiane. Per un'ipotesi sulla destinazione d'uso della stanza della preghiera', in A. Zaccaria Ruggiu (ed.), *Le abitazioni dell'insula 104 a Hierapolis Di Frigia*, Hierapolis Di Frigia, 12 (Istanbul: Ege Yayınları), pp. 683–96.

Cameron, A. and J. Herrin. 1984. *Constantinople in the Early Eighth Century: The 'Parastaseis Syntomoi Chronikai'; Introduction, Translation and Commentary*, Columbia Studies in the Classical Tradition, 10 (Leiden: Brill).

Canazza, A. 2019. 'Sculture e arredi in marmo', in A. Zaccaria Ruggiu (ed.), *Le abitazioni dell'insula 104 a Hierapolis Di Frigia*, Hierapolis Di Frigia, 12 (Istanbul: Ege Yayınları), pp. 535–75.

Collins-Clinton, J. 1977. *A Late Antique Shrine of Liber Pater at Cosa*, Études préliminaires aux religions orientales dans l'Empire romain, 64 (Leiden: Brill).

Cutler, A. 1998. 'Barberiniana: Notes on the Making, Content and Provenance of Louvre, OA. 9063', repr. in A. Cutler, *Late Antique and Byzantine Ivory Carving*, Variorum Collected Studies Series, 617 (Aldershot: Ashgate), pp. 329–39.

D'Andria, F. and others. 2006. 'L'iscrizione dipinta con la Preghiera di Manasse a Hierapolis di Frigia (Turchia): introduzione', *Rendiconti della Pontificia accademia romana di archeologia*, 78: 349–449.

Delbrück, R. 1929. *Die Consulardiptychen und verwandte Denkmäler* (Berlin: De Gruyter).

Dunbabin, K. M. D. 2018. 'The Transformations of Achilles on Late Roman Mosaics in the East', in L. Audley-Miller and B. Dignas (eds), *Wandering Myths: Transcultural Uses of Myth in the Ancient World* (Berlin: De Gruyter), pp. 357–95.

Elsner, J. 2020. 'The Death of the Figurine: Reflections on an Abrahamic Abstention', in J. Elsner (ed.), *Figurines: Figuration and the Sense of Scale*, Visual Conversations in Art and Archaeology (Oxford: Oxford University Press), pp. 130–81.

Ensoli Vittozzi, S. 1993. 'Le sculture del "larario" di S. Martino ai Monti. Un contesto recuperato', *Bullettino della Commissione archeologica comunale di Roma*, 95: 221–43.

Feuser, S. 2013. *Monopodia, figürliche Tischfüsse aus Kleinasien: Ein Beitrag zum Ausstattungsluxus der römischen Kaiserzeit*, Byzas, 17 (Istanbul: Ege Yayınları).

Frankfurter, D. 2015. 'Female Figurines in Early Christian Egypt: Reconstructing Lost Practices and Meanings', *Material Religion*, 11: 190–223.

Gazda, E. K. 1981. 'A Marble Group of Ganymede and the Eagle from the Age of Augustine', in J. H. Humphrey (ed.), *Excavations at Carthage Conducted by the University of Michigan*, IV (Ann Arbor: University of Michigan), pp. 125–78.

Hannestad, N. 1994. *Tradition in Late Antique Sculpture: Conservation-Modernization-Production*, Acta Jutlandica Humanities Series, 69.2 (Aarhus: Aarhus University Press).

——. 2007a. 'Late Antique Mythological Sculpture. In Search of a Chronology', in F. A. Bauer and C. Witschel (eds), *Statuen und Statuensammlungen in der Spätantike*, Kunst im ersten Jahrtausend. Reihe B: Studien und Perspektiven, 23 (Wiesbaden: Reichert), pp. 273–305.

——. 2007b. 'Skulpturenausstattung spätantiker Herrschaftshäuser', in A. Demandt and J. Engemann (eds), *Konstantin der Grosse: Geschichte, Archäologie, Rezeption* (Trier: Rheinisches Landesmuseum Trier), pp. 195–208.

Jacobs, I. 2010. 'From Production to Destruction? Pagan Statuary in Late Antique Asia Minor', *American Journal of Archaeology*, 114: 267–303.

——. 2016. 'Old Habits Die Hard. A Group of Mythological Statuettes from Sagalassos and the Afterlife of Sculpture in Asia Minor', in T. M. Kristensen and L. M. Stirling (eds), *The Afterlife of Classical Sculpture: Late Antique Responses and Practices* (Ann Arbor: University of Michigan Press), pp. 93–117.

——. 2019. 'Reconstructing the Sixth-Century Statuary Record of Asia Minor', in I. Jacobs and H. Elton (eds), *Asia Minor in the Long Sixth Century: Current Research and Future Perspectives* (Oxford: Oxbow), pp. 29–43.

——. (forthcoming). 'Statuary, the Secular and Religious Powers in Late Antiquity', in J. Stenger, K. Ritari, and W. Van Andringa (eds), *Being Pagan, Being Christian in Late Antiquity and Early Middle Ages* (London: Routledge).

Jacobs, I. and L. Stirling. 2017. 'Re-using the Gods. A 6th-c. Statuary Display at Sagalassos and a Re-evaluation of Pagan-Mythological Statuary in Early Byzantine Civic Space', *Journal of Roman Archaeology*, 30: 196–226.

Jacobs, I. and M. Waelkens. 2014. 'Five Centuries of Glory. The Colonnaded Street of Sagalassos in the First and the Sixth Century AD', *Istanbuler Mitteilungen*, 63 [2013]: 219–66.

——. 2017. '"Christians Do Not Differ from Other People". The Down-to-Earth Religious Stance of Late Antique Sagalassos (Pisidia)', in W. Amelung (ed.), *Die Christianisierung Kleinasiens in der Spätantike*, Asia Minor Studien, 87 (Bonn: Habelt), pp. 175–98.

James, L. 1996. 'Pray Not to Fall into Temptation and Be on your Guard: Pagan Statues in Christian Constantinople', *Gesta*, 35.1: 12–20.

Jeffreys, E., M. Jeffreys, and R. Scott. 1986. *The Chronicle of John Malalas*, Australian Association for Byzantine Studies. Byzantina Australiensia, 4 (Melbourne: Australian Association for Byzantine Studies).

Jobst, W. 1986. 'Ein spätantiker Strassenbrunnen in Ephesos', in O. Feld and U. Peschlow (eds), *Studien zur spätantiken und byzantinischen Kunst, Friedrich Wilhelm Deichmann gewidmet* (Bonn: Habelt), pp. 47–62.

Jones, A. E. 2011. '"Lord, Protect the Wearer": Late Antique Numismatic Jewelry and the Image of the Emperor as Talismanic Device' (unpublished doctoral thesis, Yale University).

——. 2016. 'Icons of Power: The Late Antique Imperial Portrait as Image and Amulet', *Ikon (Rijeka)*, 9: 129–40.

Kaufmann-Heinimann, A. 1998. *Götter und Lararien aus Augusta Raurica: Herstellung, Fundzusammenhänge und sakrale Funktion figürlicher Bronzen in einer römischen Stadt*, Forschungen in Augst, 26 (Augst: Römermuseum).

Kinney, D. 2002. 'The Horse, the King and the Cuckoo: Medieval Narrations of the Statue of Marcus Aurelius', *Word & Image*, 18: 372–98.

Kristensen, T. M. 2012. 'Miraculous Bodies: Christian Viewers and the Transformation of "Pagan" Sculptures in Late Antiquity', in B. Poulsen and S. Birk (eds), *Patrons and Viewers in Late Antiquity*, Aarhus Studies in Mediterranean Antiquity, 10 (Aarhus: Aarhus University Press), pp. 31–66.

——. 2013. *Making and Breaking the Gods: Christian Responses to Pagan Sculpture in Late Antiquity* (Aarhus: Aarhus University Press).

Laflı, E. 1998. 'Les figurines romaines en terre cuite de Seleucia Sidera en Pisidie (Turquie)', *Orient-Express: notes et nouvélles d'archéologie oriéntale*, 1998.3: 73–78.

Lavan, L. 2011. 'Political Talismans? Residual "Pagan" Statues in Late Antique Public Space', in L. Lavan and M. Mulryan (eds), *The Archaeology of Late Antique 'Paganism'*, Late Antique Archaeology, 7 (Leiden: Brill), pp. 439–77.

Leader-Newby, E. 2004. *Silver and Society in Late Antiquity: Functions and Meanings of Silver Plate in the 4th to 7th Centuries* (Aldershot: Ashgate).

Lepelley, C. 1994. 'Le musée des statues divines. La volonté de sauvegarder le patrimoine artistique païen à l'époque théodosienne', *Cahiers archéologiques*, 42: 5–15.

——. 2001. 'Recherches sur les diverses formes de paganisme dans l'Afrique romaine tardive. Les témoignages épigraphiques du IVe siècle. Compte-rendu du séminaire tenu en 1999–2000', *Annuaire de l'école pratique des hautes études: section des sciences religieuses*, 108: 283–87.

——. 2010. 'The Use of Secularised Latin Pagan Culture by Christians', in D. Gwynn and S. Bangert (eds), *Religious Diversity in Late Antiquity*, Late Antique Archaeology, 6 (Leiden: Brill), pp. 477–92.

Lichtenberger, A. 2017. 'Jews and Pagans in Late Antique Judaea. The Case of the Beit Nattif Workshop', in R. Raja (ed.), *Contextualizing the Sacred in the Hellenistic and Roman Near East: Religious Identities in Local, Regional, and Imperial Settings*, Contextualizing the Sacred, 8 (Turnhout: Brepols), pp. 191–211.

Liebeschuetz, W. 1995. 'Pagan Mythology in the Christian Empire', *International Journal of the Classical Tradition*, 2.2: 193–208.

Machado, C. 2009. 'Religion as Antiquarianism: Pagan Dedications in Late Antique Rome', in J. Bodel and M. Kajava (eds), *Religious Dedications in the Greco-Roman World: Distribution, Typology, Use* (Rome: Institutum Romanum Finlandiae), pp. 331–53.

Mägele, S. 2005. 'Ein besonderer Ort für Votive. Bemerkungen zu einem ungewöhnlichen Befund dreier Statuen in Sagalassos', *Istanbuler Mitteilungen*, 55: 289–308.

——. 2009. 'Die Skulpturen von Sagalassos: Funktionen und Kontexte' (unpublished doctoral dissertation, University of Leuven).

Mango, C. 1963. 'Antique Statuary and the Byzantine Beholder', *Dumbarton Oaks Papers*, 17: 55–75.

Markus, R. 1986. 'The Sacred and the Secular: From Augustine to Gregory the Great', *The Journal of Theological Studies*, 36: 84–96.

——. 1990. *The End of Ancient Christianity* (Cambridge: Cambridge University Press).

——. 2006. *Christianity and the Secular*, Blessed Pope John XXIII Lecture Series in Theology and Culture (Notre Dame: University of Notre Dame Press).

Marsengill, K. 2014. 'The Christian Reception of Sculpture in Late Antiquity and the Historical Reception of Late Antique Christian Sculpture', *Journal of the Bible and its Reception*, 1.1: 67–101.

Muth, S. 2001. 'Eine Kultur zwischen Veränderung und Stagnation. Zum Umgang mit den Mythenbildern im spätantiken Haus', in F. A. Bauer and N. Zimmerman (eds), *Epochenwandel? Kunst und Kultur zwischen Antike und Mittelalter* (Mainz: Von Zabern), pp. 95–118.

Nixey, C. 2017. *The Darkening Age: The Christian Destruction of the Classical World* (London: Macmillan).

Panayides, P. 2016. 'Villa of Theseus, Nea Paphos: Reconsidering its Sculptural Collection', in R. Maguire and J. Chick (eds), *Approaching Cyprus: Proceedings of the Post-Graduate Conference of Cypriot Archaeology (PoCA) Held at the University of East Anglia, 1st–3rd November 2013* (Newcastle: Cambridge Scholars), pp. 228–43.

——. (forthcoming). *The Lives and Afterlives of Classical Sculpture: Statues, Religion, Economy, and Society in Late Antique Cyprus* (Wiesbaden: Reichert).

Ritti, T. 2019. 'L'iscrizione dipinta con la *Preghiera di Manasse*', in A. Zaccaria Ruggiu (ed.), *Le abitazioni dell'insula 104 a Hierapolis Di Frigia*, Hierapolis Di Frigia, 12 (Istanbul: Ege Yayınları), pp. 667–82.

Sanders, G. D. R. 2003. 'Recent Developments in the Chronology of Byzantine Corinth', in C. K. Williams II and N. Bookidis (eds), *Corinth, The Centenary: 1896–1996*, Corinth, 20 (Princeton: American School of Classical Studies at Athens), pp. 385–99.

——. 2004. 'Problems in Interpreting Urban and Rural Settlement in Southern Greece, AD 365–700', in N. Christie (ed.), *Landscapes of Change: Rural Evolutions in Late Antiquity and the Early Middle Ages* (Aldershot: Ashgate), pp. 163–93.

Saradi-Mendelovici, H. 1990. 'Christian Attitudes toward Pagan Monuments in Late Antiquity and their Legacy in Later Byzantine Centuries', *Dumbarton Oaks Papers*, 44: 47–61.

Sauer, E. W. 2003. *The Archaeology of Religious Hatred in the Roman and Early Medieval World* (Stroud: Tempus).

Stirling, L. M. 2005. *The Learned Collector: Mythological Statuettes and Classical Taste in Late Antique Gaul* (Ann Arbor: University of Michigan Press).

——. 2007. 'Statuary Collecting and Display in the Late Antique Villas of Gaul and Spain', in F. A. Bauer and C. Witschel (eds), *Statuen in der Spätantike: Akten des internationalen Workshops in München am 11. und 12. Juni 2004*, Kunst im ersten Jahrtausend. Reihe B: Studien und Perspektiven, 23 (Wiesbaden: Reichert), pp. 307–21.

——. 2008. 'Pagan Statuettes in Late Antique Corinth', *Hesperia*, 77: 89–161.

——. 2016. 'Shifting Use of a Genre. A Comparison of Statuary Décor in Homes and Baths of the Late Roman West', in T. M. Kristensen and L. M. Stirling (eds), *The Afterlife of Classical Sculpture: Late Antique Responses and Practices* (Ann Arbor: University of Michigan Press), pp. 265–89.

Sturgeon, M. C. 2004. *Sculpture: The Assemblage from the Theatre*, Corinth, 11.3 (Princeton: American School of Classical Studies at Athens).

Talloen, P. 2011. 'From Pagan to Christian: Religious Iconography in Material Culture from Sagalassos', in L. Lavan and M. Mulryan (eds), *The Archaeology of Late Antique 'Paganism'*, Late Antique Archaeology, 7 (Leiden: Brill), pp. 575–607.

——. 2019. 'The Rise of Christianity at Sagalassus', in S. Mitchell and P. Pilhofer (eds), *Early Christianity in Asia Minor and Cyprus: From the Margins to the Mainstream*, Ancient Judaism and Early Christianity, 109 (Leiden: Brill), pp. 164–201.

Tulunay, E. T. 2005. 'Soloi Pompeiopolis heykelleri (2000–2003)', *Araştırma sonuçları toplantısı*, 22.2: 23–30.

Van Dam, R. 2007. 'Bishops and Society', in A. Casiday and F. W. Norris (eds), *The Cambridge History of Christianity*, II: *Constantine to c. 600* (Cambridge: Cambridge University Press), pp. 343–66.

Visconti, C. L. 1885. 'Del larario e del mitreo scoperti nell'Equilino presso la chiesa di S. Martino ai Monti', *Bullettino della Commissione archaeologica comunale di Roma*, 8: 27–41.

Waelkens, M. and others. 1997. 'The 1994 and 1995 Excavation Seasons at Sagalassos', in M. Waelkens and J. Poblome (eds), *Sagalassos*, IV: *Report on the Survey and Excavation Campaigns of 1994 and 1995*, Acta archaeologica Lovaniensia. Monographiae, 9 (Leuven: Leuven University Press), pp. 103–216.

White, D. 2006. 'Foreign Schrecklichkeit and Homegrown Iconoclasm: Two Faces of Communal Violence at Cyrene', in E. Fabbricotti and O. Menozzi (eds), *Cirenaica: studi, scavi e scoperte*, I: *Nuovi dati da città e territoria* (Oxford: Archaeopress), pp. 191–204.

Zaccaria Ruggiu, A. (ed.). 2019a. *Le abitazioni dell'insula 104 a Hierapolis Di Frigia*, Hierapolis Di Frigia, 12 (Istanbul: Ege Yayınları).

——. 2019b. 'Casa dell'isrizione dipinta', in A. Zaccaria Ruggiu (ed.), *Le abitazioni dell'insula 104 a Hierapolis Di Frigia*, Hierapolis Di Frigia, 12 (Istanbul: Ege Yayınları), pp. 99–131.

11. The Dancing Deity: Diminishing the Goddess Libertas on the Palatine

Elisabeth Begemann

In an earlier paper, I proposed that Cicero, in his speech *De domo sua*, argued that because the cult of Libertas on the Palatine was a strictly personal cult of P. Clodius Pulcher, it did not concern the public at large and could safely be removed.[1] The cult statue of Libertas which Clodius had set up there could likewise be removed. I will here draw on that earlier research but explore an aspect I had not taken into account: domestic religion and the juxtaposition of Cicero's household deities and Clodius's 'intruder'. In portraying Clodius's Libertas as another deity which may be worshipped privately within the house, Cicero employs a rhetoric that both diminishes the deity on site in a *lararium* context and greatly enlarges her in the rhetoric of tyranny employed throughout the speech. I will also suggest a possible iconography of the deity in question, based upon the ritual with which it was supposedly dedicated and set up within the *porticus Clodii* in that place which was formerly Cicero's house.

The cult of Libertas on the Palatine was introduced by P. Clodius Pulcher as tribune of the people in 58 BC after he had, with the aid of the two consuls and — to Cicero's chagrin — the at least tacit support of the senate,[2] successfully ousted Cicero from Rome and Roman politics in protest against his handling of the Catalinarian affair as consul in 63 BC, especially regarding the execution of four of the supposed conspirators — Roman citizens — without a trial. In 58, Clodius was finally successful in introducing the necessary laws that drove Cicero into exile. Cicero's house on the Palatine, bought at great cost,[3] but with a keen eye to the semantics of visuality,[4] was seized and demolished.[5] Somewhat later, Clodius dedicated a part of what had been Cicero's house to the goddess Libertas in order to permanently remove the site from human ownership as a *res sacra*. Whether this was a prank or part of the initial consideration is disputed.[6]

Once Clodius had clashed with Pompey and lost his political support, Cicero's friends managed to get a law passed (57 BC) which enabled Cicero to be recalled to Rome. He was naturally eager to have the monument of Libertas removed and the site returned to him.[7]

---

[1] This paper was first presented at the Annual Spring Conference of the IGS 'Resonant Self–World Relations in Ancient and Modern Socio-Religious Practices', 'Measuring the World against the Body: Materialities and Meaning of Magnification and Miniaturization in Religious Communications in Antiquity and Modernity', at the Max-Weber-Kolleg of the University of Erfurt. I cordially thank the participants at the conference as well as the participants in the research colloquium at the Max-Weber-Kolleg for their invaluable input, especially Richard L. Gordon and Jörg Rüpke. Special thanks go to Anna-Katharina Rieger, with whom I discussed the paper at various stages from beginning to end.

[2] Tatum 1999, 156.

[3] Cic., *Fam.* v.6.2; *Att.* 1.16.10; 1.13.6; Gell., *NA* xii.12.

[4] Cic., *Dom.* 103. Cf. Allen 1944, 2; Wiseman 2012, 658; Cooper 2007, 5.

[5] Cf. Davies 2019 on architectural language and destruction.

[6] As a prank: see Berg 1997, 133. As part of the initial consideration: see Stroh 2004, 368. The wording of the senate's decision that the house could be returned to Cicero since Clodius, as the person who had dedicated it, had not been issued by the people to do so *by name* would implicate the latter reading. Cf. Cic., *Att.* iv.2.3.

[7] In speaking of *monumentum*, I in fact follow Cicero's terminology in *De domo sua* — at no point does he admit that there had been a *templum*, *delubrum*, or *aedes Libertatis* (where *aedes* is used, it refers only to Cicero's house); likewise, the statue of Libertas is always only a statue. I am aware that this term is thus, necessarily, loaded. Cf. in this context also Duday and Van Andringa 2017 and Van Andringa 2018, who stress that the *monumentum* placed upon the grave was 'primarily an expression of the social memory of the individual' (Duday and Van Andringa 2017, 73). Thus, Cicero's juxtaposition between *monumentum* and *sepulcrum* lies in the shrine not being only a marker (*monumentum*) of a grave, but the very grave (*sepulcrum*) — on which is written 'the name of my enemy' (Cic., *Dom*. 100). Richard L. Gordon suggests (in personal conversation) that the statue may indeed have already come with another (Greek) inscription: *Eleutheria* — thus marking the grave of a freedwoman who took pride in dying as a free person. Clodius's transgression would thus be more that he elevated an unfree human being, i.e. a woman of the lowest social status, to prominence in the heart of Rome, rather than that the statue itself was taken from a graveside. The transposition of the statue with an inscription from Boeotia

The Roman culture was a highly visual one, something Cicero had learned early on and which had been reinforced in his mind time and again.[8] Between his and Clodius's house (the two were neighbours) lay the *porticus Catuli*, another historically charged site of the Roman visual memorial culture. It had been built from the spoils of the Cimbrian campaign on the ruins of the house of M. Fulvius Flaccus (consul in 125 BC) following electoral riots, while Flaccus had been declared an enemy of the state because he had acted, as his enemies alleged, with C. Gracchus 'contra salutem rei publicae'.[9] Clodius had in turn torn down the *porticus Catuli* as well as (parts of) Cicero's house and built in its stead a larger *porticus*, the *porticus Clodii*, in which the image of Libertas was on display.[10] Of course Cicero could not let this stand: the site was far too prominent (overlooking the forum and across from the Capitol) and connected with the earliest history of Rome,[11] a history into which Cicero yearned to inscribe himself. It was now connected to the site of an earlier enemy of the state and branded as such,[12] and the choice of deity itself was a further slap in the face.[13] After the suppression of the Catalinarian uprising,[14] Cicero had marketed himself as the *custos urbis* — and now *he* was to be branded as the tyrant?[15]

He rose to the challenge with his speech *De domo sua*, delivered to the assembled *pontifices* of Rome on 29 September 57 BC.[16] The *pontifices* assembled were willing to side with Cicero. The meeting had been carefully prepared, and negotiations in both the senate and the pontifical college had created a favourable atmosphere, something that is reflected by the fact that Cicero was to have the last word after his opponent Clodius had spoken.[17] The speech was 'throughout directed to the emotions' of the audience,[18] chiefly fear, a sense of piety, and outrage. As Rüpke has demonstrated, what was at stake was the inviolability of private property: 'dedications can only take place when they do not disadvantage any single person.'[19] This was clearly the case in the matter of Cicero's house, and, I would like to add, he was not the only one who was put to a disadvantage: his *lares* were also driven out.

Throughout the *De domo sua*, Cicero paints the threat that Clodius poses in the direst terms. He is a danger to the community of all good people (48), he is the true tyrant as he stands against everyone else (26), where he is, violence follows (passim), he does not have the support of the free people, only of slaves and mercenaries (e.g. 6, 53, 89, 110), he is motivated by personal hatred (61). Against this is set the orderliness that the involvement of Cicero in Roman politics brings, most clearly formulated in *Dom.* 17: when Cicero was driven out of Rome, chaos followed; when he returned, peace, concord, and plenty also returned. The roles are clearly assigned.

---

to Rome and its elevation to a deity would indeed fit with the few traces we have of a possible cult of *libertas* before Clodius installed his shrine on the Palatine (cf. Tatum 1999, 165), while the Greek inscription might serve to underline the *humanitas* of the dedicant and his *paideia* as a member of the Roman elite.

[8] Vasaly 1993.

[9] Cic., *Dom.* 102.

[10] Cicero is so vague about what exactly has been dedicated on the Palatine that we do not know what kind of monument has been put up there.

[11] Cf. Tagliamonte 1999. The Emperor Augustus saw the advantages also and chose to build his house here, see Zanker 2009.

[12] Cf. Roller 2010.

[13] On the discourse of kingship on late Republican Rome, see Baraz 2018.

[14] Cf. Gruen 1974.

[15] *Custos urbis*, cf. Cic., *Dom.* 7 and 102. This is also to be read against the background that there was a cult of Jupiter Libertas established in Rome in 238 BC (Liv. XXIV.16.19; Fest. 121). This, however, was initially a cult that celebrated, not the freedom of the *res publica*, but the personal freedom of former slaves. It is surely no coincidence that this is exactly what Cicero keeps stressing in his oration, implying that by establishing the cult of Clodian Libertas, Clodius reduced the rest of the populace of Rome to the status of slaves, while his supporters are made up entirely of slaves and former slaves with not an honourable soul between them (cf. Tatum 1999, 165). The case could furthermore be made that Cicero once again

---

turns Clodius's argument on its head, on top of all the scorn he pours on Clodius in *Dom.* 92. While he does not so much deny Clodius's claim that he had likened himself to Jupiter as gleefully note Clodius's purported lack of education in referring to Minerva as Jupiter's sister, in portraying Clodius as *custos libertatis*, Cicero feminizes Clodius once more. While the traditional cult of *libertas* in Rome was one of a male deity, Clodius himself, ever depraved, prefers to submit to a woman, the female *libertas*; cf. Arena 2020, 74.

[16] With the exception of both Caesar and L. Pinarius Natta, against both of whom Cicero was expected to launch attacks: Caesar as the one who had facilitated the transfer of Clodius into the *plebs*, thus making it possible for him to hold the office of *tribunus plebis*, an office which had given him great power in the city of Rome (cf. Tan 2013); and Natta, who had aided Clodius in performing the dedication on the Palatine (cf. Rüpke 2019, 300).

[17] Cf. Stroh 2004, 321. On establishing consensus in the Roman senate, a point which is certainly also applicable to the college of pontiffs, see Timmer 2019.

[18] Stroh 2004, 339.

[19] Rüpke 2019, 309.

The fear of arson and fire is also repeatedly raised (12, 25, 62, 89), a justifiable fear in the densely settled Rome, in which fires broke out and destroyed parts of the infrastructure on a regular basis. Against this, Cicero sets a much calmer fire, one that is regulated, necessary, and sanctified by religious scruple: the fire at the hearth.[20] The combination *arae, foci, di penates* occurs four times in the *De domo sua* in this order (1, 106, 108, 143), opening and closing the speech and prominently in that part of the speech which actually deals with Cicero's house.[21] At the hearth, the *lares familiares* were worshipped. And it seems to me telling that Cicero throughout the speech continuously evokes household gods, but mentions the *lares* by name only once: in the very instance in which they were driven out of their home by Clodius's supposed Libertas. That this was not, in fact, *libertas* is made clear in the opening of the oration, in which Cicero calls upon the *pontifices* to protect *dignitas, salus, libertas, arae, foci, di penates, bona, fortunae, domicilia* — if *libertas* has moved in at the Palatine, how was *libertas* then to be entrusted to and protected by the pontifical college?

But who then was the deity that was installed in what was formerly Cicero's house on the Palatine? Cicero is happy to supply the answer:

> At unde est ista inventa Libertas? quaesivi enim diligenter. Tanagraea quaedam meretrix fuisse dicitur. Eius non longe a Tanagra simulacrum e marmore in sepulcro positum fuit. Hoc quidam homo nobilis, non alienus ab hoc religioso Libertatis sacerdote, ad ornatum aedilitatis suae deportavit; etenim cogitarat omnis superiores muneris splendore superare.

> (But from whence was that Liberty brought? For I sought for her diligently. She is said to have been a prostitute at Tanagra. At no great distance from Tanagra a marble image of her was placed on her tomb. A certain man of noble birth, not altogether unconnected with this holy priest of Liberty, carried off this statue to decorate his aedileship. He had in truth cherished the idea of surpassing all his predecessors in the splendour of his appointments.)[22]

We need not take Cicero's word at face value, he loves to exaggerate and contort — anything to win his case.[23] The passage is interesting, however, for the reasons given as to why this 'Libertas' is so unfitting for the *populus Romanus* and could not possibly be a deity: she is a prostitute (*meretrix*), and thus socially unacceptable; a foreigner (*a Tanagra*); from a grave (*in sepulcro*), and thus religiously unacceptable, tainted by death and obtained in violation of the inviolability of graves; and stolen goods. At first glance, the last might not carry great weight. Romans were used to taking whatever they pleased from the provinces to adorn their own houses — as Cicero himself had detailed in the Verrine orations.[24] Yet the manner in which Appius Claudius Pulcher, brother of Clodius, collected Greek artwork no longer displays taste or connoisseurship, but plain greed, and it thus constitutes a *topos* of invective: *avaritia*.[25] In this manner, the fact that the statue was stolen, too, makes her unacceptable to the audience.

Lennon has already outlined how Cicero employs the notion of impurity to taint his political opponent, beginning with the Bona Dea scandal and happily making use of any sexual allusion he can think of in connection with Clodius. That he terms 'the Clodian' deity now a *meretrix* follows logically: Who else would be willingly found in Clodius's company?[26] She is a fitting consort for a man who is 'woman among men, man among women' (*Dom.* 139), who has seduced his own sister (*Dom.* 92), and who walks the forum as 'everyone's whore' (*Dom.* 49).[27] I have earlier argued that in calling the statue *tua pulchra libertas*, Cicero connects the deity via the cognomen of the family, Pulcher, directly with Clodius himself.[28] I had missed, however, another nuance, which is that male prostitutes were also referred to as *pulchri* — another pun, certainly not unintended by Cicero, which plants an image into the minds of the audience that fosters their willingness to side with the plaintiff.[29]

---

20 Flower 2017, 33; see also Cic., *Dom.* 109.

21 See Kenty 2018 on the structure of the speech, which has confused many modern readers and left them feeling aggravated at Cicero's assertion that this was one of his best speeches in the political context of the time (*Att.* IV.2.2).

22 Cic., *Dom.* 111 (trans. Yonge 1891).

23 Cf. Gildenhard 2011.

24 Cf. Kaufmann-Heinimann 2007.

25 See Craig 2004.

26 See also Varhelyi 2017, 89 on the equation of statue, person, and divinity.

27 In Cic., *Leg.* II.42, Cicero speaks of a *templum licentiae* put up by Clodius on the Palatine. The matter was settled by then, and he needed no longer to fear calling a spade a spade, i.e. a shrine a *templum*.

28 Begemann 2015.

29 Cf. Leigh 2004, who uses the example of the *Pro Caelio* to show beautifully how Cicero uses humour to win his case.

A further nuance was also certainly intended: prostitutes in Rome were likely to be slaves.[30] This also would be most appropriate, since throughout the speech the only ones who are to be found in Clodius's company are slaves. They form his troops, the fill up his *contiones*, they stand in for the Roman people when votes are to be taken. Cicero binds Clodius and slaves tightly together; the *collegia* also are, in Cicero's interpretation, entirely made of up them, though it is highly doubtful that their masters would have granted them this much freedom.[31] And with these, he oppresses the *libera res publica*: though none of the *boni* are on his side, Clodius rules with his slave troops and through sheer terror. In reading Seneca, Dolansky argues that because most of those who could afford it were in fact slave holders, there would have been a permanent latent fear of living among slaves and entrusting them with the safety of their families, a fear that was to be alleviated by festivals like the Saturnalia, in which the ties of bondage would be loosened for a while.[32] In continuously painting the picture of slaves flooding the forum, slaves filling the *contiones*, and slaves committing acts of violence within Rome, Cicero fosters a fear of slave risings, of those aliens who lived among the Romans but had none of their freedoms and rights, though they did most of their work — an uneasy situation, which most of the upper class Romans must have been aware of. In setting up a slave *meretrix* as deity on the Palatine, i.e. in the most prominent part of the city, Clodius creates a nice little oxymoron: the slave as queen. He installs (in Cicero's interpretation) a visual reminder to the Romans of what they now are: slaves to the tyrant Clodius, who rules by the force of the unfree.

I will pass over (mostly) the statue's supposed provenance as coming from a grave. In my eyes, the only intention in claiming it to have been a grave marker is, on the one hand, to emphasize its unsuitability as the image of a true deity and on the other, to underline the avarice of Appius Claudius, who would not even let the dead rest in peace but robs them of what little they have left, just as P. Clodius robs Cicero of what he has.[33] The reference also underlines Clodius's utter disregard for any sense of piety and makes it seem even more ridiculous that he presents himself to the *pontifices* as a devout Roman heedful of religious sentiment.[34] Cicero does not dwell much on this point, though he does use the opportunity to make sure his listeners understand that in transferring *this* statue, Clodius has also transferred the funereal context to the Palatine: not a *monumentum*, but a *sepulcrum* in the heart of the city — not only a grave marker, but a true grave where the true liberty of the people is buried.[35]

What I find much more interesting is Cicero's passing mention of the city from which this statue was stolen: Tanagra in Boeotia. In the nineteenth century, this city became famous for the little figurines that were unearthed there and soon flooded the antiquities markets, both ancient artefacts and cunningly made modern forgeries.[36] They depict mostly women and children in different poses, standing or sitting, playing, and dancing. Their posture and attire belong to the festival (thus religious) context, conveying a festive mood, both playful and elegant, and quite clearly set apart from everyday life. Hats, fans, wreaths, ribbons, fruits, and mirrors in their hands show a casual attitude that makes this group of artefacts stand out. The type was likely not developed in Tanagra but adopted from someplace else, presumably Athens rather than Thebes.[37] The figurines were made of clay, and the use of moulds allowed for great variation. While the body was put together from two moulds (front and back), the head and arms could be added separately, set onto the body at different angles or with a slightly different inclination, or else holding different objects. This wide variety of form was quite popular and soon developed into types.[38] The statuettes came mostly from domestic contexts but were also abundantly found in graves. They were likely deposited there (though somewhat carelessly, it seems)[39] after the death of young women and children as depictions of what might have been: the beautiful young women, the young bride, the happily playing child — now lost to the living, a symbol of a broken promise of happiness.

Of course Cicero and his contemporaries did not know these statuettes as 'Tangara figurines', the name under which they are now known.[40] And while they were in vogue in mainland Greece and south Italy in the

---

[30] Weiler 2018; Pesendorf 2018.

[31] Ausbüttel 1982, 41. On *collegia* as socializing opportunities, see Rüpke 2002.

[32] See Dolansky 2011, 497. See also the very enlightening autobiography of the former slave and abolitionist Frederick Douglass (1855, 177) on this point.

[33] Cf. Cic., *Dom.* 62–63.

[34] Cf. Cic., *Dom.* 104, 127.

[35] Cic., *Dom.* 100. See above, n. 7.

[36] On detecting forgeries and colouring: Mau 1993.

[37] Zimmer 1994a, 21.

[38] Bell 1993.

[39] Higgins 1987, 56.

[40] Cf. Zimmer 1994b.

fourth and third centuries BC, the name 'Tanagra' would not have evoked the same image to Cicero's audience as it does to us.[41] But upper-class Romans were keenly aware of matters of Greek art,[42] and the image is tempting: the young women and girls for which Tanagra became so famous later on were often depicted as dancing.[43] They were studies in the way a dress, and particularly its folds, wrap themselves around a body in motion (Fig. 11.1).

In Rome, dance was highly ambiguous.[44] On the one hand, dancers and their skills were part of the regular entertainment at *convivia* (i.e. the dance of slaves), while at the same time, the fact that a member of the *nobilitas* danced at a *convivium* was a matter for invective:

> Quis te illis diebus sobrium, quis agentem aliquid quod esset libero dignum, quis denique in publico vidit? cum conlegae tui domus cantu et cymbalis personaret, cumque ipse nudus in convivio saltaret; in quo cum illum saltatorium versaret orbem, ne tum quidem fortunae rotam pertimescebat.
>
> (Who in those days ever saw you sober, who ever saw you doing anything which was worthy of a free man; who in short, ever saw you in public at all? While the house of your colleague was resounding with song and cymbals, and while he himself was dancing naked at banquet; in which even then when he was going round in the circle of the dance, he seemed to have no fear of any revolution of fortune.)[45]

It is indeed hard in this instance to decide whether the fact that Gabinius was naked (and drunk) was supposed to rile Cicero's audience, or that he danced — or both.

On the other hand, dance was part of ritual, as Fless and Moede outline.[46] The *tripudium* was part of the ritual of both the Salian priesthood and that of the Arval brethren.[47] It was a step sequence which could become quite vigorous and was employed by a number of notables: M. Furius Camillus, L. Vitellius — and P. Clodius Pulcher.[48]

---

[41] I must assume that it does not. It has, in any case, never been picked up in research on *De domo sua*.

[42] Cf. Hallett 2023.

[43] They were well known in the Hellenistic world, cf. Piccioni 2018.

[44] Naerebout 2009, 149; Erker 2018, 318.

[45] Cic., *Pis.* 22 (trans. Yonge 1891); see also *Dom.* 60.

[46] Fless and Moede 2007.

[47] Regarding the ritual of the Arval brethren, see Wissowa 1917; Scheid 1990.

[48] Cf. Patzelt 2018, 176.

Figure 11.1. Terracotta statuette of a girl dancing, *c.* 299–200 BC, 24.1 × 10.2 × 8.3 cm. Metropolitan Museum of Art, New York, inv. no. 12.232.13. AKG7340994. © AKG.

Figure 11.2. Dancing *lar*. Bronze, Roman, third century AD. H: 30.8 (23) cm. The J. Paul Getty Museum, Villa Collection, Malibu, California, inv. no. 96.AB.200. Gift of Barbara and Lawrence Fleischman. © The J. Paul Getty Museum.

In a recent article, Maik Patzelt argues that Clodius employed just such a *tripudium* when he dedicated the *monumentum* of his Libertas in the *porticus Clodii*. Cicero was of course not an eyewitness to the dedication; he had left the city and was retrospectively exiled. Others were eyewitnesses, perhaps even members of Cicero's audience during the oration, though Cicero would deny it. In fact, he does not seem too certain about the visibility of the scene. In *Dom.* 139, he claims the ritual to dedicate his house had taken place *furtim*; in *Dom.* 140, he states that everyone talked about it — so presumably, people had seen. In either case, though he himself had not been witness to the scene, he gives an entertaining account of the dedication that took place. While Natta, himself newly come to the honour of a priesthood, acted uncertainly and only under the pressure of his mother, sister, and (effeminate) brother-in-law,[49] Clodius himself rushed through the process, stumbling over the very words, ignoring *omina*, and doing everything differently than it had been done before.[50] While this is usually read as ritual transgression, which should make the dedication void, Patzelt argues that Clodius did not fail but responded to audience expectations that demanded adaption to 'the changing tastes of the audience',[51] while Scipio Africanus himself provides the precedent for performing a *tripudium*, i.e. dancing, outside the usual ritual context.[52]

We know of another deity that is depicted dancing, one which Cicero sets in opposition to the supposed deity that moved into his house after he had been robbed of it: the *lar* (Fig. 11.2).[53] These deities are to be understood as the deities most intimately connected to the home:

> These gods are so closely related to the very concept of 'home' that they are often evoked either to conjure up a sense of security and belonging or to describe its opposite, notably loss of the home or exile from one's native place.[54]

---

[49] Patzelt 2019, 276.

[50] Cf. Lisdorf 2005, 453.

[51] Patzelt 2018, 180.

[52] Patzelt 2018, 178.

[53] The seminal work on the *lares* and their cult is Flower 2017. It must be noted that *lares* in the plural seems to be a later development and the standard in the Republic is a single *lar*. Multiple *lares*, however, are mentioned by Plautus. Flower (2017, 36) holds that we cannot, in this case, assume a linear development.

[54] Flower 2017, 63. See also Bodel 2008, 264: '*Lares* were more

In Cicero's speech, they are only mentioned once: when Libertas takes up residence in what used to be their home: 'Ista tua pulchra Liberias deos penatis et familiaris meos lares expulit, ut se ipsa tamquam in captivis sedibus conlocaret?' (Did that beautiful Liberty of yours turn out my household gods and the eternal divinities of my hearth (*lares*), in order to be established there herself by you, as if in a conquered country?)[55] In all other instances, Cicero does not name his *lares* outright; he instead refers to the place where they are worshipped, the hearth, as I have already indicated above.[56] In placing the hearth rhetorically between the altar and the *di penates*, however, the meaning of the phrase is clear. Cicero does not speak of a mundane place within the house where his meals are prepared or where one may sit cosily by the fire after a long day's work, he speaks of the central cult place of his *familia*. Foss states, 'fire equaled life';[57] thus the loss of fire at the hearth, e.g. in exile, resulted quite literally in social death. By the *Lex Clodia de exilio Ciceronis*, Cicero had been denied that fire: he was no longer part of the community but was considered dead to them. But he was quite alive, and he reclaimed the place where his *lares* had once been.

Cicero might not mention his *lares* before they were driven out by Libertas, but he generally refers to them obliquely throughout the speech. By holding back actual mention of them until late in the speech, he builds up expectation in his audience, an expectation that is fulfilled in a highly emotional passage in which the house itself is presented as the most religious site of all:

> Quid est sanctius, quid omni religione munitius quam domus unius cuiusque civium? Hic arae sunt, hic foci, hic di penates, hic sacra, religiones, caerimoniae continentur; hoc perfugium est ita sanctum omnibus ut inde abripi neminem fas sit.

> (What is there more holy, what is there more carefully fenced round with every description of religious respect, than the house of every individual citizen? Here are his altars, here are his hearths, here are his household gods: here are all his sacred rites, all his religious ceremonies are preserved. There is the sanctuary of every one, so holy a spot that it is against divine law to drag any one from it.)[58]

All of that, Cicero argues, will come to naught if Clodius is given his way and his Libertas not removed. But in juxtaposing this Libertas with his *lares*, Cicero introduces another motif. *Lares*, says Flower, are deities of place. Libertas had driven out Cicero's *lares* and took up residence in the space herself, thus becoming, *de facto*, a new *lar* in place of the old one.

Another matter must be taken into account: Clodius destroyed (and partly burned or watched burn) Cicero's house on the Palatine, also taking down the *porticus Catuli*, to rebuild them on a grander scale.[59] Supposedly, this was to provide the Roman people with an open walkway. In fact, says Cicero, Clodius merely wanted to live large: 'habitare laxe et magnifice voluit duasque et magnas et nobilis domos coniungere' (he wished to dwell splendidly and magnificently, and to unite two large and noble houses).[60] According to Cicero, he did this by incorporating the house of Seius, the house of Cicero, and the *porticus Catuli* into his own house, the *domus Clodiae*. If the statue of Libertas was then put up not in a public space, but in what was to be seen as the entrance hall to Clodius's grand mansion, she is not only irrelevant to the community at large. She becomes an item of personal devotion, the deity that keeps the *domus Clodiae* in place — she becomes a deity of place, Clodius's *lar*.[61]

If Cicero knew the kind of terracotta figurines that are today known as Tanagra figurines, and if his mentioning the name of the city from where the statue of Libertas came evoked for the Romans the same mental image it does for us and was not merely meant as a marker of the foreign,[62] on the one hand, and the un-

---

closely tied to the concept of "home" than to "house."'

55 Cic., *Dom.* 109 (trans. Yonge 1891).

56 That *lares* and *di penates* are more or less to be understood as the same is argued by Rüpke 2016, 258–62: the former as impersonal and deities of place (the *domus*, more family and edifice), and the latter as a collective of deities worshipped within the family.

57 Foss 1997, 198.

58 Cic., *Dom.* 109 (trans. Yonge 1891).

59 Cicero (*Dom.* 115) also alleges that Clodius killed his neighbour Q. Seius in order to get at his house and grounds.

60 Cic., *Dom.* 115. Cf. Tatum 1999, 161: 'Clodius's *domus* was destined to become perhaps the largest property on the Palatine. This was by design, since it cannot be doubted that Clodius recognized the status to be gotten from acquisitions developed on a grand scale, especially in so elite and restricted a neighborhood.'

61 It is a standard of invective to ascribe deviant sexual behaviour to the opponent. Thus, a prostitute as the item of personal devotion would, in the context of invective, not seem out of place at all but quite fitting.

62 One could argue with *Leg.* II.19 that Cicero would count Libertas among the foreign gods which had not been passed on by the fathers. It is another religious transgression, of which the life of Clodius seems to be full — not only the Bona Dea scandal, but also

urbane, on the other,⁶³ I would propose the following reading: Cicero meant to evoke the image of a dancing *meretrix* (not unusual), dedicated as a personal deity by a dancing magistrate, to become a dancing deity: a *lar*.

That is a big *if*, of course: we do not know what kind of statue Clodius dedicated on the Palatine, how tall it was, what it looked like, and which movements it depicted, if any. We do not even know about the layout of the houses on the Palatine in the Late Republic. Everything was later built over, and all traces are now lost. Cicero is not precise enough for us to reconstruct the situation in his day, so any speculation must remain that: speculation. Moreover, he is not explicit in the imagery he evokes — his argumentation is subtle. Then again, his household deities, his *lares* and *di penates*, are relevant for the college of priests to consider, and they pop up throughout the speech again and again in different allusions.

But if Cicero meant to evoke a certain kind of statue or statuette by locating her origin in Boeotia, this reading is reinforced. Clodius's Libertas would conform to the standard depiction of Roman *lares*, dancing. She would not even be all that unusual in the context of domestic devotion. Cicero himself had a small statuette of Minerva which he carried to the Capitol before his exile and dedicated there as *custos urbis*.⁶⁴ In his house, she would have been part of his *lararium*, the family shrine in which a personal — and inherited — selection of deities was venerated in addition to the *lares*.⁶⁵ She would have been part of a cult that was worshipped in the more public part of the house rather than the hearth at which the *lares* were worshipped — a cult which was, within the larger *domus*, the responsibility of the unfree part of the *familia*, the servants or slaves.⁶⁶

We do hit a certain snag. Cicero mentions the material from which the statue was fashioned: 'eius non longe a Tanagra simulacrum **e marmore** in sepulcro positum fuit' (At no great distance from Tanagra a marble image of her was placed on her tomb).⁶⁷ Neither the Tanagra figurines nor the household *lares* were, as far as can be determined, commonly fashioned from this material. In fact, *lares* were often not portable figurines, but painted on the walls and niches of their worship.⁶⁸ However, that was the task of Cicero's oratory: to reshape reality. He cannot deny that there was a cult of Libertas on the Palatine, as much as he would like to restrict that cult to one person only;⁶⁹ he cannot deny that a dedication had taken place and that it was valid — he did not even really claim that the dedication was invalid due to ritual mistakes, though he implies so strongly. He would also have to accept that people knew exactly what that statue on the Palatine looked like and what it was fashioned of — after all, the *monumentum* of Libertas was put up in a public space, in a *porticus* which was accessible to any passer-by.

He could diminish her rhetorically, however. By setting her against his *lares*, he shrinks her in size. She becomes no more than another statuette in a (personal) *lararium* that could be moved. In fact, she had been moved before: Appius Claudius had brought her from Greece to Rome, and when he no longer had any use for her, he gave her to his brother to adorn his own house with. If she is portable and can so easily be passed from one brother to the next, she cannot be hard to transport. And if she is a mere item in a personal *lararium*, she can be moved again, which is what Cicero requests.

That she is no more than an item in a personal shrine he, in fact, infers in *Dom.* 132:

> Si quid deliberares, si quid tibi aut piandum aut instituendum fuisset religione domestica, tamen instituto maiorum vetere rem ad pontificem detulisses
>
> (If you deliberated at all, if you had anything you wished to expiate, or any domestic sacrifice which you desired to institute, still according to the ancient practice of other men you should have referred the matter to the priests.)

If this is so, there is no ritual transgression. Clodius had wanted to dedicate something in the context of personal

---

the fact that he left the *gens Claudia* and its deities behind, but did not adopt, as he should have upon his own adoption, the family gods of the *gens Fonteia* (*Dom.* 35).

63 Tanagra in the first century BC was less relevant than it had been, but was, with Thespiae, one of two cities in Boeotia that were more than 'ruins and a name' (τῶν δ' ἄλλων ἐρείπια καὶ ὀνόματα λέλειπται, Str. ιx.2.25).

64 Cic., *Leg.* ιι.42.

65 Bodel 2008, 250, referring to Cic., *Leg.* ιι.19.

66 Maybe it was for this reason also more suitable for Cicero to name the *di penates*, as these would have been worshipped by himself, rather than the *lares*, who would have been worshipped by his slaves to a greater extent than he did.

67 Cic., *Dom.* 111 (trans. Yonge 1891). Higgins 1987, 25, states that the prosperity of the city of Tanagra in the fourth century BC was reflected in the sculpted gravestones and figurines.

68 Flower 2017, 2. Hallett 2023 argues that in substituting portable bronzes for the traditional painted images, the Roman upper class followed a trend to set themselves apart and prove their knowledge of fine arts and artefacts.

69 Begemann 2015.

cult and had asked *a pontifex* to be present and aid him.⁷⁰ Moreover, he had not asked *any* priest to aid him, but a member of his family, his brother-in-law Natta. The deduction that the *pontifices* are actually dealing with a matter of personal cult could not have been stronger in this instance. But then again, because Clodius is the tyrant of Rome, what is strictly personal may have become relevant for the entire populace upon the imminent return of his political enemy.

In this context, it is also relevant to have the audience imagine that Clodius danced as part of the dedication — although, in Cicero's words, he could not even do that right, but rather stumbles through it. I have mentioned above that the *tripudium* was relevant in two cult contexts, that of the Salii and that of the Arval brethren. And while Patzelt would rather connect the Clodian *tripudium* with the Salii, I lean towards the Arvals. In their ritual, they worshipped the Dea Dia, but in their prayer, they called on Mars, the Semones — and the *lares*.⁷¹ Moreover, part of their ritual involved the sacrifice to the *Mater Larum*, the mother of the *lares* in their *lucus* outside Rome,⁷² which in one tradition is equated with Acca Larentia, a former prostitute (fittingly) who brought up the twins Romulus and Remus.⁷³ It is true that this is a later restoration and probably an invention by Caesar Octavian, who would become Augustus. But for the introduction of this cult as part of, as Scheid sees it, his imaginative propaganda battle against M. Antonius,⁷⁴ Augustus also must have had a source, something on which to base his knowledge of this 'old' cult or old priesthood.⁷⁵ A very likely candidate is M. Terentius Varro, who extensively collected arcane knowledge about the Latin language as well as *rerum humanarum et divinarum*.⁷⁶ Indeed, there is a mention of the priesthood in the *De lingua Latina*: 'fratres Arvales dicti qui sacra publica faciunt propterea ut fruges ferant arva: a ferendo et arvis Fratres Arvales dicti' (5.85). At this point, it is important to recall that Cicero addressed himself to the collective of *pontifices* in Rome, members of the Roman elite who were involved in their own systematization and rationalization.⁷⁷ Cicero's audience, then, would not have been entirely ignorant of such a thing as the *fratres Arvales*, even if only as an ancient and abandoned, and thus entirely academic, brotherhood.⁷⁸ It was not necessary that the rituals were still practised; Cicero only needed his audience to be aware of their practices, to paint a certain image in the minds of his listeners that would influence their decision to his advantage. He thus weaves another thread into the image of his oratory. Not only is it fitting that the dedicator should dance if the deity to which he dedicates the site dances; in copying the dance step employed by the Arval brethren, the implication is that he calls upon the same deities they do — the *lares*.

In thus connecting a rather typical type of statue known to be dancing with a dance step employed (faultily) in the dedication and with the common and well-known iconography of dancing *lares*, which belonged, moreover, to the domestic and not to the public sphere, Cicero evokes an image in the minds of his audience to support his argumentation that the actual ritual transgression could not be blamed on him, but was to be blamed on Clodius. Not only was Clodius *impurus* and had proven himself to be demonstrably so throughout his career, but Cicero himself had always acted to protect the gods and their possessions, just as the gods — the *lares* and *di penates* evoked in his oration — are meant to protect the houses of the Romans. To be clear, the entire exercise of appealing to the pontifical college shows that Cicero did not ask for ritual transgression in having the shrine removed and did not aim to overthrow traditional Roman custom; he instead indicated the way in which the *pontifices* could concur that no ritual transgression could take place because the shrine's establishment did not bind the Roman people. Thus, no transgression would take place by having it removed — *lares*, after all, were movable deities.

Rhetorically, Libertas thus becomes a mere personal deity, just as Cicero's Minerva was to him. It did not matter that he had not seen her. It would not matter if he described her faultily because he had not seen her. This might even have been believable to the audience,

---

⁷⁰ Of course, Cicero's point is also that if this had been more than a personal dedication, the entire college should have been present; cf. Nisbet 1979, 180.

⁷¹ Cf. Flower 2017, 23. The cult of the Arval brethren was an Augustan restoration of which we do not really know much, see Scheid 2019.

⁷² Cf. Scheid 1990, 578–98.

⁷³ Liv. 1.4.7 with Flower 2017, 18–22; Graf 2006.

⁷⁴ Scheid 2019, 56.

⁷⁵ Cf. Rüpke 2014, 260.

⁷⁶ Scheid 2019 bears me out in this point, as he follows Georg Wissowa in assuming 'Gelehrte im Pontifikalarchiv' to have found mention of this deity from the circle of Ceres. Wissowa himself based his own presentation of Roman religion on Varro's *Antiquitates*, cf. Rüpke 2003, 34; Momigliano 1984.

⁷⁷ Cf. Rüpke 2012, 144–51.

⁷⁸ See also Cic., *Dom.* 33 and Rüpke 2009, 75.

for what cause would Cicero have to visit the site of his shame, the shrine to Libertas on the Palatine where once his house had been?[79] The *pontifices* might assume that he had avoided the place since his return, given also how emotionally he now spoke of the matter. Thus, by replacing the marble statue of Libertas set up in a shrine on public grounds with a statuette of a dancing *meretrix* in a personal *lararium*-like context within the *domus* (not *porticus*) *Clodiae* in the minds of his audience, Cicero diminishes the deity. She becomes much smaller than she was in reality, both religiously and in terms of her physical being.

At the same time, Libertas remains overwhelmingly large if the *pontifices* do not follow Cicero in his appeal to their religious and proprietary conscience. Because she is the personal deity of the tyrant of Rome, set up in the most prominent part of the city, she is a matter of public concern as a mockery of that which the Roman people no longer have: their freedom. As long as Clodius and Libertas rule over them with their armies of slaves, the oppression of the dancing girl would be felt in every corner of the city and in every aspect of life. She looms much larger than the simple statue in its shrine on the hill would let one suppose.

None of this can, of course, be proven. But is there need? As Craig demonstrates, in the context of invective, proof was not what the Romans were after in their courts. You were right if the jurors bought the arguments you presented. The matter of Cicero's house was, in the end, decided on legal grounds, but who can say that the rich imagery which he wove into his passionate speech that sang the praises of the sanctity of the Roman house did not to some degree persuade the *pontifices* that he also had just cause on the emotional and religious levels?

---

[79] Cic., *Dom.* 100.

Works Cited

Allen, W. Jr. 1944. 'Cicero's House and Libertas', *Transactions and Proceedings of the American Philological Association*, 75: 1–9.
Arena, V. 2020. 'The God Liber and Republican Notions of *Libertas* in the Late Roman Republic', in C. Balmaceda (ed.), *'Libertas' and 'res publica' in the Roman Republic* (Leiden: Brill), pp. 55–83.
Ausbüttel, F. M. 1982. *Untersuchungen zu den Vereinen im Westen des Römischen Reiches* (Kallmünz: Lassleben).
Baraz, Y. 2018. 'Discourse of Kingship in Late Republican Invective', in N. Panou and H. Schade (eds), *Evil Lords: Theories and Representations of Tyranny from Antiquity to the Renaissance* (Oxford: Oxford University Press), pp. 43–60.
Begemann, E. 2015. '*Ista tua pulchra libertas*: The Construction of a Private Cult of Liberty on the Palatine', in C. Ando and J. Rüpke (eds), *Public and Private in Ancient Mediterranean Law and Religion* (Berlin: De Gruyter), pp. 75–89.
Bell, M. 1993. 'Tanagras and the Idea of Type', *Harvard University Art Museums Bulletin*, 1: 39–53.
Berg, B. 1997. 'Cicero's Palatine Home and Clodius' Shrine of Liberty', *Latomus*, 8: 122–43.
Bodel, J. 2008. 'Cicero's Minerva, *Penates*, and the Mother of the *Lares*: An Outline of Roman Domestic Religion', in J. Bodel and S. M. Olyan (eds), *Household and Family Religion in Antiquity* (Malden: Blackwell), pp. 248–75.
Connolly, J. 2001. 'Mastering Corruption: Constructions of Identity in Roman Oratory', in S. R. Joshel and S. Murnaghan (eds), *Women and Slaves in Greco-Roman Culture* (London: Routledge), pp. 130–51.
Cooper, K. 2007. 'Closely Watched Households: Visibility, Exposure and Private Power in the Roman Domus', *Past & Present*, 197: 3–33.
Craig, C. 2004. 'Audience Expectations, Invective, and Proof', in J. Powell and J. Paterson (eds), *Cicero, the Advocate* (Oxford: Oxford University Press), pp. 187–214.
Davies, P. J. E. 2019. 'Vandalism and Resistance in Republican Rome', *Journal of the Society of Architectural Historians*, 78: 6–24.
Dolansky, F. 2011. 'Celebrating the Saturnalia: Religious Ritual and Roman Domestic Life', in B. Rawson (ed.), *A Companion to Families in the Greek and Roman Worlds* (Malden: Wiley-Blackwell), pp. 488–503.
Douglass, F. 1855. *My Bondage and my Freedom*, repr. 2019 (Oxford: Oxford University Press).
Duday, H. and W. Van Andringa. 2017. 'Archaeology of Memory: About the Forms and the Time of Memory in a Necropolis of Pompeii', in C. Moser and J. W. Knust (eds), *Ritual Matters: Material Remains and Ancient Religion*, Memoirs of the American Academy in Rome Supplementary Volume, 13 (Ann Arbor: University of Michigan Press), pp. 73–85.
Erker, M. 2018. 'Der Tanz in der römischen Kultur', in K. Schnegg (ed.), *Antike Welten: Althistorische Forschungen in Österreich; Akten des 16. Österreichischen Althistorikerinnen-Tages in Innsbruck, 17.–19. November 2016* (Innsbruck: Innsbruck University Press), pp. 309–29.
Fless, F. and K. Moede. 2007. 'Music and Dance: Forms of Representation in Pictorial and Written Sources', in J. Rüpke (ed.), *A Companion to Roman Religion* (Malden: Blackwell), pp. 249–62.
Flower, H. 2017. *The Dancing Lares and the Serpent in the Garden: Religion at the Roman Street Corner* (Princeton: Princeton University Press).
Foss, P. W. 1997. 'Watchful Lares: Roman Household Organization and the Rituals of Cooking and Eating', in R. Laurence and A. Wallace-Hadrill (eds), *Domestic Space in the Roman World: Pompeii and Beyond* (Portsmouth, RI: Journal of Roman Archaeology), pp. 197–218.
Gildenhard, I. 2011. *Creative Eloquence: The Construction of Reality in Cicero's Speeches* (Oxford: Oxford University Press).
Graf, F. 2006. S.v. 'Acca Larentia', *Brill's New Pauly* <https://dx.doi.org/10.1163/1574-9347>.
Gruen, E. S. 1974. *The Last Generation of the Roman Republic* (Berkeley: University of California Press).
Hallett, C. H. 2023. '"Corinthian Bronzes": Miniature Masterpieces – Flagrant Forgeries', in J. Hopkins and S. McGill (eds), *Beyond Deceit: Valuing Forgery in Ancient Rome* (Oxford: Oxford University Press), pp. 44–92
Higgins, R. 1987. *Tanagra and the Figurines* (Princeton: Princeton University Press).
Kaufmann-Heinimann, A. 2007. 'Religion in the House', in J. Rüpke (ed.), *A Companion to Roman Religion* (Malden: Blackwell), pp. 188–200.
Kenty, J. 2018. 'The Political Context of Cicero's Oration *De domo sua*', *Ciceroniana Online*, 2.2: 245–64.
Leigh, M. 2004. 'The *Pro Caelio* and Comedy', *Classical Philology*, 99: 300–35.
Lisdorf, A. 2005. 'The Conflict over Cicero's House: An Analysis of the Ritual Element in *De domo sua*', *Numen*, 52: 445–64.
Mau, L. A. 1993. 'A Pigment Analysis of Greek Hellenistic Tanagra Figurines', *Harvard University Art Museums Bulletin*, 1: 55–62.
Momigliano, A. 1984. 'The Theological Efforts of the Roman Upper Class in the First Century BC', *Classical Philology*, 79: 199–211.
Naerebout, F. G. 2009. 'Das Reich tanzt ... Dance in the Roman Empire and its Discontents', in O. Hekster, S. Schmidt-Hofner, and C. Witschel (eds), *Ritual Dynamics and Religious Change in the Roman Empire* (Leiden: Brill), pp. 143–58.
Nisbet, R. G. (ed.). 1979. *M. Tulli Ciceronis: De domo sua ad pontifices oratio* (New York: Arno).
Patzelt, M. 2018. 'The Rhetoric of Roman Prayer: A Proposal for a Lived Religion Approach', *Religion in the Roman Empire*, 4.2: 162–86.

———. 2019. 'Praying as a "Woman among Men": Reconsidering Clodius' Failed Prayer in Cicero's Speech on his House', *Religion in the Roman Empire*, 5.2: 271–91.

Pesendorf, P. 2018. '*Ne serva prostituatur*: Sklavinnen als Prostituierte im Römischen Recht', in I. Fischer and D. Feichtinger (eds), *Sexualität und Sklaverei* (Münster: Ugarit), pp. 45–62.

Piccioni, A. 2018. 'Mimesis for a Cult: The Case of Western Greek Clay Figurines of Female Dancers', in H. L. Reid and J. C. DeLong (eds), *The Many Faces of Mimesis* (Sioux City: Parnassos), pp. 339–55.

Roller, M. B. 2010. 'Demolished Houses, Monumentality, and Memory in Roman Culture', *Classical Antiquity*, 29.1: 117–80.

Rüpke, J. 2002. 'Collegia Sacerdotum: Religiöse Vereine in der Oberschicht', in U. Egelhaaf-Gaiser and A. Schäfer (eds), *Religiöse Verein in der römischen Antike* (Tübingen: Mohr Siebeck), pp. 41–67.

———. 2003. 'Libri sacerdotum: Forschungs- und universitätsgeschichtliche Beobachtungen zum Ort von Wissowas "Religion und Kultus der Römer"', *Archiv für Religionsgeschichte*, 5: 16–39.

———. 2009. 'Antiquar und Theologe: Systematisierende Beschreibung römischer Religion bei Varro', in A. Bendlin (ed.), *Römische Religion im historischen Wandel: Diskursentwicklung von Plautus bis Ovid* (Stuttgart: Steiner), pp. 73–88.

———. 2012. *Rationalization and Religious Change in Republican Rome* (Philadelphia: University of Pennsylvania Press).

———. 2014. 'Historicizing Religion: Varro's *Antiquitates* and History of Religion in the Late Roman Republic', *History of Religions*, 53.3: 246–68.

———. 2016. *Pantheon: Geschichte der antiken Religionen* (Munich: Beck).

———. 2019. 'Roman Gods and Private Property: The Invention of State Religion in Cicero's Speech *On his House*', *Religion in the Roman Empire*, 5.3: 292–315.

Scheid, J. 1990. *Romulus et ses frères: le collège des frères arvales, modéles du culte public dans la Rome des empereurs* (Paris: De Boccard).

———. 2019. *Ad Deam Diam: Ein heiliger Hain in Roms Suburbium*, Spielräume der Antike, 5 (Stuttgart: Steiner).

Stroh, W. 2004. '*De domo sua*: Legal Problem and Structure', in J. Powell and J. Paterson (eds), *Cicero, the Advocate* (Oxford: Oxford University Press), pp. 313–70.

Tagliamonte, G. 1999. S.v. 'Palatium, Palatinus Mons', in E. M. Steinby (ed.), *Lexicon topographicum Urbis Romae*, IV (Rome: Quasar), pp. 14–22.

Tan, J. 2013. 'Publius Clodius and the Boundaries of the Contio', in C. Steel and H. van der Blom (eds), *Community and Communication: Oratory and Politics in Republican Rome* (Oxford: Oxford University Press), pp. 117–32.

Tatum, W. J. 1999. *The Patrician Tribune: P. Clodius Pulcher* (Chapel Hill: University of North Carolina Press).

Timmer, J. 2019. '*Summo studio magnoque consensus*. Konsensus im Senat der römischen Republik', in L. Dohmen and T. Trausch (eds), *Entscheiden und Regieren: Konsens als Element vormoderner Entscheidungsfindung in transkultureller Perspektive* (Bonn: V&R Unipress), pp. 57–80.

Van Andringa, W. 2018. 'Le monument et la tombe: Deux facons de mourir à l'époque romaine', in M.-D. Nenna, S. Huber, and W. Van Andringa (eds), *Constituer la tombe, honorer les défunts en Méditerranée antique* (Alexandrie: Centre d'études alexandrines), pp. 381–402.

Varhelyi, Z. 2017. 'Statuary and Ritualization in Imperial Italy', in C. Moser and J. Knust (eds), *Ritual Matters: Material Remains and Ancient Religion* (Ann Arbor: University of Michigan Press), pp. 87–98.

Vasaly, A. 1993. *Representations: Images of the World in Ciceronian Oratory* (Berkeley: University of California Press).

Weiler, I. 2018. 'Antike Sklaverei und Sexualität in der vergleichenden Geschichtswissenschaft', in I. Fischer and D. Feichtinger (eds), *Sexualität und Sklaverei* (Münster: Ugarit), pp. 3–43.

Wiseman, T. P. 2012. 'Where Did They Live?', *Journal of Roman Archaeology*, 25: 656–72.

Wissowa, G. 1917. 'Zum Ritual der Arvalbrüder', *Hermes*, 52.3: 321–47.

Yonge, C. D. (ed. and trans.). 1891. *The Orations of Marcus Tullius Cicero*, Harper's New Classical Library (London: Bell).

Zanker, P. 2009. *Augustus und die Macht der Bilder*, 5th edn (Munich: Beck).

Zimmer, G. 1994a. 'Frauen aus Tanagra', in G. Zimmer (ed.), *Bürgerwelten: Hellenistische Tonfiguren und Nachschöpfungen im 19. Jahrhundert* (Mainz: Von Zabern), pp. 19–28.

———. 1994b. 'Tanagra und Myrina: Die Entdeckung der hellenistischen Terrakotten', in G. Zimmer (ed.), *Bürgerwelten: Hellenistische Tonfiguren und Nachschöpfungen im 19. Jahrhundert* (Mainz: Von Zabern), pp. 11–18.

12. *Di Penates*: From Small Objects to Anthropomorphic Gods

Peter Scherrer

Introduction

Although the *Di Penates* have their place among the oldest and most important gods of Rome, as they are responsible for the *gentes* and their households, religious historians have paid relatively little attention to them until now. As far as I can see, only one monograph has been devoted to them, dealing mainly with their cult in Lavinium and the city of Rome.[1] But the Roman Empire grew rapidly from the second century BC onwards, and the cult of the *Di Penates* spread out into the provinces, becoming part of the lived religion of Roman citizens from Britain to Africa and the Near East. In the Late Republic and Imperial periods, not only did high dignitaries of the city of Rome itself have to take an oath of office, but so too did all the municipal and colonial magistrates. Furthermore, every Roman soldier had to pledge his loyalty by invoking Jupiter *optimus maximus* and the *Di Penates*, at least after Marius's reforms. The need to integrate large numbers of people with no (political, ethnic, or other) Roman background and traditions and to grant them civil rights (*civitas Romana*) must have broadly influenced the development of the cult of *Di Penates*. One set of questions, largely correlated to the Roman army's ability to move rapidly, concerns how the *Di Penates* could be integrated into the army on a personal level, how the *cultores* could take the representations of these gods with them, and how these representations had to evolve to generate positive and — in the best case — resonant relationships. For this purpose, I must here revisit an earlier thesis of mine, investigating how the *Di Penates* became (at least partly) anthropomorphic without losing their original outlet as tangible objects of aniconic status. Ultimately, I will stress the size factor, trying to explain why the *Di Penates* (probably in very much the same way as other personal gods like the *Lares* and *genii*) never became monumental. The reason may, at first glance, be transportability, but this alone does not explain everything.

A First Definition of the Di Penates in the Environment of Other Household Gods

The commentary on Virgil's *Aeneid* by the pagan author Maurus Servius Honoratus, which was written around AD 400, delivers a short and seemingly clear message: 'Penates sunt omnes di qui domi coluntur'.[2] This sentence obviously influenced many modern researchers' understanding of the *Di Penates* as a comprehensive denomination of household gods, including the whole assemblage, which we know from so many Roman houses from the Late Republic onwards. They were mostly kept in little shrines, nowadays known as *lararia*. The word *lararium* is not used in Rome, however, before Late Antiquity — for example, in the *Life* of Alexander Severus (AD 222–235),[3] which was probably not written before *c.* AD 400. Thus, it seems to be more an expression stemming from the influence of Christianity than a *terminus technicus* of the venerators of these gods in the Republican and Imperial Eras themselves. Relating to this, it is no accident that *lararia* occurs again in another late commentary on the *Aeneid* regarding a shrine: 'ubi

---

* This article is dedicated to Eleni Schindler Kaudelka, to whose friendship, hospitality, and knowledge I owe so much.

[1] Dubourdieu 1989. One of the earliest substantial overviews of the *Di Penates* was given by G. Wissowa in 1887 (see Wissowa 1904); among the latest is McDonough 2012.

[2] Serv., *Aen*. II.514. The text of Verg., *Aen*. II.512–14, describing the situation inside Troy, says: 'Aedibus in mediis nudoque sub aetheris axe ingens ara fuit iuxtaque veterrima laurus incumbens arae atque umbra complexa penatis' (In the centre of the halls, and under the sky's naked arch, was a large altar, with an ancient laurel nearby, that leant on the altar, and clothed the household gods with shade), trans. A. S. Kline.

[3] SHA, *Alexander Severus* XXIX.2; see also *TLL* VII.2, 967. For a comment to the meaning see Rüpke 2016b, 261.

Lares Penates habitant'.[4] Actually, the focus of these authors was not the clear distinction between the *Di Penates* and the *Lares* or the differences between them and other household gods or goddesses.

A monograph by A. Dubourdieu, however, took Servius's late definition seriously and caused others to follow her with various modifications.[5] J. Bodel argues that the *Lares* and the *Di Penates* were mixed up in many households in practice in the first century AD; furthermore, in the so-called *lararia* in the provinces, it was not the *Lares* but the *Di Penates* that were stored and venerated.[6] Bodel's first assumption might be partly true, but it still would mean a serious change in cult practice, as I will try to show in this paper. More importantly, it seems that Bodel, along with R. Parker, merges all the gods and goddesses who appear in the so-called *lararia* (Vesta, Fortuna, Bacchus, and Mercury, among many others) into the *Di Penates*.[7] J. Rüpke has also recently argued in this direction, stating that, in general, the household gods form one large and broadly defined group, with the different names such as *Di Penates* or *Lares* only used in different situations for diverse tasks.[8] As we have seen, this might have been the case in Late Antiquity, but it took many centuries to arrive at this point.

Indeed, if we trace back our sources regarding the household gods in the Roman Republic and the Augustan periods, we may state that we may arrive at quite a different result from an archaeological point of view, by closely examining the surviving archaeological records in context and comparing the depictions and other material items with what is said by authors about the materials, the appearance, and the place of veneration of these household gods. To summarize briefly, in archaeological terms it is very clear that the *Lares*, at least from the second century BC onwards, had a static iconography of a 'dancing' male youth, while the *genius loci*, present in their company on many paintings, is represented by a relatively large snake.[9] But what did the *Di Penates* look like and what was — in cultic terms — their place and function in the house? The main task of this article is to address this question, while another is to stress the differences between the appearance and function of these personal *Di Penates* and the *Di Penates publici* in the Late Republic and the Imperial periods.[10] And for close parallels, it will be helpful to glance briefly at Greek household religion with the *Agathos Daimon* (corresponding to the *genius loci*), *Zeus Ktesios* (coinciding with the *Penates*), and *Zeus Herkeios* (corresponding to the *Lares*).

In addition to these special household gods, several other (tutelary) gods or goddesses could be placed in different areas of the house, standing freely or in shrines. To give only two examples: we know about a special statuette of Minerva, which Cicero loved and venerated.[11] But at the other end of society, Trimalchio had a small marble statue of Venus in the *armarium* near the *Lares*, which were made of silver.[12] But we should not conclude — especially because no ancient author or inscription tells us — that these gods and goddesses were part of the group of *Lares* or *Di Penates*; instead, they are always mentioned separately.

The Origin and Function of the Di Penates

The beginning of the cult is linked to the prehistory of Rome.[13] When fleeing Troy, Aeneas had to carry his father, guide his son, and take the *Di Penates* with him.[14]

---

[4] Gloss. *Aen.* XII.199 (ed. Hagen 1902). But Vergil here uses the neutral term *sacrarium*.

[5] Dubourdieu 1989, esp. 1–2; see also Dubordieu 2012, 36.

[6] Bodel 2008, 258–64.

[7] Parker 2015, 75, following Dubordieu and T. Fröhlich, although the latter had reservations about this merging, cf. Fröhlich 1991, 37–48.

[8] Rüpke 2016b, 258–62. D. G. Orr had already made a similar argument, cf. Orr 1978, 1563.

[9] See Fröhlich 1991; Flower 2017.

[10] For the written sources and a broad discussion of them as well as the history of research, see Dubourdieu 1989.

[11] For the close emotional engagement of single persons to a god(dess) in general, see Chaniotis 2011, esp. 275; for Cicero's Minerva: Bodel 2008, 252–64; see also the contribution of E. Begemann (p. 8–9) in this volume.

[12] Petron., *Sat.* XXIX.8.

[13] Naevius, frg. 3, gives the *sacra Penatium* a prominent role soon after Anchises' *augurium*.

[14] Verg., *Aen.* III.148–49: 'effigies sacrae divum Phrygiique penates, quos mecum a Troia mediisque ex ignibus urbis extuleram' (The sacred statues of the gods, the Phrygian Penates, that I had carried with me from Troy, out of the burning city), trans. A. S. Kline. See also Liv. 1.1.9: 'Inde foedus ictum inter duces, inter exercitus salutationem factam. Aeneam apud Latinum fuisse in hospitio; ibi Latinum apud penates deos domesticum publico adiunxisse foedus filia Aeneae in matrimonium data' (A formal treaty was made between the leaders and mutual greetings exchanged between the armies. Latinus received Aeneas as a guest in his house, and there, in the presence of his tutelary deities, completed the political alliance by a domestic one, and gave his daughter in marriage to Aeneas), trans. Rev. C. Roberts. For the manifold sculptural works depicting the group, see Quaranta 2016, 6–192.

Aeneas brought the *Penates* to Lavinium, where they were venerated in a temple; even in the Late Republic, Rome's leading officials had to go there and sacrifice to them after doing the same in the Capitol in Rome itself.[15] In Rome, however, the *Di Penates publici* had a temple of their own on the Velian Hill, but at the same time they were kept in the *penus Vestae*.[16] This location is directly linked with their name, which derives from that word *penus* (in a narrower sense, 'the inner', broadened in meaning to 'pantry', located in the innermost and thus best-protected part of the house).[17] In the very beginning, the *Di Penates* might have been the personal tutelars of the king and his palace, where all essentials of the people were stored.[18] But in aristocratic Rome, after the fall of the monarchy, every *pater familias* (probably in early times only the leading families, the *patricii*) had his own *Di Penates* to protect his *domus* in the double sense of the built house with the pantry and the family, related by kinship, forming the house in the genealogical sense.[19] At the same time, they protected the *res publica* as the *Di Penates publici*.

Thus, the *Di Penates* were principally similar to the Greek *Zeus Ktesios* in function (as Dionysius of Halicarnassus also states),[20] because he too was worshipped by the family in the narrower sense and not by servants or guests.[21] Dionysius's uncertainty in his translation of the name and thus in the functional sense of the *Di Penates* shows that by his lifetime, the borders between the *Lares* (*Zeus Herkeios*), who protected the estate, the *genius* (close to the *Theoi Patroioi*), who gave the power of life from generation to generation, and the *Di Penates*, who allowed the *pater* and his family to flourish,[22] were blurred and little understood.[23] At Rome in the Late Republic, there were also two explanations for the name *Penates*. On the one hand, the *Di Penates* were derived from *penus* (pantry), especially from the innermost part of the *templum Vestae*, where the eternal fire of Rome was kept,[24] while on the other hand they derived from living in the inner part of our body and giving us breath and rational spirit.[25] Thus, a direct personal and possibly resonant connection between a Roman citizen and his *Di Penates* was established.[26]

Whereas Aeneas had brought his tutelary gods with him and kept them safe during his long journey to the Italian shores, the opposite happened to Ovid when he

---

15 Macrob., *Sat.* III.4.11; Serv., *Aen.* II.296 and III.12. See also Bodel 2008, esp. 254–55.

16 For the temple, priests, and public offerings, see Castagnoli 1946; Dubourdieu 1989, part II. Dion. Hal., *Ant. Rom.* LXVIII.1; Varro, *Ling.* v.54; Liv. XLV.16 (167 BC): 'The temple of the Penates on the Velia had been struck by lightning.' It was again rebuilt by Augustus, see *R. Gest. div. Aug.* 19. For more mentions in the epigraphic record, see *AE* 2010, 23 and *CIL* VI 32501 = 37173a = *InscrIt* XIII 2.20. On the *penus Vestae*: Fest. 296 L; Tac., *Ann.* XV.41; Dion. Hal., *Ant. Rom.* II.66.

17 Orr 1978, 1563.

18 For the monarchic period of Rome and the Early Republic, two main opinions, exist, which I am not going to discuss in detail here. For the history of research, see Dubourdieu 1989, 59–60. Linderski 2000, 514, along with some earlier authors, thinks that the *Penates* were closely connected to the king (originally Aeneas) and that in the Republic their function was split into the public deities (in fulfilling the former duties of the king by magistrates) and the private ones of every *pater familias* of the (leading) families. Dubourdieu 1989 (e.g. 523) and others argue that the *Di Penates publici* derived from the private deities in the house, especially the *penus*, and the existence of the *penus Vestae* was the reason why (and place where) the *Penates* became public.

19 Plaut., *Merc.* 834; Dion. Hal., *Ant. Rom.* 1.67.3. See also Liv. II.40.7, when Coriolanus in Veji is remembered by his mother to the Di Penates inside the walls of Rome and in his *domus*, when he plans to wage war against the city: 'Non, cum in conspectu Roma fuit, succurrit: Intra illa moenia domus ac penates mei sunt, mater, coniunx liberique?' (Did you not say to yourself when your eye rested on Rome, 'Within those walls are my home, my household gods, my mother, my wife, my children'?), trans. Rev. C. Roberts. For the metonymical use of *Di Penates* for *domus*, see Dubourdieu 1989, 53–56.

20 Dion. Hal., *Ant. Rom.* 1.67.3: τοὺς δὲ θεοὺς τούτους Ῥωμαῖοι μὲν Πενάτας καλοῦσιν· οἱ δ' ἐξερμηνεύοντες εἰς τὴν Ἑλλάδα γλῶσσαν τοὔνομα οἱ μὲν Πατρῴους ἀποφαίνουσιν, οἱ δὲ Γενεθλίους, εἰσὶ δ' οἳ Κτησίους, ἄλλοι δὲ Μυχίους, οἱ δὲ Ἑρκείους. ἔοικε δὲ τούτων ἕκαστος κατά τινος τῶν συμβεβηκότων αὐτοῖς ποιεῖσθαι τὴν ἐπίκλησιν κινδυνεύουσί τε πάντες ἀμωσγέπως τὸ αὐτό (As for these gods, the Romans call them Penates. Some who translate the name into the Greek language render it Patrooi, others Genethlioi, some Ktesiori, others Mychioi, and still others Herkeioi. Each of these seems to be giving them their name from some one of their attributes, and it is probable that they are all expressing more or less the same idea).

21 Isaeus VII.16.

22 Gell., *NA* IV.1.1–23; for the aspect of feeding the *Di Penates* compare also Mart. VII.27, who said that the meat of the hunted wild boar would 'fatten the Penates'; cf. Hor., *Carm.* III.23.19–20: 'mollivit aversos Penatis farre pio et saliente mica' (they'll mollify hostile Penates, with the sacred corn, and the dancing grain).

23 For this, see also Bodel 2008. This explains why in many households with only cursory Roman traditions, the *Penates* and *Lares* might be mixed.

24 Fest. 296 L.

25 Inner part of the body, Cic., *Nat. D.* II.68; breath and rational spirit: Macrob., *Sat.* III.4.7. Note, however, that like Servius (see above), Macrobius wrote at a late period (around AD 390), when philosophical interest was centred around responding to Christianity, not the origins of Roman religion.

26 For resonance as a positive relation between one being and his environment ('Weltbeziehung'), see Rosa 2016.

was exiled by Augustus to Tomis on the Black Sea coast. Ovid describes his wife, who was not allowed to follow him, mourning heavily before the *Lares* and — at the hearth — the lonely (*desertos*) *Penates*.[27] Thus, being relegated truly implied being expatriated: the separation from his wife prohibiting any possibility for future legal children, the absence from Rome making him unable to take part in elections, the loss of the *Di Penates* excluding him from the Roman community in cultic and juridical ways, because he very likely could not even swear an oath (*ius iurare*) any longer.[28]

The casual occurrence of *Di Penates* in grave inscriptions is also striking in its ultimate meaning. Even if it cannot be proved, the obvious explanation for their appearance is that the deceased had no blood-related heir in direct line, no children or grandchildren, who would inherit and continue the *domus* as part of Roman civil society.[29] In those circumstances, the *sacra* would vanish, together with the last *pater familias* — or more generally, the last male in the family — not only in case of death, but also if he was adopted into another *gens*, as Cicero explicitly states.[30]

The *Di Penates publici*, as common gods of all Roman citizens in the (later) Republic, had their main function — at least as much as we can conclude from our sources — as co-recipients of the vows and oaths of all *magistratus* besides Jupiter.[31] Not only in Rome itself but in all *municipia* and *coloniae*, elected office-holders had to *iurare per Iovem deosque Penates* at least from the late second century BC onwards. In the Imperial Era, this formula was broadened to include all deified emperors (*divi Augusti*) and the *genius* of the reigning emperor(s), as is easily seen in the many fragments of their foundation laws.[32] It is common opinion that the loyalty pledge of soldiers was very similar if not identical,[33] at least after the reforms most closely connected with C. Marius in the late second century BC.[34] The vows were connected with libations, both the vows taken at the assumption and conclusion of a public office and at the entrance into the Roman army, as well as those taken at multiple other opportunities to renew the oath, such as the birthday of the emperor or his *dies imperii*, the *natalis* of the legion on 10 June (*dies aquilae*), or New Year's Day. This reminds us of Cicero, who mentions *Di Penates* and *sacra* in one direct line.[35]

Whatever function the *Di Penates* originally had in private households, it seems clear that the *Di Penates publici* were of great importance for the state as gods of oaths, common to all Roman citizens and exclusively to them.[36] They linked Romans to their mythical forefather

---

[27] Ov., *Tr.* 1.3.41–46: 'Hac prece adoravi superos ego, pluribus uxor, | singultu medios impediente sonos. | illa etiam ante Lares passis adstrata capillis | contigit extinctos ore tremente focos, | multaque in aversos effudit verba Penates | pro deplorato non valitura viro' (I spoke to the gods in prayer like this, | my wife more so, sobs choking her half-heard cries. | She threw herself before the Lares, hair unbound | touching the cold hearth with trembling lips | poured out words to the Penates, before her | not destined to help the husband she mourned). Further on, *Tr.* 1.3.91–96: 'Illa dolore amens tenebris narratur obortis | semianimis media procubuisse domo, | utque resurrexit foedatis pulvere turpi | crinibus et gelida membra levavit humo, | se modo, desertos modo complorasse Penates, | nomen et erepti saepe vocasse viri' (Maddened by grief they say she was overcome | by darkness, and fell half-dead in the midst of the room | and when she rose, hair fouled with filthy dust | and lifted her body from the cold ground | she wept for herself, and the deserted Penates | and often called her lost husband's name), trans. H. D. Riley.

[28] For this item, see also the report of Livy on the year 460 BC and the discussion on slaves and exiled citizens (below with n. 41).

[29] The *EDCS* database lists only nine grave inscriptions, as far as I can see. I give here only three case examples. *CIL* XI 45, Ravenna, a marine soldier, departed at the age of eighteen years: *Basus Virti | f(ilius) an(nos) XVIII d(omo) | Neptuno IIII(quadriere) | dis P(enatibus) hic sit(us) | est*. The elaborate epitaph (*CIL* VI 1779 = *AE* 2008, 150) of Vettius Agorius Praetextatus (around AD 384–387), gives his *cursus honorum* (highest positions: *praefectus urbi, praefectus praetorio II Italiae et Illyrici, consul ordinarius designatus*), numerous priesthoods (among them *augur* and *pontifex Vestae*) and then reads: [...] *Vettius Agorius Praetextatus | Paulinae coniugi | Paulina veri et castitatis conscia | dicata templis atq(ue) amica numinum | sibi maritum praeferens Romam viro | pudens fidelis pura mente et corpore | benigna cunctis utilis penatibus | cae[le]s[tium iam sede semper mec]u[m e]ri[s* [...]. This highest official may consciously have used the *Di Penates* as a counterpart to Christianity. Another special case is a marble plate on the front wall of a grave *aedicula* in Pompei (see Kropp 2008, no. 1/5/4/3), which invites his guest-friends to linger at the site but also curses his enemies, willing them into the power of the *Di Penates* and evil underworld spirits: *Hospes paullisper morare | si non est molestum et quid evites | cognosce amicum hunc quem | speraveram mi(hi) esse ab eo mihi accusato|res subiecti et iudicia instaurata deis | gratias ago et meae innocentiae omni | molestia liberatus sum qui nostrum mentitur | eum nec Di Penates nec inferi recipient*.

[30] Cic., *Dom.* 34–35; Cic., *Leg.* 51.

[31] Cic., *Sest.* 30.

[32] See e.g. *CIL* I² 582 (*oppidum Lucanum*) and 2924 (Tarentum), both from 130–100 BC; cf. Cic., *Acad.* 2 65. In the Hispanic provinces, a relatively high number of such laws from the time of Caesar onwards is preserved; for example, see the relevant passages of the so-called *lex Irnitana* (Crawford 2016).

[33] Compare Mommsen 2009, 101 and 507; Herrmann 1968, esp. 46 and 113.

[34] See, e.g. Pollard and Berry 2012, 19–23.

[35] Cic., *Verr.* 2 2.13; also see Cic., *Verr.* 2 4.48.

[36] Parker 2015 has already argued in favour of an overlap of

Aeneas (and by him to his descendant Julius Caesar and his heir Octavian, later Augustus) and defined, among many other privileges, the group of possible legionaries and civil office-holders. This made a substantial difference to other inhabitants of the Roman Empire, who were lacking civil rights (*peregrini*). Veterans of auxiliary units in particular, who became full Roman citizens regularly with the *honesta missio* and settled down in the provinces in most cases, could now show their new status by the *tria nomina* and the veneration of the *Di Penates* at their hearth.[37] A similar situation was beginning to take place for the thousands of freedmen who acted in Italian and provincial towns as well as in settlements close to military camps (*canabae legionis* and so-called *vici*) in the name of their patrons, upon whom they depended in juristic terms in various ways.[38] As they were limited in their civil rights, especially in cultic affairs, most likely they also lacked their own *Di Penates*; only their descendants would be able to sacrifice to them.[39] In any case, inscriptions of freedmen are almost completely missing in the epigraphic sources and slaves were definitely not involved.[40] That slaves had no right to participate in the cult of the *Di Penates* is emphasized also by Livy, who describes how in 460 BC the Capitol Hill, with the central sanctuary of the city, was occupied by a mob of exiles and slaves, and the senator P. Valerius proclaimed to the *tribuni plebis*: 'Iuppiter optimus maximus, Iuno regina et Minerva, alii dei deaeque obsidentur; castra servorum publicos vestros Penates tenant'.[41]

The Development of the Di Penates from Aniconic Tangible Items to Anthropomorphic Gods

According to Servius and to Ovid, the place of cult for the private *Di Penates* was the hearth (with its public counterpart in the *templum Vestae*), but we might propose that the *penus* (pantry) might also have been an appropriate place for them, as for *Zeus Ktesios* in Greece.[42] But, as Cicero mentions that the *Di Penates* were occasionally closely tied to the *sacra* of private men,[43] we may guess that they were on display in upper-class households in a chest or shrine in the dining room, and were placed on the table during meals to receive their portion of food.[44] This is also indicated by some

---

'private' and 'public' cults with many convincing arguments. Thus, in this paper it is all the more important to stress the actual differences and diverging developments for the 'private' *Di Penates* and the *Di Penates publici*.

37 By this, it seems not an accident that a good portion of the relatively few (I could find only around twenty-five in *EDCS*) 'private' votive inscriptions to the *Di Penates* — commonly linked with Jupiter, Fortuna, *Lares militares* or other military gods, and the gods of the house, *Lares* and Vesta — are from officers and soldiers. The concurrent involvement of *di hospitales* also gives a hint in this direction: the new Romans could impress their guests with their new gods. See e.g. *CIL* VII 237 = *RIB* I 649 (Eburacum/York, later second or third century AD): *I(ovi) O(ptimo) M(aximo) | dis deabusque | Hospitalibus Pe|natibusq(ue) ob con|servatam salutem | suam suorumq(ue) | P(ublius) Ael(ius) Marcian/us praef(ectus) coh(ortis) | aram sac(ravit) ac ded(icavit)*. *IDR* III.5.1.299 (Apulum/Alba Iulia, end of the second century AD): *Dis Penatibus Lari/bus Miltaribus Lari | Viali Neptuno Saluti | Fortunae Reduci | (A)esculapio Dianae | Apollini Herculi | Spei Fa(v)ori P(ublius) Catius | Sabinus trib(unus) mil(itum) | leg(ionis) XIII G(eminae) v(otum) l(ibens) s(olvit)*. *CIL* XI 1920 = *CIL* IX *00358,1 (Perusia/Perugia): *T(itus) Annius L(uci) f(ilius) Larg<u = I>s | Dibus Penatibus | ob rem militarem | votum solvit l(ibens) m(erito)*. *CIL* XIII 6709 (Mogontiacum/Mainz): *Numinib(us) Aug(ustis) | I(ovi) O(ptimo) M(aximo) Fortu/[nae] Vestae D[3]/[3] Laribus | Penatib[u]s | L(ucius) Sallusti(us) | Sedatus | [hospe]s v(otum) s(olvit) [l(ibens)] m(erito) ||] Ve[stae 3] | [3] Laribus | Penatibus | L(ucius) Sallustius | Sedatus hos|pes v(otum) s(olvit) l(ibens) m(erito)*.

38 Roth 2018, esp. 59–90.

39 If we look at the cognomen, this could likely be the case with *CIL* V 514 = *InscrIt* X.4.351: (Tergeste/Trieste, first century AD): *Dis deabus | et deis Penatibus | T(itus) Veturius Eudaemon | pro se et suis posuit*. *CIL* X 331 = *InscrIt* III.1.124 (Atina/Atena Lucana,

first century AD): *Iovi et | dis Penatibus | P(ubli) Nanoni Dio|phanti Augusta|les Atinates*. It looks as if the friends were celebrating the new *Di Penates* of a freedmen or his descendant.

40 For the possible example from Atina, see above, n. 39. Another likely freedman could appear in *CIL* V 561 (Rome, first century AD): *Di{i}s | Penatibus | Hermes disp(ensator) | d(onum) d(edit)*. But in no case is the social status of being a freedman explicitly mentioned.

41 Liv. III.17.1–5: 'Jupiter *optimus maximus*, Juno *regina* and Minerva, and other gods and goddesses, are besieged; a camp of slaves holds your public Penates (as their prisoners).'

42 The hearth: Serv., *Aen.* II.211; see also e.g. Mart. VII.27; Ov., *Tr.* 1.3.41–46, 1.3.91–96 (cf. n. 27). I still cannot see any reason to place them into the so-called *lararia* in the *atrium* of the house, unless the different tutelary gods were mixed together. The common mixture of statuettes with dishes, drinking cups, or other vessels, which were adorned with busts or figures of gods or goddesses, whose function will be discussed below, also points in this direction; cf. Kaufmann-Heinimann 1998, with many examples in the catalogue. The problem is that most collections were not found in place (in the provincial houses) but hidden in depots to keep them safe. So, if a mixture of valuable objects that did not belong together in function, such as different household gods and tableware or even money, was kept in a cache, we can no longer detect the original settings.

43 Cic., *Verr.* 2 2.13; also see Cic., *Verr.* 2 4.48.

44 It might be a very old tradition, if Naev. frg. 3 can be interpreted in this way: 'Postquam avem aspexit in templo Anchisa | Sacra in mensa Penatium ordine ponuntur' (After Anchises had caught sight

houses in the region around Mount Vesuvius, where so-called *lararia* were found not only in the *atrium* and/or in the kitchen but also in more distinguished rooms where guests were welcomed or meals served.[45] During each meal, some food was sacrificed to the *Di Penates* and collected in a *patella* or *patera*, an open dish, and placed on the table. After having been strewn with salt and flour, the offerings were put into the fire.[46] Especially informative are two passages in Cicero's second speech against Verres, which we have already mentioned above. After listing three men from whom Verres had stolen a *patera*, a *patella*, and a *turibulum*, Cicero writes:

> Cn. Pompeius est Philo, qui fuit Tyndaritanus. Is cenam isti dabat apud villam in Tyndaritano. Fecit, quod Siculi non audebant; ille, civis Romanus quod erat, impunius id se facturum putavit; adposuit patellam, in qua sigilla erant egregia. Iste continuo, ut vidit, non dubitavit illud insigne penatium hospitaliumque deorum ex hospitali mensa tollere, sed tamen, quod ante de istius abstinentia dixeram, sigillis avulsis reliquum argentum sine ulla avaritia reddidit.

> (There is a man named Cnaeus Pompeius Philo, who was a native of Tyndaris; he gave Verres a supper at his villa in the country near Tyndaris; he did what Sicilians did not dare to do, but what, because he was a citizen of Rome, he thought he could do with impunity, he put before him a dish on which were some exceedingly beautiful figures (*adposuit patellam, in qua sigilla erant egregia*). Verres, the moment he saw it, determined to rob his host's table of that memorial of the Penates and of the gods of hospitality. But yet, in accordance with what I have said before of his great moderation, he restored the rest of the silver after he had torn off the figures; so free was he from all avarice!)[47]

With this testimonial we may be sure that the *Di Penates* were not individual figures, but the dish itself, which was adorned with some anthropomorphic representations, possibly in the form of a relief. Another story about Verres points in the same direction, when

> Mamertinorum legatus, istius laudator, non solum istum bona sua, verum etiam sacra deosque penatis a maioribus traditos ex aedibus suis eripuisse dixit.

> (that same ambassador of the Mamertines, his panegyrist, said that he had not only robbed him of his private property, but had also carried away his sacred vessels, and the images of the Di Penates, which he had received from his ancestors, out of his.)[48]

In this case, like in the previous one, 'sacra deosque penatis' should be interpreted as a strongly tied unity. The *deos penatis* are of the same kind as the other objects (*sacra*), meaning dishes (but specially adorned). Cicero is not referring to statues or other objects; he deals only with dishes in both statements. This coincides well with other sources that will soon be mentioned, which testify that (among) the *Di Penates* (*publici*) were vases (dishes or pots of optional materials ranging from clay to silver). We shall return to this point again later.

An open question remains regarding the descriptions of meals and the use of these *Penates*-dishes given by Cicero. As stated above, it is relatively clear that the *Di Penates* had their place at the hearth and very likely also in the *penus*, the storeroom. But how might we explain their role in a fine symposium in the *tablinum* or *triclinium* with honoured guests, far away from the kitchen and the hearth?[49] Of course, during meals it was necessary to place some food inside the dish representing the *Di Penates*, which in earlier times had been kept in the central room with the cooking hearth. At the end of the dinner, the offerings were burned in the fire. This would only have been feasible during meals in dining rooms if we take into account the use of portable hearths, which are clearly attested in nearly all Greek and Roman households. The vessel then had to be deposited on or close to this hearth. The other possibility was to place some food in small dishes and carry them to the *Di Penates* at the hearth or in the pantry (we shall come back to this point later on).

Otherwise we know very little about what these *Di Penates* looked like. Most Roman authors write quite generally about them. Additionally, it seems we have to distinguish between different types of *Penates*. The *Di Penates publici* in the Temple of Vesta are called *sacra*

---

of the bird in the temple, the *sacra* of the Penates on the table were put in [right] order). For the portability and storage of these 'small gods' in the frame of storage possibilities (e.g. pantries) in a Roman house, see van Oyen 2021, 91–121.

[45] For a list of these houses, see Giacobello 2008, 230–94; see also Schörner 2016, who discusses this phenomenon, but as he does not include the *Di Penates* as a different group, his conclusions are not convincing.

[46] Varro, *Sat. Men.* 265; Hor., *Carm.* III.23.17–20; Pers. III.24–26; Arnob. II.67.

[47] Cic., *Verr. 2* 4.48, trans. C. D. Yonge.

[48] Cic., *Verr. 2* 2.13, trans. C. D. Yonge.

[49] For the role of *sacra* during dinner, see Kaufmann-Heinimann 1998, 191–95, though she speaks only of statues without discerning between the *Lares* and *Penates*. See also above, n. 44.

Figure 12.1. Denarius of C. Sulpicius C.F., 106 BC.
Obverse: *D(i) P(enates) P(ublici)*; garlanded busts of two young men.
Reverse: Lavinian Sow (image © Johny Sysel, CC BY-SA 3.0
<https://commons.wikimedia.org/w/index.php?curid=30924428>
[accessed 12 February 2023]).

Penatium by Naevius,[50] similar to what Cicero may have had in mind,[51] whereas Livy uses *pignora imperii* (signs of sovereignty) in the *penus Vestae*.[52] We learn somewhat more from Dionysius of Halicarnassus,[53] who says the *Penates in Lavinium* were 'caducei of iron and bronze and an earthen vessel', while Varro calls them *sigilla* made of wood, stone, and clay.[54] Pliny mentions a *fascinus* (human phallus),[55] and Cicero states that among the *Di Penates* was the *palladium* from Troy.[56]

We only have an eyewitness for the *Di Penates publici* in the small temple on the Velia; Dionysius describes them as follows:

> In this temple there are images of the Trojan gods which it is lawful for all to see, with an inscription showing them to be the Penates. They are two seated youths holding spears, and are pieces of ancient workmanship. We have seen many other statues also of these gods in ancient temples and in all of them are represented two youths in military garb.[57]

While Dionysius in the Augustan Age compares their clothing to that of the *Dioscuri*, other authors see similarities to the *Cabiri* of Samothrace, but the actual difference in the appearance of all these groups is small, if existent at all.[58]

---

50 Naev., *Bell. Pun.* 3 FPL.

51 Cic., *Verr.* 2 2.13; also see Cic., *Verr.* 2 4.48. See above, with ns 35 and 43.

52 Liv. XL.7–10.

53 Dion. Hal., *Ant. Rom.* I.67.4.

54 Schol. Verg., *Aen.* II.717.

55 Plin., *HN* XXVIII.39.

56 Cic., *Scaur.* 48. But see for that below with n. 65.

57 Dion. Hal., *Ant. Rom.* I.68.2.

58 Serv., *Aen.* I.78; II.325; III.12; III.148; Macrob., *Sat.*

The Professional Army since the Late Republic and its Role in the Spread of the Cult of the Di Penates

With these descriptions in mind, we turn our attention to a silver coin (denarius) of C. Sulpicius (Fig. 12.1),[59] minted in the year 106 BC, when Rome had a never-ending need for soldiers, a time best symbolized by the desperate defensive wars against the Cimbri and Teutons on the one side and the *bellum Iugurthinum* on the other. On the obverse, two garlanded busts of young men are depicted, very similar to the ones of the *Dioscuri* on other denarii, the most prominent currency for paying soldiers, of this time. The inscription *D(i) P(enates) P(ublici)* is clear, and the connection to Aeneas and the temple of the *Penates* in Lavinium is given on the reverse with two warriors with spears framing the Lavinian Sow.[60]

It is far from a coincidence that this new type of coin appeared the year after Marius, as consul (107 BC), had recruited his whole army for the Numidian War out of *capite censi* and — according to Plutarch — (former?) slaves from Rome and also from among the *socii rei publicae*,[61] while his co-consul, L. Cassius Longinus, took the 'regular' army to Cisalpine Gaul to fight the Cimbri and the Teutons. These partly lower-class and partly new citizens had to be trained in Roman ideo-

---

III.4.8–10. Following these sources, Orr 1978, 1562–63, has stated that the *Disocuri* were the *Penates* or their cults were fused.

59 Sydenham 1952, 572; Crawford 1974, 312/1. In numismatic scholarship there is a discussion about whether a denarius of Mn. Fonteius in 108–107 BC (Crawford 1974, 307/1a) already depicted the *Di Penates publici* on the obverse. Depicted are the typical conjoined laureate heads of the *Dioscuri* looking right, *X* below chin, stars above. But before the faces are two letters, *P* and *P*, which are often interpreted as *Penates Publici*. The ship on the reverse is said to bring the *Penates* to Italy. But I hardly ever find *Penates* written in Latin literature (a certain exception is Livy, but he mentions *dei deaeque* in the sentence before; see above with n. 41) or inscriptions without having *D(e)i* before. Thus, we should set aside the coin depicting the *Castores* and look for another meaning of the *P* and *P*.

60 This is the traditional interpretation of the image on the reverse. But it might also be considered to be Numa Pompilius and the Sabinian king sacrificing a sow to conclude the war between their peoples; this scene could be a further clear sign for the former Gauls that they were now Romans and all animosities belonged to the past. For this very interpretation of the so-called Aeneas panel of the *Ara Pacis*, see Rehak 2001. As Rehak convincingly argues that neither Aeneas nor the temple of the *Di Penates* is shown here, the *Ara Pacis* is excluded in this article as a monument of interest for these gods. For the opposite, traditional interpretation of the *Ara Pacis* panel, see e.g. Quaranta 2016, 645, 652–54.

61 *Capite censi*: Plut., *Marius* IX.1; *socii rei publicae*: Sall., *Iug.* LXXXIV.

Figure 12.2. Denarius of C. Antius C.f., 47 BC (Westfalenmuseum Muenster); reverse: busts of two youths with the legend *DEI PENATES*; obverse: Hercules (Westfalenmuseum Münster) (image © Robert Dylka (CC BY-NC-SA) <https://archaeologie.uni-muenster.de/ikmk/image/ID164/vs_exp.jpg> [accessed 12 February 2023]; reproduced with permission of Westfalenmuseum Münster).

logy; therefore, the picture of the *Di Penates* on their pay reminded them to whom their *fides* had to be directed.

Most areas of Cisalpine Gaul (from 41 BC onwards, the northern Italian regions) were (politically) Romanized and gained some civil rights from the second century BC onwards, until the completion of that process by Julius Caesar in the year 49 BC with his *lex de civitate*.[62] So it does not seem coincidental that in 47 BC a denarius was again struck which showed two jugate busts of young men and the legend *DEI PENATES* (Fig. 12.2).[63] It has been assumed that these special editions were initiated by the master of the mint, C. Antius Restio, but it is much more plausible to see it as a reaction from Julius Caesar himself and his administration to welcome the many new citizens in the north of Italy, especially if we consider that the earlier issue of 106 was either driven by Marius himself or was a product of the senate's reaction to his recruitment. In the same year (or the year before, 48/47 BC) another denarius was minted by Caesar himself, which showed Aeneas carrying his father Anchises and the *palladium* out of burning Troy.[64] This edition reminded the public of Caesar's descent from Aeneas. At the same time, it made people aware that his pious forefather had saved the *palladium* and the *Di Penates* and connected Caesar himself with these deeds.[65] Thus, Caesar's minting could constitute some-

thing like a tradition. But one difference is important. In the later version, the *Di Penates* were the ones of single citizens, not the *publici* of the Roman Republic. In the earlier instance, the *Dei Penates publici* served as a seal of Rome to remind the former *peregrini* and new Roman soldiers to be loyal to the *res publica Romana*. The new coins linked this entire regional society to one person, their new *patronus*, who had given them full civil rights.

Cisalpine Gaul and the also greatly Romanized Transalpine Gaul from that time onwards formed major territories for Roman legionary recruitment for more than two centuries.[66] If it is correct that soldiers had to swear to Jupiter and the *Di Penates* and to make a libation to these gods at some point at the beginning of their service — at the latest when switching from recruit (*tiro*) status to a full member of the legion (*miles*), then the veneration of the *Di Penates publici* was a decisive act for the new soldiers, but they had no (personal) tradition accorded to them. Thus, it is no wonder that the silver coins (*denarii*) used to pay soldiers depicted and named these unfamiliar gods and gave them an appearance evocative of the traditional guardians of the Roman army, the *Dioscuri*. A direct path leads from here to the (Augustan-era or even earlier) statues in the temple on the Velia described by Dionysius of Halicarnassus. The need to familiarize these new Roman citizens with the *Di Penates* and to forge inner links to them as symbols of the new citizenship was more easily fulfilled if there was an anthropomorphic image instead of merely aniconic items such as *phalloi*, *caducei*, or dishes. Interestingly, it took less than a century to complete the development from busts on coins to fully anthropomorphic and at least life-size statues in a temple. But this process is only valid when considering the *Di Penates publici*; the personal *Di Penates* of single citizens persisted principally in their original design as relatively small, in any case portable items (*sacra*) — apparently dishes but with adopted anthropomorphic features. This is clearly stated in Cicero's descriptions of the *Di Penates* stolen by Verres.

---

62 Strobel 2011, 199–202.

63 Crawford 1974, 455/2a Antia 1; Sydenham 1952, 971: on the reverse, Hercules advancing right, holding club, trophy, and cloak; this again was surely meant to suggest associations with Caesar.

64 Crawford 1974, 458/1.

65 The separate but concerted minting of the two coins with *Di Penates* and the *palladium* gives a strong argument that these objects were different, even if closely connected to one another.

66 Braithwaite 2007, esp. 318–26: 'There seems little doubt that the face beakers are an Italian tradition, and that when they occur in the provinces in the first century, they are closely associated with Roman legionaries' (p. 325). Even though Hadrian started the process of regularly filling the legions with local people from the surroundings of the *castra* (or *hiberna*) and other provincials, Marcus Aurelius still recruited two full legions (*legio II* and *III Italica*) around AD 165 from northern Italy.

12. *DI PENATES*: FROM SMALL OBJECTS TO ANTHROPOMORPHIC GODS

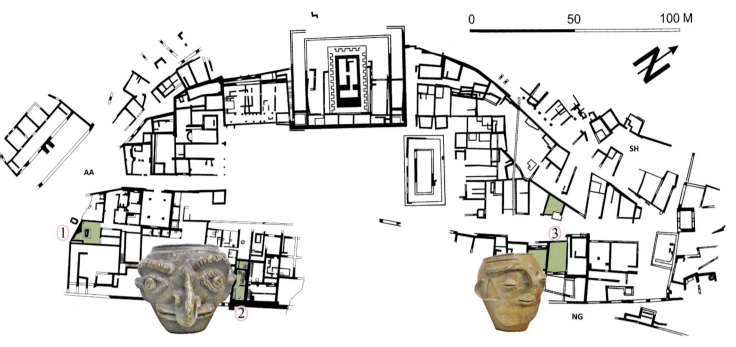

Face Beakers as sigilla in the Cult of the Di Penates

Here we might turn our attention again to the new Roman soldier-citizens from the Gallic regions. It has been proved that beakers with (partly archaic grotesque) masks came into vogue in northern Italy (formerly Cisalpine Gaul) around the mid-first century BC — that is, at precisely the time when all inhabitants there received Roman citizenship and Antius minted his denarius. Over time, these beakers were brought to many provinces, such as Spain, Britain, and the areas around the Rhine and the Danube, and they were especially frequent in military camps and settlements where veterans were resident.[67] I have earlier suggested that these face beakers (often also called mask-beakers) were used for the soldier's oath of allegiance and the mandatory libation.[68] Afterwards the soldiers kept them as a personal keepsake and probably used them for other vows or even when drinking in a symposium with their comrades.[69] This argument stands in strong opposition to the common scholarly opinion up to now, where these face beakers are often connected with Celtic traditions or at least Celtic taste, even if there are no discernible role models in pre-Roman La Tène settlements to support these assumptions.[70]

Figure 12.3. Map of the settlement on Magdalensberg (Noricum; Carinthia) with find-spots of face beakers: 1) kitchen in the high-security building; 2) *fabrica auraria imperialis*; 3) storeroom of a Roman merchant (image © Landesmuseum Kärnten and Eleni Schindler Kaudelka; reproduced with permission of Landesmuseum Kärnten and E. Schindler Kaudelka).

That these face beakers were produced and distributed professionally in larger quantities by the early first century AD in Italy and beyond is attested by the inventory of a destroyed pottery shop in the settlement at Magdalensberg in Noricum. This emporium of Roman and Italian merchants was founded around the mid-first century BC in the central area of east-alpine Noricum, and additionally became the Roman administrative centre with the seat of the *procurator Augusti regni Norici* after the occupation around 16/15 BC until the reign of Claudius.[71] From the late Augustan and Tiberian periods onwards, the city-like settlement was strongly divided into two functional areas (Fig. 12.3). The excavation area AA housed an administrative centre with an imperial *fabrica* for the production of gold ingots, situated to the west and south of a central forum. The civil production

---

67 Braithwaite 2007, 325–50 and 403.

68 Scherrer 2021, 237 and 239.

69 This conforms to Orr 1978, 1588: 'Roman household worship followed the Roman into military service.'

70 See e.g. Braithwaite 2007, 320–26 and 384. The same is to be said about the snake-vessels (see below); cf. Schmid 1991, 67–68.

71 The literature on Magdalensberg is plentiful. For an overview of the settlement, see Piccottini and Vetters 2003, esp. 127–30 (*fabrica*). For the duration of the settlement (mid-first century BC to mid-first century AD) see Ardis, Mantovani, and Schindler Kaudelka 2019, esp. 82–88 figs 5–11. For the *procurator Aug. regni Norici*, see Scherrer 2020.

Figure 12.4. Face beakers from Magdalensberg (Carinthia, Austria), Tiberian period. a) upper row: trading goods from the warehouse; b) lower row: beakers from the high-security building — the two in the centre were deposited on the hearth of the big kitchen (image © Landesmuseum Kärnten; reproduced with permission of Landesmuseum Kärnten).

and trade centre, which was under the direction of the freedmen of Italian trading houses, was located east of the forum, in excavation areas SH and NG.

In the settlement, face beakers of two different types belong to the common finds from the period of Tiberius's reign onwards. In a store's warehouse (areas SH/4, SH/5, and NG/43), which burned down in the late Tiberian period, were found thousands of imports with many pieces of so-called Italian Terra Sigillata. Among these, fragments of at least seventy face beakers were counted, six of which have been restored nearly completely so far (Fig. 12.4b).[72] Apart from this shop, no face beakers of this type have been identified in the layers of the civil town. Nevertheless, the supply can be taken as a clear sign of demand among the population.

There are also known about fifteen–twenty more face beakers in a much more elegant style with very expressive faces (Fig. 12.4a). Except for seven fragments, they come exclusively from the high-security building complex surrounding the imperial *fabrica*. Two complete mugs were found on a stove in the AA/18 central kitchen. Two beakers were detected in the gold ingot workshop AA/41 and one (or two?) in the smaller gold ingot workshop AA/41A. These precise find-spots support the hypothesis of a use exclusively among military personal (see Fig. 12.3). From the extremely fragmented beakers discovered out of the high-security building, one is likely to be a chance find from the area of the graveyard.[73]

The archaeological record provides us with the rare possibility of a detailed analysis. The supply alongside trading goods can be taken as a clear sign of demand among the local population. Among the customers, nearly all seem to have been soldiers on duty to supervise the production of the gold ingots or needed to cover their transport to Italy. In addition, the representatives of the great Aquileian and other Italian merchant houses, most of them freedmen, could have been consumers, but the lack of evidence for beakers in their lodgings does not support such considerations; we should instead view

---

[72] Schindler Kaudelka, Butti Ronchetti, and Schneider 2000; Braithwaite 2007, 192–94 nos 21–22. For the dating (local distribution in the second quarter of the first century AD), see Ardis, Mantovani, and Schindler Kaudelka 2019, esp. 88 fig. 11. I am very grateful to E. Schindler Kaudelka for providing me with much additional information on the distribution and exact find-spots of face beakers in the town, the relevant horizontal and vertical stratigraphy, and absolute dating.

[73] Unpublished journal of findings of Hedwig Kenner from 1949, nos 317 and 345 (with thanks to E. Schindler Kaudelka).

this archaeological record as a confirmation of the lack of freedmen in the epigraphical record discussed above.[74] In contrast to the dominant role of face vessels in graves in excavation reports and analytic publications,[75] the single beaker in the Magdalensberg graveyard is an exception, but their use in closed (perhaps exclusively military) living or working spaces and in particular in the large kitchen area is significant.

Face Pots with or without Additional Features

From the mid-first century AD onwards, new types of larger vessels, mainly pots of different sizes and shapes, emerge in the same provinces and areas. Some show only faces or masks, others are richly decorated with additional *phalloi* or *caducei*; they may have small censers (*turibula*) or other dishes attached;[76] and frequently snakes crawl on the outside, their heads appearing to be about to plunge into the vessel to drink or eat from it (Fig. 12.5). These snakes may have the same function as in the numerous so-called *lararia*, representing the *genius loci* or similar gods (compare the Greek *Agathos Daimon*).[77] The occurrence of snakes on these vessels symbolizing the *genius loci* is a close analogy to the paintings of the *Lares* with the *genius* snake between them that were painted in the Delian and Italian houses, beginning in the (mid-) second century BC.[78] Even if these snake-vessels have up to now been explained mostly in terms of the customs and rituals in so-called oriental cults, especially the cult of Mithras,[79] the higher prob-

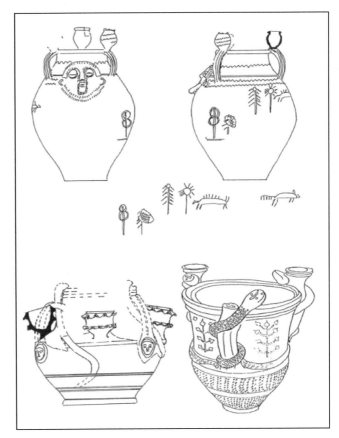

Figure 12.5. Above: face pot from a tumulus grave in Kematen/Ybbs, Noricum, with three miniature vessels attached at the upper part of the handles, and engraved animals, plants, and *caduceus* on the body (image © Austrian Academy of Sciences). Below: so-called snake-vessels. Left side: from Pocking, Raetia, with small faces at the lower part of the handles and miniature *turibula* (image © Archäologische Statssammlung München); right side: Vindonissa, Germania Superior, with tree-like plants on the body and small dishes as upper end of the handles (image © Vindonissa Museum; reproduced from Braithwaite 2007, 201 fig. G7, with permission of Austrian Academy of Sciences, Vindonissa Museum and Archäologische Staatssammlung München).

ability might be that they simply appear wherever meals are held. The original function of these snake-vessels is to be seen in the merging of the cult of the *Lares* and/or the *Di Penates* with the *genius loci* in households,[80] but later

---

74 See above with ns 39 and 40.

75 See for that below with ns 82 and 83.

76 For the use of miniature vessels in cult, see K. Rieger in this volume.

77 For the meaning of these snakes, Fröhlich 1991, 56–61. For *turibula* and snake-vessels in the compositions of so-called *lararia* in the provinces, see Kaufmann-Heinimann 1998, esp. 159–62 and 319. For snake-vessels in general: Schmid 1991. For the connection of *Zeus Ktesios* as a vessel and the *Agathos Daimon* symbolized by a snake in a fourth-century BC house in Halieis (Boeotia), see Bowes 2015, 215. In the same way the frequent occurrence of pots placed in depressions in floors in Greek houses, especially in supposed dining rooms, could be explained as emanations of *Zeus Ktesios*, instead of so-called building-sacrifices, which in fact seem not to have existed in Greek and Roman house constructions: see an overview in Scherrer (forthcoming); for newly discussed evidence from Eretria, see Gex 2019, 39–40.

78 Fröhlich 1991; Anniboletti 2011; Flower 2017.

79 A good overview of different cults in Braithwaite 2007, 481–87. The newest publication (known to me) discussing the use of these vessels in households as well as in (semi-private) sanctuaries is Berger-Pavić and Stökl 2018. But the authors also tend to connect the use of these vessels with so-called oriental cults like Mithras, Sabazios, and Jupiter Heliopolitanus, as Schmid 1991, 65–68 already did.

80 Already mentioned briefly as one possibility by Schmid 1991, 63–65 and 68: 'Wie bereits angesprochen, spielten die Schlangentöpfe der Gruppe A — vielleicht zusammen mit den Räucherkelchen — eine wichtige Rolle bei der Ausübung eines Privatkultes im familiären Rahmen; am ehesten im oder beim Lararium. Obwohl wir den Inhalt dieses Kultes und die genaue Aufgabe der Kultgefässe nicht kennen, ist eine Deutung der Schlangen als Symbol des Schutzes, als beschützender Geist des Hauses und der Familie naheliegend.'

Figure 12.6. Face pot from Bonn, found in 2018 inside a wooden barrel in a private Roman house (image © Jürgen Vogel, LVR-LandesMuseum; reproduced with permission of LVR-LandesMuseum).

they also expanded within different cultic communities, where the common meal was a decisive ritual. In fact, we find these snake-vessels in households long before Mithras appeared in the western Roman Empire.[81]

Many of these face pots, like the face beakers, have been found in military camps, in private houses, and in graves. In older archaeological reports, vessels from graves are dominant in the archaeological record because they were better preserved than in settlement excavations.[82] In new, more systematic publications, we see a stronger presence in households and private dwellings (including military barracks). The recent case study for Vindobona (Vienna) in Pannonia Superior, incorporating all fragments in the depots of the Wien Museum (Vienna, Austria), shows a distribution mainly among residential buildings and working areas but only a relatively small number in graves.[83] The relation of certain find-spots is four times as many in the *canabae* and *municipium* settlements (including private working areas) as in either the legionary living plus working areas and graves. That means that, in reality, much less than 20 per cent of face pots and beakers may have been (perhaps secondarily) used as grave goods.

Yet inside both military and apparently civilian household locations, a certain tendency can be observed for pantries and cellars (Fig. 12.6).[84] In one exceptional case in Aelium Cetium in Noricum (today St Poelten in Lower Austria), in a house that had been suddenly destroyed by fire, a face pot was found situated directly on top of the hearth, which can be compared to the two face beakers in the Magdalensberg settlement, discussed above.[85] These vessels are not to be associated with Dionysiac or oriental cults, as has often been suggested,[86] but are to be seen as emanations of the *Di Penates* being venerated at the fireplace and guarding the pantries. This usage would fit much better with the whole range of additional decorative motifs, which are attested by ancient authors as connected to the *Di Penates* (*phalloi, caducei*) or which are found in combination with face pots in household shrines (*turibula*, snake-vessels), instead of stressing the importance of the *phalloi* as Dionysiac or the *caducei* as Mercury's attributes.

The miniature vessels on top of large pots (see Fig. 12.5), symbolizing the *Di Penates*, are also easily explained. If the face pots (or in many other cases just pots without faces) were fixed in a pantry or situated at the hearth, a symbolic portion of meals or an object representing value would have been brought to them in small dishes or these miniature vessels, and the miniature vessel would have been deposited subsequently inside the pot. Such deposits have indeed frequently been found. Here, I give only one example of a face pot

---

[81] Schmid 1991, 56–61 dates the vessels' main distribution to largely between the second half of the first century and the first half of the second century AD, with even earlier examples from the first century AD and some continuing into the third century AD.

[82] Braithwaite 2007, 403, based on quite selected material — because the older publications only presented (nearly) whole vessels — states: 'The most frequently identified find spots for both face jars and face beakers are graves.'

[83] Stökl 2020 lists the following numbers in different locations: legionary fortress: five individuals; legionary brickworks: six; *canabae legionis* (settlement): thirty-two (seven more from *canabae* settlements or nearby burial grounds); *municipium* (dwelling areas): twelve; *municipium* cemeteries: ten; unknown context in the *municipium* (settlement or graves): eleven.

[84] A list is given by Braithwaite 2007, 391–92. In particular, the regional type from Gallia Belgica, with a large variety of masks, including three-heads and gods as Mercury, are regularly found in basements, see Braithwaite 2007, 429–37.

[85] Scherrer 2021, 233–34 and 241.

[86] There is a long discussion in Braithwaite 2007, 351–84 (see esp. 382–84) and 407–21. But other authors, both earlier and later than Braithwaite, are also convinced of Dionysiac rituals behind the mask-vessels, e.g. Wagner 1996; Siepen 2019.

Figure 12.7. Italian Terra Sigillata with face or mask applique (image © Eleni Schindler-Kaudelka; reproduced with permission).

from a house in Trier, half dug into the floor of the pantry cellar, in which a small cup with an *as* of Emperor Commodus (AD 183) was deposited.[87] A similar situation with a miniature vessel inside a *dolium* is described by Jacobs and Jeffrey for Roman Sagalassos in Pisidia.[88] It seems clear from these examples that the small vessels on top of face pots (Fig. 12.5) reflect these rituals of bringing goods and — at certain occasions, such as during expiating and cleansing rituals — also incense to the *Di Penates*.

Matching the described archaeological record in Trier very well are single or few coins in different types of pots in floors, as are often found during excavations in houses and have occasionally been interpreted as building sacrifices.[89] But, as the results of a comprehensive study by G. Gorini has demonstrated, these depositions are mostly closely connected to nearby household shrines or other *sacra privata*. Gorini deduced that these depots evoke the power of the household gods, especially the *Di Penates*, who were in charge of the wealth and health of the family.[90] These coins were substitutes for deposits of grain, food, or other natural materials, thus symbolizing *pecunia* at a very general level. From this perspective, the minting of denarii with *Di Penates* would make sense, especially considering the background of their protective function of the soldiers' salaries.

Unlike the face beakers, which cannot be derived from direct prototypes of Hellenistic manufactures with regard to the dominating faces or masks from a probably Etruscan tradition,[91] the face pots and their main decoration can be traced back to the second century BC with high plausibility. When Cicero mentions the vases with their figurative adornment in his speeches against Verres, we get a first hint that he is referring to the so-called Corinthian bronzes.[92] Even if none of those metal examples have survived,[93] we may compare other dishes in the Hellenistic tradition with older face pots, such as the one from Pocking in Bavaria (Fig. 12.5, lower part, left side) with small faces at the handles. Many of the bronze prototypes, used in household-cults in the early Imperial period, have such faces (or whole figurines) as appliqués at the same spot, as Kaufmann-Heinimann has convincingly shown.[94] But we can also see similar small masks or faces (Fig. 12.7) fairly frequently on so-called Italian Terra Sigillata (or Samian Ware), which was produced in the area of the Po River (Padanian Ware) from the beginning of the first to the middle of the second century AD.[95] The coincidence in time and place with the emergence of the face pots is striking. It is impossible here to discuss details of these metal and pottery productions with necessary depth, but I hope to have made clear the outline of a development in the central Hellenistic-Roman cultural area that is much more likely than an independent and sudden appearance in a Celto-Roman environment.

---

[87] Pfahl 2000, esp. 251–52; Wilburn 2019, 570–71. The ensemble (as many others in similar situations) was wrongly interpreted as a construction offering, but for the regular non-existence of those rituals in Greek and Roman cultures, see Scherrer (forthcoming).

[88] See the contribution of Jacobs in this volume, esp. Fig. 10.3.

[89] For one special example in German Fleinheim, strongly influencing the interpretation in Trier, see Pfahl 2000, 260. But see above, n. 88.

[90] Gorini 2011.

[91] Braithwaite 2007, 43–48 gives examples from south of the Po Valley in Italy and argues (pp. 360–64 and 403) for an Italian or rather Etruscan tradition. For this, see now also Martelli 2021, 93–95, 358, who lists one face beaker and two face pots from Ostia and mentions many more from the city of Rome with references.

[92] Hallett (forthcoming). — I am very thankful to Christopher Hallett for the friendly information.

[93] But a glimpse of the layout of this fine tableware can be seen in the contemporary ceramic drinking cups, richly adorned with mythological scenes, produced from the second half of the second century BC to the end of the third/beginning of the fourth century AD. They were primarily produced in Corinth and traded to Italy via the harbour of Ostia, and also distributed in Africa and other western provinces. For the dating and production centre, see Malfitana 2007, 35–46.

[94] Kaufmann-Heinimann 1998, 37–43.

[95] Schindler Kaudelka, Fastner, and Gruber 2001, esp. 51–55 for the dating. The forms (see pp. 114–18) with applied masks are predominantly plates (form Conspectus 20.4) and large dishes (form Conspectus 34).

The Development of Anthropomorphism and Size as Matters of Function

We have seen in our discussion that a significant change in the veneration and cult of the *Di Penates publici* took place from the late second century BC onwards. Together with the diffusion of the cult into first Italian and later provincial cities and military sites,[96] the beginnings of anthropomorphism can be observed. The coins from 106 and 47 BC show two busts of young males, and at some point in the first century BC (at the latest in the early Augustan Era), life- or over-life-sized statues were installed in the temple on the Velia. For this entire development, the old army gods, the *Dioscuri*, stood as sponsors. Thus, we may say that it did not take too much time for the *Di Penates publici*, once they had gained anthropomorphic features (busts), to develop into full statuary types with at least some monumentality.

In private spheres, by contrast, the magic artefacts called *Di Penates* remained as dishes or other objects (*sacra*), while faces (masks) or even full-body statuettes (if we could interpret Cicero in this manner) were only attached to adorn them.[97] In any case the items were portable and small in size, while the anthropomorphic features were even smaller. We may guess that an archaic and somewhat unusual appearance was intended to signify the *Di Penates* as a supernatural or chthonic apparition, as is shown in the face beakers of the military environments of northern Italy and the provinces. In the household, the *Di Penates* at the hearth or in storage rooms provided security against catastrophes such as fire, disease, and hostile raids. They guaranteed that the house (*domus*) and the family flourished. But it is also possible that they were used frequently as grave goods or even as guardians of the graves, especially if there were no blood-related heirs remaining.

Additional pictorial adornment on these vessels, especially *phalloi* (Fig. 12.6) and *caducei* (Fig. 12.4),[98] which were originally potentially magic items of their own (the *caduceus* may have had possible wand-like functions), accentuated the vessels' chthonic functions and guaranteed wealth, fecundity, and fertility. The frequent snakes (Fig. 12.4) on these pots or dishes and the translation of Dionysius of Halicarnassus combine the *Di Penates* with the Greek *Zeus Ktesios*.[99] But obviously the dishes themselves remained the emanation of the *Di Penates* in the private sphere, and the figurative depiction could not become independent from them. The faces facilitated the Romanization of persons, towns, and peoples who gained Roman rights. But the domestic cult was not diluted by non-Roman elements in its central character; indeed, quite the opposite: it served as a feature of 'being Roman'. The portable character of face beakers was necessary for soldiers and travellers, like merchants, to take their *Di Penates* with them, to make libations or display Roman customs to friends and comrades in symposia. Over the course of time, larger and more elaborately decorated pots at hearths inside houses showed familiarity with Roman traditions, but the aspect of portability was retained. Partly this might have been necessary because in more humble houses the *Di Penates* had to be carried from the kitchen hearth to the dining room in the case of fine dinners with honoured guests. In any case, in private environments, the *Di Penates* could not develop into full anthropomorphic images and certainly not into large statues, and not even into unaffiliated small statuettes like the *Lares* or the diverse *genii*, as the form of a vessel was part of the nature of the *Di Penates*.

Besides practical reasons, such as portability, there is also a systematic question, as presented by other papers in this symposium.[100] Private religion may connect personal relations and resonant feelings to these small artefacts, especially when eating and drinking wine with good friends;[101] while public cult and the demand for

---

[96] Even though inscriptions mentioning the *Di Penates* outside Italy are scarce (and some belong to Roman officers), they are found in most regions of the empire: Eburacum (York) in Britannia: *CIL* VII 237 = *RIB* I 649; Mogontiacum (Mainz) in Germania sup.: *CIL* XIII 6709; unknown site in Gallia Narbonensis: *CIL* XII 5413; Octodurus (Martigny) in Alpes Poeninae: *AE* 1988, 853 = *AE* 1993, 1097; Apulum (Alba Iulia) in Dacia: *IDR* III 5.1, 202 and 299; Teos (Seferihisar) in Ionia: *CIL* III 423; Cillium (Kaasserine) in Africa proc.: *CIL* VIII 212 = 11300b. Additionally, for Spain (especially Baetica but also more generally), see the many fragments of municipal laws, which surely also played an important role in the distribution of the knowledge and cult of the *Di Penates*.

[97] See above, with ns 36–48.

[98] For an overview of *phalloi* as talismans in and outside houses or even in city walls, see Fehling 1998. It seems that two — originally independent — magic arrangements were combined, at least before the later first century AD, as Plin., *HN* XXVIII.39 proves (see above with n. 55).

[99] Dion. Hal., *Ant. Rom.* 1.67.3.

[100] See the contributions of e.g. A.-K. Rieger and E. Begemann in this volume.

[101] In the terms of Rosa 2016, all three axes of resonance could easily emerge here: vertical (to the gods, the *Di Penates*), horizontal (to the guests, friends, other Roman citizens), and diagonal (to the fine and tableware representing the *Di Penates*, of which the owners were very proud).

prestige leads to full anthropomorphism and (at least some) monumentality. The agency (the German expression *Wirkungsmacht* is even more applicable) of these same gods is presented in differentiated manners in different spheres of society, the measurable material size of the god(s) being adequate to the particular situation or process.[102] A single person or a family requires only a small god with limited power for his or her concerns, and may prefer to trust the god instead of fear him; on the other hand, a mighty state needs monumental gods to convince its own people as well as the outer world of its power and authority.

Conclusions

G. Braithwaite, in her important standard book on Roman pottery with faces, has convincingly shown that face beakers occurred at the earliest in the late second century BC and had a broader distribution in central and northern Italy from the mid-first century AD onwards, arriving in military garrisons in the provinces in the early first century AD at the latest.[103] The military connection — in the light of the new interpretation of these beakers as emanations of the *Di Penates* — is strengthened by coins from 106 and 47 BC showing busts of two male youths and legends stating D P P for *Di Penates publici* or *Di Penates*. These face beakers were used by legionaries with relatively new Roman citizenship as individual possessions, most probably for the oath of allegiance and the combined libation — and then later throughout their lifetime. The cult of the *Di Penates* as a privilege exclusively for free-born Romans among these legionary soldiers is first encouraged by those denarii as a top-down measure, while the use of the beakers was their individual expression of close ties to the *res publica Romana*. Even if the beakers were a new invention or reactivation of an Etruscan tradition for these military personnel, they seem to have been strongly influenced by the already existing dishes with figural adornment in Roman households, as Cicero's predications in the speeches about Verres prove. The invention of the 'Corinthian bronzes' in the later second century BC and their mass imitation in fine-ware pottery made this development possible. Thus, the later occurrence of larger face pots (mid-first century AD) for use in military communities (*contubernia*) and households of the veterans is a logical consequence, showing their exclusive rank as Roman citizens and even more as *honestiores* among the provincial population.

The results of a survey of the period from the second century BC to the Augustan Era in relevant contemporary literature, in combination with the interpretation of face beakers and face pots, clearly show that the cult of the *Di Penates* was exclusively for (most likely only freeborn) Roman citizens and thus differs from the *Lares*, who were also regularly venerated by slaves and freedmen. The *Di Penates* were the tutelary gods of the *pater familias* and his blood relatives, and they protected this group (*domus*) and their possessions, like *Zeus Ktesios* in Greece, while the *Lares* (like the Greek *Zeus Herkeios*) guarded the estate and the house(s) built on it. From the late second century BC onwards, the *Di Penates* became important markers of identity for new Roman citizens in Cisalpine Gaul and then in the provinces, where legionaries and former servants of auxiliary units with *honesta missio* and their descendants formed a significant if not the main group of Roman citizens. The (partial) loss of civil rights, for example by exile, caused the separation of the involved person from his *Di Penates* as a sign of no longer being a member of the Roman community. On the other hand, if a family died out due to lack of sons, the last *pater familias* could take his *Di Penates* with him into his tomb.

While the *Di Penates publici* could develop from mere objects via busts on coins (106 and 47 BC) to full anthropomorphic statues in a temple on the Velia (by the first half of the reign of Augustus), the private or personal *Di Penates* of Roman citizens remained in the form of dishes, frequently — but of course not as a rule — adorned with faces and, in far fewer cases, with additional representations of other items which were connected to these gods, such as *phalloi* and rarely *caducei*. These vessels were carried around in or outside the house, on journeys and military operations. Thus, they regularly stayed small in size; only when they were installed in pantries or used exclusively at the hearth did they sometimes attain a larger size. Nevertheless, their material size was not indicative of their importance, but quite the contrary: their small scale was necessary for their portability — a necessity to fulfil their function.

---

[102] For agency, e.g. Rüpke 2016a, 23–24; Klöckner 2019, 82.

[103] For this and the following conclusions, see Braithwaite 2007, esp. 315–24.

Works Cited

Anniboletti, L. 2011. '*Compita vicinalia* di Pompei e Delo: testimonianze archeologiche del culto domestico di theoi propylaioi', in M. Bassani and F. Ghedini (eds), *Religionem significare: aspetti strutturali, iconografici e materiali di Sacra Privata; atti dell'Incontro di Studi (Padova, 8–9 giugno 2009)*, Antenor: Quaderni, 19 (Rome: Quasar), pp. 57–78.

Ardis, C., V. Mantovani, and E. Schindler Kaudelka. 2019. 'Trent'anni di "Quaderni": riflessioni attorno alcune forme in ceramica grezza e depurata', *Quaderni di archeologia friulani*, 29.1: 79–115.

Berger-Pavić, I. and S. Stökl. 2018. 'Neue Schlangengefäße aus der Zivilstadt Carnuntum. Ein Beitrag zur Problematik der Schlangengefäße und ihrer Verwendung im Kult/Hauskult', in A. Pülz (ed.), *Carnuntum Jahrbuch 2017* (Vienna: Verlag der Österreichischen Akademie der Wissenschaften), pp. 97–125.

Bodel, J. 2008. 'Cicero's Minerva, Penates, and the Mother of the Lares: An Outline of Roman Domestic Religion', in J. Bodel and S. Olyan (eds), *Household and Family Religion in Antiquity* (Malden: Wiley-Blackwell), pp. 248–75.

Bowes, K. 2015. 'At Home', in R. Raja and J. Rüpke (eds), *A Companion to the Archaeology of Religion in the Ancient World* (Chichester: Wiley-Blackwell), pp. 209–19.

Braithwaite, G. 2007. *Faces from the Past: A Study of Roman Face Pots from Italy and the Western Provinces of the Roman Empire*, British Archaeological Reports, International Series, 1651 (Oxford: Archaeopress).

Castagnoli, F. 1946. 'Il Tempio dei Penati e la Velia', *Rivista di filologia*, 74: 157–66.

Chaniotis, A. 2011. 'Emotional Communities through Ritual', in A. Chaniotis (ed.), *Ritual Dynamics in the Ancient Mediterranean: Agency, Emotion, Gender, Representation* (Stuttgart: Steiner), pp. 263–90.

Crawford, M. H. 1974. *Roman Republican Coinage*, II (Cambridge: Cambridge University Press).

——. 2016. 'Tabula Irnitana', *Oxford Classical Dictionary* <https://doi.org/10.1093/acrefore/9780199381135.013.6197>.

Dubourdieu, A. 1989. *Les origines et le développement du culte des Pénates à Rome*, Collection de l'École française de Rome, 118 (Rome: École française de Rome).

Dubordieu, A. 2012. 'Les cultes domestiques dans le monde romain', *Thesaurus cultus et rituum antiquorum*, VIII (Los Angeles: Getty Publications), pp. 32–43.

Fehling, D. 1998. 'Phallische Demonstration', in A. K. Siems (ed.), *Sexualität und Erotik in der Antike*, Wege der Forschung, 605 (Darmstadt: Wissenschaftliche Buchgesellschaft), pp. 282–323.

Flower, H. 2017. *Dancing Lares and the Serpent in the Garden: Religion at the Roman Street Corner* (Princeton: Princeton University Press).

Fröhlich, T. 1991. *Lararien- und Fassadenbilder in den Vesuvstädten: Untersuchungen zur 'volkstümlichen' pompejanischen Malerei*, Mitteilungen des Deutschen Archaeologischen Instituts, Römische Abteilung, 32 (Mainz: Von Zabern).

Gex, K. 2019. *Im Zentrum der Stadt: Klassische und hellenistische Strukturen und Funde aus dem Grundstück Bouratza (Ausgrabung 1979–1981)*, Eretria, 23 (Gollion: Infolio).

Giacobello, F. 2008. *Larari Pomepeiani: iconografia e culto dei Lari in ambito domestico* (Milan: LED).

Gorini, G. 2011. 'L'offerta della moneta agli dei: forma di religiosità privata nel mondo antico', in M. Bassani and F. Ghedini (eds), *Religionem significare: aspetti strutturali, iconografici e materiali di Sacra Privata; atti dell'Incontro di Studi (Padova, 8–9 giugno 2009)*, Antenor: Quaderni, 19 (Rome: Quasar), pp. 245–56.

Hagen, H. (ed.). 1902. *Servii Grammatici qui feruntur in Vergilii carmina commentarii*, III.2 (Cambridge: Cambridge University Press).

Hallett, C. (forthcoming). 'Ancient Bronzes as Art Objects: Roman Collectors and "Corinthian Bronzes"'.

Herrmann, P. 1968. *Der römische Kaisereid* (Göttingen: Vandenhoeck et Ruprecht).

Kaufmann-Heinimann, A. 1998. *Götter und Lararien aus Augusta Raurica: Herstellung, Fundzusammenhänge und sakrale Funktion figürlicher Bronzen in einer römischen Stadt*, Forschungen in Augst, 26 (Augst: Römerstadt Augusta Raurica).

Klöckner, G. 2019. 'Wie wird ein Bild zum Gott? Zur Medialität kaiserzeitlicher Götterbilder', in T. Schattner and A. Guerra (eds), *Das Antlitz der Götter: Götterbilder im Westen des Römischen Reiches = O rosto das divindades: Imagens de divindades no Ocidente do Império romano* (Wiesbaden: Reichert), pp. 79–88.

Kropp, A. 2008. *Defixiones: Ein aktuelles Corpus lateinischer Fluchtafeln* (Speyer: Brodersen).

Linderski, J. 2000. 'Penates (Di Penates)', in H. Canick and H. Schneider (eds), *Der Neue Pauly: Enzyklopädie der Antike*, IX (Stuttgart: Metzler), pp. 514–15.

Malfitana, D. 2007. *La Ceramica 'Corinzia' decorata a matrice: tipologia, cronologia ed iconografia di una produzione ceramica Greca di età imperiale*, Rei Cretariae Romanae Fautores acta Supplement, 10 (Bonn: Rei Cretariae Romanae Fautores).

Martelli, E. 2021. *Terracottas from Roman Ostia: Snapshots of Everyday Life; Their Production and Use in Domestic, Ritual and Funerary Contexts*, Monographies instrumentum, 72 (Drémil-Lafage: Mergoil).

McDonough, C. M. 2012. 'Penates, di penates', in R. S. Bagnall and others (eds), *The Encyclopedia of Ancient History* <https://doi.org/10.1002/9781444338386.wbeah17329>.

Mommsen, T. 2009. *Römisches Staatsrecht*, online repr. of 1888 edn (Cambridge: Cambridge University Press).

Orr, D. G. 1978. 'Roman Domestic Religion. The Evidence of the Household Shrines', *Aufsteig und Niedergang der römischen Welt*, II, 16.2: 1557–91.

Oyen, A van. 2021. *Socio-economics of Storage: Agriculture, Trade and Family* (Cambridge: Cambridge University Press).

Parker, R. 2015. 'Public and Private', in R. Raja and J. Rüpke (eds), *A Companion to the Archaeology of Religion in the Ancient World* (Chichester: Wiley-Blackwell), pp. 71–80.

Piccottini, G. and H. Vetters. 2003. *Führer durch die Ausgrabungen auf dem Magdalensberg*, extended from 1978 edn (Klagenfurt: Landesmuseums für Kärnten).

Pfahl, S. F. 2000. 'Ein römisches "pars pro toto"-Doppelbauopfer mit Gesichtstopf der Zeit um 200 n. Chr. aus dem Keller eines Wohnhauses des Augusta Treverorum', *Trierer Zeitschrift*, 63: 245–61.

Pollard, N. and J. Berry. 2012. *The Complete Roman Legions* (New York: Thames & Hudson).

Quaranta, P. 2016. 'A Troia a Lavinio. Il mito di enea nell'arte privata Romana di età imperiale. Schemi, modelli e significati' (unpublished doctoral thesis, University of Heidelberg).

Rehak, P. 2001. 'Aeneas or Numa? Rethinking the Meaning of the Ara Pacis Augustae', *The Art Bulletin*, 83.2: 190–208.

Rosa, H. 2016. 'Was heißt Resonanz? Annäherungen an einen Modus der Weltbeziehung', in L. Scheuermann and W. Spickermann (eds), *Religiöse Praktiken in der Antike: Individuum, Gesellschaft, Weltbeziehung*, Keryx, 4 (Graz: UPG Unipress), pp. 13–19.

Roth, D. 2018. *'Revocatio in servitutem': Die rechtliche Beständigkeit der Freilassung vor dem Hintergrund der 'actio ingrati'*, Europäische Hochschulschriften Rechtswissenschaft, 6025 (Berlin: Lang).

Rüpke, J. 2016a. 'Ein neuer Religionsbegriff für die Analyse antiker Religion unter der Perspektive von Weltbeziehungen', in L. Scheuermann and W. Spickermann (eds), *Religiöse Praktiken in der Antike: Individuum, Gesellschaft, Weltbeziehung*, Keryx, 4 (Graz: UPG Unipress), pp. 21–35.

——. 2016b. *Pantheon: Geschichte der antiken Religionen* (Munich: Beck).

Scherrer, P. 2020. 'Patrimonium oder Procurator Regni Norici: Anmerkungen zur Verwaltungsreform der Provinz Noricum unter Marcus Aurelius', in G. E. Thüry (ed.), *Domi Militiaeque: Militär- und andere Altertümer; Festschrift für Hannsjörg Ubl zum 85. Geburtstag* (Oxford: Archaeopress), pp. 125–37.

——. 2021. 'Di Penates – Wie die römischen Hausgötter ein Gesicht erhielten', in R. Ployer and D. Svoboda-Baas (eds), *Magnis itineribus: Festschrift für Verena Gassner zum 65. Geburtstag* (Vienna: Phoibos), pp. 233–46.

——. (forthcoming). 'Hausopfer. Bauriterale und Bauopfer', in J. Bremmer, G. Petridou, and J. Rüpke (eds), *Religion in Context: Graeco-Roman Religious Practises in their Socio-cultural Milieu*, Der Neue Pauly Suppl. (Heidelberg: Metzler).

Schindler Kaudelka, E., U. Fastner, and M. Gruber. 2001. *Italische Terra Sigillata mit Appliken in Noricum*, Archäologische Forschungen, 6 (Vienna: Verlag der Österreichischen Akademie der Wissenschaften).

Schindler Kaudelka, E., F. Butti Ronchetti, and G. Schneider. 2000. 'Gesichtsbecher vom Magdalensberg im Umfeld der Funde aus Oberitalien', *Rei Cretariae Romanae Fautores acta*, 36: 271–77.

Schörner, G. 2016. 'Domestic Cults in the Roman House: Can Archaeology Detect Individuality? The Case of the Casa dei Vettii', in L. Scheuermann and W. Spickermann (eds), *Religiöse Praktiken in der Antike: Individuum, Gesellschaft, Weltbeziehung*, Keryx, 4 (Graz: UPG Unipress), pp. 111–20.

Schmid, D. 1991. *Die römischen Schlangentöpfe aus Augst und Kaiseraugst*, Forschungen in Augst, 11 (Augst: Romermuseum Augst).

Siepen, M. 2019. 'Römische Gesichtsgefäße aus den Gräberfeldern von Krefeld-Gellep und ein eventueller Bezug zum Dionysoskult', in J. Meurers-Balke, T. Zerl, and R. Gerlach (eds), *Auf dem Holzweg... Eine Würdigung für Ursula Tegtmeier*, Archäologische Berichte, 30 (Heidelberg: Propylaeum), pp. 245–50.

Stökl, S. 2020. '"Die Lust an absonderlichen Darstellungen" – Gesichtsgefäße aus Vindobona', *Fundort Wien*, 23: 74–107.

Strobel, K. 2011. 'Zwischen Italien und den "Barbaren": Das Werden neuer politischer und administrativer Grenzen in Caesarisch-Augusteischer Zeit', in T. Kaizer and O. Hekster (eds), *Frontiers in the Roman World: Proceedings of the Ninth Workshop of the International Network Impact of Empire (Durham, 16–19 April 2009)*, Impact of Empire, 13 (Leiden: Brill), pp. 199–232.

Sydenham, E. A. 1952. *The Coinage of the Roman Republic* (London: Spink).

Wagner, P. 1996. 'Silenus ex sepulcro. Eine Urne aus dem römischen Brandgräberfeld von Thorr', *Archäologie im Rheinland*, 1995: 72–74.

Wilburn, A. T. 2019. 'Building Ritual Agency: Foundations, Floors, Doors, and Walls', in D. Frankfurter (ed.), *Guide to the Study of Ancient Magic*, Religions in the Graeco-Roman World, 189 (Leiden: Brill), pp. 555–602 <https://doi.org/10.1163/9789004390751_021>.

Wissowa, G. 1904. 'Die Überlieferung über die römischen Penaten', in G. Wissowa (ed.), *Gesammelte Abhandlungen zur römischen Religions- und Stadtgeschichte* (Munich: Beck), pp. 95–121.

THE FRAGMENTED AND
THE AUGMENTED BODY

13. The Eyes Have It: Materialities, Monumentality, and Meanings in Eye-Shaped Modern Greek *tamata* and Ancient Greek *anathemata*

Georgia Petridou

Any elementary analysis of the ways in which human beings come to relate to the world, experience and perceive it, act and orient themselves within it, cannot but begin with the body.[1]

This paper looks afresh at the socio-religious practice of gift-giving to the divine in the critical context of illness. In terms of methodology, this study draws inspiration from Rosa's sociological theory of resonant self–world relations and its strong emphasis on bodily relationships,[2] as well as on recent studies on embodiment and visual culture,[3] lived religion,[4] and monumentality.[5] It also brings together my earlier research interest in the concept of the 'lived body',[6] as well as current research work on bodily fragmentation, fusion, and trans-formation, pursued in the context of the 'De/Constructing the Body: Ancient and Modern Dynamics' project.[7]

More specifically, this paper offers a comparative study between modern Greek anatomical *tamata* ('dedications' in Modern Greek) and ancient Greek *anathemata* ('dedications' in ancient Greek) in terms of their magnitude, materiality, and the meanings ascribed to them by their dedicants. The comparison reveals a paradoxical coexistence of processes of miniaturization and magnification in both Antiquity and modernity, which is central to the meaning-making mechanisms of these objects. Despite both types of objects being effectively miniaturized versions of human bodies or body parts (internal and external alike), they exercise monumental power in the eyes of both the dedicants and the deities to whom they are offered. This last premise is fleshed out further by a close comparison between modern and ancient eye-shaped *tamata* dedicated to St Paraskevi (Fig. 13.4) and the analogously shaped ancient Greek *anathemata* dedicated to Demeter and Kore (Figs 13.5 and 13.6).

The first part of the paper discusses ancient and modern anatomical votives as objects that are arresting, diachronically resonant, and highly invested with agency, albeit an agency that is not always easy to conceptualize. These objects have a monumental impact on the representation and signification of bodily relational dynamics despite their modest dimensions — few are more than 20–30 cm in length and most fit comfortably in the palm of one's hand. In the second part, I offer some reflections on the role and typology of modern Greek *tamata* in the Christian healing cult of St Paraskevi, along with a brief survey of other female Christian saints who both preside over eyesight and are closely connected to light. The third part of the paper looks at ancient Greek eye-shaped votives (*anathemata*) that were found in temples dedicated to Demeter and Kore. Extra emphasis is given to the problem of reconciling Demeter's 'double' identity as a healer of ophthalmological illness and as a culture-bringing goddess who revealed the gifts of agri-

---

* I would like to thank wholeheartedly the co-organizers of the conference, in which a first draft of this paper was presented, as well as all fellow speakers for all their useful feedback. Special thanks to Lizzie Begemann for all her insightful comments on the paper, to Paul Scade for his expert help in the language department, and to Taylor Grace FitzGerald for her eagle-eyed editing and valuable corrections. All translations, unless otherwise noted, are my own.

[1] Rosa 2019, 47.

[2] See the epigraph of this paper.

[3] Morgan 2012.

[4] Albrecht and others 2018; McGuire 1990; 2008; Osborne 2014; Raja and Rüpke 2015; Rüpke 2018; Gasparini and others 2020; Rüpke and Woolf 2021.

[5] Osborne 2014.

[6] The 'lived body' is a line of inquiry that resulted from research conducted within the framework of the 'Lived Ancient Religion' (LAR) project, an ERC project led jointly by Jörg Rüpke and Rubina Raja. More on the concept of 'lived body' in Petridou 2020.

[7] The project (2019–2021) was jointly led by Esther Eidinow and myself, and it was generously funded by the Wellcome Trust: <https://wellcome.org/grant-funding/people-and-projects/grants-awarded/deconstructing-body-ancient-and-modern-dynamics> [accessed 12 February 2023].

culture to humanity. This apparent tension, I suggest, can be resolved easily if viewed through the prism of the goddess's principle 'mode of action', i.e., that of initiation, the revealing of the hidden and the leading into the light.[8]

In addition to the similarities revealed by this comparative approach, there are also very important differences between ancient and modern eye-shaped votives. While in the modern Greek Orthodox tradition eye-shaped votives explicitly allude to St Paraskevi's martyrdom and her main sphere of divine expertise as the guardian against ophthalmological illness, the ancient Greek eye-shaped dedications to Demeter and Kore attest to a wholly different conceptualization of illness and healing, which are both seen through the prism of initiation into the *mysteria*, the initiatory rites held in honour of the two goddesses. Thus, comparing these seemingly incomparable eye-shaped dedications, as the final part of the paper argues, allows for an *ad fontes* analysis of the *lived experience of ophthalmological illness*, in particular, and the culture-specific framings of both health and illness, more generally.

Ancient and Modern Anatomical Votives: Materials, Methods of Production, Magnitude, and Meanings

Most of the modern anatomical Greek *tamata* are small objects that depict miniaturized forms of female or male human bodies or body parts (external and internal alike). They are typically either cut out in the shape of the body part they portray (especially external body parts) or made out of thin, rectangular plaques of metal — such as silver, gold, bronze, copper, iron, tin, and alloys (Fig. 13.1) — which are incised, pressed, or cast in moulds. They often come with a suspension hole at the top, by which they can be pinned onto or hung from holy icons depicting Greek Orthodox saints. Whether made from precious metals or cheaper materials, the modern Greek anatomical dedications have a number of things in common: they are light-reflecting, eye-catching miniaturized representations of the human body or of its constituent parts. The arresting quality of these objects remains undimmed by time, despite time endowing silver or silver-plated examples with a yellowish tint and those made of alloys with a brown-red colour, both results of the oxidation of the metal.

According to Sophia Handaka, who has studied and published extensively on the Mikes Paidousis collection of Greek Orthodox *tamata* (one of the richest collections of modern Greek votives, currently housed in the Benaki Museum in Athens):

> [T]he word τάμα refers to an offering, usually directed to a particular saint, in reciprocation for the granting of a favour. It is a promise in the form of a prospective offer, entered into when a person or his close kin are in danger or in sickness, or an act of thanksgiving afterwards. The word τάμα (plural τάματα) signifies both the act of offering and the object itself, the votive offering. It derives from the verb τάσσω (now τάζω), which means 'to promise to give to the divine', 'to offer', 'to keep or execute', 'to provide something as an offering' [...] In different ways, the semantics of the word contain the idea of a response to a vow.[9]

The Mikes Paidousis collection of *tamata* comprises 1174 votive objects from all over modern Greece. In terms of materiality and production methods, Handaka has identified six categories of *tamata*: those that are dotted (στικτά), incised (εγχάρακτα), chased (σκαλιστά), embossed (εμπίεστα), pressed (πρεσαριστά), and cast in moulds (χυτά).[10] A little more than half of these are miniature representations of humans and objects related to everyday life, while 522 depict internal and external body parts, including several that depict single eyes or pairs of eyes.

Modern Greek anatomical votives closely resemble the ancient Greek anatomical votives in terms of methods of production, materiality, and, to an extent, cultural meanings.[11] In short, ancient Greek anatomical votives are dedications, primarily in the shape of external body parts (ears, eyes, genitals, breasts, etc.), which were variously dedicated prior to the healing act or afterwards, either as requests for a cure or as thanksgiving offerings.[12] Therefore, anatomical votive offerings become in turn the material evidence for, if not the act of healing itself, then certainly the worshippers' steadfast expectation of it.

---

[8] 'Mode of action' is, of course, a concept originally developed G. Dumézil but popularized by two eminent figures of the l'École de Paris, M. Detienne and J.-P. Vernant, in their celebrated *Les ruses de l'intelligence: la Mètis des Grecs*, published in 1974.

[9] Handaka 2018, 148. Sophia Handaka was the curator of the 2006 exhibition of these objects at the Benaki Museum and the editor of the resulting bilingual publication *Λατρείας Τάματα/Tokens of Worship*.

[10] Handaka 2018, 148.

[11] See Petridou 2017.

[12] Forsén 1996; De Cazanove 2009; Dasen 2013; Schörner 2015; Draycott and Graham 2017; Hughes 2008; 2017a; 2017b.

Figure 13.1. Modern Greek *tamata* from the author's collection. Image: author.

More importantly, anatomical votives, like other votives, reveal a great deal about the socio-cultural norms of their production, the artists/artisans, and the dedicants and their hopes and expectations. Anatomical votives (modern and ancient alike) are indispensable in the study of the history of religions and the socio-cultural history of medicine. Studying ancient and modern eye-shaped votives in particular, as this study argues, offers a unique insight into the individual's lived experience of ophthalmological illness and healing. Nonetheless, one needs to weigh individuality (individual suffering and individual needs for expression and communication with the divine) carefully against the overall formulaic features and the mass production of these anatomical votives. We can imagine, for example, that the majority of the votive dedications excavated in ancient sanctuaries were produced *en masse* by artisans in workshops very like the modern one owned by Yiannis and Dimitris Yiagtzis shown in Figure 13.2.

The Yiagtzis workshop, which is located in Pangrati, a neighbourhood in the centre of Athens, is one of the very few left in modern Greece in which artisans (τεχνίται) engage in the ancient art of making *tamata*. Yiannis and Dimitris Yiagtzis, father and son, continue a family trade that stretches back more than a hundred years. The modern anatomical votives they craft are usually produced using moulds or are carved on precious or semi-precious materials to meet the more individualized needs of the customers.

Figure 13.2. Top: Yiannis and Dimitris Yiagtzis in their workshop in Athens; bottom: Yiannis Yiagtzis polishes a modern Greek eye-shaped *tama* from the Yiagtzis workshop. Image: <https://www.jewelpedia.com/news-39-2313-ta-tamata-kai-oi-mastoroi.html> [accessed 12 February 2023].

The *tamata* produced by the Yiagtzis workshop, just like other modern Greek examples, are small, handheld objects, which nevertheless have a monumental impact in the eyes of their dedicants. The paradoxical coexistence of modest dimensions and monumental impact in meaning-making processes is not really difficult to grasp, especially if we are willing to redefine the concept of monumentality and disassociate it from measurable size. Osborne quotes an extract from the Sotheby's pre-auction description of the highly compact Guennol Lioness,[13] which describes the item as tiny in proportions and yet monumental in terms of impact on the beholder's visual field, and poses the all-important question of whether monumentality is indeed a correlative to size.[14]

---

13 The minute Guennol Lioness is a proto-Elamite statue that depicts a hybrid figure, half-human and half-lion, dates to *c.* 3000 BC, and is only about 8.25 cm in height.

14 Osborne 2014, 2–3.

Osborne concludes that this is not the case and proposes a much more fruitful definition of monumentality as 'an ongoing, constantly renegotiated relationship between thing and person, between the monument(s) and the person(s) experiencing the monument'. In the manner of the Guennol Lioness, the modern Greek *tamata* themselves become monuments (from the Latin verb *monēre*, 'to remind') of divine providence (πρόνοια in Modern Greek)[15] in moments of health crisis despite their small size — or perhaps precisely because of it.

The handheld *tamata* are, in fact, a *sine qua non* in the whole process of health crisis management via magico-religious means. The affected body or body part is typically miniaturized and artistically portrayed on a thin and more or less expensive metal plaque. The very act of conceptual abstraction and the often over-schematic representation of the ailing body and its constituent parts restore some degree of control and cohesiveness — two qualities that were already synonymous with healthy and fully functional bodies in the mind of the dedicant, as attested in classical medical and philosophical discourse.[16] What previously seemed to be ever-changing and unconstrained now, through the process of schematic depiction and representation, can be stabilized and made to fit within the palm of one's hand. What was previously mobile, and the cause of immeasurable pain now becomes immobile, measurable, and, above all, manageable, at least in the etymological sense of the word (from the Latin *manus*, 'hand', which is in turn derived from the PIE root *man- (2) 'hand'). However, it is only the socio-religious act of the sacred dedication (τάζω in Modern Greek) of these anatomical votives to the modern Greek saints who preside over various kinds of somatic and mental illness that activates their potential and ascribes them with concrete cultural meanings, transforming them from generic miniaturized representations of ailing bodies and body parts into individualized monuments of mortal–immortal communication and sacred healing.

Regardless of their materials, magnitude, and methods of production, modern Greek τάματα speak volumes about the pain and disease that fragment the human body. They also reveal much about the unwavering expectation of their dedicants for divine intervention and assistance in the context of health crisis. In a similar vein, if we are to believe Aelius Aristides, the famous second-century AD orator and frequent incubant at the Pergamene Asclepieion, ancient Greek anatomical *anathemata* encapsulate stories of natural bodily fragmentation and hopes for the fusion of the fragmented body parts at the instigation of the divine healer, who is portrayed here as a sort of divine craftsman whose help is required for the reinstatement of bodily health and wholeness:

ἀλλὰ καὶ μέλη τοῦ σώματος αἰτιῶνταί τινες, καὶ ἄνδρες λέγω καὶ γυναῖκες, προνοίᾳ τοῦ θεοῦ γενέσθαι σφίσι, τῶν παρὰ τῆς φύσεως διαφθαρέντων. καὶ καταλέγουσιν ἄλλος ἄλλο τι, οἱ μὲν ἀπὸ στόματος οὑτωσὶ φράζοντες, οἱ δὲ ἐν τοῖς ἀναθήμασιν ἐξηγούμενοι. ἡμῖν τοίνυν οὐχὶ μέρος τοῦ σώματος, ἀλλ' ἅπαν τὸ σῶμα συνθείς τε καὶ συμπήξας αὐτὸς ἔδωκε δωρεάν, ὥσπερ Προμηθεὺς τἀρχαῖα λέγεται συμπλάσαι τὸν ἄνθρωπον.

(But some, I mean both men and women, even attribute to the providence of the god the existence of parts of their body, when their natural bodily parts have been destroyed; others list other things, some in oral accounts, some in declarations of their votive offerings. For us it is not only a part of the body, but it is the whole body which he has composed and put together and given as a gift, just as Prometheus of old is said to have fashioned man.)[17]

The next two sections of this paper examine anatomical votives that relate to ophthalmological illness in Greece across the centuries. Comparing the seemingly disparate but structurally comparable eye-shaped modern Greek Orthodox *tamata* with eye-shaped ancient Greek *anathemata* reveals much about the prevalence and lived experience of ophthalmological illness in both Antiquity and modernity. Above all, this process of comparing the seemingly incomparable anatomical votives of the past and the present can help us to recover, at least to an extent, cultural components of the very act of sacred dedication that might otherwise have remained unfathomable.

St Paraskevi and Ophthalmological Illness in Modern Greece

Let us take a modern example of eye-illness related dedication that is very close to my heart: my brother, Yiorgos Paraskevas Petrides, was born with a fairly rare birth defect in his left eye, known as a *unilateral coloboma iridis*.[18] Coloboma (which literally means 'defect' in ancient Greek) is a congenital defect of the iris, the clinical picture of which often includes a longer pupil with the iris

---

15 The same term is used to refer to the divine providence of Asclepius, cf. Aristid., *Or.* 42.7 below.

16 Betegh 2020.

17 Aristid., *Or.* 42.7, trans. Behr 1968.

18 Coloboma iridis occurs in about 1 in 10,000 births.

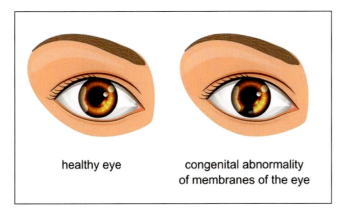

Figure 13.3. Coloboma (lit. meaning 'defect' in Greek) is a congenital defect of the iris, which usually means that the pupil is longer than it should be, occasionally acquiring a keyhole-like shape. Source: Shutterstock.

acquiring a keyhole-like shape (Fig. 13.3). The choroid fissure normally closes during the seventh week of the embryo's development, and failure of closure results in the formation of this distinctive cleft in the iris, which is known as *coloboma iridis*. The visual acuity, reading and navigational vision of infants born with coloboma iridis depend on many variants, but it is widely accepted that children affected with iris coloboma only (coloboma can also be accompanied by microphthalmos with cyst or microcornea) will probably have fairly good vision. Iris coloboma is often accompanied by light sensitivity (photophobia), however, which in turn can cause discomfort and affect the quality of vision.[19]

This sort of medical information may or may not have been conveyed to my mother, who, in a fit of panic about her newborn being rushed into intensive care, dedicated two large white candles (λαμπάδες), as well as her own infant son, to St Paraskevi. She named her baby after the saint (Paraskevas is the female form of Paraskevi) and vowed to fast every Friday (Παρασκευή in Greek), the day of the week that bears Paraskevi's name, for the rest of her life.[20] To this day, she has kept her promise.[21]

St Paraskevi, who is usually depicted as holding a pair of eyes or her own decapitated head, presides over short-term and long-term ophthalmological illness in the Greek Orthodox Church precisely because her martyrdom was related to eyesight impediment and blindness. St Paraskevi was, according to the Greek Synaxarion, born in Rome in *c.* AD 117 to Greek Christian parents named Agathon and Politeia. During the reign of the Antonines, she was persecuted for her Christian faith and was ordered to worship the idols. She refused to do so, quoting verses from Jeremiah: 'Let the gods who have not made heaven and earth be banished from the earth'.[22] The emperor ordered her imprisonment and eventually her decapitation in AD 140. The Russian Orthodox Synaxarion lays greater emphasis on her martyrdom and an extensive list of cruelties she endured after her imprisonment and trial by Antoninus Pius (AD 138–161), but the emphasis on her close links with ophthalmological illness and blindness is still discernible: apparently after enduring torture by beasts, she was forced to wear a burning helmet and was thrown into a cauldron of boiling oil and pitch. When Antoninus saw that Paraskevi remained unscathed, he accused her of using magic, and in return she flicked a bit of the boiling mixture onto his face. The emperor was immediately blinded but subsequently cured by Paraskevi.

There are several other local traditions that heavily debate the locale of St Paraskevi's martyrdom. According to a well-known modern Greek tradition, for example, the place of her martyrdom was not Rome but Thesprotia in Greece, where local officials are said to have dragged the saint to the River Acheron, one of the ancient Greek entrances to the underworld, to behead her. St Paraskevi clung so tightly to a rock that a handprint was left upon it. The rock is proudly exhibited today near her tomb, which once hosted her holy relics, at the Monastery of Pounta in Parga. Today, however, the modern visitor can only find St Paraskevi's headless body in the tomb, while her head is preserved and worshipped at the Petraki Monasteri in Athens. Other holy relics, such as part of her right hand, are preserved in other churches across Greece. The Koutloumousiou Monastery of Mount Athos, for example, preserves a portion of her holy skull, while the Dionysiou Monastery of Mount Athos and the Monastery of Prophet Elias on Thira also have relics of the saint.

St Paraskevi remains closely linked with eyesight and ophthalmological illness. Her memory is honoured on the 26th of July in many parts of modern Greece with prolonged festivities (lasting up to a week long), which usually culminate in the sacred procession (περιφορά) of her holy icon through the streets of Greek cities and villages. Some of these icons and/or churches are thought

---

[19] Hornby and others 2000.

[20] Paraskevi literally means 'preparation' in Modern Greek.

[21] I was too young to remember any other medical details delivered to the family, except, of course, the high levels of anxiety my parents experienced when they were told that their baby son had to be moved to intensive care for further tests to assess whether his eyesight was severely impacted by the condition.

[22] Jer 10.11.

to be miracle-making (θαυματουργοί) and consequently attract pilgrims from all over the country.

However, the most impressive votives dedicated to St Paraskevi are perhaps the infants, like my brother, who are born with ophthalmological illnesses and eyesight impairments and because of that were dedicated to her. Just like the *tamata* we saw earlier, these children are testaments — indeed, living testaments — both to the deep-rooted belief that the human body is safe in the hands of the gods and to the culture-specific nature of ophthalmological illness.

Light features prominently in the modern Greek conception of ophthalmological illness and is reflected in the precious materials used for the *tamata*. Indeed, so important is this focus on light that, in some parts of modern Orthodox Greece, it is not St Paraskevi who looks after eyesight but rather St Photeini (from φως, 'light'). Similarly, there are many female saints who preside over eyesight and ophthalmological illness in the Catholic Church. One of the best know of these is St Lucia (from *lux*, 'light'),[23] who, like St Paraskevi, is depicted as holding a pair of eyes.

In both Orthodox and Catholic Christianity, certain images and icons — like those of St Lucia of Belpasso and St Paraskevi of Komotini (Fig. 13.4) — were thought of as especially efficacious and prolific as far as the miraculous healing of ophthalmological illnesses was concerned. These icons are usually heavily adorned with precious metals and *tamata*, which may include anatomical votives, rings, other pieces of jewellery, and personal belongings.[24] The dedicants of these *tamata* probably spent a considerable amount of time debating and negotiating the exact position of their votive offerings in relation to the image of the miracle-working saint, while making vows to these saints in the hope of securing the ophthalmological health of their loved ones or themselves.

To return to our comparison between ancient and modern dedications, we can clearly see how much of this process of the personal and emotional investment of the ancient dedicant in the very act of dedication is now lost to the modern viewer of ancient dedications. When we encounter ancient anatomical votives, it tends to be in large museum collections, such as those in the Archaeological Museum in Corinth, the Acropolis Museum in Athens, the Archaeological Museum of Komotini in Thrace, or the National Archaeological Museum in Athens, the last of which we shall return to shortly.

---

[23] More in Cassell 1991.
[24] See Hughes 2017a.

Demeter, Kore, and Ophthalmological Illness in Ancient Greece

Some of these ancient eye-shaped dedications have been subjected to over-realistic readings and subsequently employed in retrospective diagnoses. Dacryorrhea (a medical condition that involves, among other symptoms, an excessive flow of tears), cataracts, glaucoma, weeping sores and ectropion, trachoma, conjunctival cysts or lesions, and 'night vision', all ophthalmological illnesses and conditions well-attested in ancient Greek ophthalmological treatises, have featured heavily in these exercises of retrospectively interpreting ancient symptomatology.[25] Although well-intentioned, retrospective diagnosis is fraught with methodological problems, especially when it concerns anatomical votives, like our eye-shaped votives, because it disregards their wider spatial and situational contexts (provenance, conditions of discovery, etc.) and, more importantly, the culture-specific meanings of health and illness.

The third part of this study focuses on ancient Greek framings of ophthalmological illness by looking at eye-shaped votives dedicated to Demeter and Kore. Demeter and Kore, like St Paraskevi, St Photeini, or St Lucia in the modern Christian Orthodox and Catholic traditions, presided over ophthalmological illnesses in ancient Greece. These eye-shaped *anathemata* resemble, in terms of typology, the anatomical votives we find in traditional healing temples, but they present us with different interpretative problems and possibilities. Are we to think of them as testaments to the healing activities of Demeter and Kore, especially with regards to ophthalmological diseases? Or are we to think of eye votives as mementos of the intense visual experiences that initiates had?

I have argued elsewhere that these votives are particularly difficult objects which defy modern categorization and even challenge commonly accepted definitions of anatomical votives.[26] Here, I am more concerned with what these objects might reveal to us about the culture-specific conceptualization of illness and healing. More precisely, I maintain that these eye-shaped votives attest to a wholly different conceptualization of ophthalmological illness and its treatment, since blindness or the impairment of vision and its healing are now seen through the prism of initiation into the mysteries of the

---

[25] On common ophthalmological illnesses and recommended procedures in the Hippocratic corpus, see e.g. Hippoc., *Vid. ac.* = L. 9.152–60 with Craik 2006; 2009; cf. Villard 2005.

[26] Petridou 2017.

Figure 13.4. The θαυματουργός 'miracle-working' icon of Άγία Παρασκευή Κομοτηνής ('St Paraskevi of Komotini'), heavily adorned with *tamata*. Image: author.

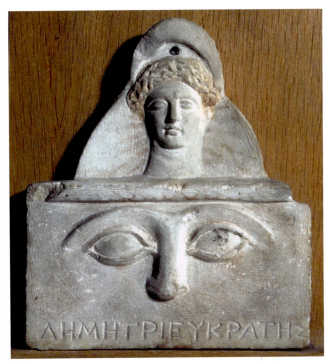

Figure 13.5. Marble votive plaque found near the Eleusinian Telestērion depicting a radiant Demeter (IG II² 4639) dated roughly to the fourth century BC. Now in the National Archaeological Museum of Athens (inv. no. 5256). Dimensions: 19.3 × 17 × 18 cm. National Archaeological Museum, Athens (photographer: Dimitrios Yalouris). Copyright © Hellenic Ministry of Culture and Sports / Archaeological Receipts Fund.

two goddesses. This sort of analysis owes much to the exploration of Demeter's *mode d'action*, that of revealing and bringing to the light.²⁷

Take the well-known relief depicted in Figure 13.5. This remarkable artefact was excavated sometime around 1800 in the area near the Eleusinian Telestērion, close to the middle round tower of the southern *peribolos*, and is dated roughly to the fourth century BC.²⁸ The votive depicts a pair of eyes with the nose and eyebrows. The name of the dedicant is revealed by the accompanying inscription: Δήμητρι Εὐκράτης, 'Eukrates (dedicates) to Demeter'.

As the votive is currently exhibited in the National Archaeological Museum in Athens, it is surrounded by several other votive offerings depicting body parts from the Athenian Asclepieion, the Amyneion, the Temple of Aphrodite at Daphne, and other healing sanctuaries. The modern spectator is encouraged to conceptualize Eukrates' relief as a typical anatomical votive. In fact, the item stands out and differentiates itself from the rest of the *anathemata* on display primarily because on the upper level of the relief is the image of a radiant female head — one would assume the head of a goddess, presumably that of a radiant Demeter.

There are two distinct levels of action in the marble relief from Eleusis: a) the rectangular plaque with the pair of eyes, eyebrows, and nose, which is already familiar to us from other eye-shaped votives, and b) the head of the light-emanating goddess on the top. The viewer is faced with the riddle of how the two levels are related to each other. Is the lower part of the relief a thanksgiving offering to commemorate successful treatment of Eukrates' eye-disease by Demeter? This could explain

---

27 Detienne and Vernant 1974.

28 On the Sanctuary of Demeter and Kore in Eleusis, see Mylonas 1961; Clinton 1993; 2003; 2004; and 2007. On the votive plaque, see Raptou 2014.

its similarities with the surrounding anatomical *ex-votos*. Does the upper face image on the rectangular plaque represent Eukrates' visual experiences in the Telestērion? Is this vision of a light-emanating Demeter or Kore what Eukrates saw in the Telestērion, perhaps during his initiation? Or was this vision of Demeter imbued in light the very first sight Eukrates had after his blindness was cured? Before answering any questions, it is important to notice that the rays of light on the relief do not originate from anything the goddess is wearing (e.g. clothes or jewellery), but they come directly out of the divine body, very much in the manner described in the *Homeric Hymn to Demeter* (189–90 and 277–79).[29]

There is, of course, nothing surprising in this. Light is, of course, a typical divine attribute and one of the most characteristic concomitant *semeia* ('signs') of divine epiphany.[30] On the other hand, we might read the radiating divine body as an allusion to the famous light of Eleusis, which was such an integral constituent element of the Eleusinian Mysteries that it ended up synechdochically denoting the rites themselves. Moreover, it is also interesting to see how marble is coloured in an artful way so as to create a light-emanating and light-reflecting effect, just like the modern Greek *tamata* made of metal plaques discussed above.

The real problem is how to reconcile Demeter, the goddess of agricultural and human fertility, with the explicit references to the healing of eye-related ailments. As hinted at above, it is possible that the relief commemorated Eukrates' physical ability to see, perhaps after a miracle cure performed by Demeter. This cure may have taken place during his initiation into the mysteries of the two goddesses, or it might just as likely have been independent of it. The fluidity, however, between the notions of physical and ritual blindness in the context of mystery cults in general and that of the Eleusinian Mysteries in particular, prevent us from determining with any certainty whether the dedicant was indeed blind or visually impaired before his encounter with the goddess.[31] The boundaries between physical and ritual vision and blindness are equally blurred in several literary sources.

For example, in an epigram from the *Anthologia Palatina* attributed to Antiphilus, we read that the narrator left behind both the literal darkness of his blindness (νυκτὶ) and the metaphorical darkness of his ignorance of the mysteries (νύκτα) on the night of his initiation into the mysteries of the two goddesses (most likely a reference to the Eleusinian Mysteries). That same night, the initiate welcomed both the light of the sun and the light of knowledge.

σκίπων με πρὸς νηὸν ἀνήγαγεν, ὄντα βέβηλον
οὐ μόνον τελετῆς, ἀλλὰ καὶ ἠελίου
μύστην δ᾽ ἀμφοτέρων με θεαὶ θέσαν, οἶδα δ᾽ ἐκείνῃ
νυκτὶ καὶ ὀφθαλμῶν νύκτα καθηράμενος
ἀσκίπων δ᾽ ἄστυ κατέστιχον Δηοῦς
κηρύσσων γλώσσης ὄμμασι τρανότερον.

(My staff led me to the temple, uninitiated as I was, | in both the secret rite and the light of the sun. | The goddesses initiated me in both; that very night I truly knew/ saw | having been purified from the night of my eyes. | Without my staff I walked down to the city proclaiming Demeter's sacred rites more vividly with my eyes rather than my tongue.)[32]

Notice the conspicuous position of the verb οἶδα in line 3, which oscillates between the semantic fields of 'vision' and 'knowledge'.[33] The cultural metaphor of 'purification' is utilized here in a twofold way: initiation into the mysteries of Demeter and Kore offered the initiate not only purity from the actual darkness of his blindness but also cleanness from his intellectual and ritual darkness. In this context, mysteric enlightenment coincided with and perhaps even facilitated the acquisition of his physical vision. The connection between the Antiphilus epigram and the Eukrates relief is an easy one to make: they both seem to pose the same sort of questions; and they both depict the image of cured physical blindness as being the structural counterpart of cured intellectual and ritual blindness. The physical ability to see and the illuminated mysteric vision acquired in the course of an initiation into the Mysteries of Demeter and Kore are closely connected to each other not only in the Eukrates relief and the epigram attributed to Antiphilus, but also in a good number of other literary and iconographical sources.[34]

One way to approach this rather modern and perhaps even overstated dilemma of physical vision/blindness versus ritual vision/blindness is to agree with the views advanced by Clinton and Petridou that the blazing *pyr* (encountered by the participants at some climactic point in the secret rites) occasionally had the power to heal physical blindness in conjunction with the neophyte's

---

[29] Clinton 2004; 2007.
[30] Petridou 2015, 32–43.
[31] On the Eleusinian Mysteries in particular, see Petridou 2013.
[32] *Anth. Pal.* 9.298.
[33] Petridou 2013.
[34] Petridou 2017.

ritual blindness.³⁵ Conversely, a preferable interpretation (and by that I refer to one that ties in well with the synchronic views of the religious insiders) might arise from resolving the artificial tension between Demeter's treatment of eye-related illnesses by assuming that, in Eleusis, Demeter was not ordinarily a healing deity, and yet she, like any other Greek deity, had the power to heal provided that the form of healing was in accordance with her 'mode of action'. Essentially, this means that when Demeter is involved in a medical activity, she still acts according to her *mode d'action*, that is rescuing and leading to light after a period of blindness/danger.

From this point of view, it is not so important to find out whether Demeter's iatric activity is attested — the anatomical *ex-votos* found in her sanctuaries show that this is clearly the case — but to see how this iatric activity is conceived of by ancient Greeks. So, the 'fluidity' between physical vision and the symbolism of light in the process of initiation does not necessarily make us think that eye-shaped anatomical votive offerings refer both to eyesight healing and to initiation, but rather that the physical healing is seen in a religious light. In short, when an individual ascribes the healing of a sight problem to the two goddesses, this process is seen through the model of the initiation. The healing must have been conceived in terms of the passage from darkness to light that the initiate undergoes during the sacred mysteries. It is equally possible that we are dealing with very sudden or spontaneous healings or with healings that are characterized by a very intense visual experience or, again, with the healing of blindness only and not milder or partial eye impairments. In either case, the problem of reconciling Demeter's 'double' identity as a healer of ophthalmological illness and as a culture-bringing goddess who revealed the gifts of agriculture to humanity can easily be resolved if seen through the prism of her principle 'mode of action', i.e. that of initiation, revealing, and leading into the light.

A further link between the mysteries and healing is provided by Pausanias in the seventh book of his *Periegesis*, in which he describes the *hydromanteion* of Patras.

τοῦ δὲ ἄλσους ἱερὸν ἔχεται Δήμητρος· αὕτη μὲν καὶ ἡ παῖς ἑστᾶσι, τὸ δὲ ἄγαλμα τῆς Γῆς ἐστι καθήμενον. πρὸ δὲ τοῦ ἱεροῦ τῆς Δήμητρός ἐστι πηγή· ταύτης τὰ μὲν πρὸς τοῦ ναοῦ λίθων ἀνέστηκεν αἱμασιά, κατὰ δὲ τὸ ἐκτὸς κάθοδος ἐς αὐτὴν πεποίηται. μαντεῖον δὲ ἐνταῦθά ἐστιν ἀψευδές, οὐ μὲν ἐπὶ παντί γε πράγματι, ἀλλ᾽ ἐπὶ τῶν καμνόντων. κάτοπτρον καλῳδίῳ τῶν λεπτῶν δήσαντες καθιᾶσι, σταθμώμενοι μὴ πρόσω καθικέσθαι τῆς πηγῆς, ἀλλ᾽ ὅσον ἐπιψαῦσαι τοῦ ὕδατος τῷ κύκλῳ τοῦ κατόπτρου. τὸ δὲ ἐντεῦθεν εὐξάμενοι τῇ θεῷ καὶ θυμιάσαντες ἐς τὸ κάτοπτρον βλέπουσι· τὸ δὲ σφίσι τὸν νοσοῦντα ἤτοι ζῶντα ἢ καὶ τεθνεῶτα ἐπιδείκνυσι.

(Demeter's sanctuary is situated in the grove; she and her daughter are standing up, but the statue of Earth is sitting down. There is a spring in front of Demeter's sanctuary with a dry-stone wall on the temple side and a downward passage to the spring on the outer side. There is an infallible oracle here, not for all purposes but for the sick. They tie a mirror onto a thin cord, and balance it so as not to dip it into the spring, but let the surface of the mirror just touch lightly on the water. Then they pray to the goddess and burn incense and look into the mirror, and it shows them the sick person either alive or dead.)³⁶

In the *hydromanteion* of Patras, we are told, people did not seek to cure their friends and relatives; what they were after was a prediction, a prognosis, regarding the outcome of the disease. They wanted to know whether their loved ones would recover or die. The prognosis was transmitted via easily perceivable visual data: the patient's friends or relatives need only look into the mirror (which was suspended over the water surface) to see whether their family member or friend would live or die.

I previously took this passage as a clear and emphatic testimony to the centrality of ocular-centric processes in the cult of Demeter and Kore, as well as evidence for the close correlation between viewing and healing in the specific *manteion*.³⁷ After further consideration, however, it now seems to me that this is yet another case of Demeter having a share of the pie as a divinity who presides over health, although only insofar as this dovetails with her principal mode of action (revealing and bringing to the light). In this case, it is not healing that she brings to the foreground (as in the cases of Eukrates and Antiphilus). Instead, Demeter reveals in the mirror (and consequently in the eyes of the suppliant) the future outcome of the illness of their beloved ones. Clearly, this combination of *hydromanteia* and *katoptromanteia* at Demeter's sanctuary in Patras does not aim at healing but rather at extracting an oracular prediction that functions here as a medical prognosis.

More significantly, we must not neglect the mysteric aspects of this rite, which, as F. Frontisi-Ducroux and J.-P. Vernant have rightly argued, closely resembles a *katabasis*.³⁸ Naturally, one thinks here of the incubatory

---

35 Clinton 2005, 110; Petridou 2017; cf. Clinton 1993; 2003; 2004; and 2007.

36 Paus. vii.21.11–12.

37 Petridou 2017.

38 Frontisi-Ducroux and Vernant 1997, 194–95.

rites practised at the Ploutonion at Acharaka (between Tralles and Nysa in Asia Minor, modern Salavatlı)[39] or near Herkyna at Trophonios's sanctuary in Leibadia.[40] Let us not forget that, according to Pausanias, Demeter with the *epiklesis* 'Europe' was one of the deities to whom one was required to sacrifice prior to consulting with the oracle of Trophonios, on the grounds that it was she who had nursed the young hero.[41] In all likelihood, Demeter's healing cult at Patras was one of those oracular and healing cults that had a distinct mysteric aspect and conceptualized natural architectural features in their vicinity, especially lakes and caves, as passages to the underworld. The cult of Demeter Thermasia ('she of the body-heat')[42] at Hermione in Argolis (modern Thermisi) may differ slightly, as it was the health-giving properties of the local hot springs that attracted sufferers. Even there, nonetheless, Demeter Thermasia may have been identified with Demeter Chthonia, as Croone postulates.[43] In all likelihood, Demeter's healing cult at Patras, as with her healing cults elsewhere, combined distinct mysteric aspects with healing and oracular dimensions.

Synopsis: 'Comparing the Incomparable' and the Lived Experience of Ophthalmological Illness

It is important to remember that neither the Antiphilus epigram nor the Eukrates reliefs are unique, in the sense that there are several other sources (both literary and material) that attest to the close links between Demeter and ophthalmology. Analogous examples of eye-shaped votives, for example, have also been discovered at, for example, the Sanctuary of Demeter in Pergamum,[44] while excavations at the small Sanctuary of Demeter next to the east wall of the city at the site of ancient Mesimvria-Zone in Thrace have yielded a good number of eye-shaped *typoi* (votive *repoussé* reliefs) made from bronze, gold, and silver (Fig. 13.6, right).[45] These *typoi* were found along with votives depicting worshippers raising their right hands in adoration (Fig. 13.6, left). The similarity between these ancient anatomical votives and the modern metallic eye-shaped *tamata*, both in terms of measurable size and modes of production, is difficult to miss. None of these votives is larger than 35–40 cm in height and yet they have a monumental impact on the eyes of the modern visitor at the Archaeological Museum of Komotini. One can imagine that they would have been of even greater importance to their original dedicants, who may have dedicated them to commemorate a sudden healing from blindness or else some form of severe visual impairment.

Moreover, a number of these ἔγκμακτοι or κατάμακτοι τύποι are also mentioned in the inventories of the Sanctuary of Demeter and Kore in Delos.[46] Some of these *typoi* are said to have been made of gold (ὀφθαλμός χρυσοῦς) and some were said to have been mounted on wooden plaques (ὀφθαλμοί ἐπί σανιδίου). One can postulate with some degree of certainty that the main reason the *typoi* mentioned in the inscriptions from Delos are now lost to us is precisely because of their precious material. Some of these *typoi* carried suspension holes like the modern *tamata* in the Benaki Museum. These *typoi* were meant to decorate the walls or other architectural features of the sanctuary and to bear witness to the immense therapeutic capacity of the presiding deity.[47] Alternatively, we may imagine them suspended from the cult statue or the images of the deity,[48] very much in the manner of the modern *repoussé* dedications found in hundreds of Catholic and modern Greek Orthodox Churches, like those of St Lucia and St Paraskevi discussed above. The modern viewer may also notice that an analogous suspension hole is also situated in the centre of the upper level (just above the goddess's head) of the Eukrates relief (Fig. 13.5): perhaps an indication that it was meant to remain in the temple and commemorate for eternity the extraordinary visual experiences of its

---

[39] Str. XIV.1.44, cf. Dillon 2003, 152.

[40] Paus. IX.39, cf. Bonnechère 2003. The Ploutonion complex was comprised out of a precinct of Kore and Plouton and a cave, the Charonion, on top of which incubation was practised by the priestly personnel on behalf of those who sought therapy either for themselves or for their relatives. The priestly personnel of the Sanctuary of Trophonios were also actively involved in decoding and reconstructing the dream experiences of the pilgrims.

[41] Paus. IX.37.3.

[42] Paus. II.34.6 and 12.

[43] Croone 1967, 229. The relationship between the curative powers of the sources and the divine presence is a problematic one, see de Cazanove and Scheid 2003, 1–6; de Cazanove 2015.

[44] Töpperwein 1976, 139–40 and 241. On the Sanctuary of Demeter in Pergamum, see Bohtz 1981; Thomas 1998; Agelidis 2011; Petridou 2017.

[45] A detailed catalogue of these objects can be found in Βαβρίτσας 1973, 77–81 and plates 93–95; cf. also van Straten 1981, 127.

[46] Bruneau 1970; Tréheux 1987; Forsén 1996, 143; van Straten 1981, 134 nos 221–22, with more bibliography.

[47] On the visual dynamic of votive offerings in sanctuaries, see Petsalis-Diomidis 2005, 187–88; Mylonopoulos 2006, 87.

[48] Van Straten 1990.

Figure 13.6. Silver votive plaques from the Sanctuary of Demeter in Mesimvria-Zone. They were discovered next to the eastern wall of the city and date to *c.* the fourth century BC. They are currently exhibited at the Archaeological Museum of Komotini. They depict (left) himation-clad worshippers raising their right hand in adoration (above) a pair of eyes, eyebrows, nose, mouth, framed by a double line on three sides and a band above.

dedicant, in both the eyes of the goddesses presiding in the sanctuary and the eyes of the other *theōroi*.

Irrespective of where they were discovered, all the eye-shaped *anathemata* discussed above point to a closer link between ophthalmological illness and the cults of Demeter and Kore.[49] Having revisited the material from the perspective of Demeter's prime mode of action, however, I am now more inclined to believe that we must interpret them as testimonies of a very culture-specific conception of ophthalmological illness as a tormenting and yet essential initiation which ultimately leads to the light (physical and ritual alike) and to the restoration of regular eyesight. Illness itself was probably thought of as a painful and life-altering experience that, with the help of the two goddesses, could lead to permanent ritual enlightenment in conjunction with physical healing, which is in turn explicitly compared to the passage from darkness to light that the initiate undergoes during the sacred mysteries. One might be tempted to speculate even further that Demeter and Kore were associated with particularly sudden healings or with healings that were characterized by very intense visual experiences or, again, with the healing of actual blindness and other acute eye-related ailments. Consequently, one could safely claim that when Demeter is involved in medical treatment of (possibly) severe eye-illnesses, she continues to act according to her *mode d'action*, that of revealing and bringing to the light.

In a similar vein, light and ophthalmological illness is central in the eye-shaped *tamata* dedicated to St Paraskevi, as mentioned above. Light is both the cause of suffering (or lack thereof) for St Paraskevi's oppressors and the medium of healing in the core narrative of her martyrdom. Unlike worshippers of Demeter and Kore, however, who probably turned to these deities only in cases of severe illness, in modern Greece, sufferers from both minor and major ophthalmological illness turn to St Paraskevi for support and healing. In both cases, the culture-specific framing of both ophthalmological health and illness is self-evident. None of these connections would have been accessible to us without the *prima facie* unorthodox comparison of ancient Greek *anathemata* to modern Greek *tamata*. As this study has shown, 'comparer l'incomparable', to quote Marcel Detienne (2000), is an indispensable methodological tool that allows for an *ad fontes* analysis of the lived experience of ophthalmological illness in both Antiquity and modernity.

---

[49] Petridou 2017.

Works Cited

Agelidis, Z. 2011. 'Kulte und Heiligtümer in Pergamon', in R. Grüßinger, V. Kästner, and A. Scholl (eds), *Pergamon: Panorama der Antiken Metropole* (Berlin: Antikensammlung, Staatliche Museen zu Berlin), pp. 177–79.

Albrecht, J. and others. 2018. 'Religion in the Making: The Lived Ancient Religion Approach', *Religion*, 48: 1–26.

Βαβρίτσας, Α. 1973. Ἀνασκαφή Μεσημβρίας, Πρακτικά τῆς ἐν Ἀθήναις ἀρχαιολογικῆς ἑταιρείας (Athens: Ἀρχαιολογική ἑταιρεία).

Behr, C. A. 1968. *Aelius Aristides and the Sacred Tales* (Amsterdam: Hakkert).

Betegh, G. 2020. 'Plato on Illness in the Phaedo, the Republic, and the Timaeus', in C. Jorgenson, F. Karfík, and Š. Špinka (eds), *Plato's Timaeus: Proceedings of the Tenth Symposium Platonicum Pragense* (Leiden: Brill), pp. 228–58.

Bohtz, C. H. 1981. *Das Demeter-Heiligtum*, Altertümer von Pergamon, 13 (Berlin: De Gruyter).

Bonnechère, P. 2003. *Trophonios de Lébadée: Cultes et mythes d'une cité béotienne au miroir de la mentalité antique* (Leiden: Brill).

Bruneau, P. 1970. *Recherches sur les cultes de Délos à l'époque hellénistique et à l'époque impériale* (Paris: De Boccard).

Cassell, A. K. 1991. 'Santa Lucia as Patroness of Sight: Hagiography, Iconography, and Dante', *Dante Studies*, 109: 71–88.

Clinton, K. 1993. 'The Sanctuary of Demeter and Kore at Eleusis', in N. Marinatos and R. Hägg (eds), *Greek Sanctuaries: New Approaches* (London: Routledge), pp. 110–24.

———. 2003. 'Stages of Initiation in the Eleusinian and Samothracian Mysteries', in M. B. Cosmopoulos (ed.), *Greek Mysteries: The Archaeology and Ritual of Ancient Greek Secret Cults* (London: Routledge), pp. 50–78.

———. 2004. 'Epiphany in the Eleusinian Mysteries', *Illinois Classical Studies*, 29: 85–109.

———. 2005. *Eleusis: The Inscriptions on Stone; Documents of the Two Goddesses and Public Documents of the Deme* (Athens: Archaeological Society at Athens).

———. 2007. 'The Mysteries of Demeter and Kore', in D. Ogden (ed.), *A Companion to Greek Religion* (Malden: Wiley-Blackwell), pp. 342–56.

Craik, E. M. 2006. *Two Hippocratic Treatises: 'On Sight' and 'On Anatomy'* (Leiden: Brill).

———. 2009. 'Hippocratic Bodily "Channels" and Oriental Parallels', *Medical History*, 53: 105–16.

Croone, J. H. 1967. 'Hot Springs and Healing Gods', *Mnemosyne*, 20: 225–46.

Dasen, V. 2013. 'Anatomical Votives', in R. S. Bagnall and others (eds), *The Encyclopedia of Ancient History* (Malden: Wiley-Blackwell), pp. 402–03.

de Cazanove, O. 2009. 'Oggetti muti? Le iscrizioni degli ex voto anatomici nel mondo roman', in J. Bodel and M. Kajava (eds), *Dediche sacre nel mondo greco-romano: diffusione, funzioni, tipologie = Religious Dedications in the Greco-Roman World: Distribution, Typology, Use* (Rome: Institutum Romanum Finlandiae), pp. 355–71.

———. 2015. 'Water', in R. Raja and J. Rüpke (eds), *A Companion to the Archaeology of Religion in the Ancient World* (Malden: Wiley-Blackwell), pp. 181–93.

de Cazanove, O. and J. Scheid. 2003. *Sanctuaires et sources dans l'antiquité: les sources documentaires et leurs limites dans la description des lieux de culte* (Naples: D'Auria).

Detienne, M. 2000. *Comparer l'incomparable* (Paris: Seuil).

Detienne, M. and J.-P. Vernant. 1974. *Les ruses de l'intelligence: la mètis des Grecs* (Paris: Flammarion).

Dillon, M. 2003. *Pilgrims and Pilgrimage in Ancient Greece* (London: Routledge).

Draycott, J. and E.-J. Graham. 2017. *Bodies of Evidence: Re-defining Approaches to the Anatomical Votive* (London: Routledge).

Forsén, B. 1996. *Griechische Gliederweihungen: Eine Untersuchung zu ihrer Typologie und ihrer religions- und sozialgeschichtlichen Bedeutung* (Helsinki: Suomen Ateenan-instituutin säätiö).

Frontisi-Ducroux, F. and J.-P. Vernant. 1997. *Dans l'oeil du miroir* (Charlieu: La Bartavelle).

Gasparini, V. and others (eds). 2020. *Lived Religion in the Ancient Mediterranean World* (Berlin: De Gruyter), pp. 237–59.

Handaka, S. 2018. 'Τάματα: μια νέα προσέγγιση μέσα από τη Συλλογή του Μικέ Παϊδούση', *Μουσείο Μπενάκη*, 2: 147–65.

Hornby, S. J. and others. 2000. 'Visual Acuity in Children with Coloboma. Clinical Features and a New Phenotypic Classification System', *Ophthalmology*, 107.3: 511–20.

Hughes, J. 2008. 'Fragmentation as Metaphor in the Classical Healing Sanctuary', *Social History of Medicine*, 21: 217–36.

———. 2017a. 'Souvenirs of the Self: Personal Belongings as Votive Offerings in Ancient Religion', *Religion in the Roman Empire*, 3: 181–201.

———. 2017b. *Votive Body Parts in Greek and Roman Religion* (Cambridge: Cambridge University Press).

McGuire, M. B. 1990. 'Religion and the Body: Rematerializing the Human Body in the Social Sciences of Religion', *Journal for the Scientific Study of Religion*, 29.3: 283–96.

———. 2008. *Lived Religion: Faith and Practice in Everyday Life* (Oxford: Oxford University Press).

Morgan, D. 2012. *The Embodied Eye: Religious Visual Culture and the Social Life of Feeling* (Berkeley: University of California Press).

Mylonas, G. E. 1961. *Eleusis and the Eleusinian Mysteries* (Princeton: Princeton University Press).

Mylonopoulos, J. 2006. 'Greek Sanctuaries as Places of Communication through Rituals: An Archaeological Perspective', in E. Stavrianopoulou (ed.), *Ritual and Communication in the Graeco-Roman World* (Liège: Presses universitaires de Liège), pp. 69–110.

Osborne, J. F. (ed.). 2014. *Approaching Monumentality in Archaeology* (Albany: State University of New York Press).
Petridou, G. 2013. 'Blessed Is He, Who Has Seen… The Power of Ritual Viewing and Ritual Framing in Eleusis', *Helios*, 40: 309–41.
——. 2015. *Divine Epiphany in Greek Literature and Culture* (Oxford: Oxford University Press).
——. 2017. 'Demeter as an Ophthalmologist? Eye-Shaped Votives and the Cults of Demeter and Kore', in J. Draycott and E.-J. Graham (eds), *Bodies of Evidence: Ancient Anatomical Votives Past, Present and Future* (London: Routledge), pp. 95–111.
——. 2020. 'The "Lived" Body in Pain. Illness and Initiation in Lucian's *Podagra* and Aelius Aristides' *Hieroi Logoi*', in V. Gasparini and others (eds), *Lived Religion in the Ancient Mediterranean World* (Berlin: De Gruyter), pp. 237–59.
Petsalis-Diomidis, A. 2005. 'The Body in Space: Visual Dynamics in Graeco-Roman Healing Pilgrimage', in J. Elsner and I. C. Rutherford (eds), *Seeing the Gods: Pilgrimage in Graeco-Roman and Early Christian Antiquity* (Oxford: Oxford University Press), pp. 183–218.
Raja, R. and J. Rüpke (eds). 2015. *A Companion to the Archaeology of Religion in the Ancient World* (Oxford: Wiley-Blackwell).
Raptou, E. 2014. 'Comments and Bibliography on Votive Plaque no. 86', in N. C. Stampolidis and Y. Tassoulas (eds), *Hygeia: Health, Illness, Treatment from Homer to Galen* (Athens: Museum of Cycladic Art), pp. 218–19.
Rosa, H. 2019. *Resonance: A Sociology of our Relationship to the World*, trans. J. C. Wagner (Cambridge: Polity).
Rüpke, J. 2018. *Pantheon: A New History of Roman Religion* (Princeton: Princeton University Press).
Rüpke, J. and G. Woolf (eds). 2021. *Religion in the Roman Empire* (Stuttgart: Kohlhammer).
Schörner, G. 2015. 'Anatomical Ex-Votos', in R. Raja and J. Rüpke (eds), *A Companion to the Archaeology of Religion in the Ancient World* (Oxford: Wiley-Blackwell), pp. 297–410.
Straten, F. T. van. 1981. 'Gifts for the Gods', in H. S. Versnel (ed.), *Faith, Hope and Worship: Aspects of Religious Mentality in the Ancient World* (Leiden: Brill), pp. 65–104.
——. 1990. 'Votives and Votaries in Greek Sanctuaries', in A. Schachter (ed.), *Le Sanctuaire grec*, Entretiens sur l'antiquité classique, 37 (Geneva: Fondation Hardt), pp. 247–84 = repr. in R. Buxton (ed.) 2009, *Oxford Readings in Greek Religion* (Oxford: Oxford University Press), pp. 191–223.
Töpperwein, E. 1976. *Terrakotten von Pergamon* (Berlin: De Gruyter).
Thomas, C. M. 1998. 'The Sanctuary of Demeter at Pergamum: Cultic Space for Women and its Eclipse', in H. Koester (ed.), *Pergamon, Citadel of the Gods: Archaeological Record, Literary Description, and Religious Development* (Harrisburg: Trinity), pp. 277–98.
Tréheux, J. 1987. 'Localisation du Thesmophorion à Délos', *Bulletin de correspondance hellénique*, 111: 495–99.
Villard, L. 2005. 'La Vision du malade dans la Collection Hippocratique', in L. Villard (ed.), *Études sur la vision dans l'antiquité classique* (Mont-Saint-Aignan: Publications des Universités de Rouen et du Havre), pp. 109–30.

14. A Triangle of Mary: Relating Religious Artefacts to Non-Religious Lorry Drivers

Manuel Moser

I'm not really a believer, but she's pretty and it's surely no harm.[1]

When answering the call for papers for contributing to this volume I was struck by its title, 'Measuring the World against the Body'. Having recently engaged with approaches from *New Materialism* and philosophies of *Speculative Realism*,[2] the title provoked a kind of feeling of smoke in my nostrils:[3] Whose 'Body' are we talking about and what 'World'?[4] If I take my own human body size as a point of reference for measuring the scales of some material beings I encounter passing through an outside world, don't I risk falling into reproducing a problematic anthropocentric worldview? To avoid this problem, I decided with my contribution to the volume not to follow a phenomenological approach of *embodied subjectivity*.[5] Instead, I will think through an example that centres primarily on an artefact as a point of reference to understand relationalities that go beyond human activity. Nevertheless, taking a non-human being as a central point for my reflection is a risky endeavour, as it comes hand-in-hand with many blind spots. I am convinced, however, that as every theory carries its internal blind spots, the usefulness of theories as well as methodologies depends on how much light they can shed on a particular problem to be studied. I hope that, thanks to an object-centred approach, I can come to an additional (and hopefully better) understanding of a particular case of extraordinariness I encounter in my fieldwork, which is the presence of many religious artefacts amid non-religious lorry drivers in the eastern parts of Germany.

Doing my fieldwork amid long-distance lorry drivers over the past two years, I myself drove articulated lorries hauling refrigerated foods across Germany. During these fieldtrips, I encountered many icons of saints (primarily the Virgin Mary) and crucifixes in the cabs of the tractor-trailers I drove as a substitute for drivers on vacation or sick leave, as well as on some bodies of lorries of fellow drivers I met on the road. This struck me as something unexpected, as I did not often encounter similar artefacts elsewhere in the urban public space of East German neighbourhoods. Indeed, it seemed — as has been argued by Detlef Pollack — that repressive politics against religious communities during the communist era were so successful that even decades after German reunification, the population of the eastern parts of Germany has not redeveloped any widespread religious interest.[6] Might it be that religious attitudes persist more strongly in the community of East German lorry drivers than elsewhere in the eastern parts of Germany, to the extent that lorry drivers should be considered an exception to this widespread secularization? When talking to fellow drivers, however, such an eventual assumption was immediately challenged and deconstructed by my interlocutors, who strongly resisted being assigned to a religious field of any kind.

---

[1] Post in a Facebook Group of German lorry drivers. Translated by the author, as are all following interview extracts.

[2] *New Materialism*: following Bennett 2010; de la Cadena 2015; Latour 2005. *Speculative Realism*: following DeLanda 2016; Harman 2017.

[3] I borrow the expression from Isabelle Stengers (2018, 103), who uses it to describe the uneasiness she feels when confronted with questions of whether she 'really' believes what she argues in her work.

[4] Advocating to think of worlds in plurality, I follow (amid others) Marisol de la Cadena and Mario Blaser (2018), who encourage us to think of 'a world of many worlds'.

[5] Jensen and Moran 2013.

[6] Pollack 1999. Obviously, this is only one of many explanations for the persistence of the secularized public space in the former GDR.

One situation I remember very well happened on the 27 August 2020, while I was looking for a parking spot in the industrial neighbourhood of Osterweddingen (Saxony-Anhalt). Having finally found an accessible road with enough space to turn around and park my articulated lorry, which was 16.5 m long, the driver of a Saxon lorry parking next to me approached. He asked if I could maintain some distance to his lorry because he had problems sleeping with the running engine of the cooling unit on my trailer so close by. I backed up a few metres, a chat followed, and the driver invited me to continue the talk in the cab of his tractor-trailer, where we discussed a wide range of topics, including our working contracts, his former life in the German Democratic Republic, and the Black Lives Matter movement.[7] Three hours and some empty beer cans later, I returned to my lorry and, before lying down to sleep for the rest of the night, scribbled in my diary:

> The first thing I noticed when entering the Saxon's cabin was two Marian icons, about 15 × 10 cm, which hang right and left in the upper corner of the windshield. On it, only visible from the inside, is a figure of Mary with a child Jesus in her arm on a golden background. [...] The Marian icons interested me a lot, but for a long time I did not dare to ask about them. At a certain point in our discussion, however, the Saxon asked me what I was studying, and I answered Religious Studies, to which he responded that religion means nonsense to him. Now I pointed at the icon in front of me and asked about it, and he explained that he brought them from Bulgaria. For him, he assured me, they do not have a religious significance.

The encounter in Osterweddingen was similar to many other interactions I had while driving lorries, when I came across icons and crucifixes airbrushed on truck bodies or placed in different versions in the cabs and on the windshields, some visible from the outside, many only visible from the inside, and a few from both sides. My chat with the Saxon driver, however, was not the only encounter in which my interlocutor strongly expressed his or her non-religiosity.

Indeed, many East German lorry drivers I spoke to performed their non-religious identities combined with othering practices towards Eastern European drivers, to whom they ascribed the identity marker 'religious'.[8] They perceived themselves as the rational opposites of these 'barbaric' drivers they localized behind the German–Polish border: they are religious, we are not! This makes the presence of 'their' religious artefacts in and on 'our' lorries quite surprising. How, then, can we make sense of this discrepancy between many lorry drivers' non-religious narratives and the expanded material culture of religious artefacts in and on their vehicles? Why do many East German lorry drivers bring religious artefacts into the cabs of their tractor-trailers while disregarding their symbolic meaning?

The quick answer would be to claim that the religious artefacts we are encountering in and on East German lorries have no longer anything to do with religion. I could simply state: these icons and crucifixes might well once have been religious artefacts for the people who produced them in Eastern European countries, but by being put in the secular space of an East German tractor-trailer they were desacralized by the driver who acquired them and are therefore no longer to be considered different in substance from any other adornment. I can identify some problems in this quick conclusion, however, because the explanation in its straightforwardness fails to take into account two central factors: first, I am not the only one who is struck by this situation; many German drivers themselves also notice the 'unruly' presence of religious artefacts in their community and experience it as a discrepancy that they struggle to make sense of.[9] I followed several discussions that arose between different drivers offline as well as in Facebook groups online, where drivers expressed different opinions on how these religious artefacts are to be understood, with some claiming that they have a religious meaning, some that they have none. In this way, individual drivers attempting to desacralize their religious artefacts are challenged by the collective (as well as the other way around). Second, regarding decorative objects, drivers explained to me that there are many other options that can be put into the cab of a trailer-tractor to make it 'beautiful', and many of these things are readier-to-hand than religious artefacts. For example, a cab can be decorated with artefacts in the national colours of one's country or region of origin, as well as those from favourite long-distance destinations. One can also refer to the logotypes of the lorry's brand

---

[7] Especially regarding the latter, I realized how strongly I am opposed to his political views. His comments favouring violence and brutality as political tools made me also feel quite frightened: I was alone in his cab, far away from any other human being. Nobody would come to my aid if something 'bad' were to happen.

[8] As I demonstrate in Moser 2022 many East German drivers perform a discriminatory collective identity in order to set themselves apart from drivers with Eastern European nationalities.

[9] Zalloua 2014.

and model to make it a nicer space. Why, therefore, take on the extra effort to find a suitable religious artefact to complement one's decorative practices?

In this article, I will develop a risky argument to find a realist but speculative answer to the collectively experienced discrepancy between religious artefacts spread amongst lorries in the Eastern parts of Germany and the non-religious identities of their drivers. To do so, I will place the religious artefacts themselves at the centre of my attention and think of the relationalities that connect them to other subparts in the lorry driving assemblages. But beforehand, I have to introduce the theoretical groundings of my approach, which relies on an entanglement of object-oriented philosophies of speculative realism (to be able to grasp and describe the stickiness between the different entities)[10] with resonance theory (to describe the quality of the sticky relationalities to be identified).[11]

Theoretical Considerations: Assemblages and Resonances

Anyone attempting to establish the definition of an assemblage starts by referring to *A Thousand Plateaus* by Gilles Deleuze and Félix Guattari.[12] Such an endeavour, however, often fails to provide a better understanding of the term because the goal of their work was to deconstruct structuralist theories. Consequently, Deleuze and Guattari do not present a concept with clear boundaries that could be easily operationalized for empirical research. It might therefore be of greater help to look into the works of contemporary philosophers that build on the paradigm of assemblage thinking and thereby clarify certain aspects that were (probably voluntarily) left open by its 'inventors'. One author I find especially useful is Manuel DeLanda, who reordered the thoughts presented in *A Thousand Plateaus* to establish an *Assemblage Theory*.[13] He cites from dialogues between Deleuze and the journalist Claire Parnet when he defines an assemblage as a 'multiplicity which is made up of many heterogeneous terms and which establishes liaisons, relations between them'.[14] An assemblage cannot be reduced to the sum of entities it is composed of, because an assemblage holds additional properties that are gained through the process of the coming together of heterogeneous entities of its composition, and these emergent properties ensure that the agency of an assemblage surpasses the properties of the parts summed up together. However, the composed assemblage alone cannot stand for all of its parts either. When different individual entities stick together to form a network of 'relations of exteriority',[15] they keep parts of their autonomies to themselves. Therefore, the totality of the composing parts summed up also surpasses the properties of the assemblage. This double irreducibility (to the total and to the parts) defines the centre of assemblage thinking.

According to DeLanda, we should include two variable 'parameters' into assemblage thinking, thereby providing grounds for distinguishing assemblages: different degrees on a continuum of coding/decoding and territorialization/deterritorialization. DeLanda thinks of these two 'parameters' not as static characteristics of individual assemblages but of processes in the fluidity of the constant reformation of assemblages. For example, an assemblage gains a higher degree of coding when it undergoes a process of standardization, which could be facilitated amid others by religion: 'a religious discourse, codifying places into sacred and profane, codifying food into permissible and taboo, codifying days of the year into ordinary and special, affects every expressive and material component of the social assemblage.'[16] In his last chapter, DeLanda discusses 'assemblages as solutions to problems', but takes uniquely mathematical problems as examples and therefore does unfortunately not provide us with a methodology of how to apply assemblage theory outside of the metalevel of philosophical thinking in empirical social research.[17] Therefore, DeLanda's *Assemblage Theory* alone does not help us to find a way to deal with our problem of the non-conforming presence of religious artefacts in the East German lorry-driving community. For a readier-to-hand understanding of what assemblages could be (in order to be operationalized for empirical research), I believe it is useful to combine it with *Actor-Network Theories*, which I, for the goal of this article, briefly present with reference to Bruno Latour's central argument.

In contrast to *Assemblage Theory*, Latour tackles more 'materialist' and 'real' problems than mathematics

---

[10] Bennett 2010; DeLanda 2016; Latour 2005. For an overview of the main currents in speculative realism, consult Morelle 2012.

[11] Rosa 2019.

[12] Deleuze and Guattari 1987.

[13] DeLanda 2016.

[14] Deleuze and Parnet 2007, 69 cited by DeLanda 2016, 1.

[15] DeLanda 2016, 10.

[16] DeLanda 2016, 56.

[17] DeLanda 2016, 165–88.

when he searches for a new 'social' paradigm that helps us deal with the global problem of the climate crisis.[18] As a cultural/natural 'hybrid', the climate crisis is directly connected to our 'modern constitution', which tries to uphold a clear line separating human entities from other material bodies and by denying the possible existence of hybrids paradoxically facilitates their development.[19] According to Latour, we are indeed wrong to think of (human/subjective) *construction* and (natural/objective) *reality* as opposites (e.g. as soon as it starts raining, no one would dare question the realness of a protecting roof).[20] Therefore, it can be harmful to try to constantly separate (Latour would say 'purify') human and non-human entities (or subjects from objects).[21] Indeed, we should approach humans and non-humans alike in a symmetrical anthropology and centre our approaches on processes of transformation (rather than focusing on intentionality): '[A]ny thing that does modify a state of affairs by making a difference is an actor.'[22] Indeed, in Latour's sociological paradigm, there is no ontological difference between humans and non-humans, but everybody/everything that acts is to be considered equally (critics would say 'human-like') as an actor/actant. Latour deconstructs the paradigm that all action is human by referring to everyday examples, such as a door-closer, which acts more responsibly than human trespassers in keeping a door closed but ready to open;[23] different strategies that ensure room tenants and hotel guests use keys correctly while according different degrees of responsibility to human and non-human entities;[24] and how audio alerts in cars train humans to drive wearing seat belts.[25] While thinking of all actor-networks (or I could say assemblages) as beings composed not of homogeneous entities but of other actor-networks, we risk an atomization that might impede the analysis of the bigger in favour of the always smaller. To deal with this risk, Latour proposes two strategies. First, he argues we should refrain from a hierarchization of scale in actor-network thinking. We should think of neither the bigger nor the smaller actor-network as more attention-worthy but should 'keep the social flat' and constantly re-shift our attention along the continuum from big to small and vice versa.[26] Second, there is the possibility of creating artificially closed systems called 'black boxes' that allow actor-networks (as well as their analytical reproductions in text) to grow:

> A black box contains that which no longer needs to be reconsidered, those things whose contents have become a matter of indifference. The more elements one can place in black boxes — modes of thoughts, habits, forces and objects — the broader the construction one can raise.[27]

It is important to never consider the black boxes as permanently closed but as temporarily summarized units that can be reopened at any stage, since Latour perceives the task of the social scientist more in questioning black boxes than in constructing a legitimization for their closedness.[28] Centring on action and mutual transformations, the *Actor-Network Theory* is a relational approach, as entities seemingly not-acting for a human observer are neglected. This is a blind spot of *Actor-Network Theory* that does not allow it to think of a radical post-human world, as has been correctly pointed out by philosophers of object-oriented ontologies.[29] However, while I agree with Jane Bennett that all 'matter' should be understood as 'vibrant',[30] I maintain that if we keep in mind that this chapter is about religious artefacts in the lorries of non-religious lorry drivers, an approach centred on relationalities (instead of *being* alone) is most befitting as a solution to the problem at hand.

Until this point, I have presented *assemblage thinking* and *actor-network theories* in order to tackle the principal problem of this article, which is to identify possibilities as to why religious artefacts are attractive to the cabs of non-religious lorry drivers. While we now have the theoretical background to analyse their presence in regard to their relationalities (without taking human superiority for granted), we have not yet located the tools to speculate on the quality of the relations that hold together the assemblages we are going to identify. Here, it comes in handy to look into *Resonance Theory*. Resonance, as it is understood for the purposes of this paper, was developed by Hartmut Rosa as antithesis to alienation and as a (potential) solution to the

---

[18] Latour 1993, 1.
[19] Latour 1993, 32.
[20] Latour 2005, 89.
[21] Latour 1993, 50–51.
[22] Latour 2005, 71.
[23] Johnson 1988.
[24] Latour 2009, 172–75.
[25] Latour 2009, 151–52.

[26] Latour 2005, 190.
[27] Callon and Latour 2015, 285.
[28] See e.g. Latour 1987, 1–17.
[29] Harman 2017, 107.
[30] Bennett 2010.

problem of acceleration in modernity.[31] Introduced as a new paradigm of critical theory, it offers us tools to identify positive ways how we can relate to the world. Even though he borrows much from phenomenological thinking,[32] Rosa leaves no doubt that he understands the concept of *resonance* not merely as the classifier of *experiences*, but defines it 'strictly as a *relational concept*'.[33] Resonance is, therefore, 'something categorically different from and independent of the *emotion* that accompanies it'.[34] In order to identify resonance, emotion is only one of four 'movements' that have to be co-present 'in interplay', the other three being affect,[35] mutual transformation (of the two resonating bodies), and double uncontrollability (*Unverfügbarkeit*).[36] Rosa always seems to place a human individual on one side of the relation, but the other side of the relation can be located on three different analytical spheres or axes: the horizontal or social axis (resonance with fellow humans), the vertical or existential axis (resonance with something transcendent), and the diagonal or material axis (resonance with things). The resonating 'Other' does need to have a voice independent of the resonating individual, otherwise no resonance could develop, but the first voice would merely be reflected back to the first individual multiplied in an 'echo chamber'.[37] Therefore, the concepts of diagonal resonance as well as vertical resonance rely on the assumption of non-human agency. Because Rosa stays vague in discussing this non-human agency, I believe it is useful to apply *Resonance Theory* empirically in combination with thoughts borrowed from object-oriented philosophies, such as DeLanda's *Assemblage Theory* and Latour's *Actor-Network Theory*, which I introduced before.

In summary, this theoretical subsection proposes to approach relationalities between different entities (such as the ones we will encounter when continuing with our case study) symmetrically, namely not distinguishing *a priori* between humans and non-humans, but considering them as equally possible agents of (trans)formations. Furthermore, it proposes not only to trace the relationalities but by inscribing itself in resonance research to also reflect on the question of how qualitatively solid these relations might be. After introducing some previous works dedicated to the appearances of religious themes in lorry driving, we will approach the field of religious artefacts in the lorry-driving communities I studied, adopting the speculative realist stance inspired by the entanglements of the different theories presented in this subsection.

Religion and Lorries: State of the Art

Contrary to comparatively many case studies in the fields of sociology and anthropology realized with lorry drivers while focusing primarily on labour conditions and gender identities,[38] there has not yet been much research about religion in lorry driving. A starting point for a religious-studies approach to lorry driving is provided by Jamal Elias, who works on Pakistani 'truck art', and his examination of the symbols and inscriptions on lorries following primarily a literary-critic approach to religion. Elias acknowledges, however, that he himself only came to the topic 'by accident'.[39] The fact that he was the first to do an in-depth study about religion around Pakistani lorries is rather surprising, as one might think that it is quite 'easy' to observe the religious charge in these lorries' decorations.[40]

Elias offers in-detail descriptions of the *aestheticscapes* of lorries from different regions in Pakistan (mainly small two-axle vehicles) and provides insights into the dynamics of cultural negotiating of symbols (e.g. through the anti-syncretism displaced on the lorries of the *Tablighi Jamaat*, a South Asian Sunni reform movement).[41] In his typology of 'decorative elements' on lorries, however, Elias differentiates between 'explicitly religiously',

---

31 Rosa 2019, 1.

32 Especially from Merleau-Ponty 2014.

33 Rosa 2019, 166.

34 Rosa 2019, 168.

35 Rosa prefers the spelling e→motion and af←fect as they show the directionality of the engagement. I simplify the spelling by eliminating the arrows as this is not important for the argumentation in this paper.

36 Double uncontrollability refers to the fact that no subject has the power to control when an experience of resonance is going to take place nor where the moment of transformation will lead to. For further information, consult Rosa 2020.

37 Rosa 2019, 220.

---

38 Labour conditions: Gregson 2018; Hamilton 2008; Ouellet 1994; Reckinger 2010; Viscelli 2016. Gender identities: Aho 2018; Balay 2018; Upton 2016; Wergen 2004.

39 Elias 2011, 2.

40 Photos e.g. in Elias 2011 and Schmid 1995.

41 Elias 2011, 138–44. Anne Koch and Katharina Wilkens developed the term *aestheticscapes* as an analytical tool in religious studies following Arjun Appadurai (1990). *Aestheticscapes* describe 'panorama[s] of aesthetic-sensory forms and elaborated codes' (Koch and Wilkens 2020, 8).

'religiously or talismanically loaded', and 'talismanic and fetish' objects as three distinct categories and thus exposes a certain uneasiness he faces as a scholar of religious studies engaging with theologically unrecognized socio-religious practices.[42] As a reader, I remain doubtful about the usefulness of his taxonomical differentiations. Due to the absence of interview passages, I assume that it could reflect more on the discussion of the binary between religion and magic that has been central in academic religious studies for a long time than on the emic realities of Pakistani lorry driving.[43] Unfortunately, no case study has yet analysed religion in Pakistani lorry driving through a social empirical research that considers the voices of lorry drivers to be as important as the art on the lorries' bodies. The disinterest of scholars of religious studies in analysing the role of religion in Pakistani lorries could be caused by boundaries between disciplines, as Anne Koch and Katharina Wilkens suspected when reflecting on a widespread academic neglect of the practice of 'drinking the Quran':[44]

> It is surprising to note, however, that this practice ['drinking the Quran'] has been neglected by Islamic studies scholars, who regard it as too 'superstitious' (if it attracts their attention at all), as well as by anthropologists, who regard it as too 'theological' and thus outside their field of competence (even though they see it practiced routinely).[45]

Religious artefacts are less visible in European than in Pakistani lorry driving. Among the technical reasons are corporate policies which strive for a standardized appearance of the fleet as well as state laws which, for security reasons, strongly restrict the possibility of adapting the outside of lorry bodies.[46] Because of these restrictions, the space for creative adaptions is limited to a large degree to the inside of the cabs, where the drivers normally have more autonomy in deciding how they want to decorate and what artefacts to hang up.[47] LED-powered crucifixes on the windshields (very popular among many drivers) are still visible from the outside, while smaller artefacts such as icons, statuettes of saints, and different (neo-)pagan talismans are often only visible from the inside of the cabs.

So far, the only mention of religious artefacts in European lorry driving in an academic article comes from André Nóvoa,[48] who, while writing an ethnography of Portuguese long-distance lorry drivers, encountered many Marian icons in the cabs of the tractor-trailers he rode in, just as I did. Nóvoa, however, interprets them exclusively as political statements favourable to the dictatorial regime of the 'Estado Novo'.[49] This argumentation appears far too simplistic in my eyes, not because it associates religion with politics — which is absolutely valid — but because Nóvoa misses the chance to discuss the complexity of the observed religious *aestheticscapes*. Just after mentioning in a half-sentence that the accompanied drivers 'feel safer when travelling under the supervision of a saint',[50] Nóvoa abandons the theme of religious artefacts and goes on to discuss food habits over several pages. I have the impression that Nóvoa, as a human geographer, feels uncomfortable touching upon the 'hot topic' of religion and therefore redirects his view away from it and onto topics on which he feels more skilled to reflect. On the following pages I will try to go deeper than Nóvoa while investigating the role of religious artefacts in German trucking assemblages.

Reassembling the Triangle of Mary

In the following subsection, I will address the relationalities of one particular assemblage of things sticking together, just as I encountered it while driving lorries across Germany. As a starting point, I will take the situation described at the beginning of this chapter when I encountered a Saxon driver with his Marian icons in Osterweddingen. That night, the two of us did not exchange our names,[51] therefore for the sake of the

---

[42] Elias 2011, 114.

[43] For further information consult e.g. Belier 1995.

[44] 'Drinking the Quran' refers to a practice of bodily 'incorporation' of Quranic verses for health reasons, which are written with ink on a plate and dissolved in water to drink by the patient, Wilkens 2020, 158–59.

[45] Koch and Wilkens 2020, 3 (parentheses and quotation marks by A. K./K. W.).

[46] The police regularly stop lorries with modifications such as extra lamps, bull bars, and additional grilles in order to control their legal status. If a modification is not approved by an official organization (TÜV), the drivers are forced to dismantle them before being allowed to continue on their route.

---

[47] Many employers provide their long-distance drivers with great autonomy to outfit their lorries as a strategy to bind them closer to the company, particularly regarding the increasing European driver shortage.

[48] Nóvoa 2014.

[49] Nóvoa 2014, 2839–42.

[50] Nóvoa 2014, 2842.

[51] Why dwell on such banalities, as we probably would not see each other again due to the hypermobility of long-distance lorry dri-

following argument I will unite him with an openly transgender Thuringian lorry driver I interviewed one month earlier called Mary. Unfortunately, I do not know if this Mary also had religious artefacts in her lorry, as we met in the public space on a free weekend and I failed to ask her. At that time, I was more interested in her experiences related to gender issues than in her religious practices.[52]

The assemblage that we are going to analyse, therefore, consists of three entities that share a common name: the first is Mary, the driver, the second is Mary, the icon, and the third is Mary, the mother of G*d (Fig. 14.1). In the following lines I shall speculate from an object-centred positioning how they might relate to each other.

A first relation unites Mary, the driver, to Mary, the icon (line I). Following the understanding of Mary, the driver, we cannot classify her relation to Mary, the icon, as a religious one, but as a relation established following an aesthetic appeal of the icon: Mary saw similar icons in the lorries of many of her international colleagues and felt a force of attraction coming from it. Once, in Bulgaria, she (Mary, the driver) gave in to this appeal of Mary, the icon, bought two of them during a break, and hung them into the windshield of her lorry with the intention of making it more 'beautiful'. By understanding Mary, the icon, in purely aesthetic and not in religious terms, Mary, the driver, challenges the religious coding of Mary, the icon, and initiates in the assemblage a process of decoding. The coding ascribed to the icon from other religious entities loses its importance, the boundaries established to determine its significance in religious terms are challenged and to a great extent removed.

The relation between driver and mother of G*d (line II), however, poses a bigger problem when we try to make sense of it, because religious studies generally call for *methodological agnosticism*,[53] therefore limiting the area of research to the human end of the relation, while

---

ving? I will, however, use changed versions of the names of all my interview partners in this article to ensure anonymization and to protect their identities.

52 While the majority of lorry drivers are cisgender men, a fast-growing part of the labour force consists of female, gay, and non-binary drivers. Many mention the search of 'freedom' from discriminatory practices experienced in family and working environments as a central reason to take on long-distance hauling jobs, which through loneliness facilitate distance from such toxic environments. LGTBIQ+ drivers form a very visible subgroup in the driving community, which seems quite well accepted (at least compared to discrimination related to nationalities).

53 Harvey 2014, 224.

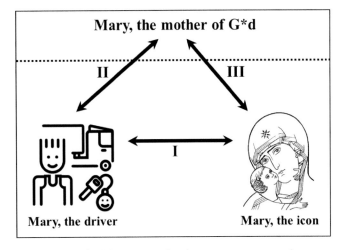

Figure 14.1. Three entities that share a common name: the first is Mary, the driver, the second is Mary, the icon, and the third is Mary, the mother of G*d. Figure by the author.

interdicting any crossing into spheres of *transcendence* (visualized in Fig. 14.1 by a dashed line). As Mary, the driver, recounts that religion means nothing to her, at first there seems to be no relation on her part to any transcendental entities. However, when Mary recounts an incident with a snapping brake hose, she explains the resulting emergency blockage of all trailer wheels as a 'braking by the Lord'. I experienced a similar situation when suddenly one of my brake hoses exploded on the highway near Cologne: the emergency blockage of the wheels, the hands cramped around the steering wheel, the trembling knees while not knowing what just happened and why the lorry resists any movement, the shaking voice while communicating with the shipper, employer, and police (who never arrive), the disengagement of trailer and lorry and the provisional repair with borrowed tools from a fellow lorry driver while experiencing continuous danger from cars overtaking on the left lane, the restarting of the engine and driving slowly to the destination, the dirty hands and the whole body covered in sweat, all while trying to restore a feeling of safety, and finally the iron bar hitting my head while I open the cargo doors, followed by sitting myself down on the asphalt with closed eyes for an instant and afterwards checking, with a minor but bleeding wound and a headache, how much of the cargo was displaced. This situation provoked by a sudden dis/assembling of these different entities felt very intense, an explanation referring to transcendental assemblages could feel very true.

The methodological problem with *transcendence*, however, intensifies when we try to elaborate on the relation of Mary, the icon, to Mary, the mother of G*d (line

III). Following assemblage thinking, simply saying the first embodies the latter, giving it a form, seems too easy a solution. To solve the problem, we must approach all entities of the assemblage from the paradigm of a 'flat ontology',[54] neglecting the possibility of hierarchical differences between divine, material, and human entities but approaching everybody/everything alike. Therefore, we do not necessarily have to reject the belief in a transcendental nature of the divine, but we must, for the goal of this investigation, push our third Mary, the mother of G*d, below the dotted line in order to be able to approach her symmetrically without having to differentiate her from other mundane actants. This softens (some might even say it contradicts) the idea of methodological agnosticism, because her divine existence (traced through actions and reactions by millions of humans) is no longer to be questioned, but she becomes an equally valid actor in the game of our assemblages. We exchange, therefore, *methodological agnosticism* for *methodological fetishism*, as proposed by Paul-François Tremlett in his call to introduce assemblage thinking in the studies of religion.[55] Following Mary, the icon, we could see how an immense actor-network links her to Mary, the mother of G*d. This actor-network or large-scale assemblage includes, among many other entities, all the devotees of Mary, the mother of G*d, who will continue to read her through a religious coding, disregarding the position of the individual driver. Mary, the driver, might partly disassemble this assemblage from the specific icon in her lorry, loosening the relation between icon and mother of G*d while reterritorializing her into a sphere of aesthetics. She will, however, never be able to decode the icon completely from her religious background of production and circulation.

That said, it seems to me that not even the most convinced atheist among drivers wishes to completely decode the religious boundaries of icons. Let us therefore conclude this subsection with a look at the opening testimony: 'I'm not really a believer but she's pretty and it surely won't harm.' This testimony comes from a Facebook post by a young female driver accompanying a photo of a rosary and a Marian statuette, which she reportedly got at a highway chapel where she stopped for a break. It was notable to see that out of more than one hundred responses from fellow lorry drivers, only one questioned

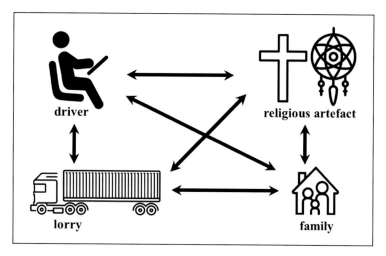

Figure 14.2. Connections between religious artefact, driver (now explicitly a particular long-distance one), lorry, and the family left at home. Figure by the author.

the value of religious artefacts, while most shared pictures of their own *Glücksbringer* (talismans) with the group. The three subjects in her testimony describe what I tried to visualize in the drawing of the assemblage: 'I'm not really a believer' narrates what I described as the relation between the driver and the (mother of) G*d. In her case, however, the adjective 'really' already significantly moderates the atheistic stance that I encountered with Mary, the driver. 'Really' makes the Facebook testimony's non-religious character an agnostic speculation rather than an ontological security. The second part 'but she's pretty' resituates the relation between driver and artefact into the sphere of aesthetics (thus decoding the assemblage religiously and recoding it aesthetically). The ending part 'and it surely won't harm', however, using an indirect pronoun, speculates on an ongoing relationality between artefact and divinity. While the driver expresses that she is not sure of the power of this relation, she believes that no harm could come from it. This last part of the sentence, therefore, again questions the decoding process in terms of religion which was initiated in the previous parts of the testimony.

Black-Boxing to Identify the Relationalities of a Quadrangle Assemblage

For the following subsection I will refocus my attention on scaling up above the triangle of Mary and knotting connections of the religious artefact to three important actants in lorry driving, thus (re)assembling an assemblage of a larger scale into quadrangular shape (Fig. 14.2) between religious artefact, driver (now explicitly a par-

---

54 DeLanda 2013, 51.

55 Tremlett 2020, 153. See also Appadurai 2013, 5.

ticular long-distance one), lorry, and the family left at home. My decision to shed additional light on the relationalities of these four actants results from my ongoing participant observation in East German lorry driving, as well as a total of twenty-three semi-structured interviews with fellow drivers, performed between January and November 2020.

For reassembling the drawn quadrangle of lorry driving, I black-boxed the above-mentioned triangle of Mary into the unit of the religious artefact. The religious artefact is, therefore, now to be considered an artificially closed unit that I locked up in order to investigate how it, as a combined assemblage, is related to the quadrangle assemblage of a larger scale, which we are going to investigate in this subsection. The reader might ask, why the driver still appears in the drawing of the quadrangle assemblage after I black-boxed her with the triangle of Mary. This is because the driver is present here in a different role, namely as a long-distance worker and predominantly physically absent family member. Mary, the driver, as a (non-)religious person is no longer considered in the new assemblage; indeed, this role of hers has been obscured into the black box of the religious artefact.

Additionally, the three other entities of the quadrangle assemblage are to be understood as black boxes because behind each one of them stands another assemblage. Let us exemplify this with the lorry. The lorry is not solely the vehicle that obviously already does only exist and function thanks to a coming together of uncountable human (e.g. assembly worker) and non-human (e.g. diesel) actants.[56] A 'lorry' only becomes a lorry, however, when it is used to transport cargo, as Mary reported in the interview with me: 'A lorry has also to earn his money.' Just as the cargo itself matters, it also matters how it is loaded onto the lorry, and an essential part of this work is done by *Ameisen* (ants), as electric pallet trolleys are known among German lorry drivers. Their official name, *Mitgängerflurförderzeuge* (literally, 'things to carry [things] across an even ground while walking together'), is one of the linguistic assemblages of the German language that, while providing a lot of background information, is in its complexity not suitable for everyday life. Therefore, all lorry drivers black-box *Mitgängerflurförderzeuge* into 'ants'. Ants play an important role in modern logistics; many drivers refuse to work without their help, fearing health problems, such as back pain, that in the long term inevitably result from loading and unloading too much heavy stuff without the help of power-driven machines. Consequently, it is one of the first words internationally driving long-distance lorry drivers learn in the local languages of their regular destinations so they can ask for one when having to unload in any foreign country.

In looking at the drawn assemblage, however, we perceive that it already has twice as many bilateral relations to explore than the triangle of Mary discussed above (respectively four times as many trilateral relations). Therefore, for the sake of the analysis of its relationalities, we shall not overload this subchapter with additional work that would result from reopening further black boxes but will respect the four entities of the assemblages as black boxes, which we will leave closed for methodological purposes. While I discuss the bilateral relations between driver and lorry as well as between religious artefact and lorry more specifically in the next subsection, I will engage shortly with the remaining relations while focalizing primarily on the role of the religious artefact.

The relation of the family to the lorry is in many cases conflictive, as the close relation between lorry and driver (discussed below) can be experienced as an endangerment of the family unit and lead to an eventual break-up, as reported by Renato: 'Many drivers are divorced several times' or Cecily, who reports that her partner cannot understand the closeness of the relation she maintains with the lorry: 'For her, it is only a tool for working.' In some cases, however, lorries also might strengthen family unions, for example when both human partners are working as drivers, or, as in the case of Allain, who grew up in a children's home and thanks to the lorry was able to find a way to relate to his father, whom he accompanied whenever possible on his trips: 'I grew up with it [the lorry] because of Dad. I did enjoy it in the past and it continues to give me joy.' In the case of a rather conflictive relation between lorry and family, a religious artefact might provide a method to tame the lorry. The religious artefact is used to obscure the danger of a 'life on the road' and to reterritorialize the tractor-trailer's cab into the safe space of a home. Thus, the lorry becomes a less dangerous space for the driver as well as its family members, because through the religious artefact (which often is a gift from people who are close to the driver) it is decoded in its role as potential destructor of the family union and as potential murderer of the loved one (which it might become in the case of an accident). In regard to the family, however, the role of the religious artefact is

---

[56] Note that to produce a standard European 4 × 2 tractor-trailer, approximately twelve thousand automotive subparts have to be assembled: Hilgers 2016, 22.

not only to prevent an accident but is equally important in mediating the absent family members into the assemblage of the moving lorry. Indeed, it seems that the religious artefact mobilizes the idea of family, by disengaging 'family' for a limited temporality from its territorial boundedness and creating a sort of deterritorialized *family-to-go*. This by no means contradicts the notion that other actants, such as 'beauty ideals' and 'divine supervisors', might continuously be present in the assemblage of the religious artefact. All assemblages (at any scale) are individual, and their subparts (that are assemblages in themselves) retain some autonomy which allows them to relate further to more entities.

Speculating on Potential Resonances Amid the Assemblages

To end this chapter, I will experimentalize with resonance theory as presented earlier and will include it in my analyses of the driver-to-lorry relation as well as in the lorry-to-religious-artefact relation. In order to go forward with a 'realist' speculation, I will have to ignore resonance's normative claims and understand it exclusively as a descriptive type.[57] For the sake of its empirical operationalization, I must flatten resonance, as I flattened religion before. Taking a flat (two-dimensional instead of three-dimensional) approach to resonance, there is suddenly a lot of data for resonance.[58] A relation is resonant (instead of mute) if the four moments of resonance (affect, emotion, mutual transformation, and double uncontrollability) come together. Contrary to a repulsive relation (which unites the same moments but alienates the resonating entities), in the result of a resonant relation, the two resonating entities move closer towards each other. In terms of assemblage thinking, we could say that resonance results in strengthening a relation.

The relation between lorry and driver is often a very close one, and in many narrations of lorry drivers, the four moments of resonance reappear. Relating affect, Renato explains that he encourages his lorry with spoken words, because it first calls to him — for example, by telling him through blinking and sound notifications that they should stop for diesel. Vera explains that she is affected by Ludmila (her lorry) speaking to her through the shining light of her lamps when Vera returns to her at night. This sight always touches Vera emotionally. The importance of lights for transmitting the voice of the lorry is also mentioned by Peter and Mary, among many others. All these long-distance lorry drivers react bodily, as well as in their actions, to what they experience as the affect of the truck, e.g. by caressing the steering wheel and reassuring the lorry through verbal communication. Many drivers comment that it is not possible to express the affect that their personal lorries have to them, nor their emotions in words, but that it is something that has to be experienced by oneself: 'It has to be felt, but you know it, you drive too.' The relation between lorry and driver results in a transformation of both entities; the lorry is personalized through interior design and verbal and nonverbal acts of communication, with the result that it becomes easier to drive in complicated situations thanks to this personal relation: 'I do need less time to back up at docking stations.' Not only does the lorry change in its relation to the driver, the driver also becomes somebody different. Many drivers report feelings of pride while driving a lorry, but also an ongoing transformation into a different person through the relation to the lorry. Tom, for example, reports that the lorry changed the way he drives cars (which also play an important role in his life), so that he now resists driving at high speeds and acts more carefully than before, but also sometimes erroneously operates the wiper, unconsciously taking it for a retarder. Emil reports that the lorry helped him figure out what he really wants in life, which led to a professional reorientation: 'In the lorry I had a lot of time to think, did I really want to do this till retiring?' Chris found his love for 'nature' through the lorry (which he used to park, whenever possible, on forest tracks), abandoning his apartment in the town centre and moving into a hut in the forest. He considers quitting his driving job to pass more time in the forest but says that his 'love for a steering wheel' is just too strong; therefore, to continue operating one, he might become a forklift operator.

The moment of double uncontrollability poses some problems for empirical research because of its inherent slipperiness, but I think that in regard to the driver-to-lorry relation, it describes quite well what happens when accidents occur. These are the moments when the voice of the lorry gets loudest, which leads to 'decoding' processes transforming the assemblages. It is not within the reach of either driver or lorry to predict when an accident will occur, but this does not mean that nobody has any influence; attentive drivers and lorries (e.g. equipped with well-functioning emergency braking assistants)

---

[57] In this 'de-normativized', purely analytical application of resonance theory, I follow Rüpke 2021, 29.

[58] For the advantages of 'flattening' meta-concepts, see again Latour 2005, 165–72.

might be able to avoid accidents in many situations, although sometimes they just happen (as for example when my brake hose exploded). It is also not controllable where the transforming process of an accident will lead the assemblage. An accident or incident might result in injuries, but not necessarily. It might result in (re)discovering religion, also not necessarily. It might result in a professional reorientation, but again not necessarily. In any case, the assemblage falls over and resurrects in a different form. If the transformative moment of an accident causes the assemblage of at least two entities interacting with each other to become more closely linked, the situation should *a posteriori* be considered as resonant. If they result in separation or alienation from each other, however, and the relationalities sticking the subparts of the assemblage together lose strength, the situation should be considered *a posteriori* as repulsive. In an object-centred application of resonance theory, it can therefore only be decided in the aftermath of each individual situation if the regrouping of a particular assemblage was resonant or repulsive.

As the accidents just described as potential resonant situations are quite close to a physical understanding of the concept of resonance,[59] the next step to speculate on, the possibility of resonance in inter-thing-relationalities between religious artefacts and lorries, might feel more applicable. The moment of double uncontrollability is rather easy to observe, as the bringing together of lorry and religious artefact is not the product of a deterministic will on the part of either entity. The mixing is facilitated by a human actor who, as a 'mediator',[60] introduces the religious artefact into the lorry. Neither can lorry and religious artefact decide when their encounter happens, nor do they control where the transformative element of them now being together leads them. The transformation is obvious; the religious artefact becomes a different one while being placed in the lorry. An icon in a monastery is not identical to an icon in a lorry. As argued before, however, it is not fundamentally different either; there is an ongoing connection between the two of them. The lorry transforms because of the religious artefact, but this process is open-ended as well. A crucifix can make a truck safer and homier, but it can also transform it into an (illusionary) police car, as stated by Renato: 'Most of the crosses are blue. From a distance, it looks like the flashing lights from a police car.'

The different roles of the religious artefact are not mutually exclusive because, as with most assemblages, its encounter with other entities is characterized by 'relations of exteriority'.[61] To come back to the initial question as to why East German drivers might introduce religious artefacts into their lorries, I think that the moment of affect can provide a suitable explanation here. Despite expressing their dislike for religion and associated orientalized Eastern European drivers, many lorry drivers from the Eastern parts of Germany realize the mutual affect between religious artefacts and their lorries. Consequentially, they facilitate their encounters by assembling them together while operating as 'mediators' and thus further diffusing the transcultural *aestheticscapes* of contemporary European long-distance lorry driving. Many lorries just call for a religious artefact to accompany them; they are not complete in their 'beauty' without it. When dealing with non-human actants, however, it becomes difficult for the emotional moment to be translated into human-produced text (even more difficult than this task already is when dealing with human emotions, which often transcend the possibilities afforded by alphabetical codes). Although it is difficult to grasp what moves a religious artefact internally, we can acknowledge that an icon or crucifix, thanks to its answering the call of the lorry, moves externally around space, while stirring up emotions in fellow humans (and maybe non-humans/more-than-humans). Maybe this non-human (loco)motion should be considered in resonance interested assemblage thinking as an analogy for human (e)motion.

Conclusion

In this paper I have discussed an observed discrepancy between an expanded material culture of religious artefacts in East German lorry driving and the narrated non-religious identities of many drivers. Inspired by the approaches of Speculative Realism and New Materialism, I was interested in the potential agency of the religious artefacts themselves in their transcultural diffusion in European lorry-driving communities. Therefore, I combined resonance theory with assemblage theory and actor-network theory and reassembled a triangular rela-

---

[59] Most prominently, the collapse of the Tacoma Narrows Bridge in 1940 exemplifies accidents caused by (mechanical) resonance (in a physical understanding of the term), but explaining the collapse as a 'resonance disaster' is an oversimplification of the events, cf. Billah and Scanlan 1991; Gunns 1981.

[60] Latour 1993, 137.

[61] DeLanda 2016, 10.

tionship between three Marys (Mary the driver, Mary the icon, and Mary the mother of G*d). I then obscured the 'triangle of Mary' as well as other sub-assemblages into black boxes in order to redraw a quadrangular assemblage linking driver, lorry, family, and religious artefact. Finally, I investigated possible qualities of the relations in the presented assemblages and concluded that in the case of a co-presence of the four moments of resonance (affect, emotion, transformation, and unavailability) the relation uniting driver and lorry as well as the relation uniting religious artefact and lorry should be considered potential resonant relations. In the case of these inter-thing resonances, I speculate that religious artefacts, due to mutual affects, might cross the paths of lorries, while the human driver merely facilitates their encounter in the role of a mediator. As such a mediator, however, the driver obviously should in no way be considered powerless (as neither are other human actors, e.g. the family), but we should acknowledge that they also attribute to the assemblage while giving the religious artefact in the lorry new additional roles — for example, as an imitation of police. Therefore, we can observe efforts to decode the assemblages around religious artefacts from the religious sphere into the sphere of aesthetics which, however, will never totally liberate the icons and crucifixes from their religious backgrounds.

Works Cited

Aho, T. 2018. 'Driving through Neoliberalism: Finnish Truck Drivers Constructing Respectable Male Worker Subjectivities', in C. Walker and S. Roberts (eds), *Masculinity, Labour, and Neoliberalism: Working-Class Men in International Perspective*, Global Masculinities (Cham: Springer), pp. 289–310.

Appadurai, A. 1990. 'Disjuncture and Difference in the Global Cultural Economy', *Theory, Culture & Society*, 7.2–3: 295–310.

——. 2013. 'Introduction: Commodities and the Politics of Value', in A. Appadurai (ed.), *The Social Life of Things: Commodities in Cultural Perspective*, repr. of 1986 edn (Cambridge: Cambridge University Press), pp. 3–63.

Balay, A. 2018. *Semi Queer: Inside the World of Gay, Trans, and Black Truck Drivers* (Chapel Hill: University of North Carolina Press).

Belier, W. W. 1995. 'Religion and Magic: Durkheim and the Année sociologique Group', *Method & Theory in the Study of Religion*, 7.2: 163–84.

Bennett, J. 2010. *Vibrant Matter: A Political Ecology of Things* (Durham, NC: Duke University Press).

Billah, K. Y. and R. H. Scanlan. 1991. 'Resonance, Tacoma Narrows Bridge Failure, and Undergraduate Physics Textbooks', *American Journal of Physics*, 59.2: 118–24.

Callon, M. and B. Latour. 2015. 'Unscrewing the Big Leviathan: How Actors Macro-structure Reality and How Sociologists Help Them to Do So', in K. Knorr-Cetina and A. V. Cicourel (eds), *Advances in Social Theory and Methodology: Toward an Integration of Micro- and Macro-sociologies*, repr. of 1981 edn (London: Routledge), pp. 277–303.

de la Cadena, M. 2015. *Earth Beings: Ecologies of Practice across Andean Worlds* (Durham, NC: Duke University Press).

de la Cadena, M. and M. Blaser (eds). 2018. *A World of Many Worlds* (Durham, NC: Duke University Press).

DeLanda, M. 2013. *Intensive Science and Virtual Philosophy*, Bloomsbury Revelations (London: Bloomsbury Academic).

——. 2016. *Assemblage Theory*, Speculative Realism (Edinburgh: Edinburgh University Press).

Deleuze, G. and F. Guattari. 1987. *A Thousand Plateaus: Capitalism and Schizophrenia*, trans. B. Massumi (Minneapolis: University of Minnesota Press).

Deleuze, G. and C. Parnet. 2007. *Dialogues*, II, trans. H. Tomlinson and B. Habberjam, rev. edn (New York: Columbia University Press).

Elias, J. J. 2011. *On Wings of Diesel: Trucks, Identity and Culture in Pakistan* (Oxford: Oneworld).

Gregson, N. 2018. 'Mobilities, Mobile Work and Habitation: Truck Drivers and the Crisis in Occupational Auto-mobility in the UK', *Mobilities*, 13.3: 291–307.

Gunns, A. F. 1981. 'The First Tacoma Narrows Bridge: A Brief History of Galloping Gertie', *The Pacific Northwest Quarterly*, 72.4: 162–69.

Hamilton, S. 2008. *Trucking Country: The Road to America's Wal-Mart Economy*, Politics and Society in Twentieth-Century America (Princeton: Princeton University Press).

Harman, G. 2017. *Object-Oriented Ontology: A New Theory of Everything* (London: Pelican).

Harvey, G. 2014. 'Field Research: Participant Observation', in M. Stausberg and S. Engler (eds), *The Routledge Handbook of Research Methods in the Study of Religion*, repr. of 2011 edn (London: Routledge), pp. 217–44.

Hilgers, M. 2016. *Gesamtfahrzeug*, Nutzfahrzeugtechnik lernen (Wiesbaden: Springer).

Jensen, R. T. and D. Moran (eds). 2013. *The Phenomenology of Embodied Subjectivity*, Contributions to Phenomenology, in Cooperation with the Center for Advanced Research in Phenomenology, 71 (Cham: Springer).

Johnson, J. 1988. 'Mixing Humans and Nonhumans Together: The Sociology of a Door-Closer', *Social Problems*, 35.3: 298–310.

Koch, A. and K. Wilkens. 2020. 'Introduction', in A. Koch and K. Wilkens (eds), *The Bloomsbury Handbook of the Cultural and Cognitive Aesthetics of Religion*, Bloomsbury Handbooks in Religion (London: Bloomsbury Academic), pp. 1–9.

Latour, B. 1987. *Science in Action: How to Follow Scientists and Engineers through Society* (Cambridge, MA: Harvard University Press).

——. 1993. *We Have Never Been Modern*, repr. of 1991 edn (Cambridge, MA: Harvard University Press).

——. 2005. *Reassembling the Social: An Introduction to Actor-Network-Theory*, Clarendon Lectures in Management Studies (Oxford: Oxford University Press).

——. 2009. 'Where Are the Missing Masses?: The Sociology of a Few Mundane Artifacts', in D. G. Johnson and J. M. Wetmore (eds), *Technology and Society: Building our Sociotechnical Future* (Cambridge, MA: MIT Press), pp. 151–80.

Merleau-Ponty, M. 2014. *Phenomenology of Perception* (London: Routledge).

Morelle, L. 2012. 'Speculative Realism: After Finitude, and Beyond? A vade mecum', in M. Austin and others (eds), *Speculations*, III (Brooklyn: Punctum), pp. 241–72.

Moser, M. 2022. 'East to West to South to North and Back: Driving Landscapes as a Thuringian Long-Distance Trucker', *Transfers*, 12.1: 20–32.

Nóvoa, A. 2014. 'A Country on Wheels: A Mobile Ethnography of Portuguese Lorry Drivers', *Environment and Planning A: Economy and Space*, 46.12: 2834–47.

Ouellet, L. J. 1994. *Pedal to the Metal: The Work Lives of Truckers* (Philadelphia: Temple University Press).

Pollack, D. 1999. 'Der Wandel der religiös-kirchlichen Lage in Ostdeutschland nach 1989', in D. Pollack and G. Pickel (eds), *Religiöser und kirchlicher Wandel in Ostdeutschland 1989–1999* (Wiesbaden: Springer), pp. 18–47.

Reckinger, G. 2010. 'LKW-Fahrer: Alles was sich irgendwie nicht ausgeht, das lastet auf den Schultern des Fahrers', in F. Schultheis, B. Vogel, and M. Gemperle (eds), *Ein halbes Leben: Biographische Zeugnisse aus einer Arbeitswelt im Umbruch* (Konstanz: UVK), pp. 238–51.

Rosa, H. 2019. *Resonance: A Sociology of our Relationship to the World*, trans. J. C. Wagner (Cambridge: Polity).

——. 2020. *The Uncontrollability of the World*, trans. J. Wagner (Cambridge: Polity).

Rüpke, J. 2021. *Ritual als Resonanzerfahrung*, Religionswissenschaft Heute (Stuttgart: Kohlhammer).

Schmid, A. 1995. *Pakistan-Express: Die fliegenden Pferde vom Indus* (Hamburg: Dölling und Galitz).

Stengers, I. 2018. 'The Challenge of Ontological Politics', in M. de la Cadena and M. Blaser (eds), *A World of Many Worlds* (Durham, NC: Duke University Press), pp. 83–111.

Tremlett, P.-F. 2020. *Towards a New Theory of Religion and Social Change: Sovereignties and Disruptions* (London: Bloomsbury Academic).

Upton, R. L. 2016. *Negotiating Work, Family, and Identity among Long-Haul Christian Truck Drivers: What Would Jesus Haul?* (Lanham: Lexington).

Viscelli, S. 2016. *The Big Rig: Trucking and the Decline of the American Dream* (Oakland: University of California Press).

Wergen, J. 2004. 'Zwischen professionellem und privatem Geschlecht: Frauen in Fahrberufen und die Geschlechterkonstruktionen westdeutscher Lkw-Fahrerinnen', in I. Miethe, C. Kajatin, and J. Pohl (eds), *Geschlechterkonstruktionen in Ost und West: Biografische Perspektiven*, Soziologie. Forschung und Wissenschaft, 8 (Münster: Lit), pp. 219–31.

Wilkens, K. 2020. 'Text Acts', in A. Koch and K. Wilkens (eds), *The Bloomsbury Handbook of the Cultural and Cognitive Aesthetics of Religion*, Bloomsbury Handbooks in Religion (London: Bloomsbury Academic), pp. 155–64.

Zalloua, Z. 2014. *Reading Unruly: Interpretation and its Ethical Demands* (Lincoln, NE: University of Nebraska Press).

Index

Page numbers in *italics* refer to figures, maps, graphs, and tables.

abstraction: 45, 61, 104, 200
anatithemai: 71
anatomical votive: 58, 62, 197–206
ancestor: 21, 87–99, 107, 121, 182
Aphrodisia: 147
assemblage: 15, 25, 34, 52, 58, 105–09, 146, 156, 159, 177, 213–22

balsamari: 47–52
binding: 129–30, 155
bodily: 39, 62–63, 87, 90, 108, 197–200, 220
body: 26–34, 43–49, 62–63, 97–111, 145, 168–69, 179, *187*, 191, 197–206, 211–21
brocche: 45, 50, 62
brochette: 52
Bucrania: 71
burial chamber: 90, 93, 96

caducei: 183–91
calici: 50–51
coin: 29, 55, 59, 63, 149–50, 183–91
compression: 45, 61–63
consecrate: 70–71, 76–77
cooperation: 74, 111
coperchi: 50–61
crucifix: 212
CTH: 51 127–29, 135–39
cult of the Lares: 53, 58, 187

diminutive: 45, 58
donation: 17, 22–29, 38–39, 70, 118
dromos: 89–97

embodied experience: 90, 100
extra–urban sanctuary: 17–22, 39
eye–shaped anathemata: 202, 207
eye–shaped votives: 198–206

face beakers: 185–91
figurine: 31–33, 46, 157, 168, 171
fragmentation: 17, 23, 29–31, 197, 200

gift: 70

healing cult: 197, 206
hearth: 167, 171–72, 180–91
heterogeneity: 14–15
hierarchy: 23, 105, 129, 136
Hittite: 128–39
household deities: 165, 172
household gods: 53, 167, 171, 178, 190

icon: 103–11, 198–205, 211–22
imagination: 107
Inter–artefactual: 43, 59, 63
intermediary: 127–39
interpretation: 21–22, 37–38, 44–63, 94, 112, 117–25, 149–50, 157–59, 168, 191, 205

katatithemai: 71

lararia: 61–62, 146, 177–78, 182, 188
lararium: 146, 165, 172–74, 177
Lares: 53–64, 166–74, 177–91
libation: 23–30, 69, 77, 91–92, 96, 100, 136, 180, 184–85, 191

materiality: 17, 22, 69, 73, 103, 109, 197–98
miniaturized pottery: 46–52, 58–61
miniaturizing: 93
Mittani treaty: 127
Mittanian: 127–29, 140
model miniature: 45
monére: 119, 200
monumentalizing: 93, 97, 104–12
Mos maiorum: 117–25

necropolis: 46–53, 88–100

ophthalmological illness: 197–207

palace: 105, 109–10, 129–34, 140, 179
phalloi: 184–91
phialai: 24–25
pinax: 71
pithos: 23–26
porticus: 165–74
procession: 22, 71, 80, 98, 106, 111, 201
protome: 29–30, *53*, 74–75

rampart: 108
religious banquet: 9–13
renovation: 59, 117–26, 152–53
ritual blindness: 204–05
ritual transfer: 37

sacralization: 54–62, 106
sacrifice: 14, 173, 179–81, 189
Sanctuary of Arsu: 10
Sanctuary of Baalshamin: 13
Sanctuary of Bel: 10–13
seal: 11–14, 76
secular: 136, 145, 154–59
shrine: 21, 46–63, 111, 137, 146, 158, 172–74, 177–81, 188–89
statue: 130, 137, 145–60, 165–74, 178, 205–06
stele: *49*, 91–94

technology: 15
temenos: 10–11, 72
token miniature: 45, 50
treasure: 24–26
tumulus: 88–99, 105, *187*

unguentaria: 47–51, 61
urbanism: 14–15, 103–10
urbanity: 103–12

vessel: 18–37, 44–63, 73–80, 145, 155, 182–91
votive: 21–22, 29, 38, 59–62, 69–80, 158
votive robes: 78

wall: 18–19, 24, 28, 34, 37, 46–47, 55–58, 88–96, 104–13, 120, 152, 157–58, 172, 205–07
wreath: *12*, 71, 76–80, 149, 168

CONTEXTUALIZING THE SACRED

All volumes in this series are evaluated by an Editorial Board, strictly on academic grounds, based on reports prepared by referees who have been commissioned by virtue of their specialism in the appropriate field. The Board ensures that the screening is done independently and without conflicts of interest. The definitive texts supplied by authors are also subject to review by the Board before being approved for publication. Further, the volumes are copyedited to conform to the publisher's stylebook and to the best international academic standards in the field.

Titles in Series

Redefining the Sacred: Religious Architecture and Text in the Near East and Egypt 1000 BC – AD 300, ed. by Elizabeth Frood and Rubina Raja (2014)

Inge Nielsen, *Housing the Chosen: The Architectural Context of Mystery Groups and Religious Associations in the Ancient World* (2014)

Anika Greve, *Sepulkrale Hofarchitekturen im Hellenismus: Alexandria—Nea Paphos—Kyrene* (2014)

Religious Identities in the Levant from Alexander to Muhammed: Continuity and Change, ed. by Michael Blömer, Achim Lichtenberger, and Rubina Raja (2015)

Phönizische, griechische und römische Gottheiten im historischen Wandel, ed. by Linda-Marie Günther & Bärbel Morstadt (2015)

Achim Lichtenberger, *Terrakotten aus Beit Nattif: Eine Untersuchung zur religiösen Alltagspraxis im spätantiken Judäa* (2016)

Expressions of Cult in the Southern Levant in the Greco-Roman Period: Manifestations in Text and Material Culture, ed. by Oren Tal and Zeev Weiss (2017)

Contextualizing the Sacred in the Hellenistic and Roman Near East: Religious Identities in Local, Regional, and Imperial Settings, ed. by Rubina Raja (2017)

Revisiting the Religious Life of Palmyra, ed. by Rubina Raja (2019)

Marlis Arnhold, *Transformationen stadtrömischer Heiligtümer während der späten Republik und Kaiserzeit* (2020)

Cultic Graffiti in the Late Antique Mediterranean and Beyond, ed. by Antonio E. Felle and Bryan Ward-Perkins (2021)